PHILOSOPHICAL FOUNDATIONS
OF CONSTITUTIONAL LAW

Philosophical Foundations of Constitutional Law

Edited by
DAVID DYZENHAUS
University Professor of Law and Philosophy, University of Toronto
and
MALCOLM THORBURN
Associate Professor of Law, University of Toronto

OXFORD
UNIVERSITY PRESS

OXFORD

UNIVERSITY PRESS

Great Clarendon Street, Oxford, OX2 6DP,
United Kingdom

Oxford University Press is a department of the University of Oxford.
It furthers the University's objective of excellence in research, scholarship,
and education by publishing worldwide. Oxford is a registered trade mark of
Oxford University Press in the UK and in certain other countries

Published in the United States of America by Oxford University Press
198 Madison Avenue, New York, NY 10016, United States of America

British Library Cataloguing in Publication Data
Data available

Library of Congress Cataloging in Publication Data
Data available

ISBN 978-0-19-875452-7 (Hbk.)
ISBN 978-0-19-875453-4 (Pbk.)

Table of Contents

List of Contributors

T. R. S. Allan is Professor of Jurisprudence and Public Law at the University of Cambridge and Fellow of Pembroke College, Cambridge.

Jack M. Balkin is Knight Professor of Constitutional Law and the First Amendment at Yale Law School.

Aharon Barak is President (ret.) of the Supreme Court of Israel; Radzyner School of Law, Interdisciplinary Center (IDC), Herzliya.

Rosalind Dixon is Professor of Law at the University of New South Wales Australia, and Director of the Comparative Constitutional Law Project at the Gilbert + Tobin Centre of Public Law.

David Dyzenhaus is University Professor of Law and Philosophy at the University of Toronto.

Evan Fox-Decent is Associate Professor in the Faculty of Law at McGill University.

Aileen Kavanagh is Associate Professor in the Faculty of Law at the University of Oxford and Fellow of St Edmund Hall, Oxford.

Cristina Lafont is Professor of Philosophy at Northwestern University.

Sanford Levinson is W. St John Garwood and W. St John Garwood Jr Centennial Chair in Law at the University of Texas Law School, and Professor of Government at the University of Texas at Austin.

Hans Lindahl is Chair of Legal Philosophy at Tilburg University, the Netherlands.

Sophia Moreau is Associate Professor in the Faculty of Law and the Department of Philosophy at the University of Toronto.

Thomas Poole is Professor of Law at the London School of Economics and Political Science.

Richard Stacey is Assistant Professor in the Faculty of Law at the University of Toronto.

Adrienne Stone is Professor of Law and Director of the Centre for Constitutional Studies at Melbourne Law School, and First Vice-President of the International Association of Constitutional Law.

Malcolm Thorburn is Associate Professor in the Faculty of Law at the University of Toronto.

Mark D. Walters is Professor of Law at Queen's University, Canada.

Introduction

David Dyzenhaus and Malcolm Thorburn

The design of a volume that deals with the 'Philosophical Foundations of Constitutional Law' faces a major problem. There is not much agreement in philosophy of law about the correct approach to that discipline. Is it a more normative prescriptive inquiry that fuses questions of ought and is, or is it, as legal positivists urge, a more descriptive conceptual analysis? This same problem, of course, affects philosophical analysis of the foundations of constitutional law, as the philosophers of law who take the conceptual approach will think that fundamental questions such as 'What is a constitution?' or 'What is constitutional law?' can be answered descriptively. In contrast, many who take the more normative approach will suppose that the answers to such questions are shaped by one's normative commitments.

For those on the normative side of this controversy,[1] there is no difference between the methodology of philosophy of law and that of prescriptive constitutional theory when it comes to answering questions about the philosophical foundations of constitutional law. From this perspective, such questions cannot be answered outside of a normative framework that seeks to understand law as a matter of principle—the fundamental or constitutional principles that structure the relationship between those who make the law and those who live under its rule.

For those on the descriptive conceptual side of this controversy, philosophy of law and constitutional theory have little to say to each other. Legal positivist philosophers of law do not think that their discipline speaks directly to the concerns of constitutional theory, for example, the legitimacy of judicial review of statutes, perhaps the central issue in constitutional theory in the United States. To make matters even more complicated, there are also a number of normative constitutional theorists who have embraced this positivist assumption. They are happy to get on with the job of defending and elaborating their explicitly normative understanding of constitutionalism without worrying about the questions that preoccupy philosophy of law, for example, 'What is law?', and 'Is there a necessary connection between law and morality?'.

The divide that the conceptual approach opens up between philosophy of law and constitutional theory has therefore had the result that much of what passes for legal philosophical inquiry into the foundations of constitutional law is hardly informed by the concerns of constitutional theory. In its insistence that philosophy of law must be a relentlessly abstract and conceptual analysis, the conceptual approach has largely

---

[1] These include Kantians, who adopt a conception of law according to which legal order is constituted by an idea of right, common law constitutionalists and others who adopt an interpretivist view of law, notably Ronald Dworkin, as well as those whose primary influence is Lon L. Fuller's conception of legality.

ignored two important developments in constitutional theory and practice. First, the wave of bill of rights constitutionalism that marked the 1990s does not figure in the conceptual approach to the philosophy of constitutional law, just as the explosion in comparative law scholarship is missing. Second, in recent years, constitutional theory has in some quarters taken what might be described as a historical turn. That is, prominent scholars have sought to tackle the fundamentals of constitutional law by taking account of their historical development, including the development of theories that were constructed to address such developments. This turn has thus brought attention to figures who were virtually unknown to Anglo-American constitutional theory some years ago, for example Carl Schmitt. But just as legal philosophical inquiry is for the most part relentlessly abstract, so it is for the most part relentlessly ahistorical and uninterested in the contribution of such figures. A curious feature of legal philosophical inquiry is then that the constitutional theory of Hans Kelsen, perhaps the most important figure in legal philosophy in the last century, plays hardly any role in it.[2]

All the chapters in this collection trample in different ways over the divide between the analysis of concepts on the one hand and the engagement with normative commitments, legal developments, and the history of ideas on the other. Their collective success is, we think, best measured by whether such trampling contributes to an understanding of the philosophical foundations of constitutional law.

In the first part of the book, 'What is a Constitution?', two chapters address the divide between philosophy of law and constitutional theory explicitly. In Chapter 1, 'The Idea of a Constitution: A Plea for *Staatsrechtslehre*', David Dyzenhaus argues that not only is joinder between philosophy of law and constitutional theory desirable but also that joinder is also already the case, as legal positivism is best understood as part of a tradition of thought in prescriptive constitutional theory—political constitutionalism. He argues in addition that once legal positivism is so understood, rival theories do better in the debates about constitutional fundamentals. But his main objective is to show that there is a productive joinder.

In Chapter 2, 'The Unwritten Constitution as a Legal Concept', Mark Walters examines the idea, often considered anathema in the positivist tradition, of the unwritten constitution. He argues that there are two camps in legal theory when it comes to such questions as whether the unwritten constitution is both legal and normative—positivistic 'linear theories of law' that trace the authority of norms back to a source and 'circular theories of law' that understand law as a 'web of strings shaped into a globe or sphere'. He deploys a mix of historical and jurisprudential arguments to support a conclusion that ultimately the divide in philosophy of law is about how we identify normative value, with the linear theorists holding that value is determined outside of law and the circular theorists holding that value is determined in a process of reasoning internal to the legal order.

The other chapters in this part do not address the divide, though their arguments do have implications for it. In Chapter 3, 'On Constitutional Implications and Constitutional Structure', Aharon Barak focuses on written constitutions. He argues that the implications of the constitutional text are as much part of the constitution as

---

[2] There is increasing interest in Kelsen in Anglo-American philosophy of law, but that interest is filtered through the preoccupations of the kind of legal positivism that was first developed by H. L. A. Hart.

the text and thus that the content of the constitution has to be ascertained in part by an interpretation that is attentive to the 'structure' of the constitution. He does not engage directly with debates in philosophy of law and he does not present his argument as part of a prescriptive constitutional theory. But as he acknowledges, those who would be most averse to accepting his claim about implications are within what Walters would term the linear camp, and his chapter does implicitly assume the kind of joinder for which Dyzenhaus and Walters both argue.

In Chapter 4, 'Reflections on What Constitutes "a Constitution": The Importance of "Constitutions of Settlement" and the Potential Irrelevance of Herculean Lawyering', Sanford Levinson argues that both philosophers of law and constitutional theorists have focused unproductively on questions about constitutional interpretation and have thus neglected questions of 'constitutional design' and in particular those parts of a constitution that are 'settled' in the way that their meaning cannot be contested in the process of legal argument before a court, no matter the skill of the lawyers and judges. These parts are thus subject to change only by amendment, a political process not well understood by philosophers of law. And these parts are, he suggests, at least as worthy of the attention of those interested in the philosophical foundations of constitutional law as those that currently occupy legal theorists. Levinson also suggests that the legal positivism associated with H. L. A Hart might prove more useful in this kind of endeavour than the normative legal theory developed by Ronald Dworkin.

Chapter 5, 'Constitutional Amendment and Political Constitutionalism: A Philosophical and Comparative Reflection' by Rosalind Dixon and Adrienne Stone might be thought to challenge Levinson's main premise. Dixon and Stone argue that the availability of amendment procedures in written constitutions can answer a significant part of the case that political constitutionalists, notably Jeremy Waldron, make against the legitimacy of judicial review of statutes. The challenge comes about because they demonstrate that the US experience with amendments is quite partial and also has not been properly located in the kind of comparative perspective that permits one to see that in other jurisdictions, what Levinson would take to be settled parts of the constitution can be quite easily unsettled through amendment. This chapter thus softens the distinction between judicial review and amendment, while at the same time issuing a more general call for an engagement between legal theory and comparative constitutional law in the inquiry into the foundations of constitutional law.

Part 2 of the book focuses on the issue of constitutional authority. In Chapter 6, 'Constitutional Legitimacy Unbound', Evan Fox-Decent argues that a theory of the constitution must include an account of its legitimacy and that such an account has to explain the distinction between citizens and non-citizens. Since that distinction cannot be explained without resort to norms of international law, he concludes that constitutionalism has to 'become unbound', that is, the constitution's authority must be 'co-constituted' by national and international law.

In Chapter 7, 'Constituent Power and the Constitution', Hans Lindahl focuses on the issue of constituent power: the capacity to enact a constitution. He thus deals with questions crucial to an understanding of the fundamentals of constitutionalism but often ignored in both legal philosophy and constitutional theory: where do constitutions come from and what bestows authority on them? Schmitt is considered to be the most important twentieth-century figure in the debate about constituent power and he espouses what we saw Walters would call a linear theory of authority. But rather in the spirit of a circular theory, Lindahl argues that the constitutive initiative taken by constituent power requires fulfilment by institutions and norms that locate the 'we' of the people within the legal order.

A somewhat similar argument is made by Richard Stacey in Chapter 8, 'Popular Sovereignty and Revolutionary Constitution-Making'. Stacey begins with the example of the Arab Spring and the wave of constitutional reforms that followed popular uprisings against authoritarian rulers. These reforms, Stacey argues, cannot be understood as involving exercises of 'unbounded sovereignty', that is, the idea that the sovereign people are unfettered in the exercise of their sovereignty at the moment at which they define a new legal and political order in the text of a constitution. Rather, in exercising the power to create a constitutional order, the sovereign people will find that the power has to be exercised in accordance with norms that flow from commitments to the rule of law, individual rights, and democracy.

The next chapter by Thomas Poole explores another neglected topic in legal philosophical inquiry into constitutional foundations: the prerogative or reason of state. In Chapter 9, 'Constitutional Reason of State', Poole explains that reason of state is associated with situations in which state action moves from one register, based on law and right, to another, based on interest and might, or we might say, from law to politics and prudence. In the latter register, it is traditionally understood as an exercise of what Stacey calls unbounded sovereignty, though it is also seen as occurring only at the margins of legal order, and thus not threatening the whole. Poole argues that the activities associated with reason of state—war and peace, commerce and empire, diplomacy and interstate relations—are hardly marginal as they shaped the formation of modern states and their constitutions. However, he also argues that prerogative and reason of state are inherently juridical categories and cannot be understood in the unbounded way that orthodoxy suggests.

Part 3 of the book addresses constitutional fundamentals, that is, some of the ideas and concepts that any inquiry into the philosophical foundations of constitutional law will encounter. In Chapter 10, 'The Rule of Law', Trevor Allan sets out his view that the rule of law has pride of place amongst constitutional fundamentals since it is only in light of an appropriate conception of the rule of law that we can understand our commitment to constitutionalism as well as other constitutional fundamentals such as the separation of powers. At bottom, the commitment to constitutionalism is the same as that entailed by the rule of law, a commitment to the related ideals of human dignity and individual liberty. The rule of law as the most important constitutional fundamental helps us to understand why a constitutional order amounts to a unified scheme of justice.

Allan's highly substantive account of the rule of law and its place in our understanding of the philosophical foundations of constitutional law contrasts rather sharply with Chapter 11, Aileen Kavanagh's 'The Constitutional Separation of Powers'. Kavanagh argues against what she calls the 'pure view' of the separation of powers, one which Allan's argument might presuppose, according to which each of the powers has an exclusive function. Rather, she suggests that we should understand the reasons for separating to some extent the powers as necessary in order to promote a productive but not exclusive division of labour between the branches of government. That understanding, however, does not suffice to explain why the powers are separated, or divided (as she prefers to put things), to the extent that they are. For we also have to take into account the role each branch plays in checking and balancing the others, even if (as she urges) we should not neglect the way in which their work has to be seen as a collaborative effort.

A central concern in the philosophy of constitutional law is how to understand the role of constitutional interpretation. In Chapter 12, 'The Framework Model and Constitutional Interpretation', Jack Balkin puts forward a view of constitutional interpretation which might contest the claims made by Barak and Levinson who assume that a written constitution has a certain fixed 'structure' (Barak) or 'settled parts' (Levinson). Balkin argues that the constitution is in a way the product of interpretation—what it is is always in the process of being constructed. At most we have a framework for that construction, but the result is always vulnerable to reconstruction over time. While, as Balkin acknowledges, his framework model has some affinity with the interpretive approach to law recommended by Dworkin (and thus also with the chapters by Walters and Allan in this volume), he distinguishes his argument from Dworkin's by emphasizing the role of politics and political movements in the construction process. In light of this role, the appearance of judicial supremacy in the US legal order is deceptive since judges are far more responsive to politics than is ordinarily appreciated, which makes political movements and the individuals in them as much interpreters of the constitution as the judiciary.

A rather different sort of political responsiveness is highlighted by Cristina Lafont in Chapter 13, 'Philosophical Foundations of Judicial Review'. Against those who contend that judicial review is a kind of trade-off between the normative goals of minority rights protection and democratic self-government, she argues that judicial review fulfils some key democratic functions, which can only be understood by setting the workings of courts within the political system. In particular, she argues that judicial review can be seen as an institution of democratic control to the extent that its justification partly derives from the right of affected citizens to effectively contest the political decisions to which they are subject. This is not, she emphasizes, an argument for giving judges the authority to invalidate statutes. Whether or not that is appropriate will depend on contingent factors about the particular legal order. Rather, the argument seeks only to remove one but very important objection to judicial review, an objection that sees the trade-off as illegitimate because it is inherently undemocratic.

The last part of the book contains two contributions on constitutional rights and their limitations. In Chapter 14, 'Equality Rights and Stereotypes', Sophia Moreau argues that equality rights have a central place in our understanding of constitutional rights because a democratic government that refused to recognize a constitutional obligation to treat individuals as equals would seem illegitimate, on most plausible conceptions of political legitimacy. It is this centrality that accounts for the fact that bills of rights, whatever else they do, prohibit discriminatory treatment. But, as she shows, understanding what amounts to discriminatory treatment is quite complex. In particular, she shows that a common understanding that discrimination relies on illicit stereotyping is misleading. Instead, we need to ask which harmful effects are relevant to the unfairness of discrimination.

Finally, in Chapter 15, 'Proportionality', Malcolm Thorburn argues that the explicit commitment to a practice of proportionality justification that is a feature of the post-war paradigm of rights protection reasoning marks a substantive difference between the understanding of rights in these constitutions and in that of the United States. In the latter, a conception of rights predominates in which rights have the legal status they enjoy because they have been enacted into law by a constituent power and they operate as absolute constraints on state action that impinges on them. When state action does not so impinge, its content can be determined by utilitarian calculation, but such calculation can never justify limiting a right. Proportionality justification, in contrast, assumes that rights are structural features of the constitutional order that both the state and the constituent power must respect. They are not, that is, external constraints on state action but regulative principles that serve to direct the activities of the state from the inside in order to ensure respect for the independence of persons. And so the question that the proportionality justification seeks to answer is whether the state's justification for limiting a right is consistent with such respect.

Together, the chapters in this collection begin the process of reconnecting the philosophy of constitutional law to a number of related areas: not only philosophy of law, but also political philosophy, comparative law, the history of ideas, and moral philosophy. Because, on the conception that dominates this volume, the philosophy of constitutional law is continuous with these other disciplines, this book's central aim is to establish and to explore these connections in ways that open up new and fruitful lines of inquiry. Rather than arguing in the abstract about whether such connections exist, the chapters of this book simply go about exploring those connections. Together, they make the case for resetting the philosophy of constitutional law back into the place it had occupied for centuries, at the crossroads of engaged normative inquiry.

We thank our editor Alex Flach for much wise advice, his team at Oxford University Press for their help throughout the production process, the Law Faculty of the University of Toronto for supporting and hosting the conference at which most of the chapters were first presented (with special thanks to Jennifer Tam), our contributors for their patience with our persistent requests, and the following Toronto law students for their assistance with getting the manuscript into Oxford house style: Dragana Rakic, Enoch Guimond, and Sam (Han Jung) Kim.

PART I

WHAT IS A CONSTITUTION?

1

The Idea of a Constitution

A Plea for *Staatsrechtslehre*

*David Dyzenhaus**

Philosophers of law and constitutional theorists generally agree that every legal order has a constitution. However, it is notoriously difficult to answer what I shall call 'the question of constitutionality': what is it that all legal orders share in having a constitution? Perhaps it is something so fundamental that every legal order has to have one, whatever the content of its actual constitution—the rules that one would collect in a textbook of the constitutional law of Canada, of Germany, of the United Kingdom, etc. For the rules of the actual constitution will vary considerably from jurisdiction to jurisdiction.

Obvious candidates for what is most fundamentally shared by legal orders are the proposals of the leading legal positivist philosophers of law of an ultimate rule or norm of legal order: H. L. A. Hart's rule of recognition—the rule of a legal order that is ultimate in that it certifies the validity of all other rules—and Hans Kelsen's basic norm—the norm that has to be presupposed in order to confer validity on the first historical constitution of the relevant legal system.[1] The rule of recognition differs from the basic norm in that its content is to be found in the settled practice of the legal officials that apply it and thus it will vary in content from legal order to legal order. In contrast, the content of the basic norm is always the same since it simply states the ultimate duty of legal order on those subject to law to comply with constitutional norms, although the content of the norms of the actual constitution will vary for the same sorts of reasons that the content of the rule of recognition varies.

However, as we will see in this chapter, it is unclear whether the rule of recognition is the constitution or, more like the basic norm, the rule that certifies the validity of the constitution. Moreover, it is unclear whether the rule of recognition is a legal rule or a rule that lies beyond legal order. Finally, both the rule of recognition and the basic norm might seem similarly reductionist in that each boils down to the rules or norms

* University Professor of Law and Philosophy, Toronto. I thank Hillary Nye for valuable research assistance, the participants in the Toronto conference and in a public law seminar in Cambridge for discussion, and Trevor Allan, Lars Vinx, and Mark Walters for written comments as well as an ongoing debate on this chapter's themes.

[1] H. L. A. Hart, 'The Foundations of a Legal System', in Hart, *The Concept of Law* 2nd edn (Oxford: Clarendon Press, 1994), ch 6; H. Kelsen, 'The Legal System and its Hierarchical Structure', in B. L. Paulson and S. L. Paulson (trans), *Introduction to the Problems of Legal Theory: A Translation from the First Edition of the Reine Rechtslehre* (Oxford: Clarendon Press, 1992), ch V.

he actual constitution with a somewhat mysteriously superadded duty on judges
l other legal officials to apply those rules.

he second difficulty is that it is not clear how, if at all, such debates in philosophy
aw relate to debates in constitutional theory, in particular, to the debate between
itical' and 'legal' constitutionalists, despite the fact that the debate in constitutional
ory is precisely about questions such as what the constitution is, what makes it
authoritative, and whether it is part of or beyond the law. Political constitutionalists
such as Jeremy Waldron and Richard Bellamy argue that the constitution is a set of
democratic principles that legitimates the legal order and they seem to suppose further
that it lies beyond the legal order in a political, not a legal constitution.[2] Conversely,
legal constitutionalists such as Trevor Allan and Ronald Dworkin argue that the constitution is legal and contains substantive principles of political morality that make up the
legitimating basis of legal order.[3]

Political constitutionalists focus on the issue of the legitimacy of judicial review of a
particular sort—what gets called either 'strong judicial review' or 'strong-form judicial
review'. Strong judicial review occurs when judges are allocated the authority to overrule the legislature and they conclude that statutory provisions violate constitutionally protected rights. This allocation of authority to judges is illegitimate in the eyes of
political constitutionalists since in their view, in a well-functioning democracy, only
our elected representatives in the legislature have the legitimacy and the competence to
settle—to have 'the last word' about—deep societal disagreements about rights.

Allan and Dworkin do not, however, see the debate as confined to a disagreement
within constitutional theory since they also contest the claim of Hart and Kelsen that
at the base of a legal order one finds either a rule of settled practice or a juristically presupposed norm. As I have indicated, in their view, at the base is a legal constitution that
contains substantive principles of political morality. It follows for legal constitutionalists that the focus of political constitutionalists on strong judicial review is misplaced,
since in every legal order judges have the duty to interpret the law in light of substantive
constitutional principles.

But legal positivist philosophers of law do not think they are in that debate. There is,
they think, no real joinder between the inquiry undertaken by philosophy of law, which
is to work out the necessary and sufficient conditions for X to be law, and constitutional
theory. Legal philosophical inquiry is, in their view, descriptive and conceptual by contrast with the politically prescriptive inquiry of constitutional theory.

My chapter argues that joinder is both possible and desirable. It is possible because
legal positivists do have commitments in constitutional theory that they share with
political constitutionalists. Most significantly, they are committed both to an understanding of the constitution according to which the constitution is a legal one that

[2] For example, J. Waldron, 'The Core of the Case Against Judicial Review' (2006) 115 *Yale Law Journal*
1346; R. Bellamy, 'Political Constitutionalism and the Human Rights Act' (2011) 9 *International Journal of
Constitutional Law* 86.
[3] T. R. S. Allan, *The Sovereignty of Law: Freedom, Constitution and Common Law* (Oxford: Oxford
University Press, 2013); R. Dworkin, *Freedom's Law: The Moral Reading of the American Constitution*
(Cambridge, Mass.: Harvard University Press, 1996).

consists exclusively of formal authorization rules—rules that delegate authority to various institutional actors—and to an understanding of the authority of the constitution that is ambivalent about whether the source of the authority is within or without the legal order. Joinder is desirable because with these commitments in view, we can see why otherwise arid-seeming questions in legal philosophy matter to fundamental questions about constitutionality, and why central questions of constitutional theory are important to a more general account of the authority of law.

I shall also argue that once we see that every legal order has a legal constitution, it is difficult to confine our understanding of the constitution of legal order to formal authorization rules or to locate authority outside of the legal order. For such rules imply substantive principles and the combination of such rules with substantive principles locates authority—in the sense of *de jure* or legitimate authority—within legal order. However, my main object is to establish the kind of joinder in which this kind of argument can be properly contested. For with that joinder, we come to see much of philosophy of law as a kind of *Staatsrechtslehre*, the theoretical tradition of public law in which Kelsen worked.[4]

As that hard-to-translate title indicates, the tradition approaches the question of constitutionality through a combination of philosophical and constitutional theory, since it is a question about the correct theory of public legal right, put differently, about the legitimacy of the legal state.[5] In the next section, I sketch the assumptions I adopt in order to get the argument started that every legal order has a legal constitution. The following sections show how these assumptions frame a space in which one can see the joinder between philosophy of law and constitutional theory because within that space legal positivism and political constitutionalism merge into a theory of the legal state and its legitimacy. Since this merger happens only within the space, the assumptions might seem to have a kind of question-begging quality to them.

But my claim is not that a legal order that failed to instantiate one or more of the assumptions would fail to be a legal order, only that all the positions in the debate accept that all of the assumptions can be instantiated without this affecting their position. But it follows from that acceptance (or so I shall argue) that the answer to the

---

[4] 'Much of' because this kind of inquiry in philosophy of law does not of course seek to answer questions about the normative structure of particular fields of private law. It is inclined, however, to give public law priority over private law in understanding legal order, for reasons I sketch in D. Dyzenhaus, 'Liberty and Legal Form', in L. Austin and D. Klimchuk (eds), *The Rule of Law and Private Law* (Oxford: Oxford University Press, 2014), 92–115.

[5] Indeed, to draw the distinction between *philosophy* of law and political or constitutional *theory* rather than between the former and political or constitutional philosophy is to beg the question along with contemporary legal positivists about the nature of legal philosophical inquiry, and I shall contest this distinction as well. There is often more than a hint of disparagement in the remarks of positivist legal philosophers about those they consider constitutional theorists, especially about Ronald Dworkin. Consider, for example, J. Gardner, 'The Legality of Law' (2004) 17 *Ratio Juris* 168, at 173, where he calls Dworkin a 'theoretically ambitious lawyer' because Dworkin is not engaged in the philosophical inquiry of searching for the necessary and sufficient conditions of law. Gardner hastens to add that he does not mean by this claim to 'underestimate the philosophical importance of . . . [Dworkin's] work', but it is unclear what else he had in mind, as might be demonstrated by the fact that he decided to change the comment somewhat when the essay was republished in his collection, J. Gardner, *Law as a Leap of Faith* (Oxford: Oxford University Press, 2012), where he now says at 184: 'Dworkin was and remains more of a lawyer than Hart', driven as his arguments are by 'parochial counterexample'.

question of constitutionality is the one offered by the legal constitutionalists—that the constitution is legal and contains substantive principles of political morality that make up the legitimating basis of legal order.

I

My first assumption has already been stated. All legal orders have a constitution and thus share something fundamental, however much their actual constitutions may differ. At this point, I want to draw out an implication of this assumption. Even if a legal order has no written or positive constitution, it will have an unwritten constitution, which is why I used 'actual' rather than 'positive' to describe the constitutional rules of a particular legal order.

The second assumption is that a legal order consists of the institutions associated with the doctrine of the separation of powers—the legislature, the executive, and the judiciary—and that there is some degree of separation between them. The legislature enacts statutes, the statutes delegate authority to the executive to implement the statutes, and judges have the main role in interpreting the law, including the statute law that delegates authority to the executive.

The third assumption is that otherwise important differences between kinds of legal order do not affect the question of constitutionality, for example, whether the legal order is federal or unitary, whether it is presidential or parliamentary, and so on. Indeed, included in this assumption is that it does not matter to answering the question whether the legal order is one in which there is parliamentary supremacy, so that the parliament can make or unmake any law it likes, or whether the order has an entrenched bill of rights and authorizes judges to invalidate legislation that they regard as violating one or more of the rights. I single out this last issue—whether a legal order is a 'parliamentary legal order' or a 'bill of rights legal order'—because while my assumption is that these features do not affect the question of constitutionality, nevertheless these two models of legal order do frame much of the debate about the question, as is illustrated in the next section of this chapter.

Notice that one can distinguish between a parliamentary legal order and a bill of rights legal order without building into one's description of the latter that judges are authorized to invalidate legislation that does not comply with the rights. As contemporary political constitutionalists envisage, an order can entrench rights or enact rights commitments in an ordinary statute without giving to judges the authority to invalidate a law that seems to violate the rights.[6] Indeed, it is precisely this kind of development that gives rise to the idea of strong judicial review. For that term is not supposed to contrast mainly with judicial review of administrative action in a parliamentary legal order. Rather, it contrasts mainly with judicial review of the kind judges perform when under section 3 of the UK Human Rights Act (1998) they read primary legislation 'in a way which is compatible with Convention rights' and when under section 4 they issue a declaration of incompatibility when a rights-consistent interpretation seems not

---

[6] For example, Waldron, above n 2; Bellamy, above n 2.

possible. Given that Parliament can enact a statute to override a section 3 interpretation and that the validity of a statute is not affected by a section 4 declaration of incompatibility, political constitutionalists suppose that Parliament retains the last word in
this kind of legal order and thus its supremacy, which is why they find the constitutional set-up unobjectionable, even desirable, given that they also suppose that a society should uphold individual rights. But my second assumption includes that in a bill —
of rights legal order, judges do have the authority to invalidate statutes.

My last assumption is that in all of the legal orders in which we pose the question of
constitutionality, judges have the authority to review state action even if their review
authority is of the weakest form possible—the authority to pronounce on whether public officials have acted within the limits of their statutory mandates, which in the parliamentary legal order of the United Kingdom is traditionally the only public law review
authority that judges are thought to have. Notice that this assumption is controversial
to the extent that it suggests that the kind of weak judicial review that is instantiated
in the field of law that goes under the name of administrative law is a kind of constitutional review. For the suggestion undermines the distinction between constitutional
law and administrative law within public law and, if it does have this effect, it also
undermines the political constitutionalist distinction between strong and weak judicial
review.

I shall indeed argue that the assumption does have these implications and that they
are salutary. But for the moment I want just to emphasize that in the debates that are the
subject of this chapter, this assumption—like the others—is not controversial in that no
one involved in the debates would think that the assumption that judges have such a
review power affects in any way their central claims. According to both legal positivists
and political constitutionalists, it is a truism that in any legal system with a rudimentary separation of powers, judges will have the authority to ensure that officials who
wield delegated powers stay within their legislative mandate and that such authority is
necessary if the rule of law is to be maintained.[7]

II

With the bill of rights legal order and the parliamentary legal order in place as our two
basic models of a legal order, we can ask what they share by way of a constitution. We
have already encountered one problem that gets in the way of answering the question
of constitutionality, whether the constitution is in or outside the legal order, that is,
whether it is a political or a legal constitution.

Another problem, as already indicated, is that there seem to be two rival versions of
the basis of constitutionality, of its fundamentality. Is it a set of *formal authorization
rules* that authorize legislators, judges, and other legal officials to make, interpret, and
implement the law or is it a set of *substantive principles* that materially limit what certain officials are permitted to do, for example, by entrenching individual rights against

[7] See J. Raz, 'The Rule of Law and its Virtue', in Raz, *The Authority of Law: Essays on Law and Morality*
(Oxford: Oxford University Press, 1983) 217, his sixth principle; and Waldron, above n 2, 1354.

the state as in a bill of rights legal order? The answer 'both authorization rules and substantive principles' is vulnerable to the following challenge. In a parliamentary legal order, there are authorization rules—the formal or procedural rules of 'manner and form' that the parliament has to follow in order to make law. But there might be no substantive principles, at least none that limits the parliament's authority to make a law with any content. So the answer to the question of constitutionality would seem to be 'necessarily authorization rules and contingently, in addition, substantive principles'. This answer will seem intuitively plausible when we consider some obvious examples of well-functioning legal orders such as the US bill of rights order which has a written constitution that entrenches rights and that requires (or at least for a long time has been asserted to require) judges to invalidate statutes that, in their view, violate those rights, and the UK order in which there is parliamentary supremacy.

With that answer, legal positivism seems to emerge victorious in its argument with thinkers in the natural law tradition who argue that there is a necessary connection between law and morality. More to the point of this chapter, the answer establishes the lack of joinder between philosophy of law and constitutional theory mentioned in the last section. Recall Austin's famous line: 'The existence of law is one thing; its merit or demerit another.' Austin follows that claim with: 'Whether it be or not is one enquiry; whether it be or not conformable to an assumed standard is a different enquiry.'[8] These two lines continue to shape legal positivism's view of legal philosophy since the distinction between philosophy of law and constitutional theory tracks the distinction between the 'is' and the 'ought' of law, the distinction stated in Hart's 'Separation Thesis' that there is no necessary connection between law and morality.[9]

However, for reasons that will become clear in a moment, I shall refer to the distinction as Hart referred to it in 1958 in his first major statement of legal positivism as the 'utilitarian distinction'[10] in recognition that Bentham and Austin who had proposed it were not only legal positivists, but also the founders of utilitarianism: a political philosophy about the common good and the design of political and legal order. Notice that to make the distinction is not to declare the second kind of inquiry to be less worth doing than the inquiry undertaken by philosophy of law. It is only to say that it falls within the domain of another kind of inquiry—political theory—of which constitutional theory is a branch.

But at least three things should make us hesitate before accepting legal positivism's apparent victory. First, political constitutionalists usually adopt a positivistic understanding of law as determined as a matter of social fact. That is, they regard as highly suspect the legal constitutionalist suggestion that judges should interpret statutes in light of their understanding of the substantive principles of their legal order. Rather, judges should adopt interpretative approaches to law that search for facts about legislative intent; and there are well-known examples of judges who profess allegiance to such approaches.[11]

[8] J. Austin, *Province of Jurisprudence Determined* 2nd edn (London: John Murray, 1861), vol 1, 233.
[9] H. L. A. Hart, 'Positivism and the Separation of Law and Morals' (1958) 71 *Harvard Law Review* 593.
[10] For example, ibid 612.
[11] See, for example, J. Waldron, 'Can There Be a Democratic Jurisprudence?' (2009) 58 *Emory Law Journal* 675, at 682ff; and Bellamy, above n 2, 91. In regard to judges, consider 'textualists' and 'originalists' in the

Second, and as Hart rather casually acknowledged in referring to the 'utilitarian distinction' between law and morality, Bentham and Austin deployed that distinction in the service of a conception of law that models legal order in such a way as to make law an effective instrument for the top-down transmission of the political judgments of utilitarian elites to legal subjects. Bentham, as we know, wished to avoid as much as possible giving judges the opportunity to impose their views on the content of legislation, whereas Austin differed mainly in that he worried that legislators are beholden to the uneducated public,[12] so he thought it desirable to give a larger role to the judicial elite than Bentham.

In other words, for Hart's positivist predecessors while the answer to the question of what the law is on a matter is not answerable to a political standard, they designed a conception of law and of legal order to make this conception so answerable. This is the standard set by utilitarianism that requires, as in political constitutionalism, that legal order should be designed in a particular way and that questions about the law of that legal order must be resolvable to the extent possible without judges having to rely on debate about the merits of that content; only interpretative methods that rely exclusively on social facts about the law are legitimate.

Third, Austin regards constitutional law not as law properly so called but as 'positive morality'—as a set of moral conventions that stand outside of the legal order and that cannot affect the validity of law.[13] But that is because, with Bentham, Austin regards as illegitimate judicial reliance on moral principles as criteria for the validity of statutes, though unlike Bentham he wants to grant judges a large interstitial law-making role.[14]

Bentham and Austin are then the original political constitutionalists, at least in the English tradition of legal thought. They differ from their descendants in Waldron and Bellamy only in that the descendants are not hostile to bills of rights, even entrenched bills of rights, as long as the legislature is recognized as the final interpreter of the rights. It might even be that if one sets contemporary positivist or 'Hartian' legal philosophy in the tradition of positivist thinking about law that stretches from Bentham to Waldron, its mode of doing legal philosophy looks rather aberrant since positivist legal philosophy before Hart and in the hands of contemporary political constitutionalists is a kind of *Staatsrechtslehre*. Indeed, as we will see below, the rule of recognition might best be understood as an unhelpful placeholder for the normative commitments of this political constitutionalist tradition.

Moreover, figures in the common law tradition have argued for centuries that the authority of a supreme lawmaker in a parliamentary legal order to legislate is controlled by substantive principles that judges discern in interpreting the legal traditions of their political community. In their view, such principles are more fundamental in the constitution of legal order than authorization rules, so if we are looking for the basis of

---

United States, such as Justices Scalia and Thomas, or in the United Kingdom, Lord Sumption. For the last, see 'The Limits of Law', available at https://www.supremecourt.uk/docs/speech-131120.pdf. In J. Gardner, 'Legal Positivism: 51/2 Myths', in Gardner, above n 5, 24, Gardner accuses those who dwell on the way that central features of legal positivism play a role in practice—his examples are Dworkin and Gerald Postema—of creating a 'fundamentally anti-philosophical climate'.

[12] See, for example, Austin, above n 8, vol 1, 65–6; and Austin, above n 8, vol 2, 348–55.
[13] Ibid vol 1, 230.   [14] Ibid vol 2, 348–55.

constitutionality, we should look to such principles. This argument has been revived in our time in the work of Allan and Dworkin as it is entailed by their and the common law tradition's *version* of the argument that the 'is' and the 'ought' of law cannot be separated in answering the question what law is, whether at the most abstract level where the question is the correct conception of law, or at the most concrete level, where in issue is the answer to a question about what the law is on a matter.

Somewhere in between these two levels, then, is the level at which the question of constitutionality is to be answered. And I emphasized 'version' because for political constitutionalists, their answer to the question at the most abstract level might appear to have the result that there is no intermediate level of legal constitutionalism. In their view, the constitution is a political one located outside of the legal order and the task of law is to transmit to those subject to law the results reached by the legislature, the primary institution of the political constitution.

Notice that while we know that political constitutionalists think that it is a political mistake to establish a bill of rights legal order, it is not clear whether they also think that even in such an order the constitution is ultimately a political and mistaken one, or whether the mistake resides in establishing a legal constitution. Austin, as Hart noted, held the former view whereas Bentham held the latter.[15] But, as we shall now see, the same kind of problem bedevils Hart's attempt to understand the fundamental or constitutional basis of legal order, that is, to answer the question of constitutionality.

Moreover, as I shall also show, although there is some ambiguity in their position, both political constitutionalists and legal positivists seem committed to the claim that the legal constitution is ultimately a formal one—one that consists only of formal authorization rules—thus establishing the promised joinder. Put differently, both political constitutionalists and legal positivists must suppose that there are rules that determine what counts as valid legislation, which goes to show that the idea of a thin legal constitution is implicit in their position. The rule of recognition and the basic norm are attempts to express that kind of normative constitutional commitment in an apparently neutral fashion.

III

In his classic essay in the 1958 *Harvard Law Review*, Hart rejected the command theory of law that he took to be advanced by his positivist predecessors, Bentham and Austin. According to that theory, the sovereign is legally unlimited and his law consists of commands backed by sanctions. Hart objected that 'nothing which legislators do makes law unless they comply with fundamental rules specifying the essential law-making procedures'. 'They lie', he said, 'at the root of a legal system' and 'what was most missing in the utilitarian scheme is an analysis of what it is for a social group and its officials to accept such rules'. Hart thus suggested that this notion of fundamental rule plus acceptance, not that of a command as Austin claimed, is the '"key to the science of jurisprudence", or at least one of the keys'.[16]

---

[15] Hart, above n 9, 599.   [16] Ibid 603.

In *The Concept of Law*, Hart elaborated his account of fundamental law by de
ing a 'primitive' society in which there are only 'primary' rules, rules that impose
on the individuals in the society, and in which problems arise in regard to: the '
tainty' about what social norms count as such rules; the 'static' nature of these
since there is no clear way of changing them; and 'inefficiency' because of the l
recognized means of determining rule violations and of rule enforcement.[17] In hi

> The simplest form of remedy for the uncertainty of the regime of primary rules is the
> introduction of what we shall call a 'rule of recognition'. This will specify some feature
> or features possession of which by a suggested rule is taken as a conclusive affirmative
> indication that it is a rule of the group to be supported by the local pressure it exerts.[18]

The static quality of primary rules is remedied by the introduction of 'rules of change'
and the problem of inefficiency by the introduction of 'rules of adjudication'.[19]

Now from the 1958 essay it might seem that the fundamental law of a legal order is
the rules of change and that their existence shows that even in a parliamentary legal
order there are legal limits on what the legislature may do, thus refuting the command
theory's claim that the sovereign is legally unlimited. But in *The Concept of Law* Hart
made it clear that it is the rule of recognition that is fundamental since it specifies the
law-making procedures.

The rule of recognition is more fundamental than the other 'secondary' rules—the
rules of change and adjudication—because the other secondary rules are not ultimate
in the way that the rule of recognition is. Indeed, that a rule of change is a rule of the
system will depend on whether it is certified as such by the rule of recognition. And the
ultimate nature of the rule of recognition is indicated by the fact that its existence is not
certified by any other rule. It exists as a matter of fact in the practice of the officials of
the system and they apply it because they take the 'internal point of view' towards it—
they regard it as providing 'a public, common standard of correct judicial decision'.[20]
Moreover, the rule does not so much limit what sovereign law-making bodies may do
as constitute them as law-making bodies, just as the rules of contract law do not so
much limit what the contracting parties may do, but make it possible for them 'to create structures of rights and duties for the conduct of life within the coercive framework
of the law'.[21]

The idea of a rule of recognition seems to enable legal positivism to account for the
existence of both parliamentary and bills of rights legal orders in a way that was not
open to Bentham and Austin, given their shared political opposition to such orders
as well as Austin's legal theoretical opposition—his claim that even in a bill of rights
legal order, the constitution amounts to no more than positive morality and that its
sanctions are moral, not legal. The rule seems to supply the answer to the question of
constitutionality that a constitution contains 'necessarily authorization rules and contingently, in addition, substantive principles'. The make-up of any actual constitution is
thus a matter of description and legal positivism itself takes no stance on whether it is
advisable to incorporate substantive principles into a constitution.

---

[17] Hart, above n 1, 92–3.   [18] Ibid 94.   [19] Ibid 95–7.
[20] Ibid 116.   [21] Ibid 27–9.

David Dyzenhaus

But ▮▮▮ of a rule of recognition turns out to be quite mysterious. While Hart often s▮▮▮▮ the rule of recognition of a legal order is its constitution, there are also indica▮▮▮▮s work and in the work of his followers that the rule of recognition is more ▮▮▮▮ the constitution. Consider, for example, the parliamentary legal order of the ▮▮▮▮ngdom described as follows on the website of the UK Parliament:[22]

> Parli▮▮▮▮ sovereignty is a principle of the UK constitution. It makes Parliament the supreme legal authority in the UK, which can create or end any law. Generally, the courts cannot overrule its legislation and no Parliament can pass laws that future Parliaments cannot change. Parliamentary sovereignty is the most important part of the UK constitution.

On this description, the rules of change for statutes—that is, formal authorization rules—are the fundamental part of the UK constitution. As a result, in an inquiry into the validity of a statute, all that a court may have regard to is whether there has been compliance with those rules. But there must be something that makes it the case that judicial inquiries into validity are so confined, and if it is the rule of recognition that makes it the case, is the rule really the constitution or is it something that lies beyond the constitution?

Hart said that this kind of question 'extracts from some a cry of despair: how can we show that the fundamental provisions of a constitution which are surely law are really law?'[23] Others, he said, 'reply with the insistence that at the base of legal systems, there is something which is "not law", which is "pre-legal", "metal-legal" or is just "political fact"'. His own solution:

> The case for calling the rule of recognition 'law' is that the rule providing criteria for the identification of other rules of the system may well be thought a defining feature of a legal system, and so itself worth calling 'law'; the case for calling it 'fact' is that to assert that such a rule exists is indeed to make an external statement of an actual fact concerning the manner in which the rules of an 'efficacious' system are identified. Both these aspects claim attention but we cannot do justice to them both by choosing one of the labels 'law' or 'fact'. Instead, we need to remember that the ultimate rule of recognition may be regarded from two points of view: one is expressed in the external statement of fact that the rule exists in the actual practice of the system: the other is expressed in the internal statements of validity made by those who use it in identifying the law.[24]

Hart also acknowledged that the consensus on which the internal point of view seems to depend could break down because there could be disagreement about the 'ultimate criteria to be used in identifying a law'.[25] In this regard, he went on to remark that when the courts have to settle such disagreements—'previously unenvisaged questions concerning the most fundamental constitutional rules'—'they *get* their authority to decide them accepted after the questions have arisen and the decision has been given. Here all that succeeds is success'.[26]

---

[22] Available at http://www.parliament.uk/about/how/sovereignty.   [23] Hart, above n 1, 111.
[24] Ibid 111–12.   [25] Ibid 122.   [26] Ibid 153 (his emphasis).

Hart's students do little, in my view, to dispel the despair. John Gardner, for example, points out that Hart was uncertain whether to classify the rules of recognition as themselves legal. In Gardner's view, rules of recognition do not 'quite belong to' their legal systems. They 'lie beyond the constitution' since one needs rules of recognition in order to identify rules as constitutional rules. 'Even the constitution needs to be constituted somehow.' 'Is it constituted by law?' Kelsen, Gardner says, thought so, but then faced an infinite regress, which the fiction of the validity of the first historical constitution was supposed to end. In contrast, Hart avoided this problem, Gardner claims, by presenting the ultimate rules of recognition as 'borderline legal rules'. They provide criteria, but 'by their nature' do not meet those criteria. They are, he says, to be found in the 'custom of law applying officials' but need not identify that custom as a source of law. 'In that sense they are above the law rather than part of it.' We can thus agree that there are 'ultimate rules of recognition that are, so to speak, above the constitution' and that 'there is no *law* that is above the constitution. Constitutional law is as high as the law goes'.[27]

Joseph Raz rejects the thought that the constitution of a country is its rule of recognition because while most constitutions can always be changed 'in accordance with procedures they themselves provide', the rule of recognition 'can change only as the practice that it is changes'. It 'cannot give way to statutory law'. It is unlike the rest of the law. 'It is the practice—that is, the fact—that the courts and other legal institutions recognize the validity, the legitimacy, of the law, and that they are willing to follow it and apply it to others.' 'It is the point...at which—metaphorically speaking—the law ends and morality begins.' 'If the rule of recognition exists...then the law exists. But only if...[the courts] are right in so conducting themselves is the law actually legitimate and binding, morally speaking.'[28]

Finally, Waldron has argued that if we are looking for the ultimate rules of a legal order, rules of change are more worthy of our attention than the rule of recognition.[29] Waldron suggests that the validity of a rule depends not on any rule of recognition but on whether the rule was made in accordance with the rules of change. He also suggests that in a parliamentary legal order the rule of recognition gets 'its distinctive content from the rule of change' that empowers the parliament to legislate and that 'it is not clear...that the rule of recognition actually does anything with that content that the rule of change has not already done'.[30] Further, contrary to the arguments made by most legal positivists, Waldron alleges that we do not need the rule of recognition to tell us that there is a duty to observe the rules of change, since the power that a rule of change confers on, say, the legislature to enact a statute implies that the duties of other actors in the system will be changed when the power is exercised. In Waldron's view,

---

[27] J. Gardner, 'Can There Be a Written Constitution?', in Gardner, above n 5, 107 (his emphasis).

[28] J. Raz, 'On the Authority and Interpretation of Constitutions: Some Preliminaries', in L. Alexander (ed), *Constitutionalism: Philosophical Foundations* (New York: Cambridge University Press, 1998), 152–93, at 161.

[29] J. Waldron, 'Who Needs Rules of Recognition?', in M. Adler and K. E. Himma (eds), *The Rule of Recognition and the US Constitution* (New York: Oxford University Press, 2009), 327–50. Waldron might be thought to have an ambivalent relationship with the positivist tradition, but that thought depends, in my view, on supposing that the tradition starts with Hart. If the tradition is seen as including Bentham and Austin, and in line with my argument as a kind of *Staatsrechtslehre*, Waldron is more of a torchbearer of that tradition than most legal philosophers who work in broadly the positivist style of legal philosophy.

[30] Ibid 342.

the claim that every legal order contains a rule of recognition might be driven by a perceived need for closure—that is, for a rule that would make it the case that a legal order
produced a kind of certainty that one might think desirable on normative or conceptual grounds. But there is, he says, 'some effrontery in the positivists' insistence that
every legal system must contain a rule cast in terms that represents the positivists' own
jurisprudential position!'[31]

Waldron could have called in aid Hart's own observation that in parliamentary legal
orders we do not need to look beyond the constitution to find a rule that puts judges
under a duty to apply the constitution: 'It seems a needless reduplication to suggest
that there is a further rule to the effect that the constitution (or those "who laid it
down") are to be obeyed.'[32] Gardner, however, thinks that the observation is mistaken
in regard to written constitutions—constitutions which are 'laid down'—though it
is true of unwritten constitutions. In the former, there is no 'needless reduplication'
but 'a separate rule of recognition without which there is no written constitution to
contain those rules.'[33]

But in this view the rule of recognition when there is a written constitution turns out
to be nothing more than Kelsen's basic norm, as Gardner seems to acknowledge.[34] And
Waldron himself reverts to Kelsen, though he suggests that we might try to understand
the basic norm as a normative practice. In line with his general argument Waldron
adds that the norm is better understood as a dynamic process than a static recognition,
since the basic norm empowers those who laid down the first constitution to make that
change.[35]

One might well ask whether Waldron's remark about the effrontery of the positivist position does not come back to bite him, given his argument. Suppose that the
fundamental or constitutional rules of a legal order are rules of change of the sort we
associate with the rules of manner and form of the UK parliamentary process. The
main constitutional task of judges when confronted with a statute is to recognize it
as valid when it complies with such rules of change. If the constitution contains only
such rules of change, its content is purely formal. It contains only those rules that are
required to enable a supreme legislature to maintain its supremacy, which is exactly
what political constitutionalists from Bentham to Waldron have thought appropriate.

Perhaps then the legal positivist answer to the question of constitutionality is that the
constitution of every legal order is fundamentally a matter of formal authorization rules
or rules of change. Precisely this thought seemed to animate Austin's reflections on the
US Constitution, the essence of which, he thought, lies in its amendment formula.[36]
Austin held the view that Gardner describes unkindly: that in the United States 'the

---

[31] Ibid 344. Note that Norberto Bobbio, one of the finest legal philosophers of the last century, held
the same view of the rule of recognition. See the illuminating discussion in R. Guastini, 'The Basic Norm
Revisited', in L. Duarte d'Almeida, J. Gardner, and L. Green (eds), *Kelsen Revisited: New Essays on the Pure
Theory of Law* (Oxford: Hart Publishing, 2013), 63–76, at 72–3.

[32] Hart, above n 1, 293.

[33] Gardner, above n 27, 109. See further P. Cane, 'Public Law in *The Concept of Law*' (2013) 33 *Oxford
Journal of Legal Studies* 649, at 669–73.

[34] Gardner, above n 27, n 51 at 109.   [35] Waldron, above n 29, 346–8.

[36] Austin, above n 8, vol 1, 222.

Presidency, Congress and the Supreme Court are ... mere administ   ies regulated by a kind of jumped up administrative law'.[37]

Political constitutionalists like Waldron and Bellamy, and perh   nam and Austin too, turn out then not to be arguing against legal constituti   but for a particular kind of legal constitution, a formal one that is not only lim   es of the manner and form sort, but also to rules that do not constrain the le   authority to effect any legal change by ordinary statute. They are then for   onstitutionalists, though for substantive reasons to do with this kind of constitutionalism's fit with the political theory of utilitarianism or with a theory of democratic legitimacy and competence that requires that the legislature have the last word when it comes to settling rights disagreements.[38] And because this fit is with some external source of legitimacy, they can understand all authority within the legal order as delegated authority, with 'the people' being the ultimate author.

It is significant that Kelsen also regarded constitutional law as jumped up administrative law.[39] In his view, the parliament in any legal order creates law at a very high level but still at a level below the constitution. So the parliament, just like an administrative body, exercises authority delegated by the level above. Indeed, Kelsen appears to think that even the constitutional level is not ultimate since states have their authority delegated to them by international law.[40] Constitutional law is then the ultra vires principle of administrative law writ large, the principle that a body that wields delegated power cannot go beyond the terms of its mandate.[41]

In this view, in every legal order there is not only a constitution but also a legal constitution, since every constitution will contain more or less complex rules of change. The choice as to such rules is, Kelsen supposes, political.[42] The question of how political power should be distributed in order to bring into being the will of the community is a political not a legal–theoretical question. But whatever the answer to that question, it will be expressed in the formal authorization rules of a legal constitution.

When the actual legal constitution contains in addition what Kelsen calls 'material norms', for example a right to freedom of expression, and gives to judges the authority to determine whether norms have been violated by the legislature, the question of whether the norm has been violated is still, according to him, formal rather than substantive or material. For in such an order, whether or not a statute that violates the

---

[37] Gardner, above n 27, 115.

[38] There are other theories of legitimacy that underpin this kind of formal constitutionalism, for example, the theory of constitutional monarchy.

[39] H. Kelsen, 'The Nature and Development of Constitutional Adjudication', in L. Vinx (ed), *The Guardian of the Constitution: Hans Kelsen and Carl Schmitt on the Limits of Constitutional Law* (Cambridge: Cambridge University Press, 2015), 22–78.

[40] Ibid 34–5.

[41] Note that Gardner himself struggles to escape this view in Gardner, above n 27, 109–16. In his view, bodies like legislatures and courts wield inherent not delegated power. In explaining why they have inherent power he suggests that originally the power was delegated to them, but at a certain point they came to be viewed by relevant officials as wielding powers that are not revocable, and from that point on they have inherent power.

[42] See Kelsen's critique of Carl Schmitt, H. Kelsen, 'Who Ought to Be the Guardian of the Constitution?', in Vinx, above n 39, 174–221.

norm is unconstitutional depends ultimately on whether it was enacted in accordance with the amendment formula.[43]

However, Kelsen warns sternly against the introduction of terms such as 'freedom' into the constitution unless these terms can be given a determinate content. If they cannot, a 'fullness of power' is conceded to judges which is 'altogether intolerable' as it involves a 'shift of power from parliament to an extra-parliamentary institution' and which might involve the judges becoming the 'exponent of political forces completely different from those that express themselves in parliament'.[44]

Notice that most features of this kind of position might seem to characterize Raz's account of the relation of the rule of recognition to the constitution. Recall that he says that most constitutions can be changed 'in accordance with procedures they themselves provide', hence, the rule of recognition cannot be the constitution. Thus he seems to envisage that the legal constitution is in most legal systems fundamentally a matter of formal rules of change. Why then is the rule of recognition necessary? Because, or so the answer seems to be, there must exist something that makes these rules authoritative for officials. But, as we have seen, it is not clear that the rule of recognition can do that job. For Raz, the source of judicial duty is morality, and so it is located beyond not only the legal order and its constitution, but even beyond the rule of recognition. Indeed, on Raz's account of authority, actual legitimacy or authority depends on whether the law is the effective instrument of moral judgments that legal subjects should follow because this will serve their interests better than if they decided for themselves. Hence, law lives up to its ideal as law when it conforms to fundamental formal norms that conduce to its service as an effective instrument of morality.[45] But then the authority of the constitution finds a moral resting point outside of law in the argument that legitimate authority inheres in the authors of the law in fact doing a better job of moral reasoning than its subjects would, if left to their own devices.

As we have seen, the political constitutionalists also find a resting point outside of law in the politics of sovereignty, though they insist that the sovereign is a supreme parliament.[46] But they have to manage the fact that the legislature is not a purely political construct—it is a legally constituted institution. They do so, as we have seen, by claiming either that it is not or that it should not be subject to substantive constitutional limits, that is, through the claim that the legal constitution is or should be limited to a particular kind of formal authorization rule. Hence for them authority becomes located both inside and outside of legal order. It is located inside in the formal rules of change of a particular kind of legal constitution, and it is located outside in what legitimates restricting the rules of change so as to ensure the supremacy of a democratically elected parliament.

---

[43] Ibid 187–8; and Kelsen, above n 39, 29.   [44] Ibid 61–2.

[45] In my view, these two lines summarize the position that comes out of a combination of J. Raz, 'Authority, Law, and Morality', in J. Raz, *Ethics in the Public Domain: Essays in the Morality of Law and Politics* (Oxford: Oxford University Press, 1994); and Raz, above n 7.

[46] For further exploration, see D. Dyzenhaus, 'Constitutionalism in an Old Key: Legality and Constituent Power' (2012) 1 *Global Constitutionalism* 229.

Similarly, both Hart and Kelsen think that behind the actual constitution is something more fundamental than positive law, something that gives rise to what Hart in a perhaps unguarded moment called 'legal legitimacy'.[47] It is what makes law into an authoritative order and not 'the gunman situation writ large'.[48] As they understand things, there has to be a source of duty and that source cannot be the constitution, because there has to be something that validates that constitution—otherwise we encounter the logical problem of an infinite regress.

However, that problem arises only for those who make what I shall term 'the assumption of linearity', after Mark Walters's perspicuous distinction in this volume between 'linear' and 'circular' theories of law.[49] Linear theories assume 'that the authority of legal norms can be traced back along a line of increasingly higher norms until an originating source is located. Law from this perspective is held up by a string, and someone or something must hold the end of that string'.[50]

Political constitutionalists differ from legal positivist philosophers when it comes to such questions as where the string ends, within or without the legal order. The best explanation for this difference is as follows. There is only one position in play but it makes its argument within two registers and it is the movement between these registers that creates ambiguity and mystery.

Legal positivism in its constitutional theory register is ambivalent about whether the constitution is political or legal, but insistent that the constitution ought to contain only formal authorization rules of the kind one finds in a parliamentary legal order. It also insists that authority, in the sense of *de jure* or legitimate authority resides outside of legal order, though when the constitution is limited to formal authorization rules it will be the case that the laws enacted by the parliament are by definition legitimate.

In contrast, in its philosophy of law register, legal positivism holds that the constitution is legal but is ambivalent about whether its authority is located in or outside of legal order. That ambivalence leads to another, about whether whatever gives the constitution authority (an ultimate rule or a basic norm) is itself in or outside the legal order. Moreover, in this register legal positivism still tends to cling to the claim that the constitution either should be or is in fact limited to formal authorization rules, though in its attempts to rise above the constitutional theory fray, it is usually compelled to concede that the constitution can contingently contain substantive principles.

The way forward for legal positivism is to merge the two registers by arguing that the constitution is legal, that it should be confined to formal authorization rules of the kind one finds in a parliamentary legal order, and that once so confined, the law made by the parliament enjoys legitimate authority. 'The people' who delegate authority from the outside can then be identified with the democratically elected legislature, and *de facto* authority becomes *de jure* authority. In other words, the way forward for legal positivism is to reconceive itself as a participant in the project of *Staatsrechtslehre*, as involved in the debate about the correct theory of public legal right.

---

[47] See H. L. A. Hart, 'Answers to Eight Questions', in Duarte D'Almeida, Gardner, and Green, above n 31, 279–98.
[48] Hart, above n 9, 603.   [49] Walters in this volume, 33.   [50] Ibid.

But, as I shall now suggest, legal positivism reconceived in this way encounters a different set of problems. Once the concession is made that the constitution is legal and that it is the locus of legitimate authority, it is difficult both to stick with a linear theory and to confine the constitution to formal authorization rules. In terms of Walters's distinction, the justification of authority becomes circular and answers the question of constitutionality with 'both authorization rules and substantive principles'. Moreover, with circularity the accusation of effrontery is stripped of its force. The values that legitimate legal order and that figure fundamentally in the theory of that order are to be found in a process of justification that circulates within the legal order.

IV

Consider the claim that the constitution has to be more than 'jumped up administrative law'. That claim is really a conclusion that depends on two premises: the major premise that the constitution can't be understood in terms of delegated power; the minor premise that there is no more to administrative law than delegated power. The first premise is correct but the second is wrong. Administrative law is constitutional law writ small, for it is not just a matter of formal authorizations, but also of values and principles that govern administrative action. And it is only if one holds a linear theory of authority that one is driven to suppose that the values and principles have to be attributed to the tacit will of some lawmaker.[51] It is for this reason that it is significant that, as I claimed earlier, legal positivists and political constitutionalists are willing to assume that in any legal system with a rudimentary separation of powers, judges will have the authority to ensure that officials who wield delegated powers stay within their legislative mandate and that such authority is necessary if the rule of law is to be maintained.

My argument starts with what will seem to many legal positivists to be two 'parochial' examples which cannot form the basis for a claim that sounds in philosophy of law, both taken from the UK parliamentary legal order.[52] The first is the great dissent in World War I by Lord Shaw in *R v Halliday*, in which he reasoned that a blanket legislative authorization to the executive to make regulations to deal with a situation of wartime emergency should be read by judges not to include the authority to make a regulation governing detention in the absence of explicit authority in the authorizing legislation.[53] In Lord Shaw's view, the Habeas Corpus Acts and other constitutional documents, for example, Magna Carta, give expression to principles that are part of the constitution. They 'in one sense confer', he said, 'no rights upon the subject, but they provide whereby his fundamental rights shall be vindicated, his freedom from arrest except on justifiable legal process shall be secured, and arbitrary attack upon liberty and life shall be promptly and effectually foiled by law'. He also said that if Parliament had intended to make this colossal delegation of power it would have done so 'plainly and courageously and not under cover of words about regulations for safety and defence'. For judges to allow the right to be abridged is to 'revolutionize' the

---

[51] See D. Dyzenhaus, 'Process and Substance as Aspects of the Public Law Form' (2015) 74 *Cambridge Law Journal* 284.
[52] See Gardner, 2012, above n 5, 184.   [53] *R v Halliday, ex p Zadig* [1917] AC 260.

constitution, perhaps, more accurately to undertake a counter-revolution. It amounts to what he called a 'constructive repeal of habeas corpus', a repeal by the executive that is then ratified by judges.[54]

Notice that in Kelsenian terms, this material or substantive norm is formally protected, because the legislature has to be utterly explicit about its intentions to override that norm in any statute. Moreover, on some definitions of strong judicial review, Lord Shaw would have exercised such review had he been able to persuade a majority of his fellow judges to join him. Waldron, for example, says such review exists not only when judges have the authority to decline to apply a statute but also when they have the authority 'to modify the effect of a statute to make its application conform with individual rights (in ways that the statute does not itself envisage)'.[55] But that is arguably what judges do much of the time in administrative law, dramatically in the *Anisminic* case in which the Judicial Committee of the House of Lords found a path to evading a provision in a statute that precluded judicial review, but less dramatically in many decisions on the validity of administrative action.[56] These are cases that political constitutionalists do not generally find problematic from the standpoint of democratic legitimacy because they take for granted that public officials must stay within their legislative mandate.[57]

As Kelsen argued, however, if one accords to judges the authority to interpret statutes in order to guarantee the legality of executive action implementing those statutes, one should likewise be committed to according to judges the authority to interpret the norms of the constitution that govern the legality of statutes. To think that a statute is the guarantee of its own legality is, according to Kelsen, a kind of nonsense,[58] a point well illustrated by my second example—*Jackson v Attorney General.*[59]

That case was on the surface about formal rules of change. The judges had to decide whether the Hunting Act 2004, which criminalized certain kinds of hunting, was a lawful Act of Parliament. The House of Lords had refused to assent to the Act. Prior to the Parliament Act 1911 such a refusal was an effective veto but the 1911 Act made it possible for the House of Commons to override the upper House after two years. The Parliament Act of 1949 reduced the period to one year, but because the House of Lords opposed the bill, it had to be enacted in accordance with the requirements of the 1911 Act.

---

[54] Ibid 293–4.   [55] Waldron, above n 2, 1346.
[56] *Anisminic Ltd v The Foreign Compensation Committee* [1969] 2 AC 147.
[57] See Waldron and Bellamy, above n 2. Political constitutionalists may object that in these cases the judges are doing something other than applying the statutes and that only if the judges were to stick to literal application would they be interpreting the statute legitimately. In other words, as I pointed out above, they hold that judges should adopt interpretative approaches to law that search for facts about legislative intent. But that of course is to adopt a controversial stance about the correct interpretative theory that cannot appeal in any non-question begging way to facts, since what the facts are is conditioned by fundamental, normative commitments. It is also, in my view, misleading to suppose as political constitutionalists do that the main issue is which institution gets the last word. Whether the legal constitution consists of substantive principles as well as formal authorization rules does not depend on whether judges are recognized as having authority to enforce the principles against the legislature. Legal positivists from Austin are misled by the same false picture.
[58] Kelsen, above n 39, 22–7.   [59] *Jackson v Attorney General* [2005] UKHL 56.

The appellants in *Jackson* argued that the 1911 Act could not lawfully be used to amend itself, that the 1949 Act was not, therefore, a validly enacted Act of Parliament, and that the Hunting Act, having been made under the amended procedure, was not an Act of Parliament. Their argument thus depended on the claim that legislation made under the 1911 Act was a species of delegated legislation which entailed that the validity of legislation made under it could be questioned in a way that the validity of primary legislation may not and the House of Commons had acted ultra vires by enlarging the powers that had been conferred on it by the 1911 Act. The argument was thus designed to meet the counterclaim that when a statute is on its face valid, the courts may not look behind it at the process by which it was enacted in order to test its validity.[60]

The government did not as a matter of fact make this counterclaim. Instead, it argued that as long as the House of Commons followed the procedure set out in the 1949 Act it could enact any statute whatsoever. Nevertheless, the judges did find it important to dismiss the counterclaim. Lord Bingham, for example, said that '[t]he appellants have raised a question of law which cannot, as such, be resolved by Parliament. But it would not be satisfactory, or consistent with the rule of law, if it could not be resolved at all. So it seems to me necessary that the courts should resolve it, and that to do so involves no breach of constitutional propriety.'[61]

Moreover, the judges agreed that Parliament as constituted under either of the Acts could not evade a prohibition in the 1911 Act against extending the life of Parliament beyond five years. Lord Bingham and two others supposed that this was the only restriction on Parliament's authority,[62] while four reserved judgment on this matter.[63] Lord Steyn and Lady Hale, in contrast, expressed their disquiet at the thought that the House of Commons as long as it waited the requisite period could do anything it liked, enacting 'undemocratic and oppressive legislation', or abolishing the upper House or judicial review in cases where governmental action affects the rights of individuals.[64]

---

[60] See ibid para 7 (per Lord Bingham).

[61] Ibid para 27, and see para 51 (per Lord Nicholls). For an argument that the judges had no jurisdiction, see R. Ekins, 'Acts of Parliament and the Parliament Acts' (2007) 123 *Law Quarterly Review* 91. En route to this conclusion, Ekins asserts that the UK Parliament was 'not constituted by law and the way in which it may act is not prescribed by law', by which he means that its 'nature and action...is not stipulated by any set of rules'; 101–2. This is question-begging as he does not take into account the possibility that it is constitutional principle that is at stake.

[62] *Jackson*, above n 59, para 31 (per Lord Bingham), para 61 (per Lord Nicholls), para 127 (per Lord Hope). It is significant that Lord Hope invoked Hart's idea of the rule of recognition in support of the claim that the 'open texture of the foundations of our legal system...defies precise analysis in strictly legal terms'. From that, he said, it followed that 'the rule of Parliamentary supremacy is ultimately based on political fact...' (ibid para 120). But he also wanted to claim that there are limits on the 'power to legislate', limits which are a 'question of law for the courts, not for Parliament'. 'The rule of law enforced by the courts is the ultimate controlling factor on which our constitution is based' (ibid para 107). The tension between these two claims—that the constitutional limits are internal legal limits and that they are external political limits—became even more palpable when he asserted both in the same sentence: 'There is a strong case for saying that the rule of recognition, which gives way to what people are prepared to recognise as law, is itself worth calling "law" and for applying it accordingly' (ibid para 126).

[63] Ibid para 139 (per Lord Rodger), para 141 (per Lord Walker), para 178 (per Lord Carswell), para 194 (per Lord Brown).

[64] Ibid paras 100–2 (per Lord Steyn), para 159 (per Lady Hale) though her remarks are inconsistent with the position she took at para 158 and with her qualification in para 159 that the 'constraints upon what Parliament can do are political...rather than constitutional'.

As Allan has said, 'Rather than treat these remarks as a threat to overthrow the established legal order, with which the courts have become disenchanted, we should interpret them—much more plausibly—as a reminder of qualifications already latent within the supremacy doctrine, awaiting elaboration if and when circumstances dictate.'[65]

In other words, Kelsen's argument is correct, but it cannot find a resting place in formal authorization rules, for it is only at the most superficial level that we can regard constitutional disputes about formal rules of change as formal in nature. They are deeply substantive disputes about the nature of democracy and the role of law and the rule of law in it, even when judges do their best to treat the disputes as formal.[66] Further, when the substance rises to the surface, we find that there is no need for judges to reach outside of the law for constitutional authority. They do not engage in linear reasoning that can find an ultimate stopping point that responds to the problem of infinite regress.

Rather, their reasoning becomes circular, because (as Walters explains):

> circular theories of authority do not need to address the problem of infinite regress. Law from this perspective is embedded within a network of interlocking strands of normative value that bend back upon themselves never reaching an end. The relevant image on this account is not a string but a web of strings shaped into a globe or sphere.[67]

Such location leads to circularity because the authority has to be sought within the legal order, which means that appeals have to be made to the resources of normative value in the public record of that order. And it leads to seeing the authority of law as legitimate because in making the appeals and in organizing them into a sustained argument about what the requirements are of the actual constitution, one is necessarily involved in a process of justification. As Neil MacCormick put the point:

> Understanding a constitution is not understanding any single rule internal to it as fundamental; it is understanding how the rules interact and cross-refer, and how they make sense in the light of the principles of political association that they are properly understood to express. If there is a fundamental obligation here, it is an obligation toward the constitution as a whole. It is the obligation to respect a constitution's integrity as a constitution, an obligation that has significance both in moments of relative stasis and in more dynamic moments.[68]

This statement picks up on Dworkin's claim that the central value of legal order is 'integrity', a value that requires legal actors to find a way of interpreting the law so that it can be understood as the expression of a unified political community.[69] The principles that

---

[65]   Allan, above n 3, 144.
[66]   This is true also of the constitutional disputes in South Africa in the 1950s, to which Hart referred when dealing with the problem of disagreement about the 'ultimate criteria to be used in identifying a law'—see Hart, above n 1, 122, 153. On these disputes, see *Jackson v Attorney General*, above n 59, para 84 (per Lord Steyn). For an elaboration of the relationship between form and substance, see Dyzenhaus, above n 51.
[67]   Walters, above n 49, 33–4.
[68]   N. MacCormick, *Questioning Sovereignty: Law, State, and Nation in the European Commonwealth* (Oxford: Oxford University Press, 1999), 93. Quoted in Allan, above n 3, 145. Note that Allan quotes these remarks in his response to Lord Hope's position in *Jackson*: Allan, above n 3, 145. See further, Allan in this volume.
[69]   R. Dworkin, *Law's Empire* (London: Fontana, 1986).

have to be invoked in public law to make sense of the law in this way are the constitutional, legitimating principles of the order.[70]

It is important to see that this idea is hardly new in philosophy of law. It goes back at
least to Hobbes, who argued that the sovereign, however constituted, has to speak with
one voice as the representative of the people who are subject to his laws. The sovereign's
subjects have to understand themselves as owning his laws as if they each had made the
laws themselves, and for that reason the laws have to be understandable as the product of a single person.[71] Put differently, the constitution of the people as a unity—as a
unified political community—depends on the sovereign's laws being understood as the
product of one person. Moreover, to understand the laws in that way is to understand
them as *de jure*, as enacted with right or legitimate.

Hobbes, of course, was concerned with the problem of infinite regress, though he
saw the issue as a practical one of not subjecting the sovereign to the rule of any other
sovereign.[72] There has to be a stopping point within legal order for questions about
what the law requires. Hobbes also argued that in the exit from the state of nature, sovereign authority comes about through the individuals in the state of nature agreeing
to be bound by the one who will act in their name.[73] But it is important to see that for
him the one who acts is an artificial person, constituted by the agreement of individuals
who on entering that agreement find themselves reconstituted from a state of individuals who make up a multitude into a unified people.

The story of exit from the state of nature becomes a just so one, though not in a
pejorative sense. It is the story one has to tell in order to make sense of the idea of the
people who are the subjects of the law being at the same time its authors and in which
authority is to be understood reflexively or as determined within legal order in the circular fashion just described. Put differently, it is the kind of story that one has to tell if
one makes the regulative assumption that legal authority is a matter that is determined
legally.

Hobbes's thought here echoes faintly in Hart in that he insists that there is only one
rule of recognition, an insistence that is undermined only because he used the metaphor of a rule to capture what it is that gives unity to a legal order. For there is no one
such rule that can do that kind of work, as Dworkin argued in two of his earliest critiques of legal positivism,[74] and as is acknowledged by Hart's students who try to save
the idea by positing a multiplicity of rules.[75] It echoes more strongly in Kelsen in that
the basic norm is a norm that has to be presupposed in order to make sense of the
hypothesis of the unity of legal order and to explain why from the perspective of the

---

[70] Dworkin at times rejected this interpretation of his position, but, as I have argued elsewhere, it is both
the natural interpretation and one that he had reason to maintain: D. Dyzenhaus, 'Dworkin and Unjust
Law', in S. Sciaraffa and W. Waluchow (eds), *The Legacy of Ronald Dworkin* (Oxford: Oxford University
Press, forthcoming).

[71] T. Hobbes, *Leviathan*, R. Tuck (ed) (Cambridge: Cambridge University Press, 1997), ch 17, 120.

[72] Ibid ch 29, 224.   [73] Ibid chs 13–17.

[74] See R. Dworkin, 'The Model of Rules I' and 'The Model of Rules II', in R. Dworkin, *Taking Rights
Seriously* 3rd impression (London: Duckworth, 1981).

[75] See J. Raz, *The Concept of a Legal System: An Introduction to the Theory of Legal System* (Oxford: Clarendon
Press, 1970) 197–200 who says at 200 that only some 'jurisprudential criterion', some 'general truth about
law' can answer the question whether a law is a law of a system.

legal official and subject, the order has to be understood as legitimate.[76] But it echoes most strongly of all in Dworkin and Allan.[77]

There are, of course, major differences between Kelsen and Hart, on the one hand, and Dworkin and Allan, on the other. Kelsen and Hart regard judicial interpretation of the law as a kind of legislation, whereas Dworkin and Allan regard judges as under a duty to give the 'one right answer' that the best principled interpretation of the law can deliver.[78] But in retrospect debate about this issue seems to have been a tremendous waste of energy. The debate makes sense if with Bentham one argues that judicial inter-pretation should be marginalized to the extent possible in legal order because from the perspective of democratic utilitarianism such interpretation is an arbitrary inter-vention in the law-making process. But from Austin on, legal positivists and political constitutionalists have conceded to judges a legitimate role in deciding cases when it is controversial what the law requires. And as Hart's take on the judicial virtues shows, discretion seems to vanish from the positivist vocabulary when it comes to describing what judges do in such cases.[79] Put differently, from the internal point of view of a legal official charged with interpreting the law, the answer has to be the judge's good faith and best shot at showing both that the legal order speaks with one voice on the ques-tion and that the answer is based on principles that justify or legitimate it to those who are affected by it.[80]

Examples such as *Halliday* and *Jackson* are thus parochial only in that they illustrate that the way in which judges in one jurisdiction dealt concretely with actual questions

---

[76] For insightful remarks along these lines, see L. L. Fuller, 'Positivism and Fidelity to Law: A Reply to Professor Hart' (1958) 71 *Harvard Law Review* 630, at 638–43. By far the majority of Kelsen scholars would reject this interpretation; see, for example, the essays in M. Troper, *Pour Une Théorie Juridique de L'État* (Paris: Presses Universitaires de France, 1994). But see L. Vinx, *Hans Kelsen's Pure Theory of Law: Legality and Legitimacy* (Oxford: Oxford University Press, 2007). See further Vinx's important argument, ibid 157–63, that seeks to make sense of Kelsen's rather bewildering set of definitions of 'constitution'.

[77] And see MacCormick, above n 68, 93, where he follows the passage quoted above with:

> This, I think, shows that Kelsen was right in thinking that any fundamental norm underlying the whole of legal order has to be conceived as external to the constitution itself. The constitution is a totality of interrelated rules or norms that is historically given and yet dynamic in providing for the possibility of its own change by processes for which it itself makes provision. As was argued in Chapter 2, however, there is no reason to follow Kelsen in treating this as a mere presupposition or transcendental hypothesis. Surely a working constitution requires this to be the kind of shared custom or convention held among those who treat the constitution as foundational of norma-tive order. That is, then, a common social practice, and it is a practice that necessarily involves shared membership in what Dworkin calls a 'community of principle', not a mere chance overlap of practical attitudes among those who hold power…. The idea of a *Grundnorm*, it is submitted, should be adapted to this sense.

> It is unclear, however, how the basic norm can in this light be considered 'external'.

[78] R. Dworkin, 'Hard Cases', in Dworkin, above n 74, 81.   [79] Hart, above n 1, 204–5.

[80] Gardner claims that Dworkin's view is 'crazy' that the constitution's meaning never changes at the hands of judges, a claim so 'crazy', he says, that he is 'reluctant' to attribute it to Dworkin. Gardner, above n 27, 38. However, far from being crazy, the claim is entailed when one adopts the internal point of view of a judge. Gardner also suggests at 37 that Dworkin possibly never held the view, referring to R. Dworkin, *Justice in Robes* (Cambridge, Mass.: Harvard University Press, 2006), 266; and that Dworkin seemed to have changed his mind when in Dworkin, above n 69, 255–63, he seems to say that the 'right answer' is 'relativ-ized to the convictions of each judge'. In *Justice in Robes*, however, at 266 n 3, Dworkin insists that he did not change his mind about the thesis and he is clear in *Law's Empire* that his view is that the right answer thesis is consistent both with recognizing that the law changes over time at the hands of judges and that judicial convictions are an intrinsic element of working out the right answer.

of constitutional law can help to answer the more abstract question of constitutionality. Put differently, that question will always be answered in the same way—by resort to both formal authorization rules and substantive principles—even though the content of the actual answers must differ according to time and place.[81] In addition, one of the ways in which the examples are parochial is significant. They show that even in a parliamentary legal order there are, following Allan, constitutional and substantive 'qualifications already latent within the supremacy doctrine, awaiting elaboration if and when circumstances dictate'. That entails that while the content of the actual answers will vary greatly, there is a limit to that variation because the ultimate addressee of the circular process of justification is the individual, who wants to understand both why the legal order speaks with one voice on the question and why its answer is based on principles that justify or legitimate it to him or her.

The answer to the question of constitutionality is thus part and parcel of satisfying what Bernard Williams called 'the Basic Legitimation Demand' that every legitimate state has to satisfy if it is to show that it wields authority rather than sheer coercive power over those subject to its rule. In order to meet that demand, Williams said, the state 'has to be able to offer a justification of its power *to each subject*'.[82]

Constitutional law, on this view, is no more than 'jumped up administrative law', as long as we understand that the implicit assumption behind this label is wrong. The assumption is that there is a qualitative difference between administrative law and constitutional law that philosophers of law have to explain because administrative law is a matter of delegated authority, or linear, whereas constitutional law is not. But this thought misperceives the quality of administrative law as did the proponents of the 'ultra vires doctrine', who argued some years ago in the United Kingdom that the grounds of judicial review of administrative action have to be sourced in a doctrine of actual legislative intent. As the critics of the ultra vires doctrine showed, administrative law is best understood as a project in which judges and other legal officials seek to work out the constitutional principles that discipline the decisions taken by those who act on behalf of the state.[83] And as Kelsen argued, there is a quantitative not a qualitative difference between this kind of review and review of statutes for their constitutionality,[84] a powerful argument as long as one grasps the quality of administrative law review. Indeed, with this qualification in place, one can go further with Kelsen and reject Gardner's assertion that '[c]onstitutional law is as high as the law

---

[81] In a bill of rights legal order when the issue is whether a statutory provision violates one of the protected rights, it might seem that only substantive principles are in play. But I think it is almost always the case that judges should consider that the legislature has issued a formal judgment on the matter, so in issue will be questions of deference and proportionality. In some jurisdictions, for example the United States, such 'formal' questions get submerged, just as in parliamentary legal orders issues of substantive principle lurk below the surface of formalistic judgments. See Thorburn in this volume.

[82] See B. Williams, 'Realism and Moralism', in B. Williams, *In the Beginning Was the Deed: Realism and Moralism in Political Argument* (Princeton: Princeton University Press, 2005) 5 (his emphasis). For relevant argument in this volume, see Lindahl in this volume; Stacey in this volume.

[83] Many of the main interventions in this debate can be found in C. Forsyth (ed), *Judicial Review & The Constitution* (Oxford: Hart Publishing, 2000).

[84] Kelsen, above n 39.

goes' because international law is higher still, and so has to be taken into account in understanding state authority.[85]

~~On this view, every legal order has to have a constitution because it comes about~~ through the complex interactions of institutions which have more or less differentiated roles to play in both producing and maintaining the order.[86] That constitution has to contain formal authorization rules that delineate the roles but it also has to contain substantive principles of two sorts. First, the formal authorization rules are themselves justified by substantive principles that will come into view when an institution is challenged on the basis that it has not performed its role. Second, the public law of the order will require interpretation and when the institution or institutions charged with interpreting it perform that role the answer they give has to present itself as the good faith and best shot answer described above.

Here too principles will come into view as a result of challenges to the way in which institutions are performing their roles. The point about challenge is important because the legal order orders relations between the individuals subject to it and legal subjects are entitled to get answers from the appropriate institution about the content of their legal rights and duties.[87] The answers have to make the good faith attempt at making sense of their subjection to law—of the claim that order exists to make it possible for them to interact under conditions of stability and security.

This rather sparse Hobbesian constraint permits a wide variety of different institutional arrangements for determining the legal will of the political community and of different content for what I called earlier the actual constitution. In a bill of rights legal order, the discussion of the content of the actual constitution will be framed but not determined by the abstract and general statements of the commitments in the bill. In a parliamentary legal order, the discussion will be framed but not determined by the public statements of rights commitments over time, notably in a common law system by judicial pronouncements.

But in both cases, the content of the actual constitution is always a matter of both form and substance and, ultimately, a matter of argument and justification. In both cases, the legal constitutionalists recognize—as did Bernard Williams in his critique of utilitarianism—that value is partly constituted by our projects.[88] And when we regard ourselves as having united our wills with others to empower a sovereign, we find that we have done more than create a mechanism through which to exercise our unbounded will. We are also a collective self that is defined (as human persons are) by commitments and projects that have normative force in our deliberations. They are not reducible to 'what we have reason to do all things considered', whether this is established by utilitarian calculation or by one or other way of moral deliberation recommended by a moral realist position. But they are binding and they confer authority on our collective

---

[85] Though the qualification requires that international law be seen as circular and thus, as E. Fox-Decent argues in this volume, as 'co-constituted by national and international law' (Fox-Decent in this volume, 139).

[86] For a basically linear account, see Kavanagh in this volume; and for a circular account, see the section on the separation of powers in Allan, above n 68.

[87] For discussion, see Lafont in this volume.

[88] B. Williams and J. J. C. Smart, *Utilitarianism: For and Against* (Cambridge: Cambridge University Press, 1973).

decisions all the same in a never-ending process of seeking to ensure the integrity of the public decisions to be found in our legal record. Coherence is a crucial aspect of 'integrity'. But another aspect which Williams highlighted is remaining true to one's long-held projects and substantive commitments.[89]

That is, the necessary connection of legality to certain constitutional substantive commitments is really part of a larger disagreement about the sources of public normativity. The legal positivist tradition, broadly understood, finds the sources outside of law and so wants to insist on a methodology for establishing value that makes it possible for law to transmit its results as a linear theory of legal authority prescribes. That builds into the legal positivism a tendency to respond to the question of constitutionality with the answer 'formal authorization rules'. In contrast, the legal constitutionalists find the sources within the law and so try to make sense of the fundamental, substantive, public commitments of their order in the way a circular theory of authority requires, and as is suggested by Williams's point about projects, commitments, and integrity.

In this light, the debate about the question of constitutionality is reconceived as one to be approached within a *Staatsrechtslehre*, a combination of philosophical and constitutional theory, since it is a question about the correct theory of public legal right, about the legitimacy of the legal state. And in that same light a productive joinder is achieved between the merger of legal positivism and political constitutionalism, on the one hand,[90] and legal constitutionalism, on the other.

---

[89] Ibid 116–17.

[90] Jeffrey Goldsworthy's work is a fine example of what I have in mind in this merger, though he may not quite see things this way. See, for example, J. Goldsworthy, *Parliamentary Sovereignty, Contemporary Debates* (Cambridge: Cambridge University Press, 2010).

2

The Unwritten Constitution as a Legal Concept

*Mark D. Walters**

'The Enlightenment hope in written constitutions is sweeping the world'—or so one prominent scholar recently stated.[1] Indeed, almost all countries today have adopted written constitutions. So why is it important to consider unwritten constitutions when examining the philosophical foundations of constitutional law?

The short answer is that the distinction between unwritten and written constitutions is contested. In neither practice nor theory does a crisp line divide the written from the unwritten constitution. In relation to the unwritten British constitution, for example, it is said that 'much (indeed, nearly all) of the constitution *is* written, somewhere'.[2] In relation to the written US Constitution, in contrast, it is said that constitutional meaning depends upon 'a dialogue between America's written Constitution and America's unwritten Constitution'.[3] To understand written constitutions we need to understand unwritten constitutions, and vice versa.

In this chapter I hope to contribute to this understanding by examining the jurisprudential idea of the unwritten constitution. My approach to this jurisprudential inquiry is interpretive. I will argue that the unwritten constitution is a legal concept and therefore a normative concept. My approach is also, in part, historical. I will argue that by locating conceptions of the unwritten constitution within the history of legal ideas we may better understand the concept's normative dimensions.

To frame my analysis, it will be helpful to begin by distinguishing between two jurisprudential camps. Within the first camp are found what I will call *linear* theories of law. These assume that the authority of legal norms can be traced back along a line of increasingly higher norms until an originating source is located. Law from this perspective is held up by a string, and someone or something must hold the end of that string. It seems sensible to allocate this job to the constitution. But who or what holds up the constitution? How, in other words, do we overcome the problem of infinite regress? Linear accounts of law answer this question in different ways, though generally they regard law's originating or constitutive source to be conceptually distinct from law itself.

In contrast, theories of law located in the second jurisprudential camp, which I will call *circular* theories of law, do not need to address the problem of infinite regress. Law

* Professor of Law, Queen's University (Canada).
[1] B. Ackerman, 'The Rise of World Constitutionalism' (1997) 83 *Virginia Law Review* 771, at 772.
[2] A. Tomkins, *Public Law* (Oxford: Oxford University Press, 2003), 7.
[3] A. R. Amar, *America's Unwritten Constitution: The Precedents and Principles We Live By* (New York: Basic Books, 2012), 19.

from this perspective is embedded within a network of interlocking strands of normative value that bend back upon themselves, never reaching an end. The relevant image
on this account is not a string but a web of strings shaped into a globe or sphere. The
legal system is held together not by an originating act or sovereign rule but by the interpretation of 'a whole set of shifting, developing and interacting standards'.[4] The constitution, on this view, is not an extraordinary entity, like some mighty Atlas holding up
the globe of normative value on his shoulders. Rather, the constitution is part of the
ordinary strands of normative value that form the sphere itself, contributing to the cen-
tripetal force that gives it a sense of integrity. Constitutional norms may have a 'written'
form, but for circular theories of law constitutionalism is ultimately 'unwritten'.

I will argue for a circular theory of the unwritten constitution. In Part I, I establish the
basis for the analysis by examining the relationship between law and writing. In Part II,
I clarify the objectives of the analysis by exploring the relationship between constitutional norms, constitutions, and constitutionalism. In Part III, I examine the problematic relationship between linear theories of law and the ideal of constitutionalism, with
particular reference to the work of Hans Kelsen and H. L. A. Hart. Based upon insights
drawn from this analysis, I will, in Part IV, identify the core features of a theory of the
unwritten constitution according to which certain legal values must obtain, regardless
of the written constitutional instruments that states have or have not adopted.

I

My argument is that the unwritten constitution should be seen as a legal concept—or
as *law*. If the unwritten constitution is law, it must of course be a kind of *unwritten* law.
The first step in the argument, then, is to identify the conception of unwritten law that
will serve as the foundation for my claim that the unwritten constitution is law. The
sense of unwritten law I have in mind for this purpose is, in fact, a very ordinary one.
I will explain it by reference to the classical common law explanation of the difference
between written and unwritten law.

Historically, English law was divided into *lex scripta*, a law drawn up in writing and
enacted, and *lex non scripta*, a common law that was said to be based on immemorial
custom or the law of nature or both.[5] But the distinction was not that simple. It was
acknowledged that unwritten law was actually revealed by 'Monuments in Writing', in
particular written reports of judicial decisions; and it was also acknowledged that while
certain old statutes that had been lost might still count as written law even though the
only evidence for them was found in reports of judicial decisions, other old statutes,
still existing, that had been subjected to prolonged judicial exposition might thereby
become part of the unwritten common law.[6] It was not writing as such, then, but the
interpretive attitude adopted in relation to different kinds of legal expression that was
important.

---

[4] R. Dworkin, 'The Model of Rules' (1967) 35 *Chicago Law Review* 14, at 41.
[5] M. Hale, *The History of the Common Law of England* 2nd edn (London: John Walthoe, 1716), 1–2, 22–3.
[6] Ibid 9, 15, 16, 23, 65.

Indeed, for common lawyers it was ultimately the 'common learning in our books'[7] that produced a meaningful sense of unwritten law. This learning was not, as the early, seventeenth-century judge John Doderidge wrote, 'expressly published in words' but rather left 'implied and included in the cases so decided'.[8] Unwritten law was a 'discourse of reason' informed by 'moral philosophy' and the ideal of 'coherence'.[9] Rules of law explicitly recognized in cases were taken to be evidence of a comprehensive body of legal principle, and both rules and principles, from the 'most ample and highest Generall, by many degrees of descent … to the lowest speciall and particular', were to be understood as holding together coherently 'as it were in a consanguinity of blood and concordancie of nature'.[10] Answers in difficult cases were found through an interpretive oscillation between law 'in *concreto*' and law 'in *abstracto*', a movement 'from the particular to the speciall' and then 'from the speciall to the generall', and finally from these 'primary principles' back to 'more speciall and peculiar assertions', 'descending' to the 'particular matter' at hand.[11] Doderidge insisted that 'unwritten law' identified through the interpretive ascent and descent of the common law secured 'equality of reason' better than 'positive' law.[12] In this way, actual experience and abstract principle were synthesized through a distinctive form of legal reason.

Gathering these ideas about written and unwritten law together, we may say that 'written law' is law set by a lawmaker using a linguistic formula that is taken to be authoritative and exhaustive of the law on the points that it purports to govern. 'Unwritten law', in contrast, is a discourse of reason in which existing rules, even those articulated in writing, are understood to be specific manifestations of a comprehensive body of abstract principles from which other rules may be identified through an interpretive back-and-forth that endeavours to show coherence between law's specific and abstract dimensions and equality between law's various applications.[13]

On this account, the rule 'no vehicles in the park' made by the town mayor is a written law whether inscribed on parchment or promulgated orally by the town crier. But the same rule, inferred from a series of judicial decisions involving nuisance actions against people driving motor vehicles and bicycles through the park, is a rule of unwritten law, even if the judge in the last of these cases states in a written judgment that the rule for which the previous cases stand is 'no vehicles in the park'. The difference is real. As a written law, the words 'no vehicles in the park', though open to interpretation, are themselves binding as the law on point. As a description of unwritten law, however, the same words are not binding as such even if the rule in the case in which the words are expressed is binding, for the rule in the case only exists within the interpretive discourse that integrates concrete with abstract senses of law and so is independent of any particular linguistic formulation.

---

[7] *The Countess of Northumberland's Case* (1598) 5 Co Rep 97b, 98a.

[8] J. Doderidge, *The English Lawyer, Describing a Method for the Managing of the Lawes of this Land* (London: I More, 1631), 244.

[9] Ibid 38, 62, 63, 64.   [10] Ibid 258; see also 64, 95, 190.

[11] Ibid 190, 237.   [12] Ibid 210, 241, 268, 270.

[13] See more generally M. D. Walters, 'Written Constitutions and Unwritten Constitutionalism', in G. Huscroft (ed), *Expounding the Constitution: Essays in Constitutional Theory* (Cambridge: Cambridge University Press, 2008), 245–76.

It might be said that there is no real difference between written and unwritten law as I define these terms. Whether the rule about vehicles in the park is written or unwritten, judges will interpret it consistently with other laws and the values underlying them and conclude that it does not prohibit, say, prams in the park. This is true. The interpretation of written law may, in certain respects at least, resemble closely the interpretive exercise that I say defines unwritten law. But there remains a basic difference. The unwritten rule 'no vehicles in the park' is one manifestation of a comprehensive set of abstract legal principles and so counts as evidence for other unwritten rules not yet acknowledged explicitly—such as (for example) 'no vehicles in the town square'. As a written rule, 'no vehicles in the park' cannot be understood in this way. That the mayor made this rule but not one for the town square is, if anything, an indication that vehicles *are* permitted in the town square. Written and unwritten law are thus distinctive forms of law.

The conception of unwritten law just sketched involves a circular interpretive enterprise; it is illustrative of the circular theory of law described at the outset of this chapter. In developing their account of law, common lawyers like Doderidge were inspired by the Renaissance humanist idea that truth in human affairs is not something external to but revealed by rhetorical and discursive methods of disputation aimed at balance between specific and general.[14] The interpretive or circular account of unwritten law is thus consistent with a more general theory of truth according to which reality about normative value exists independently of specific things that people write or accept or acknowledge or assume from time to time, but that this reality cannot exist independently of the *interpretation* of what is written, accepted, acknowledged, or assumed in light of the sphere of normative value within which human thoughts and actions exist.[15] Whether or not this is an attractive theory of normative truth in general is a question beyond the scope of this chapter. My argument here, however, is that it is the basis for an attractive theory of constitutionalism.

II

It is one thing to say that a distinctive kind of law exists that is unwritten. It is a very different thing to say that an entire constitution can be law in this distinctive sense. As we shift our focus from unwritten law to the unwritten constitution, it will be important to distinguish between 'the constitution' in its entirety and individual 'constitutional norms'. The entire constitution embraces various institutions, rules, rights, principles, and values, but it has an identity that is more than the sum of its parts. For any particular constitutional question, the constitution provides answers in the form of specific normative propositions or 'constitutional norms'. This is not to say that the constitution is a discrete 'system' consisting of linked 'individuated' norms.[16] It is simply to say that

---

[14] M. D. Walters, 'Legal Humanism and Law as Integrity' (2008) 67 *Cambridge Law Journal* 352.
[15] Compare with R. Dworkin, 'Objectivity and Truth: You'd Better Believe It' (1996) 25 *Philosophy and Public Affairs* 87.
[16] See eg J. Raz, *The Concept of a Legal System: An Introduction to the Theory of Legal System* (Oxford: Clarendon Press, 1970).

the entire constitution has sufficient shape or identity as to enjoy a character as written or unwritten distinct from the written or unwritten character of the constitutional norms it embraces.

It is also important at this stage to confront the relationship between 'constitution' and 'constitutionalism'. The two ideas are intimately connected. For present purposes, I will define constitutionalism in rough terms as the ideal of government established by law and limited by law from exercising arbitrary power. Constitutionalism in this sense is related to the ideal of the 'rule of law' or 'legality'. In this chapter, I will assume that a modern state that embraces the ideals of constitutionalism and the rule of law will have an institutional structure established by law in which legislative, executive, and judicial functions are distinguished, the legislative function being focused upon the making of general rules for the common good consistently with the equal dignity of each member of the community, the executive function on the implementation of laws and the development of policies through specific decisions and orders authorized by law, and the judicial function on the impartial and independent interpretation of law. I will assume, in other words, that the supremacy or rule of law requires, at the very least, the supremacy of the legislative over the executive function and the independence of the judicial function from both.

Like constitutional norms and entire constitutions, constitutionalism can be understood as written or unwritten. 'Unwritten constitutionalism' could be taken to mean the theory of how legality is to be understood within an unwritten constitution; conversely 'written constitutionalism' could be taken to be the theory of legality within a written constitution. However, unwritten constitutionalism might also be taken more ambitiously to refer to a theory of how legality is to be understood within both written *and* unwritten constitutions. In this chapter, I sketch the basis for an ambitious theory of unwritten constitutionalism.

In building this argument, I will begin by considering individual constitutional norms. Thomas Grey has argued that constitutional norms may be examined from *three* aspects: *first*, in terms of *status*, constitutional norms can be extralegal or legal, and legal constitutional norms can be part of regular law or a supreme law; *second*, in terms of *enforcement*, constitutional norms may be enforced through informal or formal processes, and formal processes may be judicial (an ordinary or constitutional court) or political (a special executive or legislative body); and, *third*, in terms of *authority*, constitutional norms may arise from *enactment* by ordinary or special legislative body or from one of two *unwritten* sources, namely, *acceptance* (or custom) or moral *truth* (or natural law).[17] Seeking to avoid 'theoretical dogmatism and parochialism about the varieties of legal culture', Grey concludes that constitutional norms do not need to have any particular set of characteristics.[18] A legal constitutional norm may or may not be judicially enforceable, a written constitutional norm may or may not be supreme, an unwritten constitutional norm may or may not be law, and so forth. Indeed, given the variety of constitutional norms typically found within a constitution,

---

[17] T. C. Grey, 'Constitutionalism: An Analytic Framework', in J. Pennock and J. W. Chapman (eds), *Constitutionalism: Nomos XX* (New York: New York University Press, 1979), 189–209.
[18] Ibid 196.

Grey argues against using the traditional classification of constitutions as written or unwritten. '[T]he primary object of discourse in the study of constitutionalism,' he concludes, 'should be constitutional *norms*, and not entire constitutions.'[19]

Grey's analysis is instructive but problematic. Considered in isolation, individual constitutional norms can enjoy any combination of qualities that he identifies (though his understanding of unwritten norms is underdeveloped). However, it is neither theoretical dogmatism nor parochialism to insist that certain arrangements of different constitutional norms will secure the value of constitutionalism and others will not. Indeed, it is not clear that a genuine constitution even exists within a modern state when, for example, all constitutional norms within the state are extralegal, or when constitutional norms, though supposedly legal, are left to the interpretation of an executive council or 'star chamber'. We need to step back from the constitutional trees to see the constitutional forest. Only through the interpretation of constitutional norms as a normative whole will constitutionalism be manifested. Understanding the jurisprudential character of the constitution in its entirety is essential.

If so, however, perhaps the classification of constitutions as written or unwritten is helpful—not as a description of the norms the constitution embraces but as a statement about the jurisprudential identity of the constitution itself. The characterization of a constitution as written or unwritten arguably captures the interpretive perspective through which its various norms may be shown to exhibit normative unity. A state with a written constitution, on this view, is one in which a theory of the written constitution brings normative unity to all constitutional norms, written and unwritten, within the system; a state with an unwritten constitution, in contrast, is one in which a theory of the unwritten constitution performs that role. So, for example, in the United States unwritten constitutional law will be seen as generated by or ancillary to the written constitution—as *implied* by,[20] *inferred* from the structure of,[21] *incorporated* into,[22] *supplemental* to,[23] or a common law discourse *initiated* by,[24] the written constitution. Conversely, in the United Kingdom, written rules of constitutional law (the Parliament Acts, the European Communities Act, etc.) will be seen as derived from and informed by the unwritten constitution—the constitution as a whole will be regarded as 'a common law ocean dotted with islands of statutory provision'.[25]

This dualist explanation has merit, but its implications should be resisted. Entire constitutions *are* a meaningful focus for jurisprudential inquiry, and written and unwritten constitutions *do* involve different approaches to achieving normative unity in law.

---

[19] Ibid 190.

[20] M. S. Moore, 'Do We Have an Unwritten Constitution?' (1989) 63 *Southern California Law Review* 107, at 117.

[21] C. L. Black, *Structure and Relationship in Constitutional Law* (Baton Rouge: Louisiana State University Press, 1969), 7.

[22] S. Sherry, 'The Ninth Amendment: Right an Unwritten Constitution' (1988) 64 *Chicago-Kent Law Review* 1001.

[23] T. C. Grey, 'The Uses of an Unwritten Constitution' (1988) 64 *Chicago-Kent Law Review* 211.

[24] D. A. Strauss, 'Common Law Constitutional Interpretation' (1996) 63 *University of Chicago Law Review* 877.

[25] S. Sedley, 'The Sound of Silence: Constitutional Law without a Constitution' (1994) 110 *Law Quarterly Review* 270, at 273.

However, the ambitious theory of unwritten constitutionalism insists that the difference between written and unwritten constitutions is one of degree not kind. The theory of constitutionalism that brings normative unity to written and unwritten constitutional norms is, at a deep level, common to both written and unwritten constitutions, and given its foundation in the circular conception of law this common approach to constitutionalism is itself best understood as 'unwritten'.

The written constitutions of countries like Australia and Canada are illustrative. These former 'Dominions' received written constitutions in the form of regular Acts of the UK Parliament but did not formally reconstitute themselves after evolving into sovereign states.[26] Their statutory constitutions thus exist within a common law context: the 'written Constitutions of the Dominions' took effect within a 'general unwritten Constitution';[27] 'the common law [w]as a jurisprudence antecedently existing' into which each constitution 'came and in which it operates'.[28] I shall call this model of constitution the 'legally embedded written constitution'. It is a model that resonates with common law sensibilities. Even in the United States, there was initially some suggestion that the written constitution took effect within an existing common law constitution.[29] An important question to address, then, is whether the model reflects a theory of the unwritten constitution that transcends specific common law jurisdictions.

III

I outlined a conception of unwritten law in Part I that can explain the status of particular constitutional norms as unwritten constitutional law. However, the objective I identified in Part II is more ambitious than that. The objective is to show how the conception of unwritten law, by virtue of its interpretive or circular orientation, offers a compelling account of entire constitutions. This is perhaps a confusing claim. I am not saying that unwritten law can explain the substantive details of each constitution. Whether the constitution establishes a unitary or federal structure, a parliamentary or presidential executive, one written constitutional instrument or thirty-one, and so on, are matters that depend on local decisions and practices. Nor is my claim that the unwritten constitution cures all defects in a constitution. My argument is ambitious but not that ambitious. My claim, rather, is that all things being equal the circular conception of the unwritten constitution offers a better account of constitutional law within the modern state than linear accounts of law do.

To advance this argument, I explore in this part the troubled relationship between linear theories of law and the ideal of constitutionalism. According to linear theories, the validity of each legal norm within a legal system derives from a higher legal norm, and the resulting line (or lines) of law within the system may be traced back to an

---

[26] P. Oliver, *The Constitution of Independence: The Development of Constitutional Theory in Australia, Canada and New Zealand* (Oxford: Oxford University Press, 2005).

[27] *New South Wales v The Commonwealth* (1926) 38 CLR 74, 87–8 (per Isaacs J).

[28] O. Dixon, 'The Common Law as an Ultimate Constitutional Foundation' (1957) 31 *Australian Law Journal* 240, at 240–1.

[29] *Henfield's Case* Whart St Tr 49 (1793), 61.

ultimate norm or originating point.[30] Within jurisprudential literature, linear theories abound. Indeed, it has been said that the principal debate in jurisprudence is one between natural law theories that trace law back to moral facts and positivist legal theories that trace law back to social facts.[31] But whether linear theorists look to social fact or moral norm or norm manifested in social fact, they agree that the originating phenomenon for law cannot be *law* in the ordinary sense. The natural law claim that 'natural law explain[s] the obligatory force ... of positive laws' assumes that positive law is not the same as natural law.[32] The positivist claim that the ultimate validity of law cannot 'without circularity' be explained 'solely by reference to another law'[33] assumes that 'the root of the legal system ... cannot be a legal norm,'[34] or if it is a 'legal' norm it cannot be (as other legal norms are) 'grounded on legal reasons'.[35] Whatever it is, law's starting point must be something other than law itself.

This conclusion presents a problem for constitutionalism. The foundations for the legal system presumably have something to do with the constitution of the system. Yet if these foundations are not law in a meaningful sense, then the ideal of constitutionalism—the ideal of the 'rule of law state'—is chimerical. To illustrate the problematic relationship between linear theories of law and constitutionalism, I look at the work of Kelsen and Hart below. To frame this discussion, however, it will be helpful first to sketch one classical legal narrative on this problem—one that flips the equation and argues that constitutionalism *requires* the linear separation of law's foundations from law itself.

This point was made by Charles Howard McIlwain who argued that the germ of modern constitutionalism lay in the 'fundamental law' narrative that emerged in Europe before the first written constitutions—that germ being the idea of a higher law separate from ordinary law defining and limiting sovereign power. '[I]n every free state,' McIlwain wrote, there is 'a marked difference between those laws which a government makes and may therefore change, and the ones which make the government itself', a distinction, that is, between 'ordinary' and 'constituent' law.[36] McIlwain traced this division to the separation of *jus publicum* from *jus privatum* in Roman law, and he explained that medieval lawyers came to see *jus publicum* as a fundamental or constitutive law grounded in the law of nature or immemorial custom or both.[37] With the emergence of the modern state, however, its orientation began to shift. The French jurist Jean Bodin encouraged a new understanding of fundamental law: the constitution of the state and the limits it imposes upon sovereign power were increasingly seen as immanent within the exercise of state sovereignty itself. The roots of modern

---

[30] For pictorial illustrations of such 'chain[s] of validity' see Raz, above n 16, 98.

[31] S. J. Shapiro, *Legality* (Cambridge, Mass.: Belknap Press, 2011), 39–43.

[32] J. Finnis, *Natural Law and Natural Rights* (Oxford: Clarendon Press, 1980), 23–4.

[33] L. Green, 'Positivism and Conventionalism' (1999) 12 *Canadian Journal of Law and Jurisprudence* 35, at 35.

[34] L. Green, 'The Concept of Law Revisited' (1996) 94 *Michigan Law Review* 1687, at 1693.

[35] J. Raz, *The Authority of Law: Essays on Law and Morality* (Oxford: Oxford University Press, 1979), 69.

[36] C. H. McIlwain, *Constitutionalism and the Changing World* (Cambridge: Cambridge University Press, 1939), 73.

[37] C. H. McIlwain, *Constitutionalism: Ancient and Modern* rev edn (Ithaca, N.Y.: Cornell University Press, 1947), 46.

constitutionalism, McIlwain concluded, lie in 'Bodin's essential distinction between the fundamental and the ordinary laws'.[38]

The theory of fundamental law sketched by McIlwain counts as a linear legal theory. It sees ordinary law as generated by something other than ordinary law. But unlike positivist legal theories, it tries to accommodate the ideal of constitutionalism by insisting that this generation is not just factual or social but legal, a product of a special and separate kind of law that somehow both generates and limits state power. However, the argument produces a paradox. If the authority of state institutions is to be established and limited by law, then, so the argument goes, that law must be a fundamental law separate from and higher than the ordinary law that state institutions make or apply; yet, as the degree of separation between fundamental law and ordinary law increases, then, it may be said, the extent to which fundamental law will exhibit the qualities that law ordinarily exhibits decreases. In other words, the more *fundamental* fundamental law is, the weaker the claim that fundamental law is *law*.

Historical examples are illustrative in this respect. Consider the critical moment in common law history when crown lawyers sought to demarcate a law of state separate from the ordinary law of the land. The Roman civil law division between *jus publicum* and *jus privatum* was invoked in the early seventeenth century to support the idea of a 'Law publique' in England establishing a 'Constitution' for the 'Commonwealth' separate from the 'Common Law',[39] one that gave the king 'absolute' prerogative power 'aboue the ordinarie course of the common lawe' to act for the 'publike estate'.[40] Crown lawyers argued that by the 'Law of State' kings could proceed by 'natural equity' to govern in relation to matters of state 'unto which the common law extends not', and so they could imprison subjects indefinitely without due process simply by claiming reason of state.[41] The common law response to this attempt to separate a public or state law from ordinary law was simply to deny the separation. The legal foundations of the commonwealth were not outside the bounds of ordinary law, wrote Sir Edward Coke, but rather 'the rules or fundamental points of the common law...in truth are the maine pillars, and supporters of the fabric of the common-wealth'.[42]

Coke understood—if only implicitly—that constitutionalism requires the rejection of linear theories of law. I return to this point later. It is important to recall first, however, the ways in which modern accounts of the linear 'law of state' tradition also challenge constitutionalism. The continental European idea of fundamental law inspired by jurists like Bodin would, over time, emerge into a distinctive theory of constitutive public law, one that was eventually associated with the work of theorists like Carl Schmitt.[43] Public law, on this view, is constitutive not just of law but of the people as a

---

[38] McIlwain, above n 36, 74; see also 40–5. See J. Bodin, *The Six Books of a Commonweale*, R. Knolles (trans) (London: G. Bishop, 1606).

[39] J. Cowell, *The Institutes of the Lawes of England, Digested into the Method of the Civill or Imperiall Institutions* (London: T. Roycroft, 1651), 1–2, 3.

[40] J. Cowell, *The Interpreter* (Cambridge: John Legate, 1607); see entries for 'Parliament', 'Prerogative', and 'King'.

[41] 'Proceedings in Parliament Relating to the Liberty of the Subject' (1628) 3 St Tr 59–234, 149–50. See also arguments in the *Case of the Five Knights* (1627) 3 St Tr 1.

[42] E. Coke, *The Second Part of the Institutes of the Laws of England* (London: W. Clarke & Sons, 1817), 74.

[43] See in general M. Loughlin, *Foundations of Public Law* (Oxford: Oxford University Press, 2010).

state capable of producing law; it is a law of state inherent within the reality of state sovereignty or political power that is made possible only through its exercise for the public good. Public law is thus a kind of extraordinary law that generates the political power that constitutes states and state institutions and their capacity to make and/or apply ordinary laws. No constitutive moment as such is necessary—the relationship between extraordinary and ordinary law is 'reflexive' and only through the exercise of constituted power is constitutive power manifested.[44] Even so, the separation remains theoretically and practically meaningful. On this account, existential questions for the state must remain matters of constitutive law not constituted law, and the supreme executive power within the state, as ultimate representative of the people's sovereignty, must therefore retain the final authority to exercise the sovereignty of the state unbounded by the rule of (ordinary) law in cases of necessity or emergency. The sovereign has the inherent power, in Schmitt's famous expression, to make the 'exception'.[45]

We are now in a position to consider Kelsen and Hart. The strand of public law theory that I just summarized—the idea of a law constitutive of the state separate from ordinary law—had a profound impact on Kelsen. I will explore Kelsen's response to that theory and compare it to Hart's jurisprudence in order to illuminate the inability of linear legal theories to explain constitutionalism—and then I will identify, in general terms at least, a solution.

Kelsen's legal theory is quintessentially linear. The line of law for Kelsen involves a series of norms each authorizing the next in line, a unidirectional projection of authority with norms proceeding 'from the general (abstract) to the individual (concrete)'.[46] Each general norm establishes the 'frame' within which more specific norms may be created, and at the end of law's line it is the judge who fills the last frame by creating an enforceable individual norm, legislating not to fill gaps in law (there are none) but to specify '*in concreto*' what has been mandated already '*in abstracto*'.[47] What is at the *other* end of the line? Kelsen insists that the validity of each legal norm 'can be traced back—directly or indirectly—to the first constitution', the status of which as a 'binding legal norm' is 'presupposed' by the 'starting point' for law, the 'basic norm' of the legal order.[48] The basic norm is not a social fact (Kelsen refuses to draw an 'ought' from an 'is'), nor a social or moral norm (Kelsen insists upon pure legal positivism), nor a metaphysical idea (Kelsen adopts a Kantian epistemology).[49] For Kelsen, the presupposition formulated by the basic norm is simply that—a presupposition or logical postulate for the existence of a valid but closed system of legal norms. The basic norm is a 'constitution' in the 'transcendental–logical sense' that makes the 'constitution'

[44] H. Lindahl, 'Constituent Power and Reflexive Identity: Towards an Ontology of Collective Selfhood', in M. Loughlin and N. Walker (eds), *The Paradox of Constitutionalism: Constituent Power and Constitutional Form* (Oxford: Oxford University Press, 2007), 9–24.
[45] C. Schmitt, *Political Theology: Four Chapters on the Concept of Sovereignty*, G. Schwab (ed trans) (Chicago: University of Chicago Press, 2005), 5.
[46] H. Kelsen, *The Pure Theory of Law* 2nd edn, M. Knight (trans) (Berkeley: University of California Press, 1967), 237.
[47] Ibid 237, 245, 246, 247–8.
[48] H. Kelsen, *The General Theory of Law and State*, A. Wedberg (trans) (Cambridge, Mass.: Harvard University Press, 1945), 114, 115.
[49] Kelsen, above n 46, 202.

in the 'positive-legal sense', whether 'written' or 'unwritten' or both, legally valid and binding.[50]

Hart's theory of law is also linear, though for him the ultimate norm, the 'rule of recognition', is a social rule constituted through official practice that determines the criteria of validity for law within the system.[51] Hart acknowledges that the rule of recognition 'resembles in some ways' Kelsen's basic norm.[52] But he identifies two important differences. First, Hart rejects the idea that the legal system could be based upon a mere presupposition. The ultimate rule is, he insists, 'an empirical, though complex, question of fact'.[53] True, when a lawyer within the system asserts that some rule is legally valid 'he does not *explicitly state* but *tacitly presupposes*' the rule's existence; however, if necessary, what is tacit can be made explicit 'by appeal to the facts, ie to the actual practice of the courts and officials of the system'.[54] Although Hart concedes at one point that the rule of recognition might be considered from the 'internal' point of view of participants within the system as 'law', he generally insists that it is a social rule and the assertion that it exists 'can only be an external statement of fact' made by the observer who tracks social practice.[55] It follows, for Hart, that judicial resolution of uncertainty about the rule's content can only be achieved *extra*legally. '[W]hen courts settle previously unenvisaged questions concerning the most fundamental constitutional rules,' he writes, 'they *get* their authority to decide them accepted after the questions have arisen and the decision has been given'; in these cases 'all that succeeds is success'.[56]

If Hart's rule of recognition contains 'the most fundamental constitutional rules' for the system, then it must have a substantive content that Kelsen's basic norm does not. Indeed, this is the second difference Hart identifies. Hart rightly observes that Kelsen's basic norm is the same for every legal system: it specifies that the constitution of the system, whatever it is, is legally valid and binding.[57] This makes no sense to Hart. 'If a constitution specifying the various sources of law is a living reality in the sense that the courts and officials of the system actually identify the law in accordance with the criteria it provides,' he states, 'then the constitution is accepted and actually exists' and it is 'a needless reduplication to suggest [as Kelsen does] that there is a further rule to the effect that the constitution... [is] to be obeyed'.[58] The fundamental rules of the constitution evidenced by social practice, not some presupposition lurking behind them, form Hart's ultimate rule of recognition.

Hart's observations confirm that he and Kelsen defend two starkly different linear accounts of law. Each identifies a source for law's normativity behind the main bulk of law within the system. However, Kelsen's source, the basic norm, is a mere sliver—a kind of *scintilla juris*—a substantively empty presupposition that leaves the entire constitution within the domain of ordinary law. Hart's source, in contrast, separates significant parts of what might otherwise be called constitutional law and exiles them to the domain of extralegal social practice. There is, he insists, a divide between 'the high constitutional matter of a legal system's ultimate criteria of validity' on the one hand and

---

[50] Ibid 200, 223, 226. See also Kelsen, above n 48, 260.
[51] H. L. A. Hart, *The Concept of Law* (Oxford: Clarendon Press, 1961), 103–4.
[52] Ibid 245.   [53] Ibid.   [54] Ibid.   [55] Ibid 107–8.
[56] Ibid 149.   [57] Ibid 245.   [58] Ibid 246.

'ordinary' law on the other.[59] What is the importance of this difference between Kelsen and Hart? The importance for my purposes is found in the reason for why Kelsen constructs his theory as he does. It is the result of neither accident nor logic but what can only be described as a normative concern for the rule of law state—or *Rechtsstaat*.

It is important to recall that Kelsen was responding not to Hart's jurisprudence but to the constitutive or public law theory (summarized above) advanced by his own contemporaries, including Schmitt.[60] In my view, however, Kelsen's argument against the idea of constitutive law applies to any linear theory of law, including Hart's, that severs fundamental constitutional norms from the rest of the legal system.[61] Kelsen thus helps us to see why linear theories of law are problematic for the ideal of constitutionalism.

At the centre of Kelsen's jurisprudence is a commitment to the 'unity' of law.[62] He accepts that there is a difference between *jus publicum* and *jus privatum*, but he argues that this difference should not be 'absolutized' and rendered 'extra-systematic' but rather 'relativize[d]' and made 'intra-systematic'.[63] To see the contrast between public law and private law as an 'absolute contrast' is, Kelsen says, to make absolute the contrast between 'state power and law'.[64] Kelsen argues that if public law occupies an extra-systematic domain separate from ordinary law—if public law is extraordinary—then within this domain of public law, including within 'the politically important constitutional and administrative law', the 'principle of law' will not be understood as 'valid' in the same sense or with the same intensity as it is in relation to 'private' or 'true' law.[65] Public law will be downgraded to the status of 'nonlaw'.[66] This tendency Kelsen resists. The 'ideology' underlying the theory of a separate constitutive public law must be opposed, he says, because it accepts that 'law in the strict sense of the word does not prevail in so-called public law' but rather the 'interest of the state' and the 'unfettered realization of the state's purposes', even if contrary to law, prevail instead.[67] Kelsen's objection is presented as one of logic. The claim that a 'legal principle' implicit within 'public law' secures 'freedom *from* law' for the 'life sphere of the state' is, he says, a contradiction.[68] Indeed, this is the paradox I identified above: the more fundamental fundamental law is the less likely it is that it will exhibit qualities ordinarily identified as law. But Kelsen's concern about the contradiction or paradox is hardly just logical; it is based upon a normative commitment to the ideal of constitutionalism. The contradiction is, in Kelsen's view, one result of the 'untenable dualism' between state and law.[69] For Kelsen, the 'state governed by law'—the '*Rechtsstaat*'—must be the subject not the creator of law.[70]

In the end, Kelsen's argument for the constitutional or rule of law state fails.[71] Because he insists that the basic norm can validate any constitution it follows that every state is a *Rechtsstaat*.[72] His theory secures a thin or formal sense of constitutionalism.[73] But

---

[59] Ibid 119.
[60] D. Dyzenhaus, *Legality and Legitimacy: Carl Schmitt, Hans Kelsen and Herman Heller in Weimar* (Oxford: Oxford University Press, 1997).
[61] For a similar conclusion arrived at through a somewhat different route, see L. Vinx, *Hans Kelsen's Pure Theory of Law: Legality and Legitimacy* (Oxford: Oxford University Press, 2007), 38, 57–8.
[62] Kelsen, above n 46, 282.   [63] Ibid.   [64] Ibid.   [65] Ibid.   [66] Ibid.
[67] Ibid.   [68] Ibid 283.   [69] Ibid.   [70] Ibid 312–13.
[71] Dyzenhaus, above n 60, 158–9.   [72] Kelsen, above n 46, 313.
[73] For an argument that Kelsen offers a substantive conception of the rule of law state, see Vinx, above n 61.

if he gets the solution wrong, he rightly diagnoses the problem. Kelsen understands at some level that jurisprudential linearity threatens constitutionalism. He therefore constructs a starting point for law, the basic norm, that dissolves the distinction between constitutive norms and ordinary law, between state and law, and he thereby produces a distinctively circular result according to which (as he concedes) 'the law regulates its own creation'.[74]

Where does Kelsen go wrong? The answer to this question is also instructive. He may contemplate circularity at law's starting point, but, still, he sees the line of law as spinning off from that point, a unidirectional projection of authority that extends outward as comprehensive norms *in abstracto* are laid down to support subsequent norms *in concreto* leaving no gaps in the legal order. However, any resemblance that this gapless picture of abstract and concrete law has with the conception of unwritten law I explained above is at best superficial. Kelsen denies that concrete norms are to be understood by some 'intellectual operation' as specific instantiations of more abstract principles, and so denies the essence of unwritten law as I have defined it; he insists, instead, that each norm is 'created by a special act of will'.[75] Law for Kelsen is wholly positive. I will argue below that to understand constitutionalism in the modern state, it is necessary to abandon the positivist understanding of law as a unidirectional projection of authority and accept in its place a circular understanding of law as emerging through an organic interaction between law *in abstracto* and law *in concreto*—through, that is, the interpretive encircling by law of the most abstract legal values or basic norms of the system with a view to producing morally defensible accounts of the entire constitution. The judge at the end of the line of law must adopt an interpretive perspective that permits that end to be arched back to encompass its sources, not once but over and over again. In one sense, Kelsen is very close to this position; in another sense, he is a world away.

The problem that Kelsen identifies with constitutive public law theory is also a problem for Hart's jurisprudence, for Hart too severs constitutive norms from ordinary law. Indeed, positivists in the Hartian tradition struggle to explain the relationship between constitutional law and law's starting point as a result.[76] One strategy, which is adopted to avoid the conclusion that there is always an unwritten constitution in the form of the rule of recognition behind the written constitution within a system, emphasizes, first, that Hart denies the status of 'law' to the rule of recognition, and then argues, second, that the bulk of the real constitution *is* law and the rule of recognition is a mere signal— almost literally the judicial act of pointing—indicating where constitutional law is to be found.[77] This solution purports to show that constitutional law qua law is possible after all; but it moves toward a Kelsen-like position that Hart rejects, one that sees the ultimate rule as a substantively empty gesture behind the (legal) constitution. A second strategy has been to argue that the rule of recognition does embrace meaningful constitutional content and is part of the law of the legal system—though a distinct practice-based or customary law different from ordinary law.[78] This approach has problems too.

---

[74] Kelsen, above n 46, 313; Kelsen, above n 48, 126, 198.   [75] Kelsen, above n 48, 114.
[76] J. Waldron, 'Are Constitutional Norms Legal Norms?' (2006–7) 75 *Fordham Law Review* 1697.
[77] J. Gardner, *Law as a Leap of Faith* (Oxford: Oxford University Press, 2012), 107.
[78] G. Lamond, 'Legal Sources, the Rule of Recognition and Customary Law' (2014) 59 *American Journal of Jurisprudence* 25.

It is reminiscent of the theory of constitutive public law that Kelsen opposes, and it may lead to the same problems for constitutionalism that it does.

These solutions do not address the real problem with linear legal theories and constitutionalism—the bifurcation of ordinary law from its supposed sources. The solution ultimately lies in the denial of that bifurcation. Common lawyers like Coke understood this point, at least implicitly, and their ideas may therefore suggest a way forward. Responding to the argument that basic constitutional issues, including the reciprocal rights and duties of crown and subject, were determined by laws of nature about which judges had no special knowledge, Coke conceded that 'the law of nature was before any judicial or municipal law'—it was a constitutive law—but he also insisted that 'the law of nature is part of the law of England'—it was, in effect, domesticated by ordinary law.[79] In the process, 'natural reason' became the 'artificial reason' of (ordinary) law, a reason for judges not kings to expound.[80] It was not an autonomous law of state, but something to be understood by ordinary judges in the ordinary way—through a consideration of 'the multitudes of examples, precedents, judgments, and resolutions in the laws of England' by those who could not be 'daunted with fear of any power above them, nor be dazzled with the applause of the popular about them'.[81] Of course, executive prerogative did not on this view disappear; however, because it was enveloped within, it could be both 'respected' *and* 'admeasured' by, the ordinary law of the land.[82] Indeed, once 'common right and reason' were seen as integrated within ordinary law, the common law might even 'controul acts of Parliament'—if only implicitly through interpretation.[83]

In fact, common lawyers like Coke emphasized ancient custom over natural law when combatting claims of absolute prerogative power, celebrating an ancient Saxon or Britannic constitution of liberty that predated and survived the imposition of a Norman constitution of despotism. It might be thought that the ancient constitution suggests a Kelsenian linear conception of law—but that would be wrong. The '*antient constitution*' defended by Edmund Burke, for example, was not a historically first constitution; rather it was a constitution that changed constantly through 'analogical precedent, authority, and example', a constitution that existed 'at one time, [and] is never old, or middle-aged, or young, but in a condition of unchangeable constancy [it] moves on through the varied tenour of perpetual decay, fall, renovation, and progression'.[84] Furthermore, the ancient constitution was, to borrow Coke's language, 'beyond the memory or register of any beginning'.[85] Occasionally a starting point for the ancient constitution was posited—like the fanciful claim that the 'Original Constitution' or 'Fundamental Laws of Great Britain' were established by covenant when the British people were led by a wise man named 'Britannus' out of the state of nature.[86] But

---

[79] *Calvin's Case* (1608) 7 Co Rep 1a, 12b–13a.   [80] *Prohibitions del Roy* (1607) 12 Co Rep 63, 65.

[81] *Calvin's Case*, above n 79, 3b–4a, 19a.

[82] 'Proceedings in Parliament', above n 41, 68, 78, 81–2, 153.

[83] *Dr Bonham's Case* (1610) 8 Co Rep 113b, 118a.

[84] E. Burke, *Reflections on the French Revolution* (London: J. Dodsley, 1791), 45, 48–9.

[85] 8 Co Rep (preface).

[86] R. Archerley, *Britannic Constitution: Or, the Fundamental Form of Government in Britain* (London: Bettesworth, Osborn, and Longman, 1727), 21–2, 28.

these claims were unusual. Within the common law tradition, the ancient constitution resisted the search for law's beginning; it was the constitution with *no* beginning, the constitution that (as Burke said) was always present 'at one time'. Finally, the ancient constitution insisted upon continuity through restoration. English constitutional history was punctuated by revolution, but in each case participants saw themselves as developing or restoring pre-existing legal and constitutional arrangements, an attitude that A.V. Dicey attributed to a distinctive legal viewpoint, 'a legal turn of mind and a love for forms and precedents'.[87] Given the 'scores of paper constitutions' that had failed in other countries, there was, Dicey thought, something valuable in the 'moral' sentiment that informed this national commitment to legality.[88]

The ancient constitution argument had polemical aspects that were easily exposed.[89] But this should not obscure the argument's theoretical importance. It was based upon a deep suspicion of the civilian separation of public law from ordinary law: through 'indigenous' influences, it was said, England 'developed its own common law free from the absolutist tendencies of Roman jurisprudence'.[90] There is nationalistic chauvinism here, to be sure, but there is an important theoretical point too—a recognition that for a culture of legality to flourish law's foundations cannot be isolated from law itself. Common law constitutionalism was a distinctively circular vision jurisprudentially in two ways: first, constitutive law was folded into ordinary law so that law had no beginning or originating source at all; and, second, the essence of this ordinary law was neither natural law nor ancient custom as such but an unwritten law that integrated moral principle and practical experience through ordinary methods of legal reasoning that attended impartially to precedent and analogy with a view to interpretive coherence between law's abstract and specific dimensions. One could say that Coke extended Doderidge's understanding of unwritten law to the entire constitution to secure what we would now call the rule of law or constitutionalism.

My account of common law constitutionalism is admittedly a stylized portrayal of one strand of a contested legal history; but, even so, it provides historical texture for the legal concept of the unwritten constitution and suggests a way forward for understanding that concept. That way lies with a group of legal theories that seek to understand the basic norms of good governance to be immanent within law itself, theories centred upon the 'internal morality of law'[91] or the 'constitution of law'[92] or, we could say, law's internal unwritten constitution. I will group these theories together and call them circular theories of law. Although certain theorists I associate together within this camp might resist the association, they do share common ground that supports the legal concept of the unwritten constitution I have in mind.

---

[87] A. V. Dicey, 'Lectures on Comparative Constitutionalism', in J. W. F. Allison (ed), *The Oxford Edition of Dicey* vol II (Oxford: Oxford University Press, 2013), 182.

[88] Ibid 187, 190.

[89] J. G. A. Pocock, *The Ancient Constitution and the Feudal Law: A Study of English Historical Thought in the Seventeenth Century* (Cambridge: Cambridge University Press, 1957).

[90] W. Stubbs, *The Constitutional History of England in its Origin and Development* vol I 3rd edn (Oxford: Clarendon Press, 1880–7), 6.

[91] L. L. Fuller, *The Morality of Law* rev edn (New Haven: Yale University Press, 1969), 96.

[92] D. Dyzenhaus, *The Constitution of Law: Legality in a Time of Emergency* (Cambridge: Cambridge University Press, 2006).

This common ground is formed by the cross-section of two closely related views. The first view, associated with the work of Lon Fuller, is what may be called the 'legality of normative order' in which law's formal promulgation as a set of prospective, general, clear rules with which official acts are congruent is considered to reflect the reciprocal nature of the project of governance by law—a reciprocity, that is, between ruler and subject.[93] The second view, reflected in the work of Ronald Dworkin, is what may be called the 'legality of normative reason', a distinctive interpretive attitude through which the ideal of equality implicit within legality is understood to flow from the interpretation of law as a coherent body of rules and underlying principles.[94] Both approaches resist the firm division between law's constitutive facts or norms and law itself. This is not to say that sovereign lawmakers will not be constituted as a matter of fact. Even a Hobbesian sovereign may be recognized within a community. It is to say, however, that a *legal* order will only emerge once the moral demands implicit within legality are respected both in terms of legal form and through legal interpretation, a point that, it has been argued, even Hobbes, despite claims to his membership in the linear camp, understood.[95] By attending to both the legality of normative order and the legality of normative reason, an unwritten constitution, or rule of reason, implicit within the law of all liberal democratic societies, whether they have adopted written constitutions or not, may be seen to emerge.[96]

It cannot be said that the circular conception of law and constitutionalism is always evident within the work of the theorists I have included within the circular camp. Dworkin focuses upon written constitutional texts, for example, and much of Fuller's work emphasizes governance by rules. But by drawing upon the broad themes that these theorists develop, core features of a circular conception of the unwritten constitution emerge.

IV

It is time now to draw the lines of thought explored in the preceding parts of this chapter together and to sketch at least the outline of a theory of the unwritten constitution. My objective is to employ the basic understanding of unwritten law identified in Part I to develop what I called in Part II the ambitious theory of unwritten constitutionalism, and to this end I will be guided by insights drawn from the examination of linear theories of law and constitutionalism in Part III. It will come as no surprise that the outline of the ambitious theory of the unwritten constitution that I will sketch is a reaction

---

[93] For developments of Fullerian thought see K. Rundle, *Forms Liberate: Reclaiming the Jurisprudence of Lon L. Fuller* (Oxford: Hart Publishing, 2012); N. Simmonds, *Law as a Moral Idea* (Oxford: Oxford University Press, 2007).

[94] R. Dworkin, *Law's Empire* (Cambridge, Mass.: Belknap Press, 1986); R. Dworkin, *Justice in Robes* (Cambridge, Mass.: Belknap Press, 2006), 168–71.

[95] D. Dyzenhaus, 'Hobbes and the Legitimacy of Law' (2001) 20 *Law and Philosophy* 461; D. Dyzenhaus, 'How Hobbes Met the "Hobbes Challenge"' (2009) 72 *Modern Law Review* 488; E. Fox-Decent, *Sovereignty's Promise: The State as Fiduciary* (Oxford: Oxford University Press, 2011), 1–22.

[96] T. R. S. Allan, *Constitutional Justice: A Liberal Theory of the Rule of Law* (Oxford: Oxford University Press, 2001); T. R. S. Allan, *The Sovereignty of Law: Freedom, Constitution, and Common Law* (Oxford: Oxford University Press, 2013).

against linear or extraordinary approaches to constitutionalism that sever law's foundations from law itself; it is, instead, a theory of constitutionalism built upon normative ideals implicit within the circular conception of law. The result is a view of the unwritten constitution as a legal concept that offers a compelling way to understand constitutionalism whether a state has adopted a written constitution or not. My analysis so far has been based mainly upon examples drawn from the common law tradition, and the argument that I will now develop borrows heavily from that tradition—but it is not tethered to it. The unwritten constitution I have in mind is a common law constitution in the broadest sense, a constitutional *ius gentium* that transcends particular legal traditions.

Constitutionalism is the basic ideal that government must be established by law and limited by law from exercising arbitrary power, an ideal that seeks to reconcile the equal dignity of individuals with the pursuit of the common good by the political community within which they find themselves. It follows that constitutionalism is dependent upon at least two basic principles, which I will call the *pervasiveness* of law and the *ordinariness* of law. The pervasiveness of law is simply the idea that law must be understood to stretch across the entire field of social and political life leaving no gaps where the exercise of power is arbitrary. Law's pervasiveness is obviously important for constitutionalism, but it is fruitless unless the law that is pervasive is also in some sense ordinary. The ordinariness of law is the principle that the law that establishes and limits government must enjoy the essential qualities that law ordinarily enjoys. Constitutional law must be *law* if constitutionalism is to mean anything. The pervasiveness and the ordinariness of constitutional law depend upon a theory of the entire constitution as a legal concept, and that theory is necessarily based upon a circular rather than a linear conception of law. We can see this point by considering the two principles of constitutionalism in turn.

First, the pervasiveness of law requires something like the interpretive approach to unwritten law identified in Part I. Explicit legal rules are, on this view, to be taken as examples of a comprehensive set of legal principles that become more abstract as one ascends from concrete to general. There can never be a point where law runs out. When the arc of legal principle reaches its zenith in abstraction on a particular issue it simply descends again following another line within a potentially limitless number of lines of legal principle. When the point is reached upon that descent at which a concrete rule is needed but has yet to be stated (or written) explicitly, the interpretive exercise will involve the articulation of a rule that shows the sphere of normative order as holding together in a compelling fashion. The entire constitution must be understood in something like this way. Where a written constitution has been adopted, its express terms cannot be taken to exhaust constitutional law if gaps are to be avoided: the pervasiveness of law means that all written constitutions are in effect 'legally embedded written constitutions'. This is, of course, a theoretical claim that may not always be obvious doctrinally. Sound approaches to textual interpretation will mean that principles otherwise found within the unwritten legal context are woven seamlessly into readings of the text. Furthermore, even when constitutional rules are considered to arise from unwritten law rather than a written and entrenched constitutional text, their normative influence may be subtler than those written constitutional provisions used by judges to 'strike down' acts of the legislature.

Second, the ordinariness of law, in the sense that I have in mind, involves the rejection of linear accounts of constitutional law that sever law's constitutive foundations from law itself. The struggle for constitutional government in seventeenth-century England, as we saw, was an effort to ensure that the foundations of legal order, whether conceived as natural law or ancient custom, were integrated into the ordinary law of the land—a process that involved the very same interpretive methods that make law pervasive. Recognizing a special 'law of state' and leaving it in the hands of a king or president or star chamber is to deny the ideal of constitutionalism. Constitutive law is only law insofar as it is ordinary, and it is ordinary only if it forms part of the law it constitutes. Again, law must be seen in a circular way.

My claim about ordinary law is potentially confusing. It is not a claim that all law is mundane. The law of habeas corpus is more important politically than the law of dentistry. Nor is it the claim, sometimes associated with Dicey, that public law is simply private law applied to public officials. Finally, it is not a claim that constitutional law can never occupy a status of supremacy over regular laws. This last point deserves explanation. As Chief Justice John Marshall famously said in *Marbury v Madison*, it is in the very nature of a written constitution that it establishes a law that is 'supreme' over 'ordinary' legislation.[97] In this sense, then, written constitutions are not ordinary law. But Marshall CJ went on to rule that ordinary judges must refuse to apply legislation that is inconsistent with the written US Constitution (a proposition that is not expressly recognized by the text of that Constitution) because it is the responsibility of the ordinary judge to enforce 'the law'—ie the general 'law of the land'—of which the written constitution is considered to form one part. In this sense, then, the written constitution is thoroughly ordinary. Dicey made a similar point in a different way. The most unEnglish of legal ideas, the constitutional review of legislation by the ordinary courts, is, Dicey insisted, a distinctively common law response to the adoption of a written constitution, for it assumes that written constitutional law, like all law, can be interpreted in the ordinary way by the ordinary courts. 'What has been here called the American system [of constitutional judicial review]', Dicey wrote, 'is in principle borrowed from the common law of England.'[98] In some legal systems, then, certain constitutional norms may have a supreme status that regular laws do not, but these supreme norms will be 'law' only if they are understood to form an integral part of the ordinary law of the land.

Can it therefore be said that constitutional law is ordinary law because it is enforced in ordinary courts? That is not my claim either. My claim, rather, is that constitutional norms are ordinary law if they can be identified and justified as law in the ordinary way. It is the method of their identification and justification as law rather than their judicial enforcement as such that makes them law. We have already discussed the distinctive way in which unwritten law is identified. Written constitutional law is not so very different. It will have a linguistic formula that is, for the most part, to be regarded as authoritative, but its language must be given a meaning that, in the ordinary legal way,

---

[97] *Marbury v Madison* 5 US (1 Cranch) 137 (1803), 177.   [98] Dicey, above n 87, 237.

allows the text to sit comfortably within the network of normative values of which written law forms an integral part. To the extent that broadly worded constitutional provisions invite special forms of interpretation (eg broad, purposive, or liberal readings of text), the resulting method may well begin to approximate the interpretive method associated with unwritten law, but it will be no less ordinary for that. Indeed, both written and unwritten law initiate interpretive strategies that require the same attention to equality, consistency, and coherence and the same independence of thought from external political pressure.

The result is a style of political or moral reasoning that is distinctively legal but also ordinarily legal. The ordinariness of constitutional law that is a requirement of constitutionalism is simply a product of the (circular) interpretive method that integrates legal ideas generally into the webbed sphere of value that forms our normative world. An independent judiciary is necessary but ancillary to this point: a sustained legal narrative by independent judges is the most effective way, but perhaps not the only way, for ordinary law to emerge.

The conception of constitutionalism that I am sketching here is broadly consistent with that theory of truth and knowledge in human affairs that, as I observed above, emerged with ideas associated with Renaissance humanism, ideas that helped early common law writers to understand the nature of their intellectual enterprise. In its modern form, the theory claims that normative truth exists independently of both social convention and metaphysical ideas, that these truths may only be identified internally within the practices of interpretive discourse that make normative community possible, and that although normative discourse may be distinctively moral, political, or legal in character, all ideas about normative value must in the end hold together within a unified theory of value.[99] The humanist insight underlying this theory of value is, simply put, the importance of *integration*—integration of rhetoric and logic, of process and substance, of ideals of balance, harmony, and proportionality with practical perceptions, conventions, practices, and experiences about or relating to truth. To see the normative world holding together as a coherent whole, with each normative assertion justified in light of a theory of more abstract value capable of justifying all normative assertions, is to see the identification of normative value as a process of interpretive evaluation and re-evaluation where truth is real but only demonstrable through reasoned justification that is attentive to context, experience, and tradition. At no point can we reach outside the circular endeavour of evaluating our specific normative claims in light of the more abstract values that they presuppose to find the truth or validity of those claims. Perhaps only a Hercules, as Dworkin would say, can demonstrate the complete unity of value within and between all branches of normative discourse. The point, however, is that there is no other way to engage rationally in the pursuit of truth than to strive toward this ideal. Hercules cannot ask Atlas to hold the globe of normative order upon his shoulders—and nor can we. '[T]here is no finally noncircular way to certify our capacity to find truth of any kind in any intellectual domain.'[100]

---

[99] Here I am following R. Dworkin, *Justice for Hedgehogs* (Cambridge, Mass.: Belknap Press, 2011).
[100] R. Dworkin, *Religion without God* (Cambridge, Mass.: Harvard University Press, 2013), 16.

It has not been my intention here to defend the interpretive theory of the unity of value. Nor have I argued that the circular conception of the unwritten constitution depends upon that theory. It is important to acknowledge, however, the historical and theoretical connections between the ideas about the constitution that I have advanced in this chapter and this broader set of ideas about normative value. In this chapter, I have sketched only the outlines of the ambitious theory of the unwritten constitution. It is a reaction against linear approaches to constitutionalism that sever law's foundations from law itself. Legality is something that is pursued circularly, and in the end constitutionalism depends not on what is written in a state's constitution but the interpretive attitude—the legal turn of mind—that allows this pursuit to unfold with humility. That is what the unwritten constitution as a legal concept is.

3

On Constitutional Implications and Constitutional Structure

Aharon Barak*

I. Presenting the Problem

This chapter deals with the legal interpretation of the written text of a formal constitution. I assume, therefore that a formal constitution exists in the country in question.[1] The formality is manifested, inter alia, in the enactment of a written text. In most cases, the text is difficult to amend. The constitutional norms extracted from it are generally of a higher legal status than regular statutes. In most cases, the court's power to overturn any law conflicting with constitutional norms is acknowledged.

Every text has two meanings: an express meaning and an implied meaning.[2] This we learn both from the linguistic field of pragmatics[3] and from doctrines of legal interpretation. According to both theories, the legal norm is extracted both from the text's express meaning and from its implied meaning. The distinction between these two meanings is not easy to make,[4] but its existence in every text, including any written constitutional text, is undisputed. An example from the theory of pragmatics, provided by Grice,[5] will illustrate: a philosophy professor is asked by one of his students to write a letter of recommendation for a teaching position; in his recommendation, he writes that the student has a good command of English and that he has regularly attended classes. It seems that we should have no difficulty in inferring from this, by implication, that the professor does not think much of the student's philosophical abilities. This meaning—a poor opinion of philosophical ability—is not learned directly from the language of the professor's statement; it is implied from the context in which it was made. The following example comes from constitutional law: the Australian High Court inferred the recognition of an implied constitutional right to freedom of political

---

* President (ret.) of the Supreme Court of Israel; Radzyner School of Law, Interdisciplinary Center (IDC), Herzliya.

[1] On this distinction see A. Tomkins, *Public Law* (Oxford: Oxford University Press, 2003), 7.

[2] See R. Dickerson, *The Interpretation and Application of Statutes* (Boston: Little, Brown, and Co, 1975), 40; J. Goldsworthy, 'Implications in Language, Law and the Constitution', in G. Lindell (ed), *Future Directions in Australian Constitutional Law* (Sydney: Federation Press, 1994), 150–84, at 170–1; J. Goldsworthy, 'Constitutional Implications Revisited' (2011) 30 *University of Queensland Law Journal* 9, at 12.

[3] See below at 69–72.

[4] See J. Kirk, 'Constitutional Implication (I): Nature, Legitimacy, Classification, Examples' (2000) 24 *Melbourne University Law Review* 645, at 647.

[5] P. Grice, *Studies in the Way of Words* (Cambridge, Mass.: Harvard University Press, 1989), 33.

expression from the structure of the Australian Constitution, even in the absence of a bill of constitutional rights.[6]

In this chapter, I shall discuss the implied meaning of the written text of the formal constitution. I am not discussing, therefore, a material constitution, meaning an implied constitution which is completely unwritten, but what is implied by a formal, written constitution.

Goldsworthy studied constitutions' implied meaning and made important contributions to this field.[7] He argued that constitutional implication is only possible if it realizes the constitutional framers' intent. He relies on Gricean pragmatics[8] to support this approach. I myself, like Goldsworthy, hold that the key to implication is to be found in constitutional interpretation. In contrast to Goldsworthy, however, I do not hold that only intentionalist interpretation can support constitutional implication. In my opinion,[9] each of the three main systems of interpretation[10]—intentionalism,[11] originalism,[12] and purposivism ('a living constitution')[13]—can support constitutional implication, although the implications recognized by each system may be different. The theory of pragmatics also supports this approach.

The concept of constitutional structure lies at the foundation of my interpretive approach to constitutional implications. The constitutional structure creates the necessary nexus between the constitutional language and the implications inferred from it. This nexus grants constitutional implication its legitimacy. Constitutional structure is based on a constitution's architecture, and its underlying presuppositions. This concept was developed extensively by Black[14] and Tribe.[15]

---

[6] See *Lange v Australian Broadcasting Corporation* (1997) 189 CLR 520.

[7] See Goldsworthy, 1994, above n 2; Goldsworthy, 2011, above n 2; J. Goldsworthy, 'Constitutional Implications and Freedom of Political Speech: A Reply to Stephen Donaghue' (1997) 23 *Monash University Law Review* 362; J. Goldsworthy, 'Unwritten Constitutional Principles', in G. Huscroft (ed), *Expounding the Constitution: Essays in Constitutional Theory* (Cambridge: Cambridge University Press, 2008), 277–312; J. Goldsworthy, 'Constitutional Cultures, Democracy and Unwritten Principles' (2012) *University of Illinois Law Review* 683.

[8] See below at 69–72.   [9] See below at 66–8.

[10] See A. Barak, *Purposive Interpretation in Law* (Princeton: Princeton University Press, 2005); P. Bobbitt, *Constitutional Fate: Theory of the Constitution* (Oxford: Oxford University Press, 1982); C. Sampford and K. Preston (eds), *Interpreting Constitutions: Theories, Principles and Institutions (Law, Ethics and Public Affairs)* (Sydney: Federation Press, 1996); S. A. Barber and J. E. Fleming, *Constitutional Interpretation: The Basic Questions* (Oxford: Oxford University Press, 2007); J. Goldsworthy, *Interpreting Constitutions: A Comparative Study* (Oxford: Oxford University Press, 2007).

[11] See J. Raz, *Ethics in the Public Domain* (Oxford: Oxford University Press, 1994), 231 ('...the identification of a rule as a rule of law...need not be on the ground that this is what the person or institution explicitly said. It may be based on an implication.').

[12] J. Goldsworthy, 'The Case for Originalism', in G. Huscroft and B. W. Miller (eds), *The Challenge of Originalism: Theories of Constitutional Interpretation* (Cambridge: Cambridge University Press, 2011), 42–69, at 50 ('Most implications...can only be inferred from the text understood in light of information about the intentions or purposes of the lawmaker that is (or was) readily available to the lawmaker's intended audience... Any evidence of a speaker's intention that is readily available to the speaker's intended audience is "public" in the relevant sense.').

[13] See below at 66–8.

[14] See C. Black, *Structure and Relationship in Constitutional Law* (Woodbridge, Conn.: Ox Bow Press, 1969).

[15] See L. Tribe, *The Invisible Constitution* (Oxford: Oxford University Press, 2008).

The interpretive model that lies at the foundation of this chapter is different from various conceptions that can be grouped under the umbrella of the unwritten constitution.[16] Thus, for example, an important body of literature considers implied constitutional principles in the absence of a formal constitution.[17] This chapter does not address this literature, as I assume the existence of a written constitutional–canonical text, and I examine what its structure implies. Some interesting literature considers the question of whether implied norms that exist above the formal constitution (such as natural law[18]) or alongside it (such as constitutional custom[19]) can be recognized. Any discussion of such *lex non scripta* would go beyond the scope of my chapter. The constitutional implication I am concerned with is implication from the text of the formal constitution. American literature that deals with non-interpretive judicial review of the constitutionality of statutes[20] is also outside the scope of my chapter, which is based on an interpretive model. Much American writing is concerned with 'the living constitution'.[21] This literature is pertinent to my chapter to the extent that it is based in the interpretation of the constitutional text. Where it is only based on common law it is beyond the limits of constitutional implication. In his book, *America's Unwritten Constitution*,[22] Akhil Amar defines an unwritten constitution as any constitutional norm that is outside the confines of the US Constitution's 8,000 words. My approach is much narrower. The implied meaning is that of the written constitution and it is part of its language as it is understood in light of the constitutional structure.

I shall open this chapter with a description of the constitutional structure-based interpretive model which lies at the foundation of my approach, distinguishing

---

[16] See S. Sherry, 'The Founders' Unwritten Constitution' (1987) 54 *University of Chicago Law Review* 1127; M. S. Moore, 'Do We Have an Unwritten Constitution?' (1989) 63 *Southern California Law Review* 107; D. Strauss, 'Constitutions, Written and Otherwise' (2000) 19 *Law & Philosophy* 451; A. Vermeule, 'The Facts About Unwritten Constitutionalism: A Response to Professor Rubenfeld' (2001) 51 *Duke Law Journal* 473; M. D. Walters, 'The Common Law Constitution in Canada: Return of *lex non scripta* as Fundamental Law' (2001) 51 *University of Toronto Law Journal* 9; M. D. Walters, 'Written Constitutions and Unwritten Constitutionalism', in Huscroft, above n 7, 245–76; E. A. Young, 'The Constitution Outside the Constitution' (2007) 117 *Yale Law Journal* 408; Goldsworthy, 2008, above n 7.

[17] See R. Cooke, 'Fundamentals' (1988) *New Zealand Law Journal* 158; T. R. S. Allan, 'The Common Law as Constitution: Fundamental Rights and First Principles', in C. Saunders (ed), *Courts of Final Jurisdiction* (Sydney: Federation Press, 1996), 146–66; T. R. S. Allan, 'Constitutional Justice and the Concept of Law', in Huscroft, above n 7, 219–44; Allan in this volume; Walters, 2001, above n 16.

[18] See E. S. Corwin, 'The "Higher Law" Background of American Constitutional Law' (1929) 42 *Harvard Law Review* 965; W. R. George, 'Is Natural Law Theory of Any Use in Constitutional Interpretation' (1994) 4 *Southern California Interdisciplinary Law Journal* 463; M. S. Moore, 'Natural Rights, Judicial Review and Constitutional Interpretation', in J. Goldsworthy and T. Campbell (eds), *Legal Interpretation in Democratic States* (Aldershot, UK: Ashgate, 2002), 207–29.

[19] See H. Wolff, *Ungeschriebenes Verfassungsrecht unter dem Grundgesetz* (Tübingen: Mohr Siebeck, 2000).

[20] See T. C. Grey, 'Do We Have an Unwritten Constitution?' (1975) 27 *Stanford Law Review* 703; T. C. Grey, 'Origins of the Unwritten Constitution: Fundamental Law in American Revolutionary Thought' (1978) 30 *Stanford Law Review* 843; T. C. Grey 'The Constitution as Scripture' (1984) 37 *Stanford Law Review* 1; M. J. Perry, 'Noninterpretive Review in Human Rights Cases: A Functional Justification' (1981) 56 *New York University Law Review* 278.

[21] See D. A. Strauss, *The Living Constitution* (Oxford: Oxford University Press, 2010); A. Vermeule, 'Common Law Constitutionalism and the Limits of Reason' (2007) 107 *Columbia Law Review* 1482.

[22] See A. R. Amar, *America's Unwritten Constitution: The Precedents and Principles We Live By* (New York: Basic Books, 2012).

between the express meaning of the constitutional text and its implied meaning (section II). Section III will present a number of typical examples of constitutional implication. I will then discuss the approach of various systems of interpretation to constitutional implication (section IV), followed by an examination of the relationship of constitutional implications to linguistics and pragmatics (section V). I shall conclude my chapter with directions of research that should be pursued to attain a deeper understanding of constitutional implication, and consequently, of constitutional interpretation in general (section VI). Indeed, this chapter is only the beginning of the journey of constitutional implication.

II. The Interpretive Model

A. Extracting legal meaning from linguistic meaning

Legal interpretation is a process of understanding a legal text.[23] Every understanding is the result of interpretation. We are concerned with the interpretation of a written constitution. Constitutional interpretation seeks to understand the normative message arising from the written constitutional text. It extracts the constitutional norm from the linguistic receptacle. It turns a constitutional linguistic text into a constitutional norm. The constitutional text has two meanings: express and implied.[24] It is not easy to distinguish between the two, and every distinction is disputed.[25] I shall now proceed to examine this distinction, which lies at the foundation of this chapter.

B. The express meaning

The express meaning of the constitutional text is the meaning obtained directly through reading the constitutional language. This is the linguistic meaning indicated by semantics and syntax. This is the dictionary meaning of the text.[26]

Often, the text of a written constitution contains language formulated as a principle. This language contains principles such as the rule of law, liberty, freedom of expression, and human dignity. The legal meaning given to this text is part of the express meaning of the constitution.[27] Thus, for example, where the constitutional text establishes the right to liberty or freedom of expression, the meaning given to the term 'liberty' or 'freedom of expression' is an interpretation based on the express meaning, because it is obtained directly from the language of the document. The interpreter extracts the constitutional norm of liberty or freedom of expression from the express meaning of the text. This is an interpretive activity, done according to the system of interpretation

---

[23] See Barak, 2005, above n 10.   [24] See Dickerson, above n 2.
[25] See Goldsworthy, 1994, above n 2, 154; Kirk, above n 4, 647.
[26] See Dickerson, above n 2, 40.
[27] See R. Dworkin, 'Unenumerated Rights: Whether and How *Roe* Should be Overruled' (1992) 59 *University of Chicago Law Review* 381; Goldsworthy, 2008, above n 7; M. Tushnet, 'Can You Watch Unenumerated Rights Drift?' (2006) 9 *University of Pennsylvania Journal of Constitutional Law* 209.

applied by the interpreter, which determines the scope of the constitutional right. This scope can operate at various levels of generality.[28] Thus, for example, the US Supreme Court derived the right to privacy at a lower level of generality from the right to liberty.[29] Women's right to abortion is derived from privacy at an even lower level of generality.[30] Similarly, the right to burn the flag is derived from the right to freedom of expression.[31] All these levels of generality are extracted from the express meaning of the expression 'liberty' or 'freedom of expression'.

The express meaning of an expression formulated as a principle must operate within the limits of the linguistic meaning of this expression. Even language designed as principle has boundaries that the interpreter may not cross. Thus, for example, broad as the scope of the right to human dignity may be, it cannot be applied to a corporation.

Many words have several dictionary meanings. A linguistic sentence is sometimes vague or ambiguous. Semantics and syntax are insufficient for extracting a single legal norm from the express meaning of the text. This is true for every text, and it is true for a constitutional text. Indeed, the language of the constitution often has several express meanings. The limitations of language, the use of generalizations, and the drafters' lack of skill contribute to this. This is true in general, and especially when it comes to constitutional generalizations. There is no single express meaning for the terms 'freedom of expression', 'liberty', or 'human dignity'. These terms have a number of dictionary meanings. In order to give legal meaning to the constitutional language—to extract the constitutional norm from the variety of express meanings—the relevant context, including the constitutional structure, must be considered.

At the foundation of this interpretive approach lie constitutional considerations of democracy, rule of law, and separation of powers. The legitimacy of interpretation draws its strength from the legitimacy of the constitution itself. The enactment of a constitution is an authorization to interpret it. A constitution cannot be understood without interpretation. This is the constitutional legitimacy for extracting a constitutional norm from the express meaning of the constitutional text. When a judge-interpreter interprets a constitutional text, including a vague and ambiguous text, the legitimacy of his or her interpretation is derived from the legitimacy of the constitutional text.

C. The implied meaning

1. Indirect meaning

Constitutional interpretation extracts the constitutional norm not only from the express meaning of the written constitutional text, but also from its implied meaning. The implied meaning of the text is obtained—like the express meaning—from the

---

[28] The level of generality is determined by the system of interpretation. See L. H. Tribe and M. C. Dorf, 'Levels of Generality in the Definition of Rights' (1990) 57 *University of Chicago Law Review* 1057.

[29] See *Griswold v Connecticut* 318 US 479 (1965) (per Harlan J).

[30] See *Roe v Wade* 410 US 113 (1973). But see Z. Robinson, claiming that Roe's case was based on an implied right: Z. Robinson, 'A Comparative Analysis of the Doctrinal Consequences of Interpretive Disagreement for Implied Constitutional Rights' (2012) 11 *Washington University Global Studies Law Review* 93, at 118.

[31] See *Texas v Johnson* 491 US 397 (1989).

language of the constitutional text. However, it is not directly obtained from the language. It is not revealed by applying the rules of semantics and syntax. The dictionary does not help us in understanding. In the example of freedom of expression in the Australian Constitution, the implied meaning concerns the question of whether there exists a constitutional right to freedom of political expression. The dictionary is useless in providing an answer to this question, because constitutional rights cannot be extracted from the express meaning of the text of the Australian Constitution. How is the implied meaning of the constitutional text determined? In the absence of meaning arising directly from the language of the constitution, what is to stop the interpreter from extracting any meaning she wishes from the constitutional language? My answer is that the implied meaning must arise from the constitutional structure. This constitutional structure, which I shall sketch below, creates the necessary nexus between the constitutional language and its implication. The implication does not have to be essential or necessary.[32] The implied meaning does not need to be obvious. The implied meaning must be reasonably inferred from the structure of the constitution.

This is the theory of constitutional implication which underlies my approach. It is based on the existence of a nexus between the constitutional language and its implication. This nexus is the constitutional structure and it is what gives constitutional implication constitutional legitimacy. Indeed, just as the constitutional text imparts legitimacy to the interpretation given to the express meaning of the constitutional language, the constitutional structure imparts legitimacy to the interpretation given to the implied meaning of the constitutional text. What can be read directly from the constitutional text can be read indirectly from the constitutional text as informed by its structure. Where the meaning is explicit, there is a direct linguistic connection between the constitutional language and its linguistic meaning. Where the meaning is implied, there is no direct nexus between the constitutional text and its meaning. The direct nexus is replaced by the constitutional structure which is the nexus between the constitutional text and its implied meaning. It enables the interpreter to establish the implied meaning. The constitutional norm is extracted from this meaning.

2. The implied meaning and the constitutional structure

The constitutional structure plays a role in interpreting both the express and the implied meaning of the constitutional text. However, the interpretive role of the constitutional structure is different in each of the meanings. Regarding the express meaning, the constitutional structure plays a role in extraction—ie the transition from the express meaning of the constitutional text to the constitutional norm. The structure is not alone at this stage, and each system of interpretation recognizes other considerations alongside it. Regarding the implied meaning, the constitutional structure plays a role in crystalizing the linguistic meaning—ie the transition from the express

---

[32] See Kirk, above n 4, 65; See Goldsworthy, 2012, above n 7, 702.

meaning of the constitutional text to its implied meaning. It is the only consideration at this stage. Once the implied meaning has been established, the constitutional
structure may be a consideration, alongside other considerations, in extraction—ie
the transition from the implied meaning of the constitutional text to the constitutional
norm. The content of the structure and its implications are decided by the theory of
interpretation.

What is the constitutional structure?[33] The structure begins, of course, with
the words, paragraphs, chapters, and sections which make up the constitutional
whole.[34] Beneath this whole lie the fundamental principles which support the constitutional text and the internal logic which unites the constitutional provisions. The
constitutional structure allows the constitutional unity to be expressed. It reflects
the functions which the constitution imposes on the various state powers. It lays
the foundation of the constitutional understanding of the relationships between the
individual and the state, and between individuals. The constitutional structure is the
'bridges overs waters that separate islands of constitutional text, creating a unified
and useable surface'.[35] The structure of the constitution is based on the fundamental assumptions upon which the constitutional text rests.[36] These are the 'postulates which form the very foundation of the constitution'.[37] Frankfurter explained
that the most fundamental question in statutory interpretation—and in my opinion
a fortiori regarding constitutional interpretation—is 'what is below the surface of
the words and yet fairly a part of them'.[38] The constitutional structure is the architecture underlying the constitutional scheme,[39] the constitutional principles which
support this scheme, and their underlying assumptions.[40] Through this structure,
the nexus between the constitutional text and its implied meaning is created. To
quote Tribe: 'The constitutional structure is...that which the text shows but does
not directly say.'[41]

---

[33] On structural interpretation, see Black, above n 14; Bobbitt, above n 10; Tribe, above n 15;
M. O. Chibundu, 'Structure and Structuralism in the Interpretation of Statutes' (1994) 62 *University of
Chicago Law Review* 1439; G. H. Taylor, 'Structural Textualism' (1995) 75 *Boston University Law Review*
321; L. H. Tribe, 'Taking Text and Structure Seriously: Reflections on Free-Form Method in Constitutional
Interpretation' (1995) 108 *Harvard Law Review* 1221; E. A. Young, '*Alden v. Maine* and the Jurisprudence
of Structure' (2000) 41 *William & Mary Law Review* 1601; A. R. Amar, 'Foreword: The Document and
the Doctrine' (2000) 114 *Harvard Law Review* 26; R. Elliot, 'References, Structural Argumentation and
the Organizing Principles of Canada's Constitution' (2001) 80 *Canadian Bar Review* 67; M. C. Dorf,
'Interpretive Holism and the Structural Method, or How Charles Black Might Have Thought About
Campaign Finance Reform and Congressional Timidity' (2004) 92 *Georgetown Law Journal* 833; C.
L. Westover, 'Structural Interpretation and the New Federalism: Finding the Proper Balance Between State
Sovereignty and Federal Supremacy' (2005) 88 *Marquette Law Review* 693.

[34] See L. Tribe, *American Constitutional Law* 3rd edn (New York: Foundation Press, 2000), 40.

[35] Walters, 2008, above n 16, 267.

[36] See *Reference re Secession of Quebec* [1998] 2 SCR 217, paras 49, 52, 161 DLR (4th) 385.

[37] See *Reference re Manitoba Language Rights* [1985] 1 SCR 721, 749, 19 DLR (4th) 1 (per Lamer CJ). See
also Tribe, above n 15, 210 ('Invoking the tacit postulates of the constitutional plan...is an enterprise that
should unite all who see the Constitution as their lodestar.').

[38] See F. Frankfurter, 'Some Reflections on the Reading of Statutes' (1947) 47 *Colorado Law Review* 527,
at 533.

[39] See A. R. Amar, 'Architexture' (2002) 77 *Indiana Law Journal* 671.

[40] See Tribe, above n 34, 55.   [41] Ibid 40.

3. *The legal basis for constitutional implication*

a. The meaning of constitutional silence

If the interpretation of the constitutional text leads to the conclusion that the text's explicit meaning does not provide an answer—affirmative, negative, or otherwise—to a legal problem which the interpreter seeks to solve, what is to be concluded from this silence? The answer is that constitutional silence 'speaks' in different voices[42] and offers several interpretive solutions which are selected according to the various systems of interpretation. The *first* solution is that in the absence of a solution to a legal problem within the limits of the explicit meaning, the solution must be external to the constitution. Thus, for example, many constitutions contain no explicit arrangement concerning remedies for unconstitutional infringement of constitutional rights. In cases like these, the interpreter is referred to laws that are external to the constitution, such as common or statutory law, under which the remedy will be determined.

The *second* solution is that the absence of a solution indicates the existence of a gap (lacuna, *Lücke*) in the constitution, which must be filled in, in accordance with the applicable 'gap-filling rules'.[43] Continental law has thoroughly developed the concept of lacuna.[44] A lacuna exists where a legal arrangement which aspires for completeness is incomplete, and this incompleteness negates its purpose. The gap-filling rules refer the judge—who is authorized to fill in the gap—to analogy, and in its absence, to general legal principles.[45] The gap-filling doctrine—as developed in continental law—is not accepted in common law countries, and this solution cannot be taken into account. When a common law jurist notes that there is a gap in a written text,[46] he or she is not referring to this gap-filling doctrine.

The *third* solution is that an implicit meaning can be inferred from the constitutional text; what seems like the silence of the constitutional text is not silence at all, rather an implied meaning,[47] which provides that a positive implication or a negative implication to the legal problem that the interpreter seeks to solve can be inferred from it. The implication will be positive if it can be inferred from the express meaning that the provision may apply to an issue that is not addressed explicitly. The implication will be

---

[42] See Barak, above n 10, 67; D. Rose, 'Judicial Reasonings and Responsibilities in Constitutional Cases' (1994) 20 *Monash University Law Review* 195.

[43] See Barak, above n 10, 66.

[44] See C. Perelman, *Le Probleme des Lacunes en Droit* (Brussels: Bruylant, 1968); W. Canaris, *Die Feststellung von Lücken im Gesetz: Eine Methodologische Studie über Voraussetzungen und Grenzen der Richterlicheu Rechtsfortbildung Praeter Legem* (Berlin: Duncker & Humboldt, 1983).

[45] See the Italian Civil Code, art 2 (1969) M. Beltremo et al. (trans); Swiss Civil Code, art 1; Austrian Civil Code, art 7.

[46] See *Reference re Remuneration of Judges of the Provincial Court of Prince Edward Island* [1997] 3 SCR 3, 95, 150 DLR (4th) 577. Chief Justice Lamer maintained that the role of the unwritten principles is 'to fill out gaps in the express terms of the constitutional scheme'. Justice Douglas's theory in *Griswold* is not based on gap-filling.

[47] Implication is different from gap-filling. Implication gives a meaning to what the constitutional text contains. Gap-filling completes what the text is missing. See J. H. Merryman, 'The Italian Style III: Interpretation' (1966) 18 *Stanford Law Review* 583, at 593 ('The problem of interpretation is to supply meaning to the norm; that of lacunae is to supply the norm').

negative if it can be inferred from the express meaning that the provision will not apply to an issue that is not addressed explicitly (*expressio unius est exclusio alterius*).

b. Implied constitutional meaning and constitutional text

The implied meaning—and the constitutional norm extracted from it—is not external to the constitutional text. No words are added to the constitution, which do not exist in it.[48] The implied meaning exists within the constitution, and is an intrinsic, inseparable part of the text used as a basis for the express meaning.[49] *Verba illata inesse videntur*. It follows that the constitutional norm extracted from the implied meaning is not a norm whose foundation is unwritten. It is not part of the unwritten constitution.[50] It can be said, metaphorically speaking—as I wrote in a judgment[51]— that 'the implicit language of the text is written between the lines in invisible ink'. Non-metaphorically speaking, it should be recognized that the implied meaning—just like the explicit meaning—is obtained from the language of the constitutional text, albeit indirectly. The implicit meaning is not written between the lines, it is the written lines themselves. There is therefore only one constitutional text, to which two meanings are attributed: explicit and implicit. From these two meanings two different constitutional norms are extracted.[52]

c. The status and characteristics of the constitutional norm extracted from the implied meaning

Every norm extracted from the linguistic meaning of a constitutional text is a constitutional norm. There is no 'express constitutional norm' nor is there an 'implied constitutional norm'. There are only 'constitutional norms'. The source of the linguistic meaning, be it express or implied, has no bearing on the nature of the constitutional norm extracted from it. The constitutional status of a norm extracted from the implied meaning is the same as that of the norm extracted from the express meaning of the constitutional text. The direct nexus which exists between the constitutional text and its meaning does not grant the norm extracted from it an elevated status in the normative hierarchy relative to a norm extracted from the implied meaning of the constitutional text in light of the constitutional structure. Both norms were enacted by the same constitutional assembly, through the same constitutional enactment. Both draw their legitimacy from the same constitution.

The constitutional qualities that characterize every type of constitutional norm extracted from the express meaning of the constitutional text characterize constitutional norms extracted from the implied meaning of the constitutional text as well. Therefore, this norm may establish values, rights, and powers. Similarly, any person who seeks to change it must act in accordance with the rules applicable to constitutional

---

[48] See Goldsworthy, 1994, above n 2; Tribe, above n 15, 29.

[49] See Goldsworthy, 2012, above n 7.

[50] *Reference re Secession of Quebec*, above n 36, para 32 (where it is stated that the implied principles are part of the 'unwritten constitution').

[51] HCJ 2257/04 *HDS-TAL Party v Chairman of the Central Elections Committee to the 17th Knesset* 56(6) IsrSC 685 (2004), 703 (Heb). See also Tribe, above n 15, 29.

[52] See Kirk, above n 4, 648.

amendments.[53] Just as a constitutional right extracted from the express meaning can be an absolute or relative, eternal or amendable, positive or negative right, so too regarding a constitutional right extracted from the implied meaning. Therefore, just as the one may confer upon the individual a right vis-à-vis the state, so can the other.[54]

When a constitutional norm extracted from the implied meaning of a constitutional text contradicts a constitutional norm extracted from an express constitutional text, the conflict is resolved according to the regular rules of resolving conflicts between constitutional norms.[55] A constitutional norm extracted from the express meaning is no different in this context than a constitutional norm extracted from the implied meaning. However, at times we may come to the interpretive conclusion that the express meaning of a constitutional text negates the existence of additional implied provisions. In this case, the law will be according to the constitutional norm extracted from the express meaning. This is not because it has any normative advantage, but rather because there is no place for the implied meaning to be inferred (*expressum facit cessare tacitum*), and thus there is no conflict.

III. Examples of Constitutional Implication

Each system of interpretation recognizes different constitutional implications. I shall discuss a number of typical examples. Some are implied by the constitutional text according to each of the three systems of interpretation that I will discuss; some are implied by the constitutional text only according to one system of interpretation.

Each constitution infers its own implications. Each constitution has a unique structure, and what is implied by one constitution is not necessarily implied by others. Silence in one constitution may be interpreted as a negative implication, while silence in another may be interpreted as a positive implication.

A. Implication of constitutional values

In many modern constitutions, constitutional values such as democracy, federalism, and the rule of law are set forth explicitly. These values are of great legal importance,[56] particularly with respect to the interpretation of the constitution. Can constitutional values that are not given explicit expression in the constitution be inferred by implication from the constitutional structure? The answer, in principle, is yes. Generally, no negative implication is to be inferred from constitutional silence regarding values that

---

[53] See J. Leclair, 'Canada's Unfathomable Unwritten Constitutional Principles' (2002) 27 *Queen's Law Journal* 389, at 429.

[54] But see *Kruger v Commonwealth* (1997) 190 CLR 1, 132 (per Gaudron J) where it was stated that implication limits the governmental power but does not grant the individual a right 'in the strict sense'. See also G. Williams, 'Human Rights and Judicial Review in a Nation Without a Bill of Rights: The Australian Experience', in G. Huscroft and I. Brodie (eds), *Constitutionalism in the Charter Era* (Markham, Ont.: LexisNexis Canada, 2004), 305–34.

[55] See A. Barak, *Proportionality: Constitutional Rights and their Limitations* (Cambridge: Cambridge University Press, 2012), 83; E. Brems (ed), *Conflicts Between Fundamental Rights* (Cambridge: Intersentia, 2008).

[56] See Dworkin, above n 27; J. Raz, 'Legal Principles and the Limits of Law' (1972) 81 *Yale Law Journal* 823.

were not expressly set forth. Of course, each system of interpretation does so according to its own approach.[57] Thus, for example, the Canadian Supreme Court recognized the values of judicial independence,[58] the rule of law, federalism, and separation of powers[59] as being implied from the basic structure of the Constitution. Similarly, the US Supreme Court[60] and the Canadian Supreme Court[61] recognized human dignity as a constitutional value, despite human dignity not being acknowledged in their constitutions as an independent constitutional right.

B. Implication of constitutional rights

Many modern constitutions contain a comprehensive list of constitutional rights which comprise the constitutional bill of rights. Can a right that is not extracted from the express meaning of the constitutional text be implied?[62] Or alternatively, is a negative implication to be inferred regarding every right which cannot be extracted from the express meaning of the constitutional text? At times there is an express constitutional provision which negates the existence of a negative implication.[63] What happens when there is no such provision? Can a constitutional right be implied by a constitution such as Australia's which does not contain a constitutional bill of rights at all? Each one of the systems of interpretation might give an affirmative answer to these questions, provided that such implication arises from the structure of the constitution.[64] Thus, for example, it seems to me that where the right of access to courts cannot be extracted from the express meaning of the bill of rights' text, this right can be extracted from the implied meaning of the text as informed by the constitutional structure. A constitution that takes human rights seriously should be interpreted in a manner recognizing a constitutional right of access to the judicial system. From the structure of the Australian Constitution, which does not contain an express bill of

---

[57] See Tribe, above n 15, 83; Walters, 2001, above n 16; Walters, 2008, above n 16; Leclair, above n 53; Black, above n 14; S. Donaghue, 'The Clamour of Silent Constitutional Principles' (1996) 24 *Federal Law Review* 133; P. Hughes, 'Recognizing Substantive Equality as a Foundational Constitutional Principle' (1999) 22 *Dalhousie Law Journal* 5; D. Mullan, 'The Rule for Underlying Constitutional Principles in a Bill of Rights World' (2004) *New Zealand Law Review* 9; B. McLachlin, 'Unwritten Constitutional Principles: What is Going On?' (2006) 4 *New Zealand Journal of Public and International Law* 147.

[58] *Reference re Remuneration*, above n 46, para 109.

[59] See *Reference re Remuneration*, above n 46 (judicial independence); *Reference re Secession of Quebec*, above n 36 (federalism, democracy, rule of law).

[60] See *Rosenblatt v Baer* 383 US 75 (1966), 92; *Planned Parenthood of Southeastern Pennsylvania v Casey* 505 US 833 (1990), 851; *Parents Involved in Community Schools v Seattle School District No 1* 551 US 701 (2007), 797.

[61] *R v Oakes* [1986] 1 SCR 103, 136, 53 OR (2d) 719; *R v Morgentaler* [1988] 1 SCR 30, 164, 63 OR (2d) 281; *Kindler v Canada (Minister of Justice)* [1991] 2 SCR 779, 814, 84 DLR (4th) 438; *Law v Canada (Minister of Employment and Immigration)* [1999] 1 SCR 497, 530, 170 DLR (4th) 1; *Nova Scotia (Attorney General) v Walsh* 2002 SCC 83, [2002] 4 SCR 325, 370.

[62] See Cooke, above n 17; D. Crump, 'How Do the Courts Really Discover Unenumerated Fundamental Rights? Cataloguing the Methods of Judicial Alchemy' (1996) 19 *Harvard Journal of Law & Public Policy* 795.

[63] See US Const Amend IX: 'the enumeration in the Constitution, of certain rights, shall not be construed to deny or disparage others retained by the people'.

[64] See W. Sinnott-Armstrong, 'Two Ways to Derive Implied Constitutional Rights', in T. D. Campbell and J. D. Goldsworthy (eds), *Legal Interpretation in Democratic States* (Aldershot: Ashgate 2002), 231–44.

rights, the High Court inferred an implied right to freedom of political expression.[65] Here too, the constitution was not interpreted as containing a negative implication regarding the right to freedom of political expression. However, implication has its limits. When implication loses the nexus between the constitutional text and its implied meaning based on the structure of the constitution, the interpretive boundary is breached.[66]

C. Implied limitation clause

Constitutional rights are often worded in 'absolute' language, which creates the impression that they cannot be limited.[67] The interpretive approach of most constitutions is that all rights—in the absence of an express contradictory meaning—are relative.[68] They can be limited. The express meaning of many constitutional texts allows for the extraction of constitutional norms which permit the limitation of the full realization of constitutional rights if the limitation is proportional.[69] But what is the rule where no 'limitation clauses' can be extracted from the express meaning of the constitutional text? Does it follow that the constitutional rights are absolute? My answer is that the constitutional text, interpreted in light of the structure, can often be interpreted to imply a limitation clause.[70] This is how the levels of scrutiny, recognized as arising from the US Bill of Rights can be understood.[71] Moreover, sometimes a special limitation clause exists regarding certain constitutional rights, while other constitutional rights are not accompanied by a specific limitation clause or they are accompanied by a provision whereby they may be limited by 'law'. Are we to infer from this the existence of negative implication regarding an implied limitations clause for those constitutional rights? The answer is not necessarily. A court may recognize implied limitation clauses for rights which either have no express limitation clause or which may be limited by 'law' provided that this recognition is based on the constitutional structure.

D. Implied judicial review

Most modern constitutions contain constitutional texts whose express meaning establishes judicial review of the constitutionality of statutes.[72] In the absence of

---

[65] See *Lange*, above n 6. The High Court refused to acknowledge an implied constitutional right to equality. See *Leeth v Commonwealth* (1992) 174 CLR 455.

[66] See *Kruger*, above n 54, 434.   [67] Regarding absolute rights see Barak, above n 55, 27.

[68] Regarding relative rights see ibid 32.

[69] See Israeli Basic Law: Human Dignity and Liberty, art 8; Federal Constitution of the Swiss Confederation of April 18, 1999, art 36; Constitution of the Republic of South Africa 1996, art 36.

[70] HJC 92/03 *Shaul Mofaz v Chairman of the Central Elections Committee* 57(3) IsrLR 793 (2003) (per Mazza J).

[71] On the levels of scrutiny, see E. Chemerinsky, *Constitutional Law, Principles and Policies* 4th edn (New York: Wolters Kluwer, 2011), 551.

[72] See Part VII of the *Constitution Act 1982*, s 52(1), being Schedule B to the *Canada Act 1982* (UK), 1982, c 11.

such a provision, can judicial review be implied from the constitutional structure? It seems to me that *Marbury v Madison*[73] can be understood as recognizing judicial review by constitutional implication.[74] This is also true for the *Mizrahi Bank* case[75] in Israel, where judicial review of the constitutionality of statutes limiting rights in Basic Law: Human Dignity and Liberty was acknowledged, despite the absence of an express provision in that regard. In both cases, the constitutional silence was not construed as a negative implication regarding judicial review. It seems that Australia took a similar approach regarding the recognition of judicial review.[76]

E. Implied eternity clauses

The express meaning of the text of a number of constitutions establishes that certain constitutional provisions cannot be changed through the general provisions regarding constitutional amendment.[77] They are 'eternal'.[78] They may only be changed by establishing a new constitution. Typical examples are a state's federal structure, and its democratic or secular nature. The German Constitution expressly includes the right to human dignity among these provisions.[79] Can the eternity of constitutional provisions be inferred by implication? India's Supreme Court developed the basic structure doctrine, according to which the basic structure of the Indian Constitution cannot to be changed via the normal procedure for constitutional amendment.[80]

It seems that a potential methodological basis for this doctrine is constitutional implication.[81] The constitutional structure leads us to the conclusion that the provisions regarding constitutional amendment assume the existence of the whole. Therefore, the implied meaning of the constitutional text does not recognize constitutional amendments that violate the basic structure of the constitution.[82] A similar approach can also be found in the case law of the Constitutional Court in South Africa,[83] and the Supreme Court in Israel.[84]

---

[73] See *Marbury v Madison* 5 US (1 Cranch) 137 (1803).

[74] See Tribe, above n 15, 30, 47; Amar, above n 33, 32.

[75] See CA 6821/93 *Bank Mizrahi v Migdal Cooperative Village* 2 IsrLR 1 (1995).

[76] See C. Saunders, *The Constitution of Australia: A Contextual Analysis* (Oxford: Hart Publishing, 2011), 75.

[77] See Basic Law of the Federal Republic of Germany (Grundgesetz), art 79(3); Constitution of the Republic of Turkey, art 4.

[78] K. Gözler, *Judicial Review of Constitutional Amendments: A Comparative Study* (Bursa: Ekin Press, 2008).

[79] See Basic Law of the Federal Republic of Germany (Grundgesetz), art 79(3).

[80] See S. Krishnaswamy, *Democracy and Constitutionalism in India: A Study of the Basic Structure Doctrine* (Oxford: Oxford University Press, 2010); M. Khosla, *The Indian Constitution* (Oxford: Oxford University Press, 2012).

[81] See Tribe, above n 15, 33. See also Allan, 1996, above n 17, 156.

[82] See A. Barak, 'Unconstitutional Constitutional Amendments' (2011) 44 *Israel Law Review* 321.

[83] See *Premier of KwaZulu-Natal v The President of the Republic of South Africa* 1996 (1) SA 769 (CC); *United Democratic Movement v President of the Republic of South Africa* 2003 (1) SA 488 (CC).

[84] See HCJ 6427/02 *The Movement for Quality Government in Israel v Knesset* 61(1) IsrSC 619 (2006) (Heb) (per Barak P); HCJ 4676/94 *Meatrael Ltd v The Knesset* 50(5) IsrSC 15 (1996) (Heb) (per Barak P).

IV. Constitutional Implication and Systems of Interpretation

A. Systems of interpretation

There are many systems of interpretation.[85] This is true of interpretation of any legal text. It is certainly true of the interpretation of a constitutional text. Underlying this diversity are various philosophies with regard to the nature of interpretation, the function of a constitution, and the role of the court interpreting the language of the constitution and extracting the constitutional norms from it. Different scholars classify systems of interpretation in different ways. According to the classification which I apply to constitutional interpretation, as well as to the interpretation of all legal texts, the basic difference is between subjective systems of interpretation and objective systems of interpretation.[86] The former seek to interpret the constitutional text based on the framers' intent (intentionalism). Others seek to interpret it according to criteria disconnected from the framers' intent. Among the others, some emphasize public understanding at the time of the enactment of the constitution (originalism), and some emphasize public understanding at the time of interpretation (purposivism). All the systems of interpretation recognize constitutional implication. Let us now examine each of them.

B. Constitutional implication and intentionalism

Intentionalism is a general name for a family of subjective theories of interpretation. Their underlying conception is that a constitution must be interpreted according to the framers' intent. This reflects an actual, not hypothetical, reality. The content of this intent is the values, aims, interests, policies, goals, and function that the framers of the constitution sought to realize. Intent can be recognized at different levels of generality and may be learned from within the constitution itself, or from any reliable external source.

The intentionalist interpreter gives the constitutional text an express meaning—ie meaning obtained directly from the language—that realizes the intent of the framers of the constitution. From the various express meanings, intentionalist interpretation chooses, inter alia, the meaning which fulfills the constitutional structure. The interpreter also gives this language implied meaning—ie meaning that is not obtained directly from the language but from the language in light of constitutional structure[87]— which realizes the intent of the constitution's framers. Let us return to the example of a formal constitution that does not contain a bill of rights.[88] The constitutional interpreter

---

[85] See above at 56–86.   [86] See Barak, above n 10, 120, 148.

[87] See *Reference re Secession of Quebec*, above n 36, 247. See also Tribe and Dorf, above n 28; J. Cameron, 'The Written Word and the Constitution's "Vital Unstated Assumptions"', in P. Thibault, B. Pelletier, and L. Perret (eds), *Essays in Honour of Gerald A. Beaudoin* (Montreal: Editions Yvon Blais, 2002), 91; B. L. Berger, 'White Fire: Structural Indeterminacy, Constitutional Design, and the Constitution Behind the Text' (2008) 3 *Journal of Comparative Law* 249; Goldsworthy, 2012, above n 7.

[88] See *Lange*, above n 6. For review and evaluation see G. Kennett, 'Individual Rights, the High Court and the Constitution' (1994) 19 *Melbourne University Law Review* 581; T. D. Campbell, 'Democracy, Human Rights, and Positive Law' (1994) 16 *Sydney Law Review* 195; G. Williams, 'Sounding the Core of Representative Democracy: Implied Freedoms and Electoral Reform' (1995) 20 *Melbourne University Law*

may conclude that the intent of the framers of the constitution was not to negate constitutional rights (no negative implication), but rather to recognize a constitutional right
to freedom of political expression. He must then turn to the constitutional structure
to see whether this intent can be realized by the implied meaning as emerges from the
structure. He may interpret the constitution, in much the same way as the Australian
High Court, as giving expression to an implied meaning concerning the recognition of
representative democracy. From there he may extract the implied right to freedom of
expression. However, if there is no implication regarding representative democracy, or
any other implication from which freedom of expression can be extracted, this norm is
not implied. In this case, the framers of the constitution may have had an intent which
the interpreter discovered from information external to the constitution, but they were
unable to give it expression—neither express nor implied. A person who seeks to realize this intent must do so through the process of constitutional amendment.

C. Constitutional implication and originalism

Originalism is a family of objective theories of interpretation, at the centre of which is
the conception that the constitutional text must be interpreted according to its original
public meaning.[89] The meaning of the constitutional language is the meaning that its
audience at the time of enactment gave to the language of the constitution. According
to several interpretational theories from this family, one must distinguish between the
interpretation of the constitutional text, which is concerned with the linguistic meaning of the text, and its construction, which is concerned with ambiguous and vague
text. In such a constitutional text the interpretation process has reached its limits.
Construction removes constitutional indeterminacy, fills gaps, and gives meaning to
constitutional silence.[90] Construction may entail a modern outlook.

The interpreter, according to the original public meaning, gives the constitutional text
an express meaning—emerging directly from the language—that realizes the original
public meaning. From the various express meanings, the originalist interpreter chooses,
inter alia, the express meaning which is inferred by the constitutional structure. He also
gives the language of the constitutional text an implied meaning—ie meaning arising
not directly from the language of the text but from the language's meaning in light of
the constitutional structure according to its original public meaning to the members of

Review 848; J. Kirk, 'Constitutional Implications from Representative Democracy' (1995) 23 *Federal Law Review* 37; L. Claus, 'Implications and the Concept of a Constitution' (1995) 69 *Australian Law Journal* 887; Donaghue, above n 57; A. Stone, 'The Limits of Constitutional Text and Structure: Standards of Review and the Freedom of Political Communication' (1999) 23 *Melbourne University Law Review* 668; Goldsworthy, 2008, above n 7; Goldsworthy, 1994, above n 2; Kirk, above n 4; J. Kirk, 'Constitutional Implications (II): Doctrines of Equality and Democracy' (2001) 25 *Melbourne University Law Review* 24.

[89] See A. Scalia, *A Matter of Interpretation: Federal Courts and the Law* (Princeton: Princeton University Press, 1997); K. E. Whittington, *Constitutional Interpretation: Textual Meaning, Original Intent, and Judicial Review* (Lawrence, Kan.: University Press of Kansas, 1999); S. G. Calabresi (ed), *Originalism: A Quarter-Century of Debate* (Washington, D.C.: Regnery Publishing, 2007); J. M. Balkin, *Living Originalism* (Cambridge, Mass.: Harvard University Press, 2011); R. W. Bennett and L. B. Solum, *Constitutional Originalism: A Debate* (Ithaca, N.Y.: Cornell University Press, 2011).

[90] See Whittington, above n 89.

society at the time of its enactment.[91] Thus, for example, it can be argued that the original public meaning at the time of the establishment of the American Constitution and the first ten amendments was that the Constitution provides, by implication, for judicial review of the constitutionality of statutes.[92] Accordingly, the *Marbury*[93] decision is implied by the language of the constitution as a whole, as it was part of the original public meaning. This original public meaning must give meaning to implications arising from the structure of the constitution. Otherwise, we must conclude that this original public meaning was mistaken.

D. Constitutional implication and purposive interpretation

Purposive constitutional interpretation[94] is a family of interpretational theories. Its members all share the conception that the guideline for extracting the constitutional norm from the linguistic receptacle is the constitution's underlying purpose. This purpose includes the values, aims, interests, policies, goals, and function that the constitutional text is designed to realize. This purpose considers the constitutional framers' intent and the original public meaning. However, the modern purpose has the greatest bearing. The constitution becomes a 'living document'[95] or 'living tree'.[96]

The purposive interpreter gives the constitutional text an express meaning that realizes the constitutional purpose. From the various meanings which realize the constitution's purpose, purposive interpretation will select the meaning which fulfills the constitutional structure. It gives the constitutional language an implied meaning—ie a meaning that is not obtained directly from the language but from the constitutional structure—that realizes the constitutional purpose.[97] Where the constitutional structure does not present an implication which realizes the constitutional purpose, the interpreter must not extract a constitutional norm realizing a constitutional purpose learned from external sources. A constitutional amendment would be required in order to give expression to the constitutional purpose.

The main difference between Goldsworthy's approach and my own is encapsulated in this system of interpretation. While Goldsworthy holds that constitutional implication can only be recognized by intentionalism, or originalism, which holds that the framers' intent is part of the original public understanding, I hold that every system of interpretation, including purposive interpretation, can recognize constitutional implication. Goldsworthy's reliance on linguistic pragmatics does not necessitate a change in my approach. We will now analyse the relationship between legal interpretation and linguistic pragmatics.

---

[91] Goldsworthy was prepared to see the founding fathers' intent as part of this original public understanding. See Goldsworthy, above n 12.

[92] See W. Treanor, 'Judicial Review Before Marbury' (2005) 58 *Stanford Law Review* 455.

[93] *Marbury*, above n 73.   [94] See Barak, above n 10, 83.   [95] See Strauss, above n 21.

[96] See *Edwards v Canada (Attorney General)* [1929] UKPC 86, [1930] AC 124, 136, 1 DLR 98 (per Lord Sankey) ('a living tree capable of growth and expansion within its natural limits').

[97] See Tribe, above n 15; Donaghue, above n 57.

V. Constitutional Implication and Pragmatics

A. Semantics and pragmatics

Semantics determines the meaning of texts. It deals with the theory of meaning. Syntax plays a central role in semantics. However the need was felt to look to context in order to give meaning to a text. Pragmatics was developed to fill this need.[98] It asserts that language must be understood with reference to its context. There are two types of context: linguistic (co-text) and extralinguistic. The linguistic context is internal. It is the language's textual surroundings. The extralinguistic context is external. It is the circumstances external to the text, including knowledge shared by the text's author and her audience, the author's abilities and preferences, and issues relevant to the audience. The implied meaning is derived from these external circumstances. There are numerous different external and internal contexts. They are, theoretically, infinite. From the multiple contexts, linguistics chooses those which are relevant to giving linguistic meaning to the text. In understanding the internal and external context, the pragmatist looks, inter alia, to the presuppositions upon which the meaning of the text is based.[99] They are important with respect to both the express and the implied meaning.

B. Grice's pragmatics

The linguistic philosopher Grice was particularly influential in the development of pragmatics.[100] One of Grice's contributions is conversational implicature. The example of the professor's recommendation, discussed at the beginning of this chapter, was taken from Grice. Grice assumes that social behaviour is rational. Therefore, he assumes that every conversation is guided by the 'cooperative principle'. According to this principle, every speaker aims to contribute to the conversation, and formulates his contribution in the way that is necessary to be effective. Each speaker in the conversation is expected to observe this principle, and the speaker assumes that every participant in the conversation observes it and that every participant in the conversation makes this assumption. Grice established four maxims which together comprise the cooperative principle:[101] quantity (provide as much information as needed, but no more); quality (describe only what you believe to be true and have evidence for); relation (say what is relevant to the conversation); and manner (avoid obscurity, ambiguity, and prolixity). In most cases, the maxims are respected. But sometimes they are violated. When the speaker flouts one of the cooperative maxims while both he and his audience still adhere to the cooperative principle, it can be inferred that he is using conversational

---

[98] See S. Davis (ed), *Pragmatics: A Reader* (Oxford: Oxford University Press, 1991); Y. Huang, *Pragmatics* (Oxford: Oxford University Press, 2007).

[99] See R. M. Harnish, 'Logical Form and Implicature', in S. Davis (ed), *Pragmatics: A Reader* (Oxford: Oxford University Press, 1991), 316–64, 329; A. Marmor, 'The Pragmatics of Legal Language' (2008) 21 *Ratio Juris* 423.

[100] See H. P. Grice, 'Logic and Conversation', in P. Cole and J. L. Morgan (eds), *Syntax and Semantics* vol 3: Speech Acts (New York: Academic Press, 1975), 41–58, at 43–4.

[101] Ibid 45–9.

implicature. If asked if the implicature reflects his intent, the speaker would answer affirmatively.

C. Pragmatics and constitutional interpretation

Is pragmatics relevant to the implied meaning of a public legal text, such as a statute or constitution?[102] Is a statute or constitution a 'conversation', guided by the cooperative principle? Is Gricean implicature relevant to constitutional implication? The Gricean method interprets the language of the participants in a fluent spoken or written conversation. In constitutional conversation, however, we only have the 'answer', which is sometimes disconnected and generations removed from the context in which it was given. What we have is an intergenerational monologue. How, then, can we apply Gricean theory to this one-sided and intergenerational answer? There is no simple answer to these questions. Some maintain that a statute or constitution is not a conversation between the constituent authority (in the case of a constitution) or the legislature (in the case of a statute) and members of society.[103] Even if we regard a statute or a constitution as a conversation, the cooperative principle is not a part of it. Some argue that Grice's theory is of limited utility in interpreting statutes and constitutions.[104] The reason for this is that the role of linguistics is to understand the linguistic text, while the role of interpretation is to extract a legal norm from this understanding. The theory of 'understanding' and the theory of 'extracting' are fundamentally different. Thus, for example, the speaker's intent is relevant to the theory of understanding (linguistics), but may not be relevant to the theory of extracting (legal interpretation).[105] Even those who maintain that in theory Grice's theory of implicature is relevant to the interpretation of constitutions and statutes, note that the cooperative principle does not always hold true for constitutions and statutes. Thus, for example, Marmor noted that the legislature sometimes employs 'strategic speech'. In these cases, the legislature (the speaker) abuses the Gricean maxims, and deliberately creates spurious implicature. While the audience (the subjects of the law enacted) believes that the speaker (the legislature) is

---

[102] See P. Amselek, 'Philosophy of Law and the Theory of Speech Acts' (1988) 1 *Ratio Juris* 187; A. Trosborg, 'Statutes and Contracts: An Analysis of Legal Speech Acts in the English Language of the Law' (1995) 23 *Journal of Pragmatics* 31; A. Marmor, 'What Does the Law Say? Semantics and Pragmatics in Statutory Language', in D. Canale and G. Tuzet (eds), *Analisi e Diritto 2007* (Turin: Giappichelli, 2008), 127–40; D. Cao, 'Legal Speech Acts as Intersubjective Communicative Action', in A. Wagner, W. Werner, and D. Cao (eds), *Interpretation, Law and the Construction of Meaning: Collected Papers on Legal Interpretation in Theory, Adjudication and Political Practice* (Dordrecht: Springer, 2007), 65–82; Marmor, above n 99; J. Visconti, 'Speech Acts in Legal Language: Introduction' (2009) 41 *Journal of Pragmatics* 393; S. Azuelos-Atias, 'Semantically Cued Contextual Implicatures in the Legal Texts' (2010) 42 *Journal of Pragmatics* 728; K. Greenawalt, *Legal Interpretation: Perspectives from other Disciplines and Private Texts* (Oxford: Oxford University Press, 2010), 19; F. Poggi, 'Law and Conversational Implicatures' (2011) 24 *International Journal for the Semiotics of Law* 21; R. Carston, 'Legal Texts and Canons of Construction: A View from Current Pragmatic Theory', in M. Freeman and F. Smith (eds), *Law and Language: Current Legal Issues* vol 15 (Oxford: Oxford University Press, 2013), 8–33.
[103] See H. M. Hurd, 'Sovereignty in Silence' (1990) 99 *Yale Law Journal* 945; Donaghue, above n 57.
[104] See M. Greenberg, 'Legislation as Communication? Legal Interpretation and the Study of Linguistic Communication', in A. Marmor and S. Soames (eds), *Philosophical Foundations of Language in the Law* (Oxford: Oxford University Press, 2011), 217–56.
[105] Ibid.

acting in accordance with the cooperative principle, the speaker (the legislature) has abandoned this principle.[106]

Grice doesn't only pose difficulties for intentionalists. Originalism doesn't align with him either as Grice bases implicature on the speaker's intent, while originalism sees intent as irrelevant. Seeing the legislature's, or constitutional framers', intent as part of the original understanding is a solution that has been proposed,[107] but it is contrived. Purposive interpretation also has difficulty implementing Grice. It seems to me, therefore, that if we have difficulty relying on Gricean pragmatics for constitutional implications, we must turn to other pragmatic theories.

As is well known, after Grice came the neo-Griceans, who developed his ideas. Thus, for example, Levinson wrote that conversational implicature does not necessarily arise from the flouting of the Gricean cooperative maxims. In his view, implicature is also possible where the speaker abides by the cooperative maxims. Other researchers questioned the very need for cooperation between the speaker and his or her addressees, the need to formulate maxims in this regard, and the centrality of an intentional violation of the maxims by the speaker. Sperber and Wilson based implication in language on the concept of relevance. According to their approach, the quest for relevance is fundamental in human thinking. This approach asserts that neither the cooperative principle nor the violation of the conversational maxims are of any importance. Others, like Kasher, based pragmatics on rationality. According to rationality, the presumption is that the author of the text acts rationally, and wants to achieve his goals through the text.[108] It seems that relevance and rationality theories reflect and facilitate constitutional implication more than Grice's theory.

It seems, then, that we are merely starting to explore this field. In my opinion, so long as the connection between pragmatics and constitutional structure has not been developed, pragmatics can help us only in the elementary understanding of constitutional implication by illuminating the idea of constitutional implication. Grice indicated linguistic principles for deciphering conversational implicature, and thus must be studied seriously. He and later scholars showed us that implication is natural to language; that we must distinguish between what is expressly stated and what is implied; that in giving implied meaning to the legal text the interpreter is performing an act that is interpretive in nature. Conferring implied meaning on a constitutional text is therefore a legitimate interpretive act.[109]

As we have seen, the speaker's intent is not the only possible source for implicature. We must be wary of the claim, which Goldsworthy made, that Grice's theory is decisive in the field of constitutional implications. Constitutional implication is a recognized phenomenon in interpretive systems which do not attribute decisive weight to the framers' intent. These systems may rely on other linguistic theories which base implicature on other sources, such as relevancy and rationality. Beyond that, further

---

[106] See Marmor, above n 102; Marmor, above n 99; A. Marmor, 'Can the Law Imply More Than It Says? On Some Pragmatic Aspects of Strategic Speech', in A. Marmor and S. Soames (eds), *Philosophical Foundations of Language in the Law* (Oxford: Oxford University Press, 2011), 83–104.

[107] See Goldsworthy, 2012, above n 7, 705.

[108] D. Wilson and D. Sperber (eds), *Meaning and Relevance* (Cambridge: Cambridge University Press, 2012). See A. Kasher, 'Gricean Inference Revisited' (1982) 29 *Philosophica* 25.

[109] See Greenawalt, above n 102, 35, 37.

research is required into the relationship between pragmatics and what is implied from the constitutional text.

VI. Conclusion

Constitutional implication is an accepted phenomenon in constitutional law. However, we do not yet have a thorough understanding of the methods and limits of implication. The limit of the express meaning is the meaning obtained directly from the language. What are the limits of implied meaning? When can we say that an implied meaning which realizes the intent, the original public meaning, or the modern purpose, emerges from the constitution? In my opinion, there are three directions of research which require exploration in order to advance the understanding of constitutional implication.

The main direction—which should be both of an analytical and comparative nature—is the development of interpretation based on the constitutional structure. The term 'structure' is metaphorical. We must give this metaphor normative content. A constitution should be interpreted holistically. However, an approach that is only holistic is unsatisfactory.[110] We must delve into the constitution's underlying fundamental assumptions,[111] the legal institutions it establishes, the relationship it creates among the branches of government and between them and the individual. This exploration will establish the required nexus between the constitutional text and its implied meaning. Important contributions in this area were made by Black[112] and Tribe.[113] Their structural approaches should be developed further. We must develop inductive and deductive methods for understanding constitutional structure; we must study the relevant levels of generality; we must decide to what extent the fundamental principles of the common law—such as substantive rule of law and due process[114]—comprise part of the constitutional structure; we must establish the limits of the constitutional structure, what it includes, and what exceeds its ambit. We must develop a comparative methodology that enables us to compare different constitutional structures and their effect on the implied meaning of the text. Each legal system and each system of interpretation must develop its own understanding of the concept of constitutional structure. Once we have a thorough understanding of this concept, the importance of the distinction between the express meaning of language and the implied meaning will progressively diminish. This will also draw originalist construction and purposive interpretation nearer to each other.[115] The interpretation that views the constitution as being a living document ('living constitution',[116] 'living tree'[117]) will be shared by a number of systems of constitutional interpretation.

The second direction of research should develop the connections between the theory of constitutional implication and the various theories that come under the umbrella of the 'unwritten constitution'.[118] Ideas and thoughts in the area of the unwritten

---

[110] See Dorf, above n 33. [111] See Walters, 2008, above n 16; Tribe, above n 15, 102, 104, 212.
[112] See Black, above n 14. [113] See Tribe, above n 15. [114] See Allan, 2008, above n 17.
[115] See above at 66–8. [116] See above at 68. [117] See *Edwards*, above n 96.
[118] See above at 54–5.

constitution, such as substantive rule of law, due process, the rules of natural justice, and other aspects of the common law, can help us reach a more profound understanding of constitutional implication. Indeed, the boundary between the interpretive model and the unwritten constitution will be delineated more clearly once significant portions of the unwritten constitution are incorporated into the interpretive model, as they are part of the fundamental assumptions included in the constitutional structure.

The third direction of research is the development of the connections between pragmatics and the theory of constitutional implication. This connection should not rely on Grice's theory alone. What is required, in this respect, is new thinking, both from the linguistic perspective and from the legal perspective. The extent to which new pragmatic theories—such as Sperber and Wilson's relevance theory which does not assume the cooperative principle and which also allows the identification of the meaning of 'strategic' texts,[119] or the rationality theory expounded by Kasher[120]—can provide a linguistic basis for the theory of constitutional interpretation must be examined.

As long as these directions of research are not developed, we must tread the paths of constitutional implication carefully. I hope that my chapter contributes to the recognition of constitutional implication's legitimacy, the importance of the required research, and the need for careful thought, so long as the interpretive picture remains insufficiently clear.

---

[119] See above at 71.   [120] See above at 71.

4

Reflections on What Constitutes 'a Constitution'

The Importance of 'Constitutions of Settlement' and the Potential Irrelevance of Herculean Lawyering*

Sanford Levinson**

I. Introduction

This chapter was prepared for, and is now being published as part of, an inquiry into the philosophical foundations of constitutional theory. In trying to give specific content to that topic, I am reminded of the fable about attempting to discern the nature of an elephant by asking six blind men to report on what their particular experiences taught them with regard to answering that question. The point of the fable, of course, is that each of them provided a perfectly reasonable answer, based on his direct sensory impressions, even as we who are gifted with sight know that their particular answers captured only one aspect of the complex pachyderm. So it is, I think, with regard to the intersection of philosophy and constitutional theory.

Consider only three quite different ways of approaching that intersection: first, is it a necessary attribute of a constitution that it accord with standards of justice, so that an 'unjust' constitution is really no true constitution at all? There is, quite obviously, a distinguished tradition in political and legal philosophy going back at least to Aristotle or St Augustine and forward to contemporary natural lawyers that the answer to this question is yes. My own view, for what it is worth, is that that answer is not helpful (and therefore should be rejected) for the simple reason that it would lead to disqualifying as 'genuine constitutions' most constitutions throughout our history. That most definitely would include the US Constitution, given its egregious collaborations with slavery. Although I can easily understand the desire to refuse to honour patently unjust constitutions with the honorific title 'constitution', I nevertheless believe that scholars are better off adopting a more positivist account that makes morality irrelevant to defining a constitution in the first place. And, as H. L. A. Hart valuably argued, the separation

* An earlier version of this chapter was prepared for presentation at the workshop on Philosophical Foundations of Constitutional Law, University of Toronto, 9–10 May 2014. I am extremely grateful to David Dyzenhaus for giving me the opportunity to participate (and for his comments on that earlier draft), and to the other participants in the roundtable for their consistently interesting observations about the broader topic. I have also benefitted from the opportunity to present revised versions of the chapter to seminars at the European University Institute in Florence (for which I am grateful to Professor Dennis Patterson) and to the Faculty of Law at Oxford University (for which I am grateful to Professors Aileen Kavanagh and Stephen Dimelow).
** W. St John Garwood and W. St John Garwood Jr Centennial Chair in Law, University of Texas Law School; Professor of Government, University of Texas at Austin.

between law and morality entitles us to denounce as 'immoral' constitutions that we do believe meet whatever criteria we apply to assess their moral worth.

A second approach, which tends to dominate the field, at least in the United States,[1] at the present time, is to take as given the existence of one or another constitution (whose moral legitimacy is unquestioned) and then to focus almost obsessively on 'constitutional interpretation', ie hermeneutic techniques of giving ostensibly definitive meaning to what might appear, at first glance, difficult or debatable patches of constitutional text. Anyone from the United States—and, it may be, even constitutional theorists around the world—will be familiar, for better and worse, with heated arguments among devotees of one or another of what Philip Bobbitt has labelled the 'modalities' of constitutional interpretation, in his own account 'text', 'structure', 'history', 'doctrine' (or 'precedent'), 'prudence' (or 'consequentialism'), and, finally, what he calls 'ethical argument'. This last modality, incidentally, refers *not* to recourse to classical (and universalistic) natural law, but, rather, to adverting to the specific norms that constitute a particular social order. I am thus strongly tempted to add a seventh modality that allows us to account for references to classical natural law or norms of justice; moreover, as Ran Hirschl has recently demonstrated,[2] there are certainly many constitutional orders around the world that include religious argumentation as an acceptable, perhaps even a primary, modality. This last point, of course, invites us to distinguish between secular and sectarian constitutions, which distinction is linked for many with the difference between liberal and illiberal constitutions.

A final potential intersection comes at the stage of *constitutional design*, which I confess has become my own primary interest in recent years. My own view is that we must always be aware that constitutions are attempts to control behaviour in what is sometimes called 'the real world'. This means that any extant constitutions will be shaped by the perceptions one has about the challenges presented by the particularities of any given instantiation of 'reality', including, but certainly not limited to, the absence or presence of significant cleavages along lines of race, ethnicity, religion, language, or possession of economic resources, to take only the most obvious examples. One of Sujit Choudhry's many contributions to the subject was an edited collection aptly titled *Constitutional Design for Divided Societies: Integration or Accommodation?*[3] To the extent that a given constitution 'succeeds' or 'fails', the reason is far more likely to involve its 'degree of fit' with the demands presented by a given social order than its adherence to, or deviation from, abstract and universalistic notions of constitutional design.

---

[1] The discussion in my presentations in Florence and Oxford highlighted the possibility that my description (and worries) about the near-exclusive focus of 'constitutional theorists' on problems of interpretation rather than institutional design may reflect my immersion in debates taking place within the United States. I am certainly sympathetic with the emphasis in the chapters by Professors Dixon and Stone on the potential distortions in the arguments of particular scholars that may be explained by 'assumptions generated by observing the jurisdictions they are most familiar with'. See Dixon and Stone in this volume.

[2] R. Hirschl, *Constitutional Theocracy* (Cambridge, Mass.: Harvard University Press, 2010).

[3] S. Choudhry, *Constitutional Design for Divided Societies: Integration or Accommodation* (Oxford: Oxford University Press, 2008).

There is, I believe, something manifestly foolish about trying to design an 'ideal constitution' as in the setting of an academic seminar that ostentatiously avoids reference to the realities of any given society. As a matter of fact, it is not clear that any significant theorist takes the enterprise of 'ideal constitutionalism' very seriously. John Rawls, for example, never imagined that anyone would actually design a constitution. He was surely well aware that no known operating constitution has ever been designed behind such a 'veil', nor is there reason to believe that he advocated any such decision procedure when confronted with the practical realities surrounding constructing a constitutional order in the actual world we live in. This, of course, does not deny that Rawls might be helpful in generating 'a theory of justice' that might be useful when *assessing* the morality or goodness of a particular constitution, even if one also goes on to explain, or even justify, the impossibility of achieving any kind of 'maximum justice' given actual circumstances facing the drafters of a particular constitution.

This suggests, ironically or not, that one consequence of a Rawlsian approach might be to highlight the conflict among different conceptions of the overall constitutionalist enterprise. Do we define that enterprise, for example, by reference to the desirability of achieving a modus vivendi that will enable potentially conflicting populations to live in a semblance of peaceful political order? Or, do we instead define it by reference to a far broader desire to achieve a very particular kind of political order instantiating norms (however derived) of justice? Rawls might perhaps be especially relevant if the framers of a constitution announce, perhaps in its preamble, that they are devoted to constructing a political system that will 'establish Justice'. With regard to the constitution that I know best (and whose preamble I am quoting from), that raises the obvious point that it was grievously flawed at the outset as the result of compromises adopted at the Philadelphia Convention and then ratified by state conventions. But that only underscores that actual 'framers', as 'constitutional designers', may have other goals besides attaining justice, save as a long-run aspiration. Another goal, for example, that of 'domestic Tranquility', at least in the short run, might be thought to require making certain compromises, perhaps even what Avishai Margalit notably labels 'rotten compromises', in the name of procuring the consent of relevant (and conflicting) elites whose accord is necessary to establish a working constitution at all.

The reference to Margalit, a distinguished philosopher in his own right, suggests two aspects of the relationship between philosophy, constitutional design, and constitutional assessment. One, perhaps the most obvious, is that the taxonomy of constitutions can run the gamut from 'just constitutions' to 'unjust ones'; for many this would be equivalent to distinguishing between 'liberal' and 'illiberal' constitutions. But Margalit's most important contribution may be to the constitutional designer herself in reminding us of the practical reality that all constitutions are the product of political struggles and concomitant compromises. And in an age where stiff-necked devotion to 'principle' has gained many admirers, it is important to be reminded of the necessity of compromise.[4]

---

[4] See eg D. Thompson and A. Guttmann, *The Spirit of Compromise: Why Governing Demands It and Campaigning Undermines It* (Princeton: Princeton University Press, 2012).

Still, it is also important to be reminded as well that some compromises are better than others and that there exists a category of what Margalit calls 'rotten compromises' that presumptively ought *never* be agreed to, save, perhaps, in the presence of what American lawyers would call truly 'compelling interests', with no practical alternative seemingly available. 'Let justice be done though the heavens fall' may not be a maxim one wants to live by if in fact the heavens *are* falling; those articulating such a view include Machiavelli, Max Weber (in 'Politics as a Vocation'), and Michael Walzer (defending the necessity to accept 'dirty hands' as part of political leadership). Even so, one might well believe that a very heavy burden of proof should be on those arguing that such a dire situation is at hand.

So what *is* a 'rotten compromise'? Margalit's definition is that it agrees 'to establish or maintain an inhuman regime, a regime of cruelty and humiliation, that is, a regime that does not treat humans as humans.'[5] It takes no great feat of imagination to view the set of compromises that basically acquiesced to the maintenance of chattel slavery within the United States as such a 'rotten compromise', in contrast, say, to the so-called Great Compromise by which small states were given equal representation in the Senate with larger states. One might well agree that the latter was a 'lesser evil' than would have been the torpedoing of the enterprise of drafting a new constitution in 1787 that would have accompanied the withdrawal from the Convention of Delaware and other states for whom the lack of equal voting power would have been a 'deal breaker'. But the 'evil' of the Senate, even if substantial,[6] certainly pales before that of slavery. One might well agree with William Lloyd Garrison that the Constitution was a 'Covenant with Death and an Agreement with Hell', though, interestingly, that might still not be conclusive as to whether it would have been 'better' for the Convention to fail—and for the new United States to disintegrate, say, into at least two, possibly three, separate countries along the Atlantic coast, with predictions of European-like endless warfare among them.[7]

There are times, after all, when one might even be obligated to make 'pacts with the devil', as was the case with regard to the Western alliance with Stalin during World War II. One should recall that even anti-utilitarian devotees of 'principles', including Ronald Dworkin, Robert Nozick, and Charles Fried, all included exceptions if adherence to principle would generate true 'catastrophes'. But, quite obviously, these debates as well require immersion in empirical materials, for how does one know, exactly, what the consequences of a given compromise will actually be? One may be overestimating the risks, after all, of failure to achieve agreement (ie a constitution).

So now let me attend to my more specific argument, which is, basically, that legal philosophers[8] are 'overinvesting' their energies in trying to resolve questions linked

---

[5] A. Margalit, *On Compromise and Rotten Compromises* (Princeton: Princeton University Press, 2009).

[6] As I have argued elsewhere. See S. Levinson, *Our Undemocratic Constitution* (Oxford: Oxford University Press, 2006), 49–62.

[7] See eg J. Jay, 'No. 3', 'No. 4', 'No. 5', in C. Rossiter (ed), *The Federalist Papers* (New York: Penguin Putnam, 1999), 9–21; A. Hamilton, 'No. 6', 'No. 7', 'No. 8', 'No. 9', in C. Rossiter (ed), *The Federalist Papers* (New York: Penguin Putnam, 1999).

[8] Readers may wish to insert 'especially in the United States' here and in any further generalizations about 'legal philosophers'.

with 'constitutional interpretation' and should address some important questions attached to the enterprise of constitutional design itself.

II. The Limits of Herculean Brilliance

Perhaps the reader will already have gathered that I am basically a pragmatist, which, I realize, for some is simply a confession of a certain lack of intellectual rigour. Perhaps because I am not a trained philosopher, I am not in quest of the one true notion—a 'necessary truth'—of constitutional identity. As with the elephant, there are undoubtedly a variety of notions competing for our attention; as a political scientist, as well as an academic lawyer, I am interested primarily in what helps us best to understand how constitutions function, as a practical matter, and what might count as strengths or weaknesses of particular exemplars. I have increasingly come to believe that constitutions—or, at least, the US Constitution—have at least *two* aspects—perhaps one might even analogize them to trunks or legs—that lead analysts down considerably different roads, even if we must ultimately recognize that the elephant does indeed consist of both (and more besides, such as the consequences of the sheer size (and weight) of elephants).

But one difference between elephants and constitutions presents itself immediately: unless one has a particular view of the world that includes a creator-God or some other strongly teleological account, it is difficult to argue that the answer to what constitutes an elephant requires assigning some *purpose* to the animal's existence. The fact that looking at elephants might give us great pleasure is a fact about us, not about why elephants exist in the world. But one really cannot make any sense of the constitutional enterprise without including an extensive account of purpose. Constitutions are not natural objects; one does not have to be a post-modernist in order to view them as socially constructed for specific ends, some of them indeed set out in the constitution's text—this is a principal function of many preambles, for example. Other purposes are easily inferred from a knowledge of the historical and social circumstances surrounding the creation of a particular constitution. We can, of course, believe that specific provisions, as they play out in the fullness of time, may in fact be counterproductive to the presumed purposes. This provides endless grist for those interested in the vagaries of 'interpretation' and the tensions between such modalities as textualism or originalism as against more 'purposive' analyses that end up being far more consequentialist in operation.

As with Robert Frost, I think that roads not taken can make 'all the difference', and I have become quite perturbed about the dominant road that defines at least the American legal academy and, I suspect, most legal academies, including philosophers of law. Thus this chapter can be read as an attempt to intervene in the ongoing conversations of legal philosophers when talking about constitutions; it is not, most certainly, an argument that traditional legal philosophy has failed to contribute mightily to understanding certain enduring issues within the constitutionalist enterprise. It most certainly has. Rather, I want to argue that legal philosophers have concentrated too much on only a limited set of such issues—a single road, as it were—rather than paying sufficient attention to other matters that merit significant discussion. In particular, I want to argue that an excessive amount of philosophical discussion focuses on questions of 'constitutional interpretation', ie how best to give meaning to certain clauses of existing constitutions whose meanings are indeed not clear. Instead, I find my own work increasingly focuses on clauses that in fact present no real interpretive dilemmas (save, as I sometimes put it, in the 'highest' of 'high theory' seminars), but where the question of the *wisdom* of these provisions is central. Should one find them unwise, then that may raise important questions of a constitution's amendability or, ultimately, the desirability even of replacing an existing constitution with a substantially new one, as occurred, for example, with regard to the Articles of Confederation within the United States.[9]

In order to elaborate my critique, I will proceed somewhat indirectly, by focusing on a posthumous essay by Ronald Dworkin published in *The New York Review of Books* under the title 'Law from the Inside Out'.[10] Whatever one's agreement or disagreement with particular facets of Dworkin's complex jurisprudence, there is presumably a consensus that he was one of the twentieth century's towering jurisprudential figures; his work must be grappled with even if only ultimately to reject it. We will, no doubt, be assessing its strengths and weaknesses for many years to come.

A central question for both admirers and critics is the extent to which a sufficiently inspired Herculean judge could at least transform, and perhaps even in a real sense amend, existing constitutions through dazzling feats of interpretive prowess that would be accepted as 'legitimate' by whatever the relevant interpretive community (or communities) might be. Such a question, of course, immediately suggests that the central question posed by a constitution is one of 'constitutional hermeneutics'. Is constitutional law in its 'interpretive dimension' sufficiently capacious to subsume every question that might be raised by a particular constitution, including those clear patches of text that, I argue, generate questions about wisdom rather than meaning? Is *all* of our political life within the domain of what Dworkin notably called 'the forum of principle'— that is, the judiciary applying recognizably legal modes of analysis to even the most wrenching of problems? I have come to believe that constitutions are complex instruments only some of which are susceptible to the traditional lawyerly skills captured by the term 'interpretation' and made most manifest by judges inhabiting their particular forum.[11]

---

[9] Again, see Dixon and Stone in this volume for the importance of amendability in understanding any given constitutional order (including the presumptive role of courts). It is certainly the case that one can scarcely understand the nature of debates within the United States without taking into account the inordinate difficulty of amending the *national* constitution. Matters are considerably different with regard to many of the fifty *state* constitutions within the United States. It is almost bizarre that discussions of the notion of 'popular sovereignty' within the United States ignore the profound differences between the decidedly different notions found in the national and state constitutions. See S. Levinson, 'Popular Sovereignty and the United States Constitution: Tensions in the Ackermanian Program' (2014) 123 *Yale Law Journal* 2644, at 2666–72.

[10] R. Dworkin, 'Law from the Inside Out', *The New York Review of Books*, 7 November 2013, at 54–5.

[11] Indeed, it is worth noting that even Dworkin, when writing, eg, about proposals to 'constitutionalize' the welfare state by innovative interpretation particularly of the Fourteenth Amendment (see eg F. Michelman, 'Foreword: On Protecting the Poor Through the Fourteenth Amendment' (1969) 83 *Harvard Law Review* 7), argued that it simply could not be done, whatever his own political sympathies with the project. See R. Dworkin, *Freedom's Law: The Moral Reading of the American Constitution* (Cambridge, Mass.: Harvard University Press, 1996), 36. Whatever his own commitments to liberal notions of 'economic equality', 'I have insisted that integrity would bar any attempt to argue from the abstract moral clauses of the

I focus on one aspect of Dworkin's self-description, which, not to put too fine a point on it, I view as exemplifying a basic deficiency, perhaps even pathology, in the way that legal philosophers have come to define their relationship with the field of 'constitutional law'. Consider, then, Dworkin's capsule description of his own career:

> When I left Wall Street to join a law school faculty, I took up a branch of law—constitutional law—that is in the United States of immediate and capital political importance. Our Constitution sets out individual rights that it declares immune from government violation. That means that even a democratically elected parliament, representing a majority opinion, has no legal power to abridge the rights the Constitution declares. But it declares these individual rights in very abstract language, often in the language of abstract moral principle. It declares, for example, that government shall not deny the freedom of speech, or impose cruel punishments, or deprive anyone of life, liberty, or property without due process or law, or of the equal protection of the law.
>
> The Supreme Court has the final word on how these abstract clauses will be interpreted, and a great many of the most consequential political decisions taken in the United States over its history were decisions of that Court. The terrible Civil War was in part provoked by the Supreme Court's decision that slaves were property and had no constitutional rights; racial justice was severely damaged, after that war, by the Court's decision that racially segregated public schools and other facilities did not deny equal protection of the law; a good deal of Franklin Roosevelt's progressive economic legislation was declared unconstitutional because it invaded property rights and so denied due process. These were the bad decisions that everyone now regrets. There have been very good decisions, too: in 1954 the Court, reversing its earlier bad decision, declared that segregated schools were inherently unequal . . . .
>
> It is therefore a crucial question how courts should interpret the abstract constitutional language: What makes a particular reading of that language correct or incorrect?[12]

There is so much that could be said about these brief excerpts. Dworkin's assignment to the US Supreme Court of 'the final word on how these abstract clauses will be interpreted' is debatable on both empirical and normative grounds, not to mention in tension with some of his own writing on civil disobedience. As to the former, it is a much-disputed issue among American political scientists whether the Supreme Court has necessarily been successful in imposing its own views of the Constitution on public officials, especially if they are recalcitrant state officials.[13] The normative issue is even more complex. There is a rich tradition in American political thought, which I denominate in my own work a 'protestant' view of institutional authority, of refusing to identify (mere) 'opinions' of the Supreme Court with the genuine 'meaning' or 'definitive

---

Bill of Rights, or from any other part of the Constitution, to any such result'. Thus, to that extent, he adopted positivistic limits, founded on the notion of 'best fit' with the realities of the American constitutional order, to the Herculean enterprise.

[12] Dworkin, above n 10, 54.

[13] See eg G. N. Rosenberg, *The Hollow Hope: Can Courts Bring About Social Change?* (Chicago: University of Chicago Press, 1991) and the literature it has spawned about the actual 'impact' of the Court in changing the behaviour of relevant officials.

interpretation' of the Constitution.[14] Among the most famous illustrations of this position is President Andrew Jackson's statement in his veto of congressional renewal of the
charter of the Bank of the United States, the constitutionality of which had been upheld in
Marshall CJ's opinion in *McCulloch v Maryland*.[15] 'The opinion of the judges has no more
authority over Congress', wrote Jackson, 'than the opinion of Congress has over the judges,
and on that point the President is independent of both. *The authority of the Supreme Court
must* not, therefore, be permitted to control the Congress or the Executive when acting in
their legislative capacities, but to *have only such influence as the force of their reasoning may
deserve.*'[16]

Similar statements can be found in the speeches and writings of many other Americans.
Indeed, Dworkin himself had notably defended a 'protestant' approach toward judicial authority. 'We cannot assume', he had written in *Taking Rights Seriously*, 'that the
Constitution is always what the Supreme Court says it is.' Judicial decisions are entitled
to respectful consideration—Jackson would presumably have agreed with this—but the
American version of constitutionalism 'does not make the decision of any court conclusive. Sometimes, even after a contrary Supreme Court decision, an individual may still reasonably believe that the law is on his side'.[17] It is possible that Dworkin believed that even
mistaken decisions nevertheless had to be respected and obeyed until the Court, on its
own, changed its view. One can, however, certainly find in his writings suggestions that he
supported civil disobedience in the face of legal mistakes that trenched on protected rights.
Thus his contribution to a 1971 anthology, *Is Law Dead*, which presented an early version
of *Taking Rights Seriously*, included his assertion that '[i]f a man believes he has a right to
demonstrate, then he must believe that it is wrong for the government to stop him, *with or
without benefit of a law*. If he is entitled to believe that, then it is silly to speak of a duty to
obey the law as such'.[18] To be sure, this statement is consistent with a view that a decision
of the Supreme Court states 'the law', but that individuals have a moral right, perhaps even
a duty, to ignore the law under certain circumstances. If this reads Dworkin correctly, then
it establishes once more elements of legal positivism even in his own jurisprudence, whatever its general identification with a critique of positivism.

What is probably more important is Dworkin's tendency to identify the US
Constitution—the subject of most of his writings—with declarations of individual
rights that are ostensibly protected against governmental override. No doubt many constitutional theorists around the world, particularly after World War II, would assert that
all constitutions worthy of respect are basically *liberal* constitutions. Besides making it
difficult to know what to do with illiberal constitutions,[19] this also invites confusion

---

[14] See S. Levinson, *Constitutional Faith* 2nd edn (Princeton: Princeton University Press, 2011).
[15] 17 US 316 (1819).
[16] A. Jackson, 'Veto Message Regarding the Bank of the United States' (Washington, 10 July 1832), available at: http://avalon.law.yale.edu/19th_century/ajveto01.asp (emphasis added).
[17] R. Dworkin, *Taking Rights Seriously* (Cambridge, Mass.: Harvard University Press, 1977), 211, 214–15.
[18] R. Dworkin, 'Taking Rights Seriously', in E. V. Rostow (ed), *Is Law Dead?* (New York: Simon and
Schuster, 1971), 168–211, at 179 (emphasis added).
[19] See eg T. Ginsburg and A. Simpser (eds), *Constitutions in Authoritarian Regimes* (Cambridge: Cambridge
University Press, 2014) (comprising a collection of articles examining constitutions in authoritarian
regimes); L.-A. Thio, 'Constitutionalism in Illiberal Polities', in M. Rosenfeld and A. Sajó (eds), *The Oxford*

about even liberal constitutions inasmuch as we focus *only* on rights provisions. Such a focus blinds us to important realities of the constitutional enterprise, especially if, as is almost (though not quite) universal in the modern world, countries rely on canonical written documents and their promises of a certain fixity. In the *ur*-text of judicial pronouncements on the US Constitution,[20] for example, Chief Justice Marshall almost obsessively reminds the reader that that Constitution is, unlike that of the country from which the United States seceded, a *written* one. It is precisely so that the basic norms of the Constitution 'may not be mistaken, or forgotten', Marshall writes, that 'the constitution is written'. He then adds what is surely for him a rhetorical question: 'To what purpose are powers limited, and to what purpose is that limitation committed to writing, if these limits may, at any time, be passed by those intended to be restrained?' No doubt many of us regard this sentence as 'mere' rhetoric, given that the central question for practising lawyers and legal academics has been the degree to which the powers of the national government are indeed 'limited'. Thus the fixation on 'constitutional interpretation' and, one might add, the concomitant acrimony among partisans of various positions as to how 'properly' to interpret the Constitution.

It is worth remembering—especially in a group that includes distinguished constitutional lawyers and philosophers from Canada, the United Kingdom, and Israel, that one does not need a written constitution in order to partake of 'constitutionalism'. Unwritten 'conventions' might well operate to protect certain rights; moreover, and far more ominously, even written patches of text may well turn out to be what James Madison referred to as 'parchment barriers' honoured at least as much in the breach, especially under conditions of perceived 'exigency', as in the observance. An obvious question, especially to political scientists, is what is gained by writing things down instead of relying on unwritten conventions. Is it really the case that written texts specifying the existence of 'individual rights'—or for that matter, even of 'states' rights' in a strongly federal constitutional order—will lead to dramatically different outcomes from those found in societies without constitutions or, as might be argued is the case in the *Canadian Charter of Rights and Freedoms*[21] or the *European Convention on Human Rights*,[22] constitutions where the assignment of a right is followed immediately by recognition of the various circumstances in which the right can be limited?

It is not, to be sure, that the US Constitution—like almost all modern constitutions—is lacking in such declarations. But I have come to believe that these provisions scarcely constitute the entirety of what is important about constitutions. I believe that we must pay far more attention than is generally the case to *structural* aspects of constitutions, even (or especially) if they rarely present the kinds of 'interpretive' dilemmas that rights provisions notoriously do. As David Haljan writes in a recent book examining the political and legal theory of secession, '[w]e tend to take the basic issue of the existence

---

Handbook of Comparative Constitutional Law (Oxford: Oxford University Press, 2012), 133–52, at 138–47 (examining 'illiberal constitutionalisms').

[20] *Marbury v Madison* 5 US (1 Cranch) 137 (1803).

[21] Part I of the *Constitution Act 1982*, being Schedule B to the *Canada Act 1982* (UK), 1982, c 11.

[22] *Convention for the Protection of Human Rights and Fundamental Freedoms* (Rome, 4 November 1950, 213 UNTS 221 at 223; Eur TS 5).

and structure of the state somewhat for granted. Its enduring and pervasive presence is simply a fact of life.' It becomes all too easy in effect to forget that 'a constitution is in the first place a structural blueprint' that 'establishes or announces the existence of a state' instantiated in given institutional structures.[23] It is these institutional structures that may well determine, as a practical matter 'how well a state does its job of governing'.[24] It is, alas, not 'unconstitutional' for a state to become significantly dysfunctional because of the ineptness of its basic institutional designs, even if the aspirations set out in a preamble or, indeed, the assignment of abstract rights, is impeccable.

Thus I have recently offered the pragmatic distinction, with regard to the US Constitution, between what I call 'the constitution of conversation' and the 'constitution of settlement'.[25] Dworkin's Constitution just *is* the 'constitution of conversation', ie the 'abstract' language that generates the obsession with developing techniques of 'constitutional interpretation' that can distinguish between 'correct or incorrect' views of the document. It would be foolish to dismiss the reality and importance of 'the constitution of conversation'. But I want to insist on the at least equal importance of the accompanying 'constitution of settlement', which is really about the most fundamental aspects of the institutional structure. To my knowledge, Ronald Dworkin, like many other contemporary legal philosophers, never had anything to say about *that* constitution, even if, no doubt, he would have conceded that, say, bicameralism or the presidential veto power—or, for that matter, article V and the hurdles it establishes to anyone seeking formal constitutional change—are all parts of the US Constitution.

One might contrast Dworkin in this respect with his adversary H. L. A. Hart, who distinguished sharply between 'primary' and 'secondary' rules. The former are rules that apply directly to individuals; tort and criminal law are standard examples. The latter, on the other hand, refer to the structures and practices by which primary rules are achieved (or changed). How legislatures operate (and pass criminal laws) involves secondary rules, as does the process by which persons can choose to enter into something we will recognize as a binding contract (that then generates and imposes primary legal obligations on those subject to the contract). Hart was interested as well in the overarching question of a 'rule of recognition' that constituted a legal system in the first place, since it cannot constitute itself by written declaration.[26] But much of the debate between Dworkin and Hart involved how one interpreted primary rules, particularly with regard to the role of 'background principles' in allowing judges to arrive at a 'right answer' instead of being forced, as Hart argued, to exercise discretion when, in effect, law ran out. Still, one can say of Hart that he recognized that there would, especially in the modern state, rarely be rules to interpret in the first place without the existence of legislatures deemed authorized (by the 'rule of recognition') to pass them. The structural provisions—ie the secondary rules—just weren't interesting enough to

---

[23] D. Haljun, *Constitutionalizing Secession* (Oxford: Hart Publishing, 2014), 36.   [24] Ibid.

[25] See S. Levinson, *Framed: America's 51 Constitutions and the Crisis of Governance* (Oxford: Oxford University Press, 2012).

[26] See, for an elegant and humorous demonstration of this point, F. Schauer, 'Amending the Presuppositions of a Constitution', in S. Levinson (ed), *Responding to Imperfection: The Theory and Practice of Constitutional Amendment* (Princeton: Princeton University Press, 1995), 145–61.

warrant extensive display of Dworkin's formidable energies, perhaps because, frankly, it is exceedingly difficult to avoid being a legal positivist when discussing them. The 'right answer' to many basic questions involving the secondary rules is often provided simply by engaging in what might be described as 'mindless (or, at least, quite unsophisticated) textualism'.

So let me suggest that 'the constitution of settlement' can be conceived as a type of 'constitution of secondary rules', especially those rules set out in what are widely thought to be intellectually unchallenging sentences or clauses. Consider only the basic reality of bicameralism, which in the United States gives a death-ray-like veto power to each house over any legislation passed by the other, not to mention, because of the assignment of 'two senators' to each state, generating a grotesquely malapportioned Senate. Nor is there any difficulty standing in the way of ascertaining the 'meaning' of such terms as 'two years', 'four years', 'six years', 'January 20', 'two-thirds', or 'three-quarters'. It is most certainly *not* the case that these clauses fail to generate debate of the highest intellectual and philosophical kind. But the debates involve not the clauses' 'meaning', but, rather, their *wisdom*. Are we as a political order well served by particular elements of the 'constitution of settlement'? If the answer is, as I believe is the case, a resounding negative, then what is to be done? Do we put our minds as lawyers to crafting arguments that say aspects of the Constitution are themselves 'unconstitutional' (because, say, they violate any cogent twenty-first-century notion of a Republican Form of Government or make far more difficult the Preamble's directive that we 'establish Justice')? Or must we instead speak as citizens and suggest that the Constitution must be formally amended, with all of the difficulties that entails inasmuch as the worst single provision of the 'constitution of settlement' within the United States is almost certainly article V itself? Even as it recognizes the possibility of constitutional amendment, it nevertheless establishes a series of such stringent 'secondary rules' necessary to achieve such amendment that it becomes near impossible, as a practical matter, to imagine the contemporary amendment of the Constitution with regard to anything that is both truly important and controversial. After all, amendments can be defeated at the outset simply by the inability to achieve two-thirds support in one of the two Houses of Congress. But even if they are proposed by Congress, there is still the more difficult hurdle of getting the support of three quarters of the states. Given that only one state is unicameral, this means that, as a minimum, those promoting change must be successful in at least seventy-five legislative houses in thirty-eight states. Opponents need only prevail in thirteen houses in separate states.

Precisely because the 'constitution of conversation' is so permeable to 'interpretation', it can relatively easily be changed over time, perhaps through reference to notions of 'purposive' or 'dynamic interpretation', to take account of fundamentally new challenges and realities. This, indeed, was one reason for Madison's scepticism about the fundamental importance of 'parchment barriers'.[27] When push came to shove, they would *not* withstand the pressures of significant political movements or what Oliver

---

[27] See J. Madison, 'No. 48', in Rossiter, above n 7, 276–81 ('Will it be sufficient to mark, with precision, the boundaries of these departments in the constitution of government, and to trust to these parchment barriers against the encroaching spirit of power?').

Wendell Holmes in a different context called the 'felt necessities' of the times registered in public opinion or, at least, the opinions of relevant political elites. There is a
reason that University of Chicago professor David Strauss offers what he describes as a
'common law' approach to constitutional interpretation in his recent book *The Living
Constitution*, which in many ways is a paean to the ability of wise judges to keep the US
Constitution in harmony with the needs of the era. Exhibit A for Strauss is the Court's
arguably innovative decision in *Brown v Board of Education*[28] that invalidated, at least
as a legal matter, the coerced separation of the races in American public education.

Structural clauses, however, seem far more impervious to 'common law' modification.
Consider only one of my favourite examples of the stupidity of the US Constitution, the
long period between election day and the inauguration of a new president. The former
is held, by congressional enactment, in early November. The latter, by command of the
Twentieth Amendment, occurs promptly at high noon on 20 January. Congress could
obviously change the date of election, but it would face very real constraints because
of another bizarre feature of the American political system. That is the formal election
of the president not by popular election, but, rather, by the vote of 'electors' chosen in
November who do not, however, cast their own votes, as a formal matter, by statute
until mid-December, and whose votes are not counted, by constitutional command,
until the newly elected Congress meets during the first week of January.

As Yale professor of law Akhil Reed Amar has suggested, one can, at least within
the seminar room, imagine 'workarounds' around this stupidity: a defeated president
could, after all, arrange first that the incumbent vice president immediately resign, the
newly elected president be appointed to succeed him or her (and, of course, immediately confirmed, as is required by the Twenty-Fifth Amendment, by both Houses of
Congress), and then the incumbent president would resign to allow the just-installed
vice president to take over the office to which he or she had actually been elected. As
hard as it is to imagine this actually happening, it is even harder—I would go so far as to
say impossible—to imagine walking into a court and successfully arguing that the sheer
stupidity of leaving the United States for eleven weeks, in the contemporary world, with
a government that lacks the true union of legal and political authority, is so stupid as to
be unconstitutional. Indeed, not only would I expect to lose the case; I might even not
be surprised to find myself sanctioned for having made such an obviously 'frivolous'
argument in violation of my ethical duties as a lawyer operating within the parameters
of the legal system. It may be worth noting, incidentally, that it is no small jurisprudential matter to be able to identify a 'frivolous', as against merely an inadequate or likely-
to-lose argument.[29] But challenging institutional structures that are clearly established
by the foundational text certainly seems ill advised. Unfortunately, Inauguration Day
is only one example of what William Eskridge and I labelled 'constitutional stupidities'
in a book that we co-edited over fifteen years ago. Perhaps they made sense at the time
they were created, perhaps they were always 'stupid', but, for a variety of reasons, not
particularly costly in the past. But today these embedded features of the political order,

---

[28] 347 US 483 (1954).
[29] See eg S. Levinson, 'Frivolous Cases: Do Lawyers Really Know Anything at All?' (1986) 24 *Osgoode
Hall Law Journal* 353.

which are impervious to Herculean feats of interpretative skill, are—or so I would argue—very costly indeed.

In our own time, I believe that the 'constitution of settlement' helps to account for the dysfunctionality of the American political system and, therefore, of the accompanying discontent and alienation from the system. Thus on 30 June 2014, the Gallup Organization announced that polls taken earlier that month demonstrated that 'Americans [Are] Losing Confidence in All Branches of US Gov't'.[30] Thus only 7 per cent of the public had confidence in Congress. Even confidence in the Supreme Court was at a historic low of 30 per cent, though that was one percentage point better than the president. I have quite seriously suggested that had polls been available in 1775, one might well have found a higher percentage of colonists who still approved of rule by the 'King-in-Parliament'. Canadians, especially, need no reminder about the numbers of American colonists who chose loyalty to the Crown over the blandishments of the purported 'patriots' seceding from the British Empire!

It is hard to look at the United States these days and not see a country suffering through far more than the 'winter of our discontent' inasmuch as discontent and alienation seems to be a year-round reality, regardless of one's particular location on the political spectrum. Does the Constitution make it more or less likely that these discontents will continue to erode further a basic trust that the national government is capable of responding adequately to *any* of the basic challenges facing the country? And will we move ever farther from the goals enunciated in the Preamble, not to mention receiving what we might have thought were the protections guaranteed by the liberal provisions of the Bill of Rights? If, as I strongly believe, our particular structures that almost pathologically 'check and balance' one another into irresolvable 'gridlock' *do* play some explanatory role in our discontents,[31] then I believe that the Dworkinian enterprise of clever, even brilliant, lawyering dedicated to mining constitutional abstractions is almost entirely irrelevant, whatever its utility with regard to the constitution of conversation. Indeed, an emphasis on Herculean lawyering and, of course, judging, encourages us to fixate on the appointment of the 'right judges' who would accept suitably brilliant arguments designed to alleviate our problems. Not only does that run into the earlier cited reality that Dworkin himself rejected the possibility of using the Fourteenth Amendment to provide 'affirmative goods' to the poor; it also misconceives the reality of important aspects of the—or perhaps *any*—Constitution, not to mention the responsibilities we should place on judges, whose professional training may ill equip them to answer basic questions about the desirability of any given constitutional design. This may be one reason why so many judges repeat banalities about the 'separation of powers' or the virtues of 'federalism' rather than engage in arduous—and perhaps frustrating—analysis of the degree to which these aspects of a political system really do have the benefits claimed for them.

Let me be clear, especially in the company of distinguished philosophers, that I am *not* making an argument based on an abstract theory of linguistics that certain

---

[30] Available at: http://www.gallup.com/poll/171992/americans-losing-confidence-branches-gov.aspx.
[31] See for a similar analysis, I. Shapiro, 'On Non-domination' (2012) 62 *University of Toronto Law Review* 293.

words just have clear meanings—in the sense of what might be termed 'operative significance'—that will be constraining in any and all circumstances. I described my views as 'pragmatic', which means, among other things, that I do not want to commit myself to such a theory of language. Indeed, all of us as common lawyers know that many otherwise clear terms of contracts can become somewhat evanescent if they are not viewed as truly 'material' to the enterprise. It may be that on occasion the promise to construct a balcony by 14 January will be dispositive in the sense of allowing rescinding the contract if, for example, the balcony in question was to be used to watch the inaugural (or coronation) parade less than a week later.[32] Most of the time, though, failure to meet the 'due date' will occasion only modest damages and, possibly, no consequences at all, and the attempt to rescind will accurately be viewed as a 'bad-faith' attempt simply to avoid a contract that one wishes one had never entered in the first place. The point is that context, rather than the words alone, will control our response to various claims.

Similarly, it is important to remember that the Philadelphia Convention itself rendered irrelevant article XIII of the Articles of Confederation, which required that any amendments to the Articles receive the approval of the state legislature of each and every one of the then-thirteen states in the Union. From one perspective, the most important article in the Constitution of 1787 was article VII, which allowed the newly proposed Constitution to come into effect upon the ratification of state *conventions* in only nine states. (Thus North Carolina and Rhode Island had not ratified the Constitution as of Washington's inauguration on 30 April 1789, and it did not matter as a constitutional matter, since eleven states *had* ratified and, therefore, legally validated the start-up of the new political order.) But article XIII was negated *not* by clever lawyerly argument about its meaning, but, rather, by appeals to the 'exigencies' of the current (1787) situation and the duty in effect to ignore the rules laid down. Article XIII itself became a 'parchment barrier' that could be breached by Holmesian 'felt necessities' to respond to, and in effect overthrow, a polity that was condemned by its opponents, including such luminaries as Alexander Hamilton, as 'imbecilic' and potentially fatal to the survival of the United States as a free and functioning country in the aftermath of its successful secession from the British Empire.

At the very least, breach of the 'constitution of settlement' places the burden of proof on the breaching party to indicate the nature of the 'exigent circumstances' requiring such an extraordinary act, whereas most issues within the 'constitution of conversation', at least as a formal matter, can be resolved by reference to what American constitutional jargon deems 'minimum rationality' and concomitant 'deference' to legislatures, administrative agencies, or, on occasion, presidents. But even 'exigent circumstances' would probably not license a judge, say, to extend the term of a president beyond 20 January simply because the incumbent is engaged in delicate negotiations with an adversary that should not be disrupted by the replacement of the incumbent with someone unknown to the negotiating parties. One can think of Jimmy Carter's negotiations with Iran at the cusp of his term in 1980–1, just before he was replaced by

---

[32] There are a spate of cases in English contract law, all provoked by the coronation of Edward VII in 1903. The leading case, *Krell v Henry* [1903] 2 KB 740, involved a lease of rooms rather than a contract to do alterations. I am grateful to my learned colleague Alan Rau for his knowledge of these cases.

Ronald Reagan, or, more dramatically, of Winston Churchill's displacement by Clement Atlee in July 1945 upon Churchill's unceremonious eviction from 10 Downing Street by the British electorate. In this latter context, we should recall as well that there had been no election for Parliament since 1935, because of the exigencies of war; the United States, on the other hand, did hold elections during World War II, just as Lincoln risked his own hold on office during the American Civil War.

The same man who almost blithely (perhaps unconstitutionally) and unilaterally suspended habeas corpus in order to preserve the Union apparently never considered even for a moment postponing the 1864 election, even though he believed, at least until the Union victory in Atlanta, that he might well lose the election. One might ask whether this particular aspect of Lincoln's undoubted 'constitutional fidelity' necessarily speaks well for him if, for example, one believes that it put into question the survival either of the Union or of the Emancipation Proclamation; there can be no doubt, though, that the four-year duration of his term and the need for a new election in order to maintain him in office was far more than a mere 'parchment barrier'. It is a paradigm example of a clause—and accompanying political psychology—that truly instantiated the 'constitution of settlement', and I suspect that it remains ignored in large part because Lincoln's gamble succeeded. That is, he was in fact re-elected and the Union was preserved with the surrender of the Confederacy. But it is possible to imagine a counter-history. Though, perhaps, had General George McClellan succeeded in defeating Lincoln and restored the Union by reversing the Emancipation Proclamation, then the fact that history is written by winners might have led us to esteem his understanding of the need for compromise and the like. Political philosophers might well participate in such debates, but, as already suggested, it is not clear to what degree the bulk of contemporary legal philosophers would have much to say.

But if the ordinary skill set of lawyers—including such skilled jurisprudes as Ronald Dworkin—is irrelevant, then to whom should we turn for insight? It is tempting to suggest that the answer is political scientists, who have been studying constitutionalism in all of its forms since the time of Aristotle. The problem, of course, is that one scarcely finds anything resembling consensus on the issues one might be most interested in as one turns from Dworkinian questions of 'constitutional interpretation' and 'meaning' to questions instead of 'constitutional design' and 'wisdom'. How truly important is it, for example, that a given country has chosen a convoluted system of 'checks and balances', including an independently elected presidency, over a parliamentary regime? For a while the late Yale political scientist Juan Linz expressed a certain kind of conventional wisdom in suggesting that presidentialism was far more apt than parliamentarianism to lead to dictatorship or military coups, but then Jose Antonio Chiebub, using highly sophisticated multiple regression analysis, seemed to demonstrate that Linz had considerably exaggerated the connection.[33] Does it really matter that Nebraska, within the United States, has liberated itself from the convention of bicameralism and opted instead for 'The Unicameral'? How important is it that almost none of the states

---

[33] See J. A. Cheibub, *Presidentialism, Parliamentarism, and Democracy* (Cambridge: Cambridge University Press, 2007), 112 (refuting the 'Linzian view of presidentialism').

within the United States has opted for a 'unitary executive' or that, perhaps as a kind of compensation, they have granted their governors considerably stronger veto powers than those granted to the president of the United States? Indeed, it is worth asking how much the oft-derided Weimar Constitution of Germany during the interwar years, including its famous article 48 allowing the invocation of 'emergency powers', really helps to account for the catastrophe that befell that country. Perhaps, as with the Articles of Confederation, we overestimate its defects, but, again, the question is how one would actually carry on such arguments about the actual importance of any given constitution.

All of these questions call for deeply empirical investigation. And there are competing conclusions that might be demonstrated. The first is that constitutional structures either do not matter at all *or* that we simply do not know with any real confidence what the consequences are. In both cases, the conclusion might be some version of 'it does not seem to be broken—or, even if it is, we cannot tell exactly what caused it—so probably the safest thing to do is to relax and do nothing'. The second possibility, of course, is that a given structure might be significant in explaining our political unhappiness and that, ideally, it should be substantially modified or perhaps even excised.

But what if the latter is the conclusion reached about article V itself (as I personally believe)? Many people *have* reached that conclusion, and this, as much as anything, explains the desire to create a theory that explains 'informal amendment' outside the boundaries of article V. The most important theorist of such amendment is Yale professor of law Bruce Ackerman, who has now devoted three impressive volumes to elaborating a complex theory explaining how constitutional amendment—which should be recognized as such by our rule of recognition—has taken place without meeting the precise demands of article V. I am a great admirer of Ackerman's project, and I think he has certainly identified important features of American constitutional development. But I believe that informal amendment—or David Strauss's 'living Constitution' or Jack M. Balkin's 'living originalism', however described—works only within the ambit of the 'constitution of conversation'. For the 'constitution of settlement', it is, to borrow Gerald Rosenberg's phrase, a hollow hope.

III. Conclusion: The Brooding Omnipresence of Carl Schmitt

The dragon of article V must be slain, but how? My own hope is that a new constitutional convention could do to article V what the framers in Philadelphia did to article XIII of the Articles of Confederation, with its requirement that proposed amendments receive the unanimous assent of all state legislatures. The framers ruthlessly ignored it and depended on what James Madison in Federalist No. 40 called the 'approbation' of the public to accept the legitimacy of the new regime (including its new amendment rule). I realize that most people, including my family and friends, are basically appalled by this suggestion, and even some who are more favourably disposed argue quite persuasively that there are insurmountable obstacles in the way of bringing about a successful convention. Optimism, therefore, scarcely seems to be merited. Thus we are left with the hope that our constitutional structures really are not so important after all and/or with the belief that God really does take special care of children and of the

United States of America (and of any other country locked into an unfortunate 'constitution of settlement').

Or, however regrettable, it may be that the more apt constitutional theorist, with regard to alleviating the 'constitution of settlement', will turn out to be Carl Schmitt. How we view Schmitt himself has certain analogues to our opening metaphor of the blind men and the elephant. It is impossible to ignore the fact that he was an apologist for the Nazi takeover in Germany and was, at least for two years or so, a member of the Nazi Party, or that he was uninterested in 'rehabilitating himself' after World War II by denouncing his role in what had occurred. And, of course, there are his particular works with their own unattractive features, including the defence of 'sovereign' dictatorship and concomitant transformation that was so useful to Nazi apologists. All of this can be—must be—readily conceded, but there is at least one other aspect of Schmitt that remains relevant to anyone interested in the philosophy of constitutional orders.[34] As Andreas Kalyvas in particular has emphasized, Schmitt was a deeply interesting—and challenging—theorist of popular sovereignty.[35] For better, and perhaps for worse, most constitutions since the American precedent in 1787 and the French counterpart in 1791 have been written in the name of 'We the People'. When James Madison in Federalist No. 40 defended the blithe setting aside of any constraints posed by the unanimity requirement of article XIII of the Articles of Confederation, it was in the name of the Declaration of Independence and the right of the people to 'alter and abolish' their systems of government whenever that was thought to be conducive to achieving public happiness.

Madison was scarcely a systematic political theorist. But Schmitt was, and he grappled extensively with the mysteries contained within the idea of rule by the demos, particularly where constitutional transformation was concerned. One might wonder, at the end of the day, how much separates, at least in the realm of constitutional theory, Schmitt's emphasis on the legitimate recourse to the constituent sovereign power that is free to ignore any restraints of an existing constitution, and Ackerman's at least rhetorical embrace of a 'popular sovereignty' that is equally entitled to ignore existing restraints. 'It is', Schmitt wrote, 'part of the directness of the people's will that it can be expressed independently of every prescribed procedure and every prescribed process.'[36] How far, one might legitimately ask, is this from the statement made on the floor of the Philadelphia Convention by Virginia's Governor Edmund Randolph (who would become Attorney General in George Washington's administration): 'There are great seasons', he told his fellow delegates, 'when persons with limited power are justified in exceeding them, and a person would be contemptible not to risk it.'[37] There was no doubt in his mind, as was true of others, that the fall of 1787 was just such a 'great season', and the imperative was to act on behalf of what was perceived as the common

---

[34] See C. Schmitt, *Constitutional Theory*, J. Seitzer (trans) (Durham: Duke University Press, 2007).
[35] A. Kalyvas, *Democracy and the Politics of the Extraordinary: Max Weber, Carl Schmitt, and Hannah Arendt* (Cambridge: Cambridge University Press, 2008).
[36] Schmitt, above n 34, 131.
[37] M. Farrand (ed), *Records of the Federal Convention of 1787* vol 1 (New Haven: Yale University Press, 1937), 362.

good of the nation rather than to adhere to what Madison, in Federalist No. 40, dismissed as 'ill-timed scruples' or a 'zeal for adhering to ordinary forms'. To paraphrase Ecclesiastes, if there is a time for legal fidelity, there is also a time for placing the law to one side and instead doing what is thought best to overcome crises. To be sure, what saved the delegates in Philadelphia from condemnation is not only the goodness of their motives, but also the fact that their proposals, in Madison's language, were 'to be submitted TO THE PEOPLE THEMSELVES' (or, more accurately, to conventions elected by a relatively wide franchise of the people, at least from an eighteenth-century perspective). Should 'the people' approve of the new constitution, this would serve to 'blot out antecedent errors and irregularities'. Ackerman, too, has devoted much of his career to limning some of the 'irregularities' with regard to adding to the American Constitution's text the so-called Reconstruction Amendments, particularly the truly transformative Fourteenth Amendment, and explaining why the process was nonetheless legitimate in terms of popular sovereignty.

To be sure, it is crucially important that Schmitt was basically contemptuous of liberalism, whereas Ackerman is a noted liberal in terms of his political theory. But political theories and constitutional theories are not always congruent with one another. Ackerman, for example, has notably rejected the idea that the US Constitution is so essentially liberal that, for example, it would be illegitimate to adopt a constitutional amendment establishing the United States as a 'Christian nation' subservient to religious law. It would, he has written, be his duty as a judge to 'uphold [such a Christianity amendment] as a fundamental part of the American Constitution'.[38] This is, one might say, constitutional positivism with a vengeance.

Perhaps the most fundamental question that hovers over constitutional (and political) philosophy at least since the seventeenth century is the degree to which one can take seriously notions of 'popular sovereignty'. After all, almost all contemporary constitutions claim to speak in the name of some group of people. It is easy enough to join the late Yale historian Edmund Morgan in his dismissal of popular sovereignty as a basically ideological 'fiction' that in actuality 'enable[s] the few to govern the many'.[39] I doubt, though, that we are prepared to jettison the concept. What would replace it? Perhaps it would be a theory of natural law or Rawlsian justice, but can anyone seriously believe that it would generate a sufficient consensus to be viewed as anything other than the attempted rule of a few self-described wise philosophers?

It is one thing to prefer 'taking rights seriously' to submission to popularly supported measures that would unduly limit those rights, but does this mean that a commitment to 'taking rights seriously' necessarily requires that in effect one reject the validity of a constitution (or amendment) drafted by a popular sovereign less committed to rights (or, at least, one's particular programme of rights that one wanted to be taken especially seriously)? One might well be tempted, of course, to adopt a contemporary German perspective and write into a constitution a so-called eternity clause that protects certain provisions (or concepts) against change in the absence of a truly revolutionary

---

[38] B. Ackerman, *We the People: Foundations* (Cambridge, Mass.: Harvard University Press, 1991), 14.
[39] E. Morgan, *Inventing the People: The Rise of Popular Sovereignty in England and America* (New York: Norton, 1988), 13.

overthrow of the current constitutional order.[40] But consider the *two* provisions protected by the German 'eternity clause'. One protects the dignitary interests of all human beings; one might well believe that if any norms are to be taken away from ordinary political processes, it would be those involving human dignity, even though one should recognize the obvious differences of opinion as to what that admirable abstraction actually requires. But the other concerns protection of the German federal system and the prerogatives of the *Länder* within that system. Does this make any real sense, at least in the absence of an implausible belief that it is always the case that a particular form of federalism will necessarily be conducive to the achievement of desired ends beyond protection of federalism itself? There is little or no reason to believe that.[41]

Nothing in my remarks should be taken as denigrating the role played by legal philosophers. They have much to contribute to debates generated by various issues of constitutional design. But I do hope that it is clear that the community of those scholars interested in constitutions as a phenomenon of government would benefit shifting from the emphasis that has been placed on how best to interpret constitutions or how best to describe the roles of model judges to a consideration of the implications of adopting given, fixed institutional structures in which change requires formal amendment rather than clever interpretation.

---

[40] For a critique of 'eternity clauses', see M. Schwartzberg, *Democracy and Legal Change* (Cambridge: Cambridge University Press, 2007).

[41] See eg F. L. Neumann, 'Federalism and Freedom: A Critique', in D. Karmis and W. Norman (eds), *Theories of Federalism: A Reader* (New York: Palgrave, 2005), 207–20.

5

Constitutional Amendment
and Political Constitutionalism

A Philosophical and Comparative Reflection

Rosalind Dixon* and Adrienne Stone**

Constitutional government entails that certain laws have a special fundamental status and the validity of other laws depends on their compliance with constitutional requirements. In many cases constitutions are contained in one, or a few, canonical documents and in such cases, constitutions are usually in some way formally entrenched—that is, they are especially hard to change via existing legal procedures.[1] These features of constitutionalism enable and limit government by providing for stable institutions identifying key constitutional norms that cannot be transgressed. But where constitutions have these features, they also include provisions for amendment. That is, the text of the constitution contains a provision that prescribes a mechanism for constitutional change.

In this chapter we consider the role that amendment plays in democratic constitutionalism generally, and particularly debates over the democratic legitimacy of judicial review by constitutional courts. Amendment procedures, we suggest, serve three broad functions or values: they allow for change of a constitution in line with changing societal needs and circumstances—and thus ensure that a constitution can respond to the changing needs of the polity it governs.[2] They provide for ongoing popular participation in constitution-making, and in doing so confer legitimacy on changes to the constitution as well as to the status quo. And they provide a means of overriding judicial interpretations of existing provisions of the constitution, thereby allowing for the reassertion of democratic decision-making in the constitutional process. Amendment procedures thus hold the promise of answering some of the central philosophical

* Rosalind Dixon is a Professor of Law at UNSW Australia, and Director of the Comparative Constitutional Law Project at the Gilbert + Tobin Centre of Public Law.

** Adrienne Stone is Professor of Law and Director of the Centre for Constitutional Studies at Melbourne Law School, and First Vice-President of the International Association of Constitutional Law. The authors thank the editors and Kristen Rundle, Theunis Roux, Denise Myerson, Helen Irving, and Carlos Bernal-Pulido for helpful comments on earlier versions of the chapter, and Melissa Vogt for excellent research assistance.

[1] There is, of course, always the possibility of constitutional change via formal constitutional replacement, or 'informal' constitutional change via procedures not explicitly recognized in the existing constitutional text: see eg B. Ackerman, *We the People: Foundations* (Cambridge, Mass.: Harvard University Press, 1991).

[2] R. Dixon, 'Constitutional Amendment Rules: A Comparative Perspective', in T. Ginsburg and R. Dixon (eds), *Comparative Constitutional Law* (Northampton, Mass.: Edward Elgar, 2011), 96–111.

difficulties posed by the phenomenon of written constitutionalism: how to justify the imposition of a constitution on later generations, and how to justify the role of courts in determining the meaning of constitutions, and specifically judicial review?

In this chapter, we focus largely on this second aspect of the relationship between amendment and democratic constitutionalism. Political constitutionalists such as Jeremy Waldron have famously objected to judicial review on democratic grounds, or as an undemocratic displacement of the will of the people expressed through legislative majorities.[3] Yet political constitutionalists often concede that democratic objections largely do not apply in 'weak-form' systems of judicial review in which legislatures can override courts simply by inaction, or by ordinary legislation.[4] Nonetheless, they generally fail to account for the possibility that constitutional amendment procedures may play a similar role in answering such objections.

This chapter explores what, if any, arguments or assumptions might support this implicit position that amendment procedures do not mitigate the anti-democratic nature of judicial review. It identifies three possible explanations: first, the practical unavailability of amendment as a means of democratic override; second, the idea that any supermajority requirement for the approval of an amendment is necessarily incompatible with democratic commitments to equality among citizens; and third, the idea that amendment procedures necessarily add too greatly to the overall length, or 'prolixity', of a constitutional document.[5] It then explores the plausibility of each argument, or explanation, in the context of the constitutional experience of two countries, India and Colombia, which otherwise generally meet the requirements, identified by political constitutionalists, of having legislative and judicial institutions in relatively good working order.[6]

In both countries, the chapter suggests, constitutional amendment procedures have played an important role in providing a means of legislative override of court decisions; and in a way that does not obviously contravene commitments to equality among citizens, or the capacity of the constitution to function as a framework for democracy. In light of these facts, the chapter further suggests, the legitimacy of judicial review should not be treated as an 'either–or' proposition with systems of weak-form judicial review preserving the legitimacy and systems of strong-form review departing from it.

Once it is recognized that various forms of judicial review fall along a spectrum from weak to strong, the question of the legitimacy of judicial review will be best approached as both one of degree, and one informed by a variety of factors.[7] The most important

---

[3] See generally J. Waldron, *Law and Disagreement* (Oxford: Clarendon Press, 1999); J. Waldron, 'The Core of the Case Against Judicial Review' (2006) 115 *Yale Law Journal* 1346; A. Tomkins, 'In Defence of the Political Constitution' (2002) 22 *Oxford Journal of Legal Studies* 157; A. Tomkins, 'The Role of Courts in the Political Constitution' (2010) 60 *University of Toronto Law Journal* 1.

[4] See Ackerman, above n 1.

[5] J. Waldron, 'Some Models of Dialogue Between Judges and Legislators' (2004) 23 *Supreme Court Law Review* 7, at 36, reprinted in G. Huscroft and I. Brodie (eds), *Constitutionalism in the Charter Era* (Markham, Ont.: LexisNexis Canada, 2004), 7–47.

[6] For India, this assumption holds true largely for the higher judiciary, though not necessarily for lower courts: see eg M. Galanter, *Law and Society in Modern India* (Oxford: Oxford University Press, 1993).

[7] Compare with A. Kavanagh, 'What's So Weak about "Weak-Form Review": The Case of the UK *Human Rights Act 1998*' (unpublished manuscript, 2014).

question, in this context, may be the range of formal mechanisms that allow legislators to override court decisions simply by way of inaction, or ordinary majority vote. But it will also be important to consider the practical availability of other mechanisms, such as powers of amendment.

The remainder of this chapter is divided into four sections. Section I considers in general terms the values that amendment procedures serve. In light of that discussion, we then revisit the democratic objections to judicial review of political constitutionalists such as Waldron, and the degree to which they view mechanisms for legislative override as answering those objections. Section II considers whether amendment procedures are necessarily inferior to those other mechanisms based on three criteria: the practical unavailability of amendment procedures, notions of equality in voting, and the tendency of such procedures to add undue length or 'prolixity' to a democratic constitutional document; and the degree to which these assumptions have plausibility in constitutional democracies such as Colombia and India, compared to the United States or the United Kingdom. Section III offers a conclusion that reflects on the relationship between constitutional theory and comparative constitutional law in this context, as well as more generally.

I. Democratic Objections to Judicial Review: The Relevance of Amendment

A. Amendment procedures: Philosophical underpinnings

A starting point for this chapter is to consider the role that amendment procedures play in the project of democratic constitutionalism. First, it should be seen that amendment procedures are a feature of a certain kind of constitutionalism: constitutions consisting of one or more canonical documents. An unwritten, common law constitution of the kind that characterizes the United Kingdom may change over time. It may even change abruptly—the UK Human Rights Act 1998 (HRA) might be one such change[8]—but we would not describe that kind of change as an amendment. When we speak of constitutional 'amendment' rather than constitutional change we are referring to change to those canonical texts.

The association of 'amendment' procedures with canonical texts brings with it an association with entrenchment. Almost all modern constitutions, and especially written constitutions, are entrenched against ordinary revision.[9] It is this rigidity that allows constitutions to serve the purpose of enabling government by settling basic questions and removing the need to revisit questions as to basic structures.[10] In addition, rigidity

---

[8] A. Kavanagh, *Constitutional Review under the UK Human Rights Act* (Cambridge: Cambridge University Press, 2009), 2.

[9] Entrenchment of this kind can, of course, be either formal/legal or informal/political in nature: see eg R. Dixon and E. A. Posner, 'The Limit of Constitutional Convergence' (2011) 11 *Chicago Journal of International Law* 399.

[10] See eg Levinson in this volume (on the 'constitutional settlement'). See also S. Holmes, *Passions and Constraint: On the Theory of Liberal Democracy* (Cambridge: Cambridge University Press, 1995); C. L. Eisgruber, *Constitutional Self-Government* (Cambridge, Mass.: Harvard University Press, 2001); R. Dixon, 'Updating Constitutional Rules' (2009) *Supreme Court Review* 319.

serves to limit government and ensure adherence to fundamental moral norms. But entrenchment brings with it practical and philosophical problems.[11] The practical problems arise from the inability of an entrenched constitution to respond to changing circumstances. A constitution may contain commitments to which a polity no longer adheres or, more prosaically, that may have failed to anticipate social or technological developments. There are related philosophical problems that arise from the imposition of a constitution on future generations. Even if a constitution has a strong claim to legitimacy with respect to its framing generation, the question of legitimacy is complicated by its imposition on later generations. Moreover, as Andrei Marmor points out, this problem persists even where a constitution is not very old, as even a new constitution purports to impose its constraints on later generations.[12] Amendment procedures respond to both problems. As a practical matter, they allow for change though within a framework that protects entrenched norms from ordinary revision. In addition, amendment procedures serve two values associated with legitimacy: popular participation and compliance with rules.

Legitimacy is a contested value in constitutional theory as elsewhere,[13] but nonetheless some minimal conditions for constitutional legitimacy are relatively uncontroversial. At its most minimal, legitimacy of any law—including a constitution or constitutional amendment—might be (at least partially) a matter of compliance with pre-existing prescribed rules.[14] Therefore amendment procedures, in so far as they provide a set of legal criteria against which the legitimacy of future changes might be judged, offer legitimacy associated with compliance with legal rules.[15]

Another condition for legitimacy of a constitution, which is more significant for our purposes and which can be stated with confidence, is popular participation in constitution-making. Although the reality of constitutional politics may not always live up to the ideal, it is almost always assumed that popular participation in constitution-making—usually filtered through a representative body—is a pre-condition for constitutional legitimacy.[16] Indeed, in a democracy, some form of popular participation in constitution-making is almost axiomatic following closely from the idea that the people hold the 'constituent power' in the constitutional order.[17] The close association between legitimacy and popular participation is reflected in the suggestion that popular participation in constitution-making has become a norm of international law,[18]

---

[11] For this reason, judges interpreting written entrenched constitutions commonly take the view that methods for constitutional interpretation should be somewhat flexible to respond to changing circumstances, even in legal cultures, like Australia and the United States, where originalism has significant judicial support. See *Australian National Airways Pty Ltd v Commonwealth* [1945] HCA 41, 71 CLR 29, 81 (per Dixon J); *McCulloch v Maryland* 17 US 316 (1818), 407, 415 (per Marshall CJ).

[12] A. Marmor, 'Are Constitutions Legitimate?' (2007) 20 *Canadian Journal of Law and Jurisprudence* 69.

[13] R. H. Fallon, 'Legitimacy and the Constitution' (2005) 118 *Harvard Law Review* 1787.

[14] Ibid.   [15] Ibid.

[16] Though an imposed constitution may gain acceptance over time, especially if it succeeds in reducing conflict or promoting prosperity: C. Klein and A. Sajó, 'Constitution-Making: Process and Substance', in M. Rosenfeld and A. Sajó (eds), *The Oxford Companion to Comparative Constitutional Law* (Oxford: Oxford University Press, 2012), 419–41, at 424.

[17] Though of course that raises the question of 'who are the people?' and 'who determines that question?': ibid.

[18] T. M. Franck, 'The Emerging Right to Democratic Governance' (1992) 86 *American Journal of International Law* 46.

or conversely, that there is a constitutional right to 'amendment'—or replacement—by plebiscite that exists irrespective of its formal recognition in constitutional text.[19] For similar reasons, amendment procedures, like modern constitution-making procedures, frequently reflect a commitment to popular participation.[20] In some cases, this will involve procedures for the proposal of amendments by citizens, and in others, a requirement that proposed amendments gain the approval of a democratic majority at a referendum. But in either event, constitutional amendment procedures will frequently involve some element of direct popular participation.

Even amendment processes that lack this element of direct popular participation will also often have important claims to democratic legitimacy. By allowing the people's elected representatives to debate, and vote on, proposed constitutional changes, such procedures ensure at least some minimal connection between such change and the 'will of the people', or the 'consent' of the governed. Thus, one way to view amendment procedures is that they offer an ongoing mechanism for constitution-making, and confer on formal constitutional change the legitimacy that popular participation confers on constitution-making. But, importantly, amendment procedures can also offer legitimacy—perhaps in a weaker form—associated with popular participation to continuing, unamended constitutions as well. In addition to the provision of this positive consent, amendment procedures can provide a weaker form of legitimacy: that which arises from a failure to amend. The failure to use amendment procedures to change the constitution, or more concretely, the rejection of proposals for amendment, can also be taken as evidence of a tacit acceptance of the constitution and thus confer legitimacy on the continuance of old constitutional arrangements.

In addition, we argue that constitutional amendments serve a further, more 'presentist' function, less directly connected to debates about intergenerational legitimacy, or the relationship between democratic actors across time. They provide a means by which, at least in some settings, democratic majorities may contribute to a process of constitutional 'dialogue' with courts about issues of *contemporary* constitutional morality. That is, they not only allow democratic majorities to 'update' or revise prior constitutional settlements. They allow democratic majorities to 'trump' or override a decision of a constitutional court they deem unreasonable or unjustified as a 'reading' of contemporary constitutional understandings, by substituting a new textual basis for subsequent acts of constitutional interpretation.[21]

This aspect of amendment is also significant for that central puzzle of modern Anglo-American constitutional theory—the democratic legitimacy of judicial review. If amendment procedures provide an effective mechanism of the reassertion of democratic decision-making, it would seem to resolve or lessen the problem posed by giving judges the power to overturn the decisions of the majoritarian arms of government.

---

[19] A. Amar, 'Consent of the Governed: Constitutional Amendment Outside Article V' (1994) 94 *Columbia Law Review* 457; S. Levinson, *Our Undemocratic Constitution: Where the Constitution Goes Wrong* (Oxford: Oxford University Press, 2008).

[20] On popular participation in constitution-making see, Klein and Sajó, above n 16, 422–6.

[21] Ibid.

To make this point in further detail we will revisit the democratic objection to judicial review raised by political constitutionalists such as Jeremy Waldron.

B. Political constitutionalism and weak-form judicial review

Political constitutionalists such as Jeremy Waldron raise serious objections based on principles of democracy to courts reviewing legislation for compatibility with constitutional norms. For Waldron, this democratic objection is particularly powerful for rights-based constitutional provisions, but potentially also applicable to judicial review of structural constitutional guarantees.[22] Judicial review for Waldron violates a fundamental commitment in liberal societies to equal citizenship. 'By privileging majority voting among a small number of unelected and unaccountable judges', Waldron suggests, judicial review of legislation 'disenfranchises ordinary citizens and brushes aside cherished principles of representation and political equality in the final resolution of issues about rights.'[23] In the face of reasonable disagreement about moral and political questions, Waldron argues, the most principled means of resolving such disagreements is by reference to a norm of majority decision-making which 'is neutral as between…contested outcomes, treats participants equally, and gives each expressed opinion the greatest weight possible compatible with giving equal weight to all opinions.'[24] Indeed, for this reason, judicial review is incompatible with rights-based constitutionalism. It is the respect for the moral autonomy of the individual, which leads us to accord individual rights that should, in Waldron's view, lead us to respect the process in which those individuals participate equally.[25]

Waldron himself, however, has conceded that it is only judicial review of a certain kind that is the target of political constitutionalists: judicial review that targets legislation rather than executive action, and which is 'final' in a formal legal sense. He explicitly notes that the democratic objection is to 'strong' forms of judicial review, or the '*final* resolution of issues about rights' by courts, *not* all or any judicial involvement in constitutional rights protection.[26] He in fact concedes there can be democratic benefits to courts exercising 'weaker' or more penultimate forms of judicial review.[27]

Our own view is that this kind of role for courts can significantly contribute to a form of constitutional government that treats citizens with equal concern and respect.[28] Consider a case in which parliament passes a law providing for the mandatory detention of any non-citizen who enters the country without a visa. Numerous laws of this kind have been passed by democratic legislatures in recent years.[29] Yet democratic legislators have also frequently overlooked the capacity for such laws to bear disproportionately on certain classes of non-citizen—those who face long delays in the processing

---

[22] Waldron, above n 5.   [23] Ibid 1353.   [24] Ibid 1389.

[25] See also Tomkins, 2002, above n 3, 173–5 (making similar arguments based on arguments from political freedom).

[26] Waldron, above n 5.   [27] Ibid. See also Tomkins, 2010, above n 3, 20.

[28] R. Dixon, 'Weak-Form Judicial Review and American Exceptionalism' (2012) 32 *Oxford Journal of Legal Studies* 487.

[29] R. Thwaites, *The Liberty of Non-citizens: Indefinite Detention in Commonwealth Countries* (Oxford: Hart Publishing, 2014).

of their applications for asylum, or other forms of complementary protection; those (such as children) who are particularly vulnerable in detention; and those who are stateless, or without proper identification, and thus practically unable to be removed or deported.[30] One argument for judicial review in these circumstances is that it can help bring these 'blind spots' to the attention of democratic legislators.[31] This kind of role is one that many political constitutionalists endorse. Waldron, for example, suggests that judicial review may play a useful role where 'the legislative majority is unsure about how far it should go in pursuing its own understanding of a provision of the Bill of Rights or about how extreme it is willing to be perceived as being in its legislation on some rights issue'.[32]

The key question for political constitutionalists, however, is whether, if and when courts perform this role, legislatures retain scope to decide whether the decision reached by a court reflects the best, and most reasonable, considered judgment about the balance between competing rights and responsibilities in a particular context. Therefore, the dividing line between strong- and weak-form judicial review for political constitutionalists depends on two key factors: first, the strength of courts' remedial powers; and second, the degree to which court decisions can be overridden by the passage of ordinary legislation.

In strong-form systems of judicial review, courts enjoy broad powers to issue declarations of invalidity, or to invalidate legislation for incompatibility with constitutional norms. Declarations of this kind also have the immediate effect (unless explicitly 'suspended' by a court) of depriving relevant legislation of legal effect. Many weak-form systems, in contrast, give courts only a much weaker power to make 'declarations of incompatibility'. In the United Kingdom, for example, section 4 of the HRA explicitly recognizes a power to make declarations of this kind; and a similar power has now been incorporated into charters of rights in the Australian Capital Territory and Victoria.[33] Further, what is defining about these remedies is that they have *no* effect on the legal rights or liability of individual parties before a court. Instead, they are designed to draw the attention of members of parliament to incompatibility between a particular statute and a constitutional rights statute. As a matter of domestic law, members of parliament are under no direct legal duty to respond to the making of such a declaration.[34] For parliament, this creates an important source of power to override the substantive constitutional interpretation of particular rights arrived at by a court: parliaments may

[30] See eg *Refugee Council of New Zealand v Attorney-General (No 1)* [2002] NZAR 717 (NZHC); *Al-Kateb v Godwin* [2004] HCA 37, 219 CLR 562; *R v Governor of Durham Prison, ex p Singh* [1983] EWHC 1, [1984] 1 All ER 983 (QB).

[31] R. Dixon, 'Creating Dialogue about Socioeconomic Rights: Strong-Form versus Weak-Form Judicial Review Revisited' (2007) 5 *International Journal of Constitutional Law* 391; R. Dixon, 'A Democratic Theory of Constitutional Comparison' (2008) 56 *American Journal of Comparative Law* 947; R. Dixon, 'A New Theory of Charter Dialogue: The Supreme Court of Canada, Charter Dialogue and Deference' (2009) 47 *Osgoode Hall Law Journal* 235.

[32] Waldron, above n 5, 31.

[33] See eg S. Gardbaum, *The New Commonwealth Model of Constitutionalism: Theory and Practice* (Cambridge: Cambridge University Press, 2013).

[34] R. Dixon, 'A Minimalist Charter of Rights for Australia: The UK or Canada as a Model?' (2009) 37 *Federal Law Review* 335; compare with L. R. Helfer and A.-M. Slaughter, 'Towards a Theory of Effective Supranational Adjudication' (1997) 107 *Yale Law Journal* 273.

exercise a power of override in this context simply by inaction or non-response—or the deliberate 'non-implementation' of a court decision.

A second source of override power under rights charters such as the HRA is the power of parliament to pass ordinary legislation overriding the effect of a particular court decision. This form of override can potentially occur in two ways: either by passage of an ordinary legislative 'sequel' to a court decision, which seeks in some way to modify or override its effect and thereby rely on a power of implied repeal (implied repeal); or by the passage of legislation expressly overriding the rights provisions relied on by courts in a particular context (express repeal).

C. Political constitutionalism and constitutional amendment

The political constitutionalist objection to judicial review is thus limited to powers of judicial review that are final and do not allow for democratic revision of judicial decisions. However, most political constitutionalists do not explicitly address formal powers of constitutional amendment as relevant to the strength or weakness of judicial review. For instance, although Waldron begins 'The Core of the Case Against Judicial Review' by mentioning the possibility of constitutional amendment as a means of revising the decision of the Supreme Court of Massachusetts' decision in *Goodridge*,[35] which recognized a constitutional right to same-sex marriage under state law,[36] he does not consider whether amendment might answer democratic concerns about the legitimacy of judicial decisions.

Considered as a matter of principle, this omission is puzzling, especially for countries that have a single or canonical document labelled 'the constitution'.[37] As we have argued, amendment procedures provide the key mechanism for formal constitutional change within a stable structure, and at the same time allow for the reassertion of democratic will. They also do so in a way that has two key advantages from the perspective of political constitutionalists. First, by making changes to the text of the constitution itself, amendment procedures generally provide a means of override that is highly decisive, and thus effective in allowing the assertion of the people's will with respect to the constitution.[38] Different judges, as one of us has noted elsewhere, will certainly differ in how much weight they ascribe to a constitution's text, as opposed to other constitutional sources.[39] But in most constitutional democracies, a near universal consensus exists that judges must pay *some* attention to the text of the constitution, in order to engage in a legitimate act of constitutional interpretation.[40] If the text of an amendment is drafted with sufficient care, it will

---

[35] *Goodridge v Department of Public Health* 798 NE 2d 941 (2003).

[36] Waldron, 2006, above n 3, 1346.

[37] For the less puzzling nature of the omission in the context of a country (such as the United Kingdom) without a written constitution of this kind, see section II.

[38] See eg R. Dixon, 'Amending Constitutional Identity' (2012) 33 *Cardozo Law Review* 1847, 'Partial Constitutional Amendments' (2010) 13 *University of Pennsylvania Journal of Constitutional Law* 643.

[39] R. Dixon, 'Partial Constitutional Codes' (unpublished manuscript, 2014).   [40] Ibid.

thus generally be sufficient to force judges to at least somewhat reconsider a prior decision—even when they continue to regard it as correct on a more all-things-considered or unconstrained basis.

Second, as a means of override, constitutional amendment procedures meet one key criterion identified by political constitutionalists for the legitimacy of judicial review—they allow for the expression of 'rights disagreements' as well as 'rights misgivings'. Waldron in particular distinguishes between two potential sources of democratic disagreement with a court decision upholding human rights: forms of disagreement or 'dissensus' about the meaning or scope of particular rights in the relevant context ('rights disagreements'); and disagreements about the primacy, or priority, of relevant rights in a particular context ('rights misgivings').[41] Both forms of disagreement are likely to arise in different contexts in a democracy, and if judicial review is effectively to preserve the capacity of the people to resolve disagreement about rights, there must be a mechanism for their expression. Political constitution-alism is directed at ensuring proper respect for reasonable disagreement about rights, and the respectful treatment of opposing views would be directly undermined by misrepresentation of the nature of these views. A particular problem will arise if all disagreements with a judicial determination as to rights are cast as rights misgiv-ings rather than rights disagreements. If the people (through participatory institu-tions) are able only to 'override' rights rather than express an alternative conception of them, there is a risk that democratic override will be cast as unprincipled disre-gard for rights. Reservations of just this kind have been expressed about the express power of legislative override provided for under section 33 of the *Canadian Charter of Rights and Freedoms*.[42] Because the power of override is expressed as a 'notwith-standing'[43] provision, it allows legislatures to express disagreement only as a prefer-ence for a competing interest that overrides the right (a right misgiving), rather than a disagreement about the proper limits and meaning of a right.[44] One important criterion for assessing the adequacy of a power of democratic override, therefore, is whether it provides a means for expressing both forms of disagreement. A power of constitutional amendment also clearly allows legislators flexibility to express both rights disagreements *and* misgivings—by allowing legislators to direct changes to the constitutional text toward the prima facie scope of relevant rights *or* relevant limita-tion clauses, or some combination of both.

What, then, explains this apparent unwillingness of political constitutionalists to include the availability of constitutional amendment as a factor relevant to assessing the strength of judicial review?

---

[41] Waldron, 2006, above n 3, 1366–9.

[42] Part I of the *Constitution Act 1982*, being Schedule B to the *Canada Act 1982* (UK), 1982, c 11 (*Canadian Charter*).

[43] Section 33 (1) of the *Canadian Charter* provides: 'Parliament or the legislature of a province may expressly declare in an Act of Parliament or of the legislature, as the case may be, that the Act or a provision thereof shall operate notwithstanding a provision included in [rights protection provisions of the *Charter*].'

[44] J. Goldsworthy, 'Legislation, Interpretation, and Judicial Review' (2001) 51 *University of Toronto Law Journal* 75.

II. Weak-Form Review and the Inferiority of Amendment as Democratic Override?

In this section, we consider three possible explanations: the practical unavailability of amendment procedures; notions of equality in voting; and the tendency of amendments to add too greatly to the overall length of a constitution. Each of these explanations, we suggest, has some real plausibility in the United States, and to a lesser extent the United Kingdom, where Waldron is writing. But in many other constitutional democracies, they seem far less relevant: at best, in these countries such explanations may suggest limits to the role of constitutional amendment in certain circumstances. They do not provide anything like a categorical basis for rejecting amendment as a tool for democratic override. Because of this, attention to such procedures would also seem directly relevant to assessing the democratic legitimacy of judicial review in these countries.

A. Practical unavailability

Perhaps the most obvious explanation for the comparative non-attention to constitutional amendment procedures by political constitutionalists is that constitutional amendment procedures may be subject to a range of obstacles, which make them an unlikely source of actual democratic override. Obstacles of this kind could take two forms: formal obstacles to amendment such as super- or double-majority requirements in the legislature, or requirements of popular ratification; or informal obstacles, such as a pattern or practice of non-use of a power of constitutional amendment.

As to formal obstacles to constitutional amendment, an implicit focus on the United States would make it entirely understandable for political constitutionalists to ignore, or overlook, constitutional amendment as a means of democratic override. While article V has been used to override decisions of the US Supreme Court, including in the case of the Eleventh Amendment,[45] no one could suggest that article V provides any kind of routine power of democratic override: for an amendment to succeed under article V, it must receive the support of a majority in Congress *and* be ratified by two thirds of state legislatures (or conventions).[46] There is some disagreement about just how difficult this makes amendment in the United States: Sandy Levinson has suggested that it is so difficult that democratic principles in fact favour an attempt to replace the entire Constitution.[47] Vicki Jackson has counselled against this extremely pessimistic view, suggesting that formal amendment may still be possible in the United States in some circumstances, given sufficient democratic mobilization for such a change.[48] But whichever of these two views one

---

[45] See eg US Const Amend XI (overriding effect of the Supreme Court's decision in *Chisolm v Georgia* 2 US 419 (1793)); US Const Amend XIV (overriding effect of the Supreme Court's decision in *Dred Scott v Sandford* 60 US 393 (1857)). See discussion in Dixon, 2010, above n 38; Dixon, above n 28. See also *Goodridge*, above n 35.

[46] US Const, art V.

[47] S. Levinson, 'United States: Assessing *Heller*' (2009) 7 *International Journal of Constitutional Law* 316. See also S. Levinson, 'Designing an Amendment Process', in J. Ferejohn, J. N. Rakove, and J. Riley (eds), *Constitutional Culture and Democratic Rule* (Cambridge: Cambridge University Press, 2001), 271–87.

[48] V. Jackson, 'Paradigms of Public Law: Transnational Constitutional Values and Democratic Challenges' (2010) 8 *International Journal of Constitutional Law* 517.

takes, no one suggests that article V is easy to satisfy. Indeed, there has been no successful attempt to rely on article V for this purpose since the early twentieth century and the passage of the Sixteenth Amendment as a means of overriding the decision of the Supreme Court in *Pollock v Farmer's Loan and Trust Co*[49] (invalidating a federal income tax). This is also despite numerous calls to invoke article V in order to override particular decisions of the Supreme Court over the last half-century.[50] Prominent examples include proposals to amend the Constitution to overturn the decision of the US Supreme Court in *Texas v Johnson*[51] and allow Congress to criminalize flag burning;[52] and to override the Court's decision in *Roe v Wade*[53] and allow broader regulation or limits on access to abortion.[54]

In most other constitutional democracies, however, the formal obstacles to constitutional amendment are considerably less onerous than in the United States. Comparing the difficulty of constitutional amendment across different jurisdictions is, of course, notoriously difficult.[55] For one, most countries have constitutional amendment procedures or requirements with multiple different stages or dimensions: amendments frequently require legislative and popular approval, but sometimes only one of the two. Legislative approval will sometimes require a majority of two houses of parliament, but in other cases, the approval of a single house may be sufficient; and some systems adopt requirements of delay, or double ratification, within the same voting body. These different requirements can also be difficult to compare in terms of stringency. Political scientists, however, have made several useful attempts to construct different indexes of comparison; and on these measures, it is clear that, given the filibuster rule in the Senate and stringent requirements for state ratification of proposed amendments, the US Constitution is now the *most* difficult of all constitutions to amend.[56] Similarly, if one focuses simply on the core dimension to amendment difficulty, namely the degree of supermajority support required for a constitutional amendment to obtain legislative approval, it is apparent that the United States is a clear outlier in global terms. A survey of global constitutions by the Comparative Constitutions Project, for example, shows that for 142 constitutions, only 15 per cent of countries have US-style supermajority requirements for the legislative approval of amendments.[57] Most have legislative voting requirements that are closer to ordinary, or weak, supermajority requirements.

[49] 157 US 429 (1895), aff'd on reh'g 158 US 601 (1895).

[50] See eg Dixon, 2010, above n 38; J. Mazzone, 'Unamendments' (2005) 90 *Iowa Law Review* 1747; J. R. Vile, *Encyclopedia of Constitutional Amendments, Proposed Amendments, and Amending Issues, 1789–2002* (Santa Barbara, Calif.: ABC-CLIO, 2003).

[51] 491 US 397 (1989).

[52] See eg S Res 12, 109th Cong (2006); HRJ Res 10, 109th Cong (2005); SJ Res 1980, 101st Cong (1989).

[53] 410 US 113 (1973).

[54] See HRJ Res 261, 93rd Cong (1973); HRJ Res 427, 93rd Cong (1973); HRJ Res 769, 93rd Cong (1973); HRJ Res 91, 94th Cong (1975); HRJ Res 294, 96th Cong (1979); HRJ Res 110, 97th Cong (1981); SJ Res 3, 98th Cong (1983).

[55] Z. Elkins, T. Ginsburg, and J. Melton, *The Endurance of National Constitutions* (Cambridge: Cambridge University Press, 2009).

[56] See D. S. Lutz, 'Toward a Theory of Constitutional Amendment', in S. Levinson (ed), *Responding to Imperfection: The Theory and Practice of Constitutional Amendment* (Princeton: Princeton University Press, 1995), 237–74; compare with J. Ferejohn, 'The Politics of Imperfection: The Amendment of Constitutions' (1997) 22 *Law & Social Inquiry* 501.

[57] Comparative Constitutions Project, http://comparativeconstitutionsproject.org/.

As to the actual record of constitutional amendment as a tool for democratic override, there is also an extensive—and quite recent—history of constitutional amendment being used as a means of overriding constitutional decisions by courts in constitutional democracies outside the United States. The experiences of constitutional amendment in India and Colombia provide two good examples. For most constitutional amendments, article 368 of the Indian Constitution[58] requires only an absolute majority in both houses of the Indian Parliament, or two thirds of members present and voting. A power of amendment has also been used on numerous occasions by the Parliament to override key decisions of the Supreme Court of India, and of lower courts, on issues such as the scope of affirmative action, or reservations for so-called backward classes of citizen, the scope for the criminalization of seditious or subversive speech, and the scope of compensation requirements for the taking of land or other property, as part of efforts at land reform or economic nationalization.

In Colombia, article 357 of the Constitution[59] provides that the legislature may amend the Constitution by ordinary majority vote—though only after twice considering or passing such an amendment. Article 358 likewise provides for amendments to be passed by popular referendum, with the support of an ordinary majority of citizens. The Colombian legislature has also successfully relied on these procedures to override several high-profile decisions of the Constitutional Court on the scope of socioeconomic rights and the lawfulness of prohibitions on illegal drug use and possession. While courts in both Colombia and India have sought to impose limits on a formal power of constitutional amendment, to date, these limits have not been applied in either Colombia or India so as to systematically frustrate attempts at democratic override by constitutional amendment.[60]

As the Colombian and Indian experiences show, constitutional amendment procedures are not only generally far less onerous than in the United States, but are also frequently used as an actual tool for democratic override in many constitutional democracies. This by itself suggests that it may be misleading to treat the strength or finality of judicial review as an either–or proposition, with systems of (formally) weak-form judicial review preserving the legitimacy and systems of strong-form review departing from it.

B. Supermajority requirements and political equality

A second response by political constitutionalists might be that to conclude that amendment procedures render judicial review democratically acceptable is nonetheless to make the wrong comparison. The point should not be that in most constitutional systems amendment is relatively more available than the practically impossible article V

---

[58] Constitution of India, 1950.   [59] Constitution of Colombia, 1991.

[60] R. Dixon and D. Landau, 'Transnational Constitutionalism and Amendment Limited Doctrine of Unconstitutional Constitutional Amendment' (working paper delivered at the ICON Symposium on 'The Challenge of Formal Amendment' at the Inaugural AALS Academic Symposium, 5 January 2014); R. Dixon, 'Constitutional Drafting and Distrust', *International Journal of Constitutional Law* (forthcoming); R. Dixon and D. Landau, 'Constraining Constitutional Change', *International Journal of Constitutional Law* (forthcoming).

procedure. Rather, the question should be whether amendment procedures are as available as ordinary legislative repeal or non-implementation. And the answer in the vast majority of jurisdictions is quite clearly 'no'. Most amendment procedures not only adopt a higher supermajority threshold. They also impose other hurdles designed to promote deliberation, or protect minority interests, such as requirements of double or delayed passage, or popular ratification.

Recall that participation as the 'right of rights' is at the heart of Waldron's argument.[61] Judicial review is necessarily democratically inferior to majoritarian decision-making because it overrules decisions made through processes in which the people have had equal rights of participation. So one response to our suggestion that amendment procedures allow for a democratic revision of judicial review is that amendment procedures which require supermajorities do not fully respect the equality of participation, instead weighting the scale in favour of the status quo.

We suggest, however, that while the argument has force in countries like the United States, such an argument has far less persuasiveness in constitutional democracies with weaker traditions of political competition, or competition between political parties. In setting up the four basic assumptions that inform 'The Core of the Case Against Judicial Review', Waldron explicitly notes the assumption that, for democratic institutions to be 'in reasonably good working order', there should be 'political parties, and that legislators' party affiliations are key to their taking a view that ranges more broadly than the interests and opinions of their immediate constituents'.[62] Implicit in this understanding seems to be the view that legislative voting should be based on some consideration of the public interest, or a form of reasoned deliberation, rather than voting based on narrow sectional interest. Another version of this idea might be the understanding that every voter should have a roughly equal chance of being pivotal on a particular legislative vote or issue; or at least not systematically advantaged or disadvantaged in having their views carried into law by virtue of their particular connection to an individual legislator or factional interest.[63] A commitment to political equality is best respected, according to Waldron, when the votes of individual citizens have 'equal weight or equal potential decisiveness'; or every individual's vote has 'equal weight...in the process in which one view is selected as the group's'.[64]

Now suppose that there is a system, such as the United States or United Kingdom, where there are two or more major political parties that are relatively evenly matched. The argument often made by political scientists is that competition between such parties will help advance this kind of goal of impartiality: competition among parties generally ensures that parties respond to the concerns of the median voter, rather than the

[61] Waldron, 1999, above n 3.
[62] Waldron suggests that the presence of political parties is a feature of the four preconditions of legislative structure necessary for the 'Core Case' to apply, but does not fully explore their relevance to correlated voting of this kind: compare with Waldron, 2006, above n 3, 1361.
[63] For the relationship between veil of ignorance ideas and constitutional design, see eg J. Rawls, *A Theory of Justice* (Cambridge, Mass.: Harvard University Press, 1971); A. Vermeule, *Mechanisms of Democracy: Institutional Design Writ Small* (Oxford: Oxford University Press, 2007).
[64] Waldron, 1999, above n 3, 114. Note that this is a more outcome-oriented conception of equality than one that emphasizes thicker or more active forms of participation by citizens in processes of democratic self-government.

views or concerns of those voters who happen to be pivotal in particular electorates, or parties, or who are less broadly representative of majority views or understandings.[65] In such a system, a commitment to a norm of ordinary majority voting in the legislature will also make sense: it will be the rule that best ensures that all voters have a roughly equal chance of being pivotal on a given question, regardless of their particular identity, or connection to any given candidate, party, or faction.

In contrast, in a system where there is greater asymmetry between parties or one party is consistently dominant, it may be far less likely that legislators will consistently consider the public interest, rather than the interests of members of their own party or electorate. Norms of majoritarian decision-making, in such circumstances, may thus no longer be the rule that best promotes norms of *substantive* equality of participation among voters.[66] Instead, the rule that best respects norms of equality may be a form of supermajority rule, which gives the non-dominant party, or citizens aligned with such a party, at least a somewhat greater chance of being pivotal in deciding on the merits of a particular issue.[67] A similar analysis applies where politics, or legislative behaviour, is dominated by particular *individuals* and families, rather than parties. The dominance of such individuals or families will often mean that, under majoritarian decision-making procedures, those aligned with particular individuals have a far greater chance of being pivotal on any given question than those outside the dominant family. A supermajority rule, which gives a greater chance of an effective veto, or being pivotal, to those without such dominant-party connections, may thus also be the form of voting rule that best promotes norms of substantive equality. In many real-world constitutional democracies, there are also numerous examples where supermajority requirements for constitutional amendment do in fact co-exist with exactly these kinds of pattern of legislative dominance by particular parties or individuals.

A good example involves the requirements for constitutional amendment in India. The Congress Party in India has dominated control of Parliament for most of India's history: since India gained independence, it has been in power for all but thirteen years.[68] This has allowed the Congress-controlled Parliament to pass numerous amendments designed to override specific decisions of the Supreme Court of India without the need to gain substantial support from non-Congress Party aligned legislators. Indeed, in India, the argument is generally *not* that amendment procedures give non-Congress Party voters too much power to block proposed amendments, or disproportionate or unequal veto over majority proposals for constitutional override. Rather, the argument is generally that amendment procedures have been too readily available to Congress Party legislators, and thus a means by which would-be authoritarian leaders from within the party, such as Prime Minister Indira Gandhi, are able to remove various

---

[65] See eg A. Downs, *An Economic Theory of Democracy* (New York: Harper & Brothers, 1957).

[66] Waldron acknowledges the possibility of a more substantive notion of equality in this context, but disagrees with its application, in the context of discussing the work of Charles Beitz: see Waldron, 1999, above n 3, 116.

[67] Compare with R. Holden, 'Supermajority Voting Rules' (working paper, 2004) (on how different distributions of voters can affect the optimality of various majority versus supermajority rules).

[68] The Congress Party was out of power March 1977–January 1980 (Janata party), November 1989–June 1991 (BJP Government), and May 1996–May 2004 (BJP Government).

democratic checks and balances. The ready availability of constitutional amendment is also one reason why the Supreme Court of India may have developed a set of implied limits on the power of amendment, which seek to protect the basic structure of the Indian Constitution from change under article 368.[69]

Of course, Waldron might respond to this by suggesting that countries such as India, or Colombia, are in fact outside the 'Core Case', or not countries that in fact have democratic institutions in truly 'good' working order. Such a response would also have some real plausibility: effective democratic competition between political parties that is robust, but not hyper-partisan or polarized may indeed be an important pre-condition for effective legislative rights-protection.[70] Such a response, however, also has the very clear effect of narrowing the scope of the 'Core Case': instead of applying to a large part of the democratic world, it would then apply at most to only a few dozen countries.[71] Even within those countries, there will also likely be cases where supermajority requirements for constitutional amendment do not offend *substantive* commitments to political equality.

We do not suggest that all supermajority requirements for successful amendment would be equivalent to requirements for ordinary legislative override, from the perspective of political equality. We simply suggest that, at the legislative stage at least, one should pause before assuming that any form of supermajority requirement will necessarily give *substantively* 'unequal weight' to the votes of individual citizens. Whether or not this is true will depend largely on the specific political circumstances, and whether there are inequalities or pathologies in legislative voting patterns that mean that ordinary majority voting rules do not necessarily further goals of substantive political equality for participants in the political process.

This argument again suggests that it is misleading to treat the strength of judicial review and its democratic legitimacy as an either–or proposition, with systems of weak-form judicial review preserving legitimacy and systems of strong-form review departing from it, regardless of the availability of constitutional amendment in a particular political context.

C. Narrowness and constitutional parsimony (versus prolixity)

A third objection that political constitutionalists might pose in response to constitutional amendment as a means of override lies in the tendency of amendment to create pressures toward 'prolixity' or codification in a constitution. Political constitutionalists themselves favour a more flexible, 'framework-like' approach to democratic constitutional drafting.[72] Almost all successful amendments will add to the overall length of a

---

[69] Dixon and Landau, 2014, above n 60.

[70] See M. Tushnet and R. Dixon, 'Weak-Form Review and its Constitutional Relatives: An Asian Perspective', in R. Dixon and T. Ginsburg (eds), *Comparative Constitutional Law in Asia* (Northampton, Mass.: Edward Elgar, 2014), 102–20 (on the need for democratic competition). See also N. Persily, *Solutions to Political Polarization in America* (Cambridge: Cambridge University Press, 2015) (on the dangers of polarization).

[71] See eg Dixon, 2008, above n 31 (on countries that could be considered sufficiently democratic for various purposes).

[72] Dixon, above n 39.

constitutional document. Though there are exceptions: some may seek to delete language that has been the basis of a disfavoured decision by a court, while others may seek to delete language that has been understood to create a limitation on government power. Most amendments, however, will seek to add at least some additional language to the existing constitutional text. This is particularly true where amendments are designed so as to overcome another potential objection to amendment as a means of democratic override—ie its potential for overbreadth, or 'unintended' interpretive consequences.

This feature of constitutional amendment has led several American constitutional scholars, including Kathleen Sullivan and Cass Sunstein, to express reservations about the too-ready use of amendment.[73] It also provides a potentially persuasive explanation for why many constitutional lawyers (though not necessarily political constitutionalists themselves) reject the idea of amendment as fully equivalent to ordinary powers of legislative override. Yet potential for prolixity can often be addressed by careful and detailed attention to constitutional language. Through careful drafting it is possible to anticipate some potential overbreadth. It is possible simply to remove a particular piece of legislation from the scope of judicial review,[74] or to limit the scope of relevant legislative disagreement by simultaneously overriding and affirming aspects of a prior court decision.[75] The price, however, is simply that the drafters of a proposed amendment must use quite detailed, code-like constitutional language.[76]

What are the likely consequences of this additional length in a constitution created by various constitutional amendments? In the United States, there is a long-standing view that too much detail and prolixity in a constitution will pose a threat to a constitution retaining its 'constitution-like' status. The most famous statement of this view is found in the decision of the US Supreme Court in *McCulloch v Maryland*,[77] where Marshall CJ argued that by definition a constitution must be somewhat abstract or non-specific, or mark only 'great outlines' or 'important objects', rather than contain more 'accurate detail'. If a constitution were too detailed, Marshall CJ suggested, it 'would partake of the prolixity of a legal code' in a way that would directly threaten its constitution-like status or 'nature'.[78]

What lies behind this view articulated by Marshall CJ, and endorsed by so many courts around the world? One potential explanation relates to the time-horizon for constitutions. Constitutions, Marshall CJ suggested, are designed to endure over the

[73] K. Sullivan, 'Constitutional Amendmentitis', *The American Prospect*, 19 December 2001, http://prospect.org/article/constitutional-amendmentitis; C. R. Sunstein, 'The Refounding Father', *The New York Review of Books*, 5 June 2014, http://www.nybooks.com/articles/archives/2014/jun/05/justice-stevens-refounding-father/.

[74] See eg Constitution of India, 1950, schedule 9.

[75] See eg on the Colombian fiscal sustainability amendments, D. Landau, 'Should the Unconstitutional Constitutional Amendments Doctrine Be Part of the Canon?' *International Journal of Constitutional Law Blog* (10 June 2013), http://www.iconnectblog.com/2013/06/should-the-unconstitutional-constitutional-amendments-doctrine-be-part-of-the-canon/.

[76] 'Code-like' here denotes the idea of additional textual specificity, or detail, not the more traditional common law–civil law distinction between different modes of regulation: see eg R. Dixon, 'Constitutional Redundancy' (unpublished manuscript, 2014).

[77] *McCulloch*, above n 11.   [78] Ibid 407.

long-term, or 'for ages to come'. The more detailed a constitution is, the more likely it also is to contain various 'immutable rules'—or long and detailed rule-like provisions—that are poorly suited to adapt to a society's changing needs and circumstances.[79] Constitutional amendment, however, as section I notes, provides at least a partial solution to this problem of constitutional updating.

Another potential explanation might be the relationship between code-like constitutional language and political participation. One of the key criteria of constitutional legitimacy, for political constitutionalists, will be whether there is an 'active and engaged, public-spirited citizenry and a deep participation in political affairs'.[80] Processes of constitutional amendment may also potentially serve as a site of public participation of this kind—providing the text of the existing constitution is sufficiently understandable and accessible to the public to allow for such participation. The more detailed or code-like a constitution, as Marshall CJ himself noted, the less likely it may also be 'understood by the public' or 'embraced by the human mind'.[81]

Similarly, political constitutionalists might argue that constitutional non-codification has distinct benefits in encouraging more active constitutional deliberation by legislators. In countries such as the United Kingdom, there is a widespread belief that constitutional non-codification has benefits. While the United Kingdom lacks a single, canonical document labelled 'a constitution', it has a long and successful history of political constitutionalism. Many commentators also draw a close connection between these facts, suggesting that political constitutionalism is enhanced when constitutional norms are expressed in general, flexible terms, rather than more narrowly codified or legalistic language.[82]

The difficulty with this argument, however, is that it clearly rests on a vision of constitutionalism that is neither generally shared across all constitutional systems and contexts, nor self-evidently normatively correct. First, there is a clear trend worldwide toward countries adopting a single, canonical document labelled 'the constitution'. Moreover, even in countries without such a document, there is a trend toward increasing codification of certain elements of the constitution, such as those regarding common law rights and liberties.[83] Among countries with written constitutions, there is also a trend toward increasing length or prolixity in constitutional drafting.[84] Developments of this kind also fundamentally change the baseline for judging notions of constitutional 'parsimony-versus-prolixity'.

To treat constitutional amendments as necessarily threatening the parsimonious or 'constitution-like' status of a constitution, therefore, would once again seem to conflate American constitutional experience with constitutional experience more generally. In the United States, the short and 'pristine' nature of the Constitution may

[79] Ibid 415.   [80] Tomkins, 2002, above n 3, 175.   [81] *McCulloch*, above n 11, 407.
[82] Compare with J. McLean, 'The Unwritten Political Constitution and its Enemies' (working paper delivered at the Symposium on Australian Constitutionalism at the Melbourne Law School, 13–14 December 2013); Gardbaum, above n 33.
[83] See eg Gardbaum, above n 33.
[84] T. Ginsburg, 'Constitutional Specificity, Unwritten Understandings and Constitutional Amendment', in A. Sajó and R. Uitz (eds), *Constitutional Topography: Values and Constitutions* (The Hague: Eleven International Publishing, 2010), 69–94; Dixon, above n 76.

mean that it would almost always seem incongruous for Congress to propose detailed amendments that sought to override particular court decisions.[85] In many other countries, in contrast, such amendments are both frequently proposed and enacted, and accepted as consistent with background norms of constitutional drafting. At the very least, the argument rests on a set of normative assumptions about constitutions—and constitutionalism—that are largely unexpressed by political constitutionalists, and which seem open to debate.

Our own view is that there are in fact a set of reasonably persuasive arguments that could be made against an overly prolix, or codified, approach to democratic constitutionalism, which could support the reluctance of political constitutionalists to treat amendment procedures as *fully* equivalent to ordinary legislative override as a means of expressing democratic disagreement.[86] But these arguments depend on a set of empirical assumptions about the relationship between constitutional language, interpretation, and political practice that are clearly open to dispute, and require justification. To rely on such arguments as a basis for rejecting the relevance of amendment procedures to the democratic legitimacy of judicial review, without providing such justification, would thus seem to us once again to be unjustified.

III. Conclusions: Constitutional Theory and Comparison

In developing 'The Core of the Case Against Judicial Review' and related arguments, Waldron suggested that 'what [was] needed [was] some general understanding, uncontaminated by the cultural, historical, and political preoccupations of each society' of the theoretical arguments for and against judicial review in a democracy.[87] Judicial review, he suggested, is a global phenomenon, which requires examination from a philosophical and not merely local–historical perspective.[88] Because of this, he further suggested, what was needed was an attempt to '[boil] the flesh off the bones' of the practical experience of judicial review in various countries, to identify various core workings about assumptions, and to use those to generate various theoretical arguments.[89]

In adopting this kind of stripped down account, however, we suggest that political constitutionalists have nonetheless been inevitably influenced by the jurisdictions they are working in, or are most familiar with. Jeremy Waldron's critique of judicial review reflects his intellectual links to the United States, United Kingdom, and his native New Zealand. Other political constitutionalists, such as Adam Tomkins, are similarly deeply connected to debates over judicial review in the United Kingdom, and other countries with UK-style parliamentary and common law traditions, such as Canada and New Zealand.[90] Evidence of this American and British focus is also apparent in the numerous references to American and British, and at times New Zealand, experience in the writings of political constitutionalists.[91]

---

[85] Compare with Sullivan, above n 73.   [86] See eg Dixon, above n 39.
[87] Waldron, 2006, above n 3, 1352.   [88] Ibid.   [89] Ibid.
[90] Tomkins, 2002, above n 3; Tomkins, 2010, above n 3.
[91] See eg Tomkins, 2002, above n 3; Tomkins, 2010, above n 3.

In the United States and the United Kingdom, it also makes a great deal of sense for political constitutionalists such as Waldron and Tomkins to overlook constitutional amendment in debates over the democratic legitimacy of judicial review. In the United Kingdom, all constitutional norms are small 'c' constitutional in nature. Some of these norms are conventional, some common law in origin, and others statutory in nature.[92] For statutory norms, at least, their origins in ordinary legislation will also mean that the Westminster Parliament has powers of amendment and express repeal that are completely co-extensive: nothing particular to the power of amendment, therefore, in any way alters the strong- or weak-form of judicial review under the United Kingdom's Constitution. The same is also true in New Zealand, about which from time to time Waldron has made similar arguments.[93]

Conversely, in the United States, formal powers of constitutional amendment could be considered irrelevant for quite different reasons. The formally onerous nature of constitutional amendment in the United States means that, for practical purposes, constitutional amendment is basically unavailable as a means of democratic override. The existence of robust political competition, at least at a national level, might mean that political constitutionalists could argue that any form of supermajority requirement for constitutional amendment violates democratic norms of political equality. (The same also holds true for the United Kingdom.[94]) Similarly, the general and parsimonious nature of the existing constitutional text in the United States may mean that long and detailed constitutional amendments seem incongruous, as a means of democratic override, and thus that any override via the amendment process will carry a necessary danger of overbreadth, of the kind warned against by political constitutionalists.

In many countries, however, these assumptions will simply not hold true, or at least not nearly to the same degree as is true in the United States or United Kingdom. In many constitutional democracies, constitutional amendment procedures are only moderately, not extremely, onerous. As the Colombian and Indian experiences make clear, legislative majorities also quite frequently invoke such procedures to override (or attempt to override) particular court decisions. The dominance of a single political party, or political figure or family, in the national legislature also often means that some (weak or moderate) supermajority requirement for the passage of such amendments affirmatively helps promote, rather than undermine, norms of political equality among voters in the face of constitutional democratic disagreement. Similarly, as the Colombian and Indian experiences also show, the existing level of detail in the text of various countries' constitutions can mean there is often nothing incongruous at all about amendments that make use of quite careful, detailed language in order narrowly to override particular court decisions.

This diversity among constitutional systems means that it may be unwarranted to treat the legitimacy of judicial review as an either–or proposition. Instead, the question

---

[92] Demarcating the bounds of a so-called unwritten constitution is, of course, notoriously difficult, and one could potentially add a number of other sources to this list, including transnational ones.

[93] See J. Waldron, 'A Right-Based Critique of Constitutional Rights' (1993) 13 *Oxford Journal of Legal Studies* 18.

[94] See P. Webb, *The Modern British Party System* (London: SAGE Publications, 2000).

of the legitimacy of judicial review may be better approached as both one of degree, and one informed by a variety of factors, including the availability, and context, for use of a power of constitutional amendment.[95] Waldron himself begins to move in this direction, by categorizing Canada as occupying a 'middle position' between strong- and weak-form judicial review.[96] Waldron also questions the degree to which true legislative–judicial dialogue can occur without some form of deference, by courts, to true expressions of democratic disagreement by legislators.[97] From this perspective, it may be that, at other times, Waldron is in fact too quick to accept the democratic legitimacy of those forms of judicial review he identifies as falling on the 'weak' side of the strong–weak dichotomy.

In other contexts, however, political constitutionalists seem to gloss over questions of the actual practical degree of strength, or weakness, under particular formal constitutional models. One potential reason for this, we suggest, is that while explicitly attempting to be general and de-contextualized in the empirical assumptions they make, scholars such as Waldron are in fact heavily influenced by assumptions about background constitutional conditions that track those found in the United States, or to a lesser degree, the United Kingdom—ie both high formal and informal barriers to constitutional amendment, strong norms of political party competition, and a background commitment to parsimonious constitutional drafting, or a framework-like constitution. None of these conditions are explicitly included in Waldron's definition of what it means to have 'judicial institutions' that resolve constitutional disputes on a 'final basis', or to have 'democratic institutions in reasonably good working order'.[98] Yet, this chapter has shown that they are also more or less necessary assumptions if we are to accept the decision by political constitutionalists largely to ignore amendment as a means of democratic override.

The focus on constitutional 'ideal-types' by political constitutionalists in this context has also arguably led them to gloss over important questions of degree in the actual strength, or weakness, of judicial review under weak-form systems of judicial review. It may even, at times, have led them quite substantially to overstate the democratic objection to judicial review in its stronger forms—by downplaying the degree to which even quite well-functioning legislative processes may be subject to certain practical limitations or 'blockages', which cause them systematically to under-protect certain kinds of rights. One of us, for example, has argued in prior work that the democratic objection to judicial review often radically understates the potential for both 'blind spots' in the legislative process, and 'burdens of inertia' of the kind that can radically undermine the degree to which legislative processes are actually responsive to democratic majority understandings.[99] These arguments would also be far more directly addressed, by political constitutionalists, if they were to adopt a more context-sensitive account of actual legislative functioning. A more general lesson to be drawn from a study of constitutional amendment and political constitutionalism in this context, therefore, is about

[95] Kavanagh, above n 7; Tushnet and Dixon, above n 70.
[96] Waldron, above n 5, 1356–8. Cf also Dixon, 2009, above n 31.
[97] Ibid.   [98] Waldron, 2006, above n 3, 1360–2.
[99] Dixon, 2007, above n 31; Dixon, 2008, above n 31; Dixon, 2009, above n 31.

the dangers of a wholly 'boiled-down' approach to actual constitutional practice in constitutional theory. Indeed, we think this is a danger that is likely to arise in many areas of constitutional theory.

Constitutional theorists, like all of us, will inevitably be influenced by assumptions generated by observing the jurisdictions they are most familiar with.[100] But the diversity of global constitutional practice, and experience, will often mean that those assumptions turn out *not* to hold more generally. Understanding why, and to what extent this is true, will also be critical to assessing the actual real-world applicability of various constitutional theoretic arguments.

In seeking to offer general theoretical arguments, therefore, we suggest that a safer course for constitutional theorists may be to make much clearer, and more explicit, the jurisdictions they are drawing on or imagining in generating the 'bare bones' assumptions on which they then base their theoretical arguments. By doing so, they would create the conditions for a natural dialogue between constitutional theorists and scholars of comparative constitutional law about the actual generality, versus specificity, of their theoretical arguments, while still allowing both sets of scholars to do what they do best—ie for constitutional theorists to focus on fundamental ideas about democracy and legitimacy, and for comparative scholars to focus on questions of context and degree of the kind we highlight in the chapter.

---

[100] Behavioural psychologists often label this tendency a form of 'availability bias'. A similar behavioural tendency is also 'representativeness bias', which involves the tendency of individuals to underestimate the degree to which the sample (of information) they are observing is, or is not, representative of a more general pattern. See eg D. Kahnemann and A. Taversky, 'On the Reality of Cognitive Illusions' (1996) 103 *Psychological Review* 582.

PART II

CONSTITUTIONAL AUTHORITY

6

Constitutional Legitimacy Unbound

*Evan Fox-Decent**

I. Introduction

Constitutions, whether written or unwritten, are conventionally perceived to have three dimensions. The first concerns a constitution's substantive elements. These elements typically include a division of powers specifying a federation or a unitary state, a separation of public powers between legislative, judicial, and administrative branches, and an institutionalized form of rights protection. Underlying these substantive elements is usually some conception of the rule of law or legal order, which may or may not—depending on the account—circumscribe fully the exercise of sovereign power. Secondly, constitutions are ordinarily regarded as the supreme law that governs relations between the state and its citizens. And finally, constitutions of democracies are thought to supply democratic and self-contained standards of legitimacy, standards that emerge from 'We the People' and thereby express their people's fundamental and enduring values. In short, this orthodox view of (liberal democratic) constitutions is that (i) their substantive content allocates public powers and protects rights within a municipal legal order; (ii) their structure supplies a paramount legal framework to state–citizen relations; and (iii) their legitimacy rests on their capacity to authorize public power in accordance with local democratic standards.

I argue that the orthodox view is incomplete along all three dimensions, and that its incompleteness is vividly exposed by reflection on boundary questions of entrance and membership to a state. In addition to the allocation of public powers and the specification of constitutional rights, constitutions must also determine over whom public powers may be lawfully exercised and who may claim standing as a right holder in the relevant political community. In other words, for the allocation of public powers and the specification of rights to play a constitutive role in the paramount legal framework of a given community, there must be some group of individuals who form that community, and there must be some way to determine that they are its members. As Michael Walzer puts it, '[t]he primary good that we distribute to one another is membership in some human community. And what we do with regard to membership structures all our other distributive choices: it determines with whom we make those choices,

* Associate Professor, Faculty of Law, McGill University. For excellent research assistance and comments, I thank Michaël Lessard and Ian Dahlman. I likewise owe a debt for helpful comments to Eyal Benvenisti, Andrew Gold, Andrew Botterell, the editors of this volume, the participants at a workshop held at the Faculty of Law, University of Toronto, 10–11 May 2014 to discuss the contributions to this volume, and the participants of the 'Fiduciary Relationships' workshop held at the University of Western Ontario, 14–15 November 2014.

from whom we require obedience and collect taxes, to whom we allocate goods and services.'[1]

It follows that the structure of a constitution must be wider than the framework necessary for the governance of state–citizen relations, since it must be capable of distinguishing citizens from non-citizens, and likewise capable of specifying how natural persons become citizens.[2] Two familiar means of specifying citizenship track the location of the individual's birth (*jus soli*) and her lineage (*jus sanguinis*). In other cases, an outsider appears at the border, or within the state, and seeks citizenship. Under the prevailing Westphalian conception of sovereignty as exclusive jurisdiction, states assert a unilateral right to determine the conditions of entrance and membership. This unilateral assertion, I contend, subverts the legitimacy of the state's constitutional order.

For a constitution to be legitimate, it must possess a cosmopolitan aspect capable of regulating municipal decisions that determine whether a foreign national can enter a state and become a citizen.[3] This cosmopolitan aspect denotes an openness to transnational legal norms, a legal duty to take such norms into account and justify adverse decisions in light of them, preparedness to submit these decisions to international institutions for review, and the presence of an underlying legal relationship between the state and foreign national that explains and informs the duty to justify adverse decisions. The state, I claim, is a fiduciary of everyone subject to its public powers, including individuals at the border. As we shall see, the state can be understood to occupy both a local and a global fiduciary position, and these combine to place it under a defeasible duty to grant entrance and eventually membership to peaceful outsiders. The state is entitled to restrict entrance and membership only if it offers a compelling and independently reviewable justification. The arguments that lead to these conclusions show that immanent to constitutional order is a public law duty to justify decisions that transgress international norms and other requirements of legality ('the duty of justification'), a duty that is owed to citizens and non-citizens alike.

In section II, I use Canada as an example to set out briefly some of the ways international law has pierced the veil of Westphalian sovereignty with respect to borders and membership, in effect entitling certain foreign nationals to remain in a host state

[1] M. Walzer, *Spheres of Justice: A Defense of Pluralism and Equality* (New York: Basic Books, 1983), 31.
[2] I am simplifying. Many constitutions stipulate rights protections that apply to foreign nationals as well as citizens, so this is a contingent reason those constitutions require a wider scope than state–citizen relations. Section 7 of Canada's Constitution Act 1982, for example, provides that '[e]veryone has the right to life, liberty and security of the person...' No constitution, however, to the best of my knowledge, supplies the same rights to non-citizens as it does to citizens. And more significantly, to the extent citizenship marks the ordinary and enduring class of persons with full membership rights in a state, the constitution *must* have resources for distinguishing citizens from non-citizens, and likewise it *must* have resources for specifying how individuals can become citizens. It must have these resources—whether or not, as a matter of fact, foreign nationals happen to enjoy numerous civil rights—since the state's constitution must be able to identify to whom the rights of citizenship attach and for whom citizenship is accessible. A similar argument can be made that distinguishes lawful from unlawful residents, since in this case too there is a crucial boundary issue, but one determined by jurisdiction over territory rather than membership.
[3] The question of whether a non-citizen can participate in ordinary (non-political) civic life by working, going to school, accessing healthcare, and so on is an intermediate boundary question of much importance too. I limit my attention to entrance and membership, and since these are both essentially boundary questions, I refer to them somewhat interchangeably, notwithstanding the many different considerations that would bear on them in practice.

against the wishes of its administration. I also offer an interpretation of the federal Crown's positive constitutional authority to deal with foreign nationals that paves the way for a cosmopolitan approach to constitutionalism. In section III, I defend the cosmopolitan approach sketched above. Part of this argument will draw on intrinsic features of legality postulated by Thomas Hobbes, and part will draw on recent scholarship of Arash Abizadeh, Mattias Kumm, and Rainer Forst. Running through all four is an aversion to unilateralism and a concern to design public institutions capable of securing conditions of non-domination. The mortar that will hold the various pieces of the argument together is taken from my prior work—much of it with Evan Criddle—and recent scholarship of Eyal Benvenisti. In my writings with Criddle, sovereigns are conceived as fiduciaries of the people subject to their power, including resident and extraterritorial foreign nationals.[4] Under this conception, sovereignty is not a veil that international law sometimes pierces. Rather, it is a relational idea to which international law contributes institutional form and substantive content. In a discussion regarding the accountability of states to foreign stakeholders, Professor Benvenisti strikingly characterizes sovereigns as 'trustees of humanity', and sees in the trusteeship model a capacious structure at the global level for limiting sovereignty in favour of foreign nationals—'the entire system of state sovereignty is subject to the duty to respect human rights'.[5] Benvenisti's trustees-of-humanity approach affirms the important idea that legal consequences follow from states possessing sovereign powers that implicate the interests of humanity at large. In section IV, I argue that the duty of justification owed to migrants applies to citizens as well, and use the case of indigenous peoples as the argument's starting point. Canadian law has long recognized that the Crown has fiduciary responsibilities to Canada's First Nations, and part of those involve a duty of justification. Because this duty is partially constitutive of the state's legal authority vis-à-vis indigenous peoples, it is intrinsic to any constitutional order in which indigenous peoples are members. And because the relations between the state and non-indigenous individuals is also fiduciary, the duty of justification is owed to them too, and so forms part of the legal order they inhabit.

---

[4] See eg E. Fox-Decent, 'The Fiduciary Nature of State Legal Authority' (2005) 31 *Queen's Law Journal* 259, at 272 ('[t]he civil or political status of the person subject to state authority does not matter'); E. Fox-Decent, 'Is the Rule of Law Really Indifferent to Human Rights?' (2008) 27 *Law and Philosophy* 533, at 543 (affirming that 'subject' within the state–subject fiduciary relationship refers to 'anyone affected by an exercise of state power, including non-citizens within or outside the state's territorial jurisdiction'); E. Fox-Decent, 'From Fiduciary States to Joint Trusteeship of the Atmosphere: The Right to a Healthy Environment through a Fiduciary Prism', in K. Coghill, C. Sampford, and T. Smith (eds), *Fiduciary Duty and the Atmospheric Trust* (Burlington: Ashgate, 2012), 253–68 (arguing that states are joint trustees of the atmosphere on behalf of humanity); E. Criddle and E. Fox-Decent, 'A Fiduciary Theory of Jus Cogens' (2009) 34 *Yale Journal of International Law* 331, at 380–2 (discussing state obligations to respect the human rights of resident non-citizens, extraterritorially detained foreign nationals, and refugees); E. Criddle and E. Fox-Decent, 'The Fiduciary Constitution of Human Rights' (2009) 15 *Legal Theory* 301, at 301 ('human rights are best conceived as norms arising from a fiduciary relationship that exists between states (or statelike actors) and the citizens and noncitizens subject to their power'); E. Criddle and E. Fox-Decent, *International Law's Fiduciary Constitution* (New York: Oxford University Press, forthcoming) (discussing inter alia the cosmopolitan rights of civilians during hostilities, detained foreign nationals, and persons seeking asylum).

[5] E. Benvenisti, 'Sovereigns as Trustees of Humanity: On the Accountability of States to Foreign Stakeholders' (2013) 107 *American Journal of International Law* 295, at 307.

II. Unilateralism under Stress

In the late nineteenth century, publicist William Hall commented that '[i]t follows from the independence of a state that it may grant or refuse the privileges of political membership... Primarily therefore it is a question of municipal law to decide whether a given individual is to be considered a subject or citizen of a particular state.'[6] The Supreme Court of Canada has echoed this view in recent years, finding that '[t]he most fundamental principle of immigration law is that non-citizens do not have an unqualified right to enter or remain in Canada.'[7] The Court draws this 'fundamental principle' from the historical position of the common law, according to which 'an alien has no right to enter or remain in the country.'[8] Without such a right in place, the Court infers elsewhere that '[t]he Government has the right and duty to keep out and to expel aliens from this country if it considers it advisable to do so.'[9] To the extent foreign nationals have rights to remain in Canada, those rights are statutory in nature and subject to legislative amendment and extinguishment.[10] Canada's naturalization process is also a creature of statute and subject to amendment.[11] In short, the basic terms of entry and residence in Canada reflect the Westphalian understanding of sovereignty. Canada, like other states, asserts and exercises unilateral control over its borders and citizenship.

In various ways, however, international law mediates the relationship between some foreign nationals seeking to remain in Canada and Canada's immigration authorities. The refugee case is perhaps the most striking. Canada has ratified the 1951 Convention Relating to the Status of Refugees[12] and the 1967 Protocol Relating to the Status of Refugees.[13] Canada's Immigration and Refugee Protection Act (IRPA) incorporates word for word many of the Refugee Convention's provisions. Canada cannot return a person to her country of origin if she has a well-founded fear of persecution arising from grounds set out in the Convention (race, nationality, religion, membership of a particular social group, and political opinion). Canada has also ratified the Convention against Torture, which prohibits deportation if there are substantial grounds to believe the individual will be tortured.[14] Although Canadian jurisprudence has left open the possibility of deporting someone to torture in unspecified 'exceptional circumstances',[15] the general rule is that Canada cannot deport if the risk of torture is established. In

---

[6] W. E. Hall, *A Treatise on International Law* 2nd edn (Oxford: Clarendon Press, 1884), 200.
[7] *Medovarski v Canada (Minister of Citizenship and Immigration); Esteban v Canada (Minister of Citizenship and Immigration)* [2005] 2 SCR 539, para 46 (citing *Chiarelli v Canada (Minister of Employment and Immigration)* [1992] 1 SCR 711, 733).
[8] *Chiarelli*, above n 7, 733 (citing *R v Governor of Pentonville Prison* [1973] 2 All ER 741, 2 WLR 949; *Prata v Minister of Manpower and Immigration* [1976] 1 SCR 376).
[9] *Kindler v Canada (Minister of Justice)* [1991] 2 SCR 779, 834.
[10] Immigration and Refugee Protection Act 2001, SC 2001, c 27.
[11] Citizenship Act 1985, RSC 1985, c 29.
[12] Convention Relating to the Status of Refugees (Refugee Convention) (Geneva, 28 July 1951, 189 UNTS 137).
[13] Protocol Relating to the Status of Refugees (New York Protocol) (New York City, 31 January 1967, 606 UNTS 267).
[14] Convention against Torture and Other Cruel, Inhuman or Degrading Treatment or Punishment (Convention against Torture) (New York City, 10 December 1984, 1465 UNTS 85).
[15] *Suresh v Canada (Minister of Citizenship and Immigration)* [2002] 1 SCR 3.

addition to these substantive provisions, Canadian law guarantees refugee claimants an oral hearing as well as written reasons in the event of a negative determination.

Another set of pertinent immigration cases involves the intersection of international law and discretionary authority provided in the IRPA. The IRPA confers on decision-makers discretionary power to permit an individual to remain in Canada on humanitarian and compassionate grounds notwithstanding that they are otherwise inadmissible (s 67), and notwithstanding that they do not have authorization to remain in Canada (s 25). In *Baker v Canada (Ministry of Citizenship and Immigration)*,[16] one of the most important cases in Canadian administrative law, the Supreme Court found that the Convention on the Rights of the Child (CRC)[17] was relevant to assessing the legality of a discretionary decision over whether to grant relief from a deportation order to a mother of four Canadian-born children who overstayed a visitor's visa for eleven years. A majority drew on the common law's presumption of conformity—a principle of statutory interpretation according to which interpretations of domestic law that conform to international law are preferred—to insist that discretionary exercises of authority must take account of fundamental values articulated in international law. The fundamental value at stake in *Baker* was a concern for the children's best interests. Two judges dissented on this point, objecting that to rely on the CRC was to let international law into the domestic sphere without the imprimatur of Parliament, and therefore illegitimately, through 'the backdoor'.[18] The argument for cosmopolitanism in section III helps explain the legitimacy of the presumption of conformity and vindicates the *Baker* majority.

It bears underscoring that refugee claimants comprise a small minority of migrants who seek to enter Canada each year. And, in the years since *Baker*, the Court has at times taken a very 'hands off' approach to review of humanitarian and compassionate decisions, sometimes declining to give any consideration at all to international law.[19] In Canada's public law, the dominant approach to foreign nationals seeking to enter or remain is that they are at the mercy of the federal Crown. Section 91(25) of the Constitution Act 1867[20] allocates to Parliament legislative power over 'Naturalization and Aliens', an authority that legal officials presume is both plenary and exclusive. The power allocated under section 91(25), however, need not be read this way.

Canada's founding document could instead be read such that (i) it is taken to distribute only those powers a municipal constitution is capable of distributing; and (ii) the distribution is undertaken strictly for the purpose of delineating federal and provincial legislative competences.[21] This alternative reading implies that the exclusivity of

---

[16] *Baker v Canada (Ministry of Citizenship and Immigration)* [1999] 2 SCR 817, 174 DLR (4th) 193.
[17] Convention on the Rights of the Child (CRC) (New York City, 20 November 1989, 1577 UNTS 3).
[18] *Baker*, above n 16, 78–81.
[19] See *Canada (Citizenship and Immigration) v Khosa* [2009] 1 SCR 339.
[20] Constitution Act 1867 (UK), 30 & 31 Victoria, c 3.
[21] I am borrowing from the interpretation urged by Patrick Macklem and Michael Asch of section 91(24) of the Constitution Act 1867 with respect to Canada's First Nations: M. Asch and P. Macklem, 'Aboriginal Rights and Canadian Sovereignty' (1991) 29 *Alberta Law Review* 498. The powers contained within the Constitution Act 1867, they argue, are distributed between federal and provincial legislatures, but the federal Crown has jurisdiction to exercise constitutional powers over indigenous peoples only to the extent that those peoples have submitted to Crown jurisdiction through a fair and open treaty process.

federal jurisdiction over foreign nationals is in relation to provincial legislative power alone, and that this jurisdiction can be no more ample than a municipal constitution has authority to grant.[22] Arguably, for instance, federal authority over foreign nationals could not be read to include the power to strip them of their foreign citizenship while they reside in their home state. This extension of the section 91(25) power would contravene the international legal principle of sovereign equality under which states enjoy a right to non-interference against other states. In the ordinary case (there are myriad exceptions), a municipal constitution is presumed to apply, in whole or in part, to a fixed territory and the citizens and non-citizens within it. A common law judge tasked with interpreting a statute that purported to authorize the removal of citizenship from an extraterritorial foreign national would struggle to read it down so as to bring it into conformity with the principle of sovereign equality.[23] If the statute were wholly unambiguous, the judge would nevertheless have good reason to find that it exceeded Parliament's legislative authority. The judge might find it ultra vires on grounds that the Constitution cannot be constructed to authorize powers that contravene the principle of sovereign equality.[24] Or, if the judge hews closely to Dicey's view of parliamentary sovereignty, she might nonetheless conclude that our hypothetical statute constitutes an abuse of right. That is, strictly speaking Parliament has authority to legislate over foreign nationals in any way it pleases, but to do so in this way is an abuse of right because it is inconsistent with the purpose for which the authority was conferred.[25] If this is so, then federal legislative authority over foreign nationals is not unlimited, but rather is regulated in part by structural requirements of international legal order and in part by limits internal to the nature of legal powers (ie it is in the nature of any legal power that, however wide, it is susceptible to abuse).

The point of the foregoing analysis, together with the refugee cases and *Baker*, is to suggest that international law is capable of influencing the scope and exercise of the public powers allocated to each of Canada's legislative, administrative, and judicial branches by the Constitution Act 1867. While the cosmopolitanism defended in section III cuts against the grain of the dominant and unilateralist approach to dealing with foreign nationals, it does so in a manner that is consistent with the reading of

---

[22] *Mutatis mutandis*, the subsequent argument in the text is applicable to any state, whether federal or unitary, and whether there is a written constitution or not, since at its crux is a conceptual claim about the inherent power of a constitution to delegate authority to exercise power over foreign nationals. The particular form of the delegation and the history behind it—eg a 'constitutional moment' or a written constitution that emerges from a constituent assembly—is irrelevant. But it is important to see how the argument can arise from a concrete institutional setting, since part of the point is to provide a theory of constitutional legitimacy that explains salient features of actual constitutional law while providing pointers to how it might evolve in practice.

[23] Compare *Slaight Communications Inc v Davidson* [1989] 1 SCR 1038, 1056, 59 DLR (4th) 416 (per Dickson CJ) (affirming that international human rights should inform interpretation of rights enshrined in the Canadian Charter of Rights and Freedoms).

[24] For discussion of international law's evolving approach to citizenship, see P. Spiro, 'A New International Law of Citizenship' (2011) 105 *The American Journal of International Law* 694.

[25] Locke gives as an example of abuse of right a military commander who has absolute authority over his soldiers—he has authority to order them to their deaths, and authority to order their deaths for disobedience—but who nonetheless would abuse his absolute right of command were he to take 'one farthing' from them for his personal use: J. Locke, *Two Treatises of Government*, P. Laslett (ed) (Oxford: Oxford University Press, 1960), bk II, ch 11, 361–2, para 139.

section 91(25) sketched above, and in a way that justifies the IRPA's implementation of the Refugee Convention and the *Baker* majority's use of the CRC.

III. Cosmopolitan Legality

The writings of Thomas Hobbes may seem a wildly unpromising starting point for the development of a theory of cosmopolitan constitutionalism. The received view of international relations is that Hobbes is an 'extreme Realist'[26] who surpasses Machiavelli in this regard by tying a celebration of realpolitik to an implacable human disposition for more and more power. Hans Morgenthau interprets Hobbes as averring 'an urge toward expansion which knows no rational limits, feeds on its own successes and, if not stopped by a superior force, will go on to the confines of the political world'.[27] The received view of his political and legal theory is hardly more encouraging. Hobbes is widely regarded as a defender of absolute state authority in which the sovereign can act extralegally at his sole discretion.[28]

Hobbes's conception of legal order, however, is eminently suited to cosmopolitan purposes, though I will give only the briefest sketch. In an early argument in *Leviathan* that captures the core of Hobbes's general argument for the state, Hobbes lays down that in the event of a controversy the parties must resort to a judge or arbitrator if their dispute is to be resolved justly.[29] The judge must abide by various 'laws of nature' or legal principles internal to adjudication: she must treat the parties as equals; she cannot be a party to the dispute; she cannot have (or appear to have) a stake in the outcome; and, if possible, she must determine the facts on the basis of independent corroborating evidence rather than rely on the parties' testimony alone.[30] When the judge is called to interpret and apply a statute or the common law, she must at all times seek an equitable construction and application of the relevant law.[31] So there are institutional, formal, and substantive aspects to Hobbes's legal theory. The institutional dimension is third-party dispute resolution, the formal element consists in principles internal to adjudication, and the substantive aspect is an orientation toward equitable outcomes.

---

[26] M. Wight, *International Theory: The Three Traditions*, G. Wight and B. Porter (eds) (Leicester: Leicester University Press, 1991), 36.

[27] H. Morgenthau, *Politics Among Nations: The Struggle for Power and Peace* 2nd edn (New York: Alfred A. Knopf, 1955), 52. For three important correctives to the received view, see N. Malcolm, 'Hobbes's Theory of International Relations', in N. Malcolm, *Aspects of Hobbes* (Oxford: Clarendon Press, 2002), 432–56; L. May, *Limiting Leviathan: Hobbes on Law and International Affairs* (Oxford: Oxford University Press, 2013); and D. Dyzenhaus, 'Hobbes on the International Rule of Law' (2014) 28 *Ethics & International Affairs* 53.

[28] See K. Hoekstra, 'Hobbes and the Foole' (1997) 25 *Political Theory* 620; T. Poole, 'Hobbes on Law and Prerogative', in D. Dyzenhaus and T. Poole (eds), *Hobbes and the Law* (Cambridge: Cambridge University Press, 2012), 68–96. For an antidote, see D. Dyzenhaus, 'Hobbes on the Authority of Law', in D. Dyzenhaus and T. Poole (eds), *Hobbes and the Law* (Cambridge: Cambridge University Press, 2012), 186–209. For my own doubts about the received view, see 'Hobbes's Relational Theory: Beneath Power and Consent', in D. Dyzenhaus and T. Poole (eds), *Hobbes and the Law* (Cambridge: Cambridge University Press, 2012), 118–44; and 'Unseating Unilateralism', in L. Austin and D. Klimchuk (eds), *Private Law and the Rule of Law* (Oxford: Oxford University Press, 2014), 116–38.

[29] T. Hobbes, *Leviathan: With Selected Variants from the Latin Edition of 1668*, Edwin Curley (ed) (Indianapolis: Hackett Publishing, 1994), ch V, 23, para 3.

[30] Ibid ch VX, 97–9, paras 23, 31–4.   [31] Ibid ch XXVI, 178–9, 183, paras 14–15, 26.

Underwriting all these features of Hobbes's legal order is a commitment to the idea that no private party is entitled to dictate terms or impose justice claims on another; justice is the domain of the public sphere alone. Sustaining this prohibition on unilateralism is a commitment to the equality of legal subjects and their interest in living together peacefully and free of domination. How might these various ideas contribute to our understanding of the requirements of legality when states and foreign nationals interact?

To see how they may, we need to reflect for a moment on the circumstances that attend the state–foreign national interaction when non-citizens attempt to cross the state's border or become citizens. To the extent that the Westphalian model of sovereignty prevails such that entrance and membership is at the discretion of the state, the relationship between the state and the outsider at the border is one of pure domination. The state has de facto control of the border and, under the Westphalian model, unfettered discretion with respect to whether or not the non-citizen can enter. The state may adopt policies that are generous to migrants, but it is under no obligation to do so. Indeed, even if a state were to adopt an open-border policy, non-citizens would still suffer domination, since the state could at any time change its policy with impunity. Like the benevolent slave master who doesn't interfere in his slave's life but could at his will, the Westphalian state holds a whip it can crack at any time.

In practice, immigration policies vary significantly from one state to the next, but they are all the same in one crucial respect: they are all enforced against outsiders through the threat or use of violence the state claims a unilateral right to deploy. It is true that law authorizes the threat or use of force, and the relevant law may have been promulgated democratically, but it is the law of a state with which the foreign national may have had no prior contact. So the legitimacy of the threat or use of legal violence against the outsider cannot issue from its democratic credentials, since it has no such credentials in relation to non-citizens. One way to address this deficit would be to posit, with Arash Abizadeh, that the demos is in principle unbounded, and therefore border policy must be determined by institutions that allow the effective participation of foreigners as well as citizens.[32] This prescription, in part, seeks to avoid domination through the construction of institutions capable of supplying a democratic justification of border policy to every person affected by it.

Hobbes's legal theory, charitably elaborated, offers a parallel diagnosis of the legitimacy deficit attending border control regimes, and more significantly for present purposes, it points to features of a constitutional framework that could address the deficit from a distinctively legal point of view. From a Hobbesian legal perspective, the legitimacy deficit flows from the state's claim to unilateral authority regarding any sort of border dispute it might have with foreigners. While the state for Hobbes is the embodiment par excellence of public authority, the state and the outsider confront each other at the border in a state of nature, for they are not subject to a common authority. Yet like private parties to a dispute in the state of nature, if their controversy is to be decided

---

[32] A. Abizadeh, 'Democratic Theory and Border Coercion: No Right to Unilaterally Control Your Own Borders' (2008) 36 *Political Theory* 37.

justly, then they must submit their controversy to a third-party adjudicator, since neither can claim unilateral authority to decide the matter.[33] The adjudicator must treat the state and the non-citizen impartially and as parties with equal standing, and must decide the issue with an eye to an equitable outcome. I will discuss momentarily some of the plausible considerations the state and the outsider might adduce to advance their respective causes, and on which party the burden of proof lies. But we can see immediately that one major argument is blocked from the get-go: the state cannot close its border on the basis that it has unilateral authority to do so. For the state to comply with the requirements of legality vis-à-vis non-citizens, it must be prepared to submit border disputes to independent review.[34]

The obvious institutional home of such review is international law. Importantly, however, this does not mean that new institutions have to be built from whole cloth. Cosmopolitan constitutionalism is not strained by the state exercising front-line decision-making power over border questions—so long as independent review is possible—since international law itself can be understood to delegate this authority to the state. Furthermore, in the event of an adverse decision, the foreigner's first course of redress is (and ought to be) the national judiciary (or in civilian jurisdictions, the Council of State) of the foreign state. As one Canadian Supreme Court judge put it, international human rights norms 'are applied consistently, with an international vision and on the basis of international experience. Thus our courts—and many other national courts—are truly becoming international courts in many areas involving the rule of law'.[35] Having exhausted all domestic avenues of recourse, the individual should be able to seek review at the international level. If the decision imperils the foreign national's human rights, she can file a complaint with the UN Human Rights Committee, assuming the state is a party to a relevant human rights treaty the Committee

---

[33] Hobbes thought that, *as a general matter*, individuals in the state of nature are not under a positive duty (a duty in *foro externo*) to abide by the laws of nature, including, presumably, the law of nature stipulating that disputants must submit their controversies to third-party arbitration. If one party were to abide by the laws of nature with no common authority in place to compel the other's obedience, then *generally* the co-operator would make herself a 'prey to others', which no party can be obligated to do. Hobbes, above n 29, ch XV, 99, para 36. Hobbes, however, also suggested that were a party in the state of nature able to perform her law-of-nature duty *without* making herself a prey to others, then she had a duty to do so. For example, in the case of second-performers of contractual duties, the second-performer cannot be played for a sucker because the other party has performed already, and so the second-performer is duty-bound to perform. Ibid ch XIV, 86, para 27. In the case of the state and the outsider, it is hard to see how the state could be made a 'prey' of the outsider by submitting the legality of its entrance and membership decisions to impartial review. If the outsider loses on review, she is liable to deportation and exclusion from membership, since she cannot impose her will on the state. The outsider's relative impotence immunizes the state from being played for a sucker, and thus places it under an obligation to submit to impartial review.
[34] Of course, Hobbes thought that peace and security could be achieved through the sovereignty of separate states, and he probably would have been hostile to the idea of independent review of border questions. Depending on the details of the institution, he may have thought that such review would place an international sovereign atop the national sovereign, dividing and weakening sovereignty. If this is right, then the argument in the text should be read simply as one grounded on Hobbesian principles concerning the requirements of legality. With this caveat in place, it is noteworthy that Hobbes laid down as a law of nature the principle that 'all men that mediate peace be allowed safe conduct'. Ibid ch XV, 99, para 29. This principle points to both support for an inchoate institution of international law and a restriction on the sovereign's authority over his borders.
[35] G. V. La Forest, 'The Expanding Role of the Supreme Court of Canada in International Law Issues' (1996) 34 *The Canadian Yearbook of International Law* 89, at 100.

oversees.[36] And, as I will argue, cosmopolitan constitutionalism supports turning the current regime of border control on its head by requiring states to discharge a weighty justificatory burden should they wish to close their border to peaceful migrants.

Mattias Kumm characterizes helpfully the relationship contemplated here between international and domestic law. He claims that the two stand in a relation of 'mutual dependence'.[37] Whereas the legitimacy of international law depends in part on states having an adequate constitutional structure, the legitimacy of national law depends in part 'on being adequately integrated into an appropriately structured international legal system'.[38] The leading standards of constitutional legitimacy—democracy, human rights, and the rule of law—are shared by national and international law alike, and are 'to be derived from an integrative conception of public law that spans the national-international divide'.[39] Crucially, because sovereign states can engage in activities that impose '*justice-sensitive* externalities' on outsiders—eg decisions about carbon emissions—and about which there is pervasive and reasonable disagreement, there can be no self-standing national constitutional legitimacy.[40] Echoing Hobbes's conception of legality, Kumm claims that international law must settle such matters because 'any claim by one state to be able to resolve these issues authoritatively and unilaterally amounts to a form of domination'.[41] Indeed, Kumm argues that just as constitutionalism at the domestic level is necessary to thwart private forms of domination endemic to the state of nature, so too is it necessary internationally, given the problem of justice-sensitive externalities.

Kumm discusses borders as a case of a structural justice-sensitive externality, one that arises as a consequence of a world with multiple sovereign states asserting territorial sovereignty.[42] Borders present a *structural* externality because they are built into the fabric of the international state system: no individual or state can avoid or eliminate them. And borders create a *justice-sensitive* externality because they limit the liberty of individuals who wish to cross them. Kumm nonetheless suggests that the general right to exclude implied by the contemporary border regime follows as an 'external corollary' of the 'claim to self-government—to use the territory within the state as is deemed desirable by "We the People" organizing our lives together'.[43] He tentatively claims that states can rightfully claim exclusive jurisdiction over territory, and unilaterally exclude

---

[36] The Committee oversees implementation of nine human rights treaties: International Convention on Civil and Political Rights (ICCPR) (New York City, 16 December 1966, 999 UNTS 171); Convention against Torture, above n 14; International Convention on the Elimination of All Forms of Racial Discrimination (ICERD) (New York City, 4 January 1969, 660 UNTS 195); Convention on the Elimination of All Forms of Discrimination against Women (CEDAW) (New York City, 18 December 1979, 1249 UNTS 13); Convention on the Rights of Persons with Disabilities (CRPD) (New York City, 30 March 2007, 2515 UNTS 3); International Convention for the Protection of All Persons from Enforced Disappearance (CPED) (Paris, 20 December 2006, UN Doc A/RES/61/177); International Convention on the Protection of the Rights of All Migrant Workers and Members of Their Families (CMW) (New York City, 18 December 1990, 2220 UNTS 3); International Convention on Economic, Social and Cultural Rights (ICESCR) (New York City, 16 December 1966, 993 UNTS 3); and Convention on the Rights of the Child (CRC) (New York City, 20 November 1989, 1577 UNTS 3).

[37] M. Kumm, 'Constitutionalism and the Cosmopolitan State' (2013) *NYU Public Law and Legal Theory Working Papers*, Paper 423, at 8.

[38] Ibid 8–9.   [39] Ibid 9.   [40] Ibid 9–10 (emphasis in original).

[41] Ibid 10.   [42] Ibid 15–17.   [43] Ibid 15.

outsiders, so long as a Lockean proviso is satisfied under which the excluded party, in a relevant sense, is made no worse off. Translating Locke's proviso on appropriation to the context of exclusionary borders, Kumm suggests that the proviso is met if 'the person denied entry [has] access to the territory of a state where, at the very least, his or her rights are not violated in a serious way'.[44]

Arthur Ripstein reaches the same conclusion on borders from a Kantian perspective. He claims that the state's right to exclude outsiders is justified because the exclusion 'does not interfere with any of their rights'.[45] When other states restrict your ability to reside within it, there is no compromise of your cosmopolitan right because 'they limit only your ability to achieve what you wish, rather than your ability to use what you have to set and pursue your own purposes'.[46] Both Kumm and Ripstein think that states must take in refugees, however, since the right to exclude has an 'internal limit' in that the foreigner must have somewhere else where she can safely go, the absence of which would make her very existence 'subject to the choice of another'.[47]

Kumm's and Ripstein's defences of a general right to exclude are suspect on several grounds. First, the simple claim to self-government over a given territory does not *ipso facto* imply a general right to exclude. It all depends on the content one invests in the idea of self-government, and to invest it upfront with the power to exclude is to beg the question rather starkly.

Second, if taken on its face, the argument could apply to citizens as much as to foreigners, so long as citizen-deportees (and perhaps their property) could be sent somewhere safe where they would enjoy full citizenship. On Ripstein's construal, the deporting state would limit only their citizens' ability to achieve what they wish. On Kumm's account, the citizen-deportee would be no worse off in the relevant sense.[48]

Third, it is unclear how one could limit the argument to states alone. Why couldn't self-governing provinces or cities assert a general right to exclude, so long as those excluded had somewhere else to go? Given the diversity in territorial extent, demographic composition, and population size of recognized states, and the accidents of history that have determined the existence of many, it is hard to imagine that states represent the unit of self-governance to which a general right to exclude would uniquely apply.

Fourth, both Ripstein and Kumm analogize territory to private property, and infer that the right to exclude constitutive of the latter is implicit in the former. But territory

---

[44] Ibid 16.
[45] A. Ripstein, *Force and Freedom: Kant's Legal and Political Philosophy* (Cambridge, Mass.: Harvard University Press, 2009), 296.
[46] Ibid 297.   [47] Ibid 298.
[48] Ripstein and Kumm could reply that the deportation of citizens denies their vested right to membership in *this* state, whereas prospective immigrants have no such vested right. The reply begs the question, however, since it assumes without more that investiture alone gives the citizen a special—if not absolute—right to remain. A defender of authoritarian state power could help herself to the resources offered by Ripstein and Kumm, and then question whether *any* individual, citizen or not, is necessarily immune to deportation, assuming respect for the deportee's human rights, person, and property. Under these assumptions, the deportee would retain her ability to use what she has to set and pursue her own purposes, albeit not in the context she 'wished' (Ripstein), and her human rights would be respected (Kumm). Note that any purported right to citizenship could be a universal human right only if the right is to world citizenship or to citizenship in some state somewhere, but not necessarily the citizenship in the state of one's birth or choice.

and property are fundamentally distinct. A state's territory is quintessentially a public domain, whereas private property is (no surprise) private. You may be deprived of the ability to 'use what you have to set and pursue your own purposes' without some exclusive rights to some private property. And private property as such, on many accounts, may lose its character as property without the owner having an entitlement to exclusive use and possession of the thing owned. But ordinarily, neither the state nor its members will be deprived of the ability to set and pursue legitimate purposes by the arrival of a peaceful migrant. Nor is there reason to think that the territory of a self-governing people will lose its character as territory—even *their* territory—by requiring the state to justify decisions to exclude outsiders. There are indeed reasons to limit immigration in certain cases, discussed below, such as when large-scale and rapid migration threatens to overrun a community. But contestable reasons such as these point to perhaps the most important objection to state assertions of unilateral authority over borders and the lack of an independent arbiter.

Kumm's and Ripstein's arguments go to the merits of the question of whether a state has a general right to exclude outsiders. Those arguments proceed as if the nature of this right were self-defining, and as if its application were self-executing. Defending the right to exclude is an especially tall order for Ripstein, since he tries to square it with Kant's insistence on a duty of hospitality that gives to every human being the right to enter foreign states for the purposes of temporary visitation.[49] But what counts as a visit, and what is the limit of temporary? Ripstein insists that the state is entitled to determine these questions unilaterally, but it is unclear why this would be any more legitimate from a Kantian perspective that honours the cosmopolitan right of hospitality than an individual enforcing his understanding of his provisional private rights in the state of nature. As between the state and the foreigner alone, there is a clash of rights and no institutional mechanism to provide for their reconciliation.

In Kumm's case, the same issue arises with respect to determining what will count as satisfying the Lockean proviso. Recall that for Locke, an appropriator in the state of nature must leave the propertyless no worse off through an act of appropriation. Kumm claims that we can interpret 'no worse off' to mean coercive deportation to a home state that does not violate the foreigner's human rights. But why should this be the metric, rather than, say, the migrant's estimation of where her best life prospects lie? And why should the state get to determine unilaterally what counts as 'no worse off'? Kumm insists that for the state to claim 'authority to resolve questions of justice concerning outsiders, who per definition have no equal standing in the domestic policy formation, is an act of domination'.[50] Arguably, a state's claim to determine the content of the Lockean proviso is one such act.

The deep structural problem with Kumm's and Ripstein's arguments lies in their implicit assumption that philosophical inquiry into the scope of national authority over foreigners is an adequate substitute for international determination of intractably contestable issues that attend border disputes. For Hobbes, by contrast, for whom '[a]ll laws, written and unwritten, have need of interpretation',[51] the institutional question

---

[49] Ripstein, above n 45, 296.   [50] Kumm, above n 37, 14.
[51] Hobbes, above n 29, ch XXVI, 180, para 21.

of 'Who decides?' is always at least as important as the substantive question 'On what basis is the decision made?'[52] The two questions are categorically distinct and cannot be collapsed into each other, for it does not follow from the fact that one has a right that one also has authority to determine its scope and legal effects. In sum, Kumm makes a compelling case that national constitutional legitimacy is not self-standing, but neglects to follow through on the institutional implications of his argument when he turns his attention to state borders. Kumm's constitutionalism with respect to borders, by its own lights, is not cosmopolitan enough.

Assuming, then, that border control policy and decisions call for the intervention of international law and independent institutions to apply it, what is the front-line or primary duty of the state to migrants? I argue that, other things being equal, if the state wishes to close its borders to peaceful migrants, then it owes them a duty of justification. In principle, the duty applies to policy formation as well as individual border decisions. As Rainer Forst argues in his recent defence of a 'constructivist' theory of human rights, 'there is at least *one* fundamental moral demand that no culture or society may reject: the unconditional claim to be respected as someone who deserves to be given justifying reasons for the actions, rules, or structures to which he or she is subject.'[53] Under Forst's theory, these justifications are to be structured by considerations of reciprocity and generality.[54] The reciprocity condition states that an individual cannot make demands for herself that she would deny her addressee; one cannot make an exception for oneself. The generality condition stipulates that 'in moral contexts the community of justification may not be arbitrarily restricted, but rather must include all those affected by actions or norms in morally relevant ways.'[55] Given the entrenched nature of the domination that pervades contemporary border regimes, borders are a 'moral context' to which the duty of justification applies, and so it applies to all who are affected, including outsiders. Significantly, the duty is borne by the state, since the state produces the moral context of domination typical of border regimes.

Forst's account is very rich and I cannot go into its details here. However, it is unclear that reciprocity and generality alone are enough to guide the development of border policy in the event of reasonable disagreement. Kumm's and Ripstein's defences of unilateral border control are fully consistent with reciprocity and generality: the claim to unilateral border control is made on behalf of states and their members with the intent that all states be equally entitled to maintain closed borders, except if doing so would leave the would-be migrant with nowhere safe to go. Similarly, at the level of implementation and review of border decisions, an official or judge tasked with justifying an

---

[52] While for Hobbes the ultimate decision-maker is the sovereign, the point of instituting the sovereign is to secure peace through the establishment of public institutions whose authority depends on their impartiality as well as their effectiveness. In the cosmopolitan context, the suggestion in the text is simply that the Hobbesian distinction between institutional and substantive matters can be extended to explain the institutional authority of international law as arbiter between states and foreign nationals. Kumm and Ripstein ultimately go wrong by collapsing the distinction in their analyses of border regimes. Moreover, were they to insist that the state necessarily confronts the outsider at the border in an intractable state of nature in which Westphalian sovereignty must be presumed, they would, in my view, give up on the possibility of legality governing the state–foreigner interaction at the border.

[53] R. Forst, *The Right to Justification* (New York: Columbia University Press, 2011), 209.

[54] Ibid 209–14.   [55] Ibid 214.

adverse decision to a migrant could point to arguments akin to Kumm's or Ripstein's to satisfy the Forstian duty of justification. Forst himself defends a right of asylum, but is silent on the more general issue of territorial borders and membership.[56] He claims that respect for and discursive use of a reciprocal and general moral right of justification can ultimately produce just legal institutions. Still, it is hard to see, from this moral theory alone, how such institutions are to guide the development of border policy or serve as more than transmission belts for whichever policy is ultimately adopted.

One might be tempted by Catherine Dauvergne's argument that liberal political theory is simply incapable of cognizing border and membership issues as matters of justice.[57] Dauvergne argues that because the self-governing state plays such a central role in liberal theory, liberalism views immigration policy through the lens of humanitarianism and charity rather than justice. Thus, liberalism appears to give no guidance on the question, 'How many migrants does justice demand we let in this year?', and generally assumes that 'we' have unilateral authority to make such decisions however we wish.[58] Border governance can become a matter of constitutional justice and legality, however, if we draw out various implications of Hobbes's institutional account of constitutionalism.

The most significant implication is relational in nature, and takes its bearings from the morally salient features of the actual relationship of authority that exists between legal institutions and the people—citizens and non-citizens alike—subject to their power. As noted in the introduction, Evan Criddle and I have defended elsewhere the idea that public authorities—states and non-state public actors—stand in a fiduciary or trust-like relation to citizens and foreign nationals subject to their power.[59] The argument for viewing states as fiduciaries begins by discerning the constitutive features of fiduciary relations from familiar cases in private law (eg trust–beneficiary, lawyer–client, parent–child, director–corporation, etc.), and then moves to posit that the state–subject relationship has these features, too. Fiduciary relations in private law arise whenever the entrusted party possesses discretionary power of a certain kind over the beneficiary or her interests, and the beneficiary is in principle or in practice unable or unwilling to exercise this power. The discretionary power at issue must be other-regarding, purposive, and institutional. It must be other-regarding in the strictly factual sense that another person is subject to it. The power must be purposive in that it is held for certain purposes, such as an agent's power to contract on behalf of her principal. Lastly, the power must be institutional in that it is situated within a legally permissible institution, such as the family. Indeed the parent–child relationship is paradigmatic: the child cannot consent to the relationship, so the law sets the terms and entrusts the parent with

---

[56] Ibid 225.

[57] C. Dauvergne, 'Amorality and Humanitarianism in Immigration Law' (1999) 37 *Osgoode Hall Law Journal* 597.

[58] There are, of course, notable exceptions: Abizadeh, above n 32; J. Carens, *The Ethics of Immigration* (New York: Oxford University Press, 2013); M. Blake and M. Risse, 'Immigration and Original Ownership of the Earth' (2009) 23 *Notre Dame Journal of Law, Ethics and Public Policy* 133; C. Kukathas, 'The Case for Open Migration', in A. I. Cohen and C. H. Wellman (eds), *Contemporary Debates in Applied Ethics* (Oxford: Blackwell Publishing, 2005), 207–20, at 208.

[59] See above n 4.

authority over the child. In these and other fiduciary circumstances, the main duty of the power holder is to act without regard to her own interests and in what she reasonably perceives as the best interests of the beneficiary. When there are multiple beneficiaries subject to the same power, the basic duty is to act selflessly, even-handedly, and with due regard for the beneficiaries' legitimate interests.

The legislative, judicial, and administrative branches of the state all possess powers that are other-regarding, purposive, and institutional. Moreover, private parties as such are not entitled to exercise these public powers, since no private party is entitled to set unilaterally the terms of interaction with another. It follows that the state and its institutions are in a fiduciary relationship to the people subject to their powers, including foreign nationals at their borders. The state's overarching fiduciary duty is to provide a regime of secure and equal freedom under the rule of law. This duty is a necessary feature of the fiduciary model because it explains the fiduciary principle's authorization of state power on behalf of every person subject to it: public power is authorized to protect individuals from unilateralism, and no such protection is universal unless every legal actor in the state, including the sovereign, is subject to law.

The state's constitutional legal authority to establish a regime of equal freedom flows from two intertwined sources: a power-conferring fiduciary principle that is intrinsic to domestic legal order, and international law. International law authorizes the state to govern domestically and represent its people internationally in a manner similar to the way municipal law authorizes parents to govern their children and directors to govern their corporations. To understand the internal constitution of parental and directorial authority, we need to examine the structure of parent–child and director–corporation relations. The dutiful state does not micromanage those relations, but rather establishes a framework within which their participants can interact with each other and with third parties on terms of equal freedom. If parents or directors breach their fiduciary obligations or wrong third parties, the state will intercede. Likewise, the principal role of international law is to establish an international legal order in which states can interact on terms of equal freedom with their citizens, with non-citizens, and with other states. So long as a state respects the sovereignty of other states and complies with the constitutional requirements of legality that arise from its fiduciary position vis-à-vis citizens and foreign nationals, its actions will be considered authorized under international law and its autonomy will be protected. Under the fiduciary theory, this is the overarching structure of cosmopolitan constitutionalism, a structure within which domestic law and international law each have a role.[60]

---

[60] Of course, when a state commits a wrong under international law against another state or a non-state actor, the intervention of international law is likely to be less systematic and effective than the intervention of municipal law in the case of an individual committing a domestic wrong. Yet so long as international law supplies public legal standards against which state action may be properly assessed, it thereby supplies authoritative standards deployable by international adjudicatory bodies, such as the UN Human Rights Committee and the International Court of Justice. Their determinations are authoritative from a Hobbesian legal point of view independently of whether they are enforceable. Furthermore, even in the absence of formal institutions, the public standards of international law arguably provide valuable resources for critical scrutiny of state action. On the possibility of a Hobbesian international law without third-party institutions, see Dyzenhaus, above n 27.

Let us turn now to the requirements of cosmopolitan legality that regulate the inter-action of states and outsiders at the border. These interactions cannot be regulated justly by national law alone because national law is foreign law to the outsider. For the state to assert unilateral and exclusive authority in this domain is akin to an indi-vidual in the state of nature insisting on authority to set the conditions on which she can appropriate common land. A Kantian sceptic might reply that the state is different because it constitutes a rightful condition of self-governing persons, and so unlike the individual in the state of nature, it has authority to take up the means necessary for maintaining a rightful condition for its people.[61] These means necessarily include ter-ritory because human beings are corporeal and require physical space. This reply, how-ever, overshoots the mark.

That the state has authority to establish a rightful condition within territorial borders does not imply that the state must have unilateral authority capable of barring outsid-ers from entering. It is perfectly conceivable for states to establish jointly an interna-tional legal regime capable of governing migration, possibly with the participation of transnational non-state actors to represent the interests of migrants, along the lines Abizadeh suggests. Indeed, the fiduciary theory of sovereignty arguably implies that states have a cosmopolitan duty to do this, since for them to fail to do so is for them to insist on unilateralism against foreign nationals at their borders. States within such an international legal order would give laws to themselves in a way that is structurally identical to the way Kantians claim that citizens in a rightful condition give national laws to themselves, thereby providing for, rather than abridging, their equal freedom.[62] I cannot defend this admittedly sweeping proposition here, and raise it only to ques-tion further the notion that states must have unilateral jurisdiction over their borders to be self-governing.

International law has moved piecemeal towards constitutionalizing a cosmopolitan regime of border control, as the Refugee Convention and the CRC discussed in section II attest. But even in the absence of a universal and comprehensive international border regime, the fiduciary theory offers valuable guidance to the cosmopolitan legal duty owed by states to would-be entrants. I argue now that states have a defeasible legal duty to let peaceful outsiders into their territory, and eventually to grant them full member-ship should they wish to acquire it. The state's duty is owed directly to non-citizens, and it is a legal duty because it is drawn from the state's dual fiduciary positions.

At the global level, states are joint trustees of the earth's surface on behalf of humanity,[63] including the individual at the border. While the state is permitted to favour its

---

[61] Nagel interprets Hobbes to the same effect, noting that Hobbes compares international relations to the state of nature, but that because states provide peace and security for their people, there is not the 'misery' in international relations one finds in the pre-political state of nature. T. Nagel, 'The Problem of Global Justice' (2005) 33 *Philosophy & Public Affairs* 113, at 117 (citing Hobbes, above n 29, ch XIII, 78, para 12). As noted, a strong reply to this interpretation is Malcolm, above n 27.

[62] Ripstein, above n 45, 182–231.

[63] See Fox-Decent, 2012, above n 4. In this paper I derived joint trusteeship of the atmosphere from the spillover effects of state regulation of carbon emissions. If borders present structural spillover effects arising from international law's collective assignment to states of territorial sovereignty over the earth's surface, as Kumm contends, then arguably joint trusteeship of the earth's surface could also be derived from global spillover effects of state sovereignty at the local level, though I will not pursue this here.

nationals in various ways for purposes of collective self-determination, its claim to territorial sovereignty can be legitimate vis-à-vis foreign nationals only if the state's claim to territory can be understood to be made *on behalf of them* as well as on behalf of its citizens. Were the state's claim to territory not made on behalf of humanity generally, it would amount to a sectional demand akin to an assertion of noble privilege. The trustee-of-humanity model[64] allows states to claim territory on behalf of humanity because individual states, in their capacity as territorial authorities, are conceived as co-representatives of humanity. As trustees as well as representatives, however, states cannot treat peaceful migrants with indifference. The state's position as trustee combines with Forst's universal right of justification to yield the following cosmopolitan and constitutional principle: the state is entitled to coercively bar peaceful outsiders from entering its territory only if it supplies a compelling justification for doing so. The idea is to extend to ordinary migrants Benvenisti's view on persons seeking 'to find refuge elsewhere' that the state, as a trustee of humanity, is under an obligation 'not to deny entry to migrants or refugees without taking into account the asylum seekers' individual concerns and without at least providing justification for their exclusion'.[65]

The state's second fiduciary position is specific to the state–outsider encounter at the border: the state stands in a concrete fiduciary relationship to the outsider because their relationship exhibits the constitutive properties of fiduciary relations. The state possesses discretionary and administrative power over the border that the outsider, as a private party, is not entitled to exercise. But for the state's possession and exercise of its border authority to be legitimate, it must satisfy the institutional and substantive requirements that flow from the state's twin fiduciary positions. The Hobbesian institutional requirement is that its authority must be reviewable by an independent institution—possibly a national court, possibly an international review body—and, substantively, this institution must have authority to hold the state accountable to international standards that do not favour, or appear to favour, either the state or the foreigner.[66] A further and more general substantive requirement, as noted above in the trustee-of-humanity discussion, is that the state's exercise of its border authority must be interpretable as an exercise of power made on behalf of all who are affected by it; that is, the state's inhabitants *and* the foreign national. This substantive requirement derives from the power-conferring fiduciary principle inherent to concrete fiduciary relations as well as international law, both of which authorize state power on behalf of

---

[64] See Benvenisti, above n 5 (positing states as trustees of humanity, in part, to provide for state accountability to foreign nationals affected by state policies).

[65] Ibid 311. See also B. Ackerman, *Social Justice in the Liberal State* (New Haven: Yale University Press, 1980), 93–5 (affirming that exclusionary decisions must be justified to those denied entry, and that such justification, to be adequate, must be grounded on the threat posed by the admission of outsiders to the viability of liberal institutions).

[66] I cannot in this chapter develop a position on the 'convergence thesis' according to which domestic courts are advised to converge on the same methods and rules of interpretation used by international forums. It would be enough for present purposes that national courts were independent of their administrations, and that they took account of international norms and the interests of foreign nationals as they held their governments to account through the duty of justification. For critical discussion of the convergence thesis, see O. Frishman and E. Benvenisti, 'National Courts and Interpretative Approaches to International Law: The Case against Convergence', Global Trust Working Paper 8/2014, available at http://globaltrust.tau.ac.il/publications.

every person subject to it. This is the crystallization of cosmopolitan constitutionalism at the border, and what it means for the state to be a trustee of humanity as well as a fiduciary of its people.

The state's defeasible duty to let in peaceful foreigners, then, follows from the outsider's call on the state's public co-stewardship of the earth's surface on behalf of humanity, and limits intrinsic to the state's fiduciary authority, limits that require all exercises of state power to be justified to the persons over whom it is exercised. Unlike the case of private property from which individuals can ordinarily exclude others on a whim,[67] the state's territory is public, and so exclusions from it cannot be made on an arbitrary basis. In the standard case, a single peaceful migrant poses no threat at all to the state. Thus, her call on the state's co-stewardship of the earth's surface together with the state's concrete fiduciary relationship to her places the state under a defeasible duty to let her in. The open-borders duty is necessarily defeasible, however, because the state is a fiduciary of its people too, and must provide for their security. But importantly, because the state-as-trustee-of-humanity cannot treat the outsider at the border with indifference, it has a legal duty to provide a public and reviewable justification of any decision to restrict a foreigner's right of entrance, a justification that must take seriously the outsider's status as an equal co-beneficiary of the state's trusteeship of humanity.

While much depends on the circumstances of the receiving state or polity, there are, in my view, a significant number of prima facie plausible justifications for refusing entry or membership to a peaceful outsider. Large-scale migration to a scantily populated polity may pose a serious threat to the survival of its members' culture or language (eg large-scale non-indigenous migration to autonomous indigenous territory, such as that carved out by the 1998 Nisga'a Agreement in favour of the approximately 6,000 Nisga'a of northern British Columbia).[68] Likewise, sudden large-scale migration may threaten to overwhelm public services such as healthcare, education, housing, and social welfare services. These sorts of concerns and others may, in appropriate circumstances, warrant restrictions on immigration. Moreover, the cosmopolitan state is entitled to make these kinds of determinations provisionally, and it is entitled to treat its people as its predominant—but not exclusive—moral concern. Under the theory of cosmopolitan constitutionalism urged here, however, the state must publicly justify these determinations, taking account of international norms, and ultimately it must be prepared to submit its justification to independent review.

A sceptic may think that this proposal goes too far, and that so long as international law ensures that everyone has somewhere to live free of abuse, then there is no reason to think that states must presumptively let in peaceful outsiders. The sceptic might grant that the state is a trustee of humanity under international law charged with co-stewardship of the earth's surface, but then insist that its mandate as a trustee should

---

[67] Here too there are limits, as attested by *Vincent v Lake Erie Transportation Co* (1910) 124 NW 221, a case in which a non-owner was found to be entitled to use another's wharf in necessitous circumstances, but held liable for damage caused to the wharf.

[68] The 1998 Nisga'a Final Agreement, available at http://www.nnkn.ca/files/u28/nis-eng.pdf. The population statistic is taken from the government of British Columbia website and available at http://www2.gov. bc.ca/gov/topic.page?id=B17E2DF38BDC4DE594115B32AA16F02D.

be understood to have essentially three parts: (i) providing legal order for its people on the territory entrusted to it; (ii) abiding by international law when the state or its people produce justice-sensitive externalities (eg carbon emissions); and (iii) letting in, exceptionally, those migrants who have nowhere else to go. This is roughly Kumm's and Ripstein's position. Motivating this view is the thought that so long as the outsider is the citizen of some country where she enjoys secure and equal freedom, why should it matter—from the standpoint of her status as a free person, at least—of which country she is a citizen? So long as she is a citizen of a democratic and human-rights-respecting country that abides by the rule of law, this seems to solve the problem of ensuring the conditions of her non-domination.

While in principle the Kumm/Ripstein account may solve the problem of ensuring the conditions of a citizen's non-domination *within* her state, it does nothing to address the problem of domination when that same person interacts with another state. The problem with this position is that it takes insufficient account of the threat and use of coercion implicit in border control. The use of physical coercion to deport someone—physical restraint, forcible confinement, and forcible transportation—is directly liberty-infringing. The standing threat of the use of such coercion, if not mediated by cosmopolitan constitutionalism, constitutes domination, since the threat of force at the border (or within the foreign state, following a negative membership determination) can materialize at any time, and most importantly, for any reason, however arbitrary (refugees excepted). In effect, the Kumm/Ripstein view rejects constitutionalism at the border in favour of granting to the state prerogative powers it can exercise at will against the peaceful outsider. That the state may only coercively deport someone to somewhere safe is irrelevant to the liberty-infringing nature of the coercive force it may rely on, and is similarly irrelevant to the domination produced by the unilateral and unreviewable power states claim to use such force.

A Kantian might reply that to deny the migrant entry is not to coerce her in the relevant sense, since to exclude a person from a place they have no right to be is to uphold equal freedom rather than impose on the trespasser an arbitrary act of will. This reply trades on a strong republican view of freedom as non-domination according to which freedom is compromised only if a person's physical liberty is threatened or actually infringed on arbitrary grounds. An uncomfortable corollary of this view is that someone dragged away in chains from a place they have no right to be suffers no compromise to her freedom. And, setting this worry to one side, if the state is a joint trustee of the earth's surface on behalf of humanity, as I have argued, then the peaceful migrant does have a right to enter the foreign state's territory, unless, of course, the receiving state can offer a compelling justification for her exclusion.

IV. Constitutional Legitimacy

It remains to gather the lessons that the fiduciary account of cosmopolitan constitutionalism might have for ordinary constitutional legitimacy, where the relevant actors are the state and its officials on one side, and citizens and denizens on the other. The relevant lessons concern the role of international law and the duty of justification.

On the fiduciary view, the state upholds its internal constitutional legitimacy by abiding by its overarching duty to provide a regime of secure and equal freedom under the rule of law. International human rights and norms of *jus cogens* supply content to this duty, making it more concrete and determinate in the various domains in which these norms apply. This does not imply a commitment to hard-core monism in which the state disappears, only to emerge as an organ of the international legal order or a world state, where subsidiarity replaces sovereignty. Foundational ideas of conventional international law such as sovereign equality and a commitment to state sovereignty are maintained, but sovereignty is reconstructed along fiduciary lines. The state's constitutional authority to self-govern and establish legal order is constructed through the combination of its internal duty to its people and the authorization it enjoys from international law to govern so long as it generally complies with that duty. The constitutional legitimacy of the state is therefore co-constituted by national and international law, which themselves, Kumm rightly asserts, are 'mutually co-constitutive'.[69] One practical implication of this approach is that municipal courts are indeed also international courts. National judges who apply the presumption of conformity to bring domestic law into line with international law, such as the majority in *Baker*, are therefore justified in doing so. They are simply acknowledging that the legitimacy of their national legal order is co-constituted by the authority vested in the state by international law.

With respect to the duty of justification—the state's duty to offer a public justification of infringements of international norms—one might think that such a duty stops at the border, that once outsiders enter the state they are properly subject to the state's laws which may or may not, at the state's discretion, provide for a duty of justification. Intriguingly, there is one case in national and international law where states are required to meet such a duty, even when the action they contemplate is legislative in nature. In Canada and under the jurisprudence of the Inter-American Court of Human Rights, states must always consult and attempt to accommodate indigenous peoples if their intended action would invade indigenous lands or compromise indigenous rights to hunt or fish.[70] In Canada, if after consultation and efforts to reach accommodation the Crown proceeds with plans that will infringe indigenous rights, it must discharge a 'heavy burden' of justification.[71] The courts assess this justification through a proportionality analysis, and without the prompt of positive law to do so. Within the Inter-American System, the Court has gone so far as to find that states must acquire indigenous consent if they intend to undertake large-scale projects that would compromise their lands.[72] Canadian courts have grounded the duty to consult, accommodate, and justify on the Crown's fiduciary position and the honour of the Crown vis-à-vis

---

[69] Kumm, above n 37, 24.

[70] See eg *R v Sparrow* [1990] 1 SCR 1075; *Haida Nation v British Columbia (Minister of Forests)* [2004] 3 SCR 511, 245 DLR (4th) 33; *Taku River Tlingit First Nation v British Columbia (Project Assessment Director)* [2004] 3 SCR 550, 234 DLR (4th) 193; *Case of the Saramaka Peoples v Suriname* [2007] Inter-American Court of Human Rights (Series C) No 174; *Case of Kichwa Indigenous People of Sarayaku v Ecuador* [2012] Inter-American Court Human Rights (Series C) No 245.

[71] *Sparrow*, above n 70, 1119.   [72] *Sarayaku*, above n 70, 164.

First Nations. In other words, part of being a public fiduciary is having an obligation to justify one's actions to stakeholders.[73]

Under the fiduciary theory, non-indigenous as well as indigenous peoples are in a fiduciary relationship to the state. While the state's non-indigenous citizens by definition do not have indigenous rights to press against the state, they do have human rights recognized by international law. And while non-indigenous individuals do not typically present their claims as nations, as do indigenous peoples, they are nonetheless like First Nations inasmuch as both are legal persons, and therefore entitled to treatment as legal equals. More pervasively, they are equal co-beneficiaries of a fiduciary state that must live up to the status of its role as public trustee. As such, legal subjects can properly expect the state to offer reasons when the state takes action that impairs their legitimate interests. In common law jurisdictions, this is reflected in the duty to give reasons of administrative law, a statute-independent duty of common law constitutionalism that is hard to explain without reference to the rule-of-law principle that the state is barred from treating arbitrarily the people subject to its power. As in the case of outsiders at the border, the duty of justification arises to ensure that individuals are not subject to domination, and that any interference with their legitimate interests must be justified to them on the basis of good reasons. Under the fiduciary theory, the parallel duties of cosmopolitan and common law constitutionalism are explained by public trusteeship's aversion to domination.

V. Conclusion

I began this chapter suggesting that the orthodox account of constitutionalism has three main elements, and that its treatment of all three is incomplete to the extent that the cosmopolitan dimensions of entrance and membership are overlooked. If the content of constitutionalism is limited to an allocation of powers and rights protection that is strictly national in substance and Westphalian in its presuppositions, then the non-citizen at the border is illegitimately subject to foreign law. Furthermore, the state is acting as judge and party of the same cause. If the structure of constitutionalism is limited to providing a paramount legal framework for the state and its citizens, then once again the outsider is subject to domination rather then the rule of law, properly understood. If the ideal of democratic legitimacy that runs through constitutional theory is restricted to a nationalist and exclusionary conception of the demos, then a state rules its borders with might but not right.

En route to these conclusions, I have argued that state legitimacy is co-constituted by national and international law. I have also claimed, with Benvenisti, that states are trustees of humanity as well as their people, and that given this dual fiduciary role,

---

[73] It bears mentioning that trusteeship models of authority have a dark legacy in international law, serving at various times to justify colonial expansion over non-Europeans. See eg A. Anghie, *Imperialism, Sovereignty and the Making of International Law* (Cambridge: Cambridge University Press, 2005). The recent jurisprudence discussed above suggests, however, that despite its colonial past, conceiving the state as a trustee or fiduciary does not entail giving it an imperial mandate. Indeed, arguably the jurisprudence aims to undo the more pernicious effects of imperialism. For discussion, see E. Fox-Decent and I. Dahlman, 'Sovereignty as Trusteeship and Indigenous Peoples' (2015) 16 *Theoretical Inquiries in Law* 507.

a state's legitimacy depends on its maintenance of a presumptively open border policy. The legitimate state can rebut the presumption, but it must be willing to respect international standards and justify its action before an independent body.

Admittedly, I have done little more than claim that states occupy the twin fiduciary positions I have ascribed to them. Some may doubt this claim. Others will doubt the (relatively) open-borders implication that I believe follows from it. Certainly I have only scratched the surface of the debate on borders that has a rich literature of its own. Be that as it may, the present Westphalian border regime tests deep-seated principles of legality that preoccupied Hobbes and find currency in contemporary public law. The best way for law to remedy this illegitimacy is for constitutionalism to become unbound.

7

Constituent Power and the Constitution

Hans Lindahl*

Constituent power is, most generally speaking, the capacity to enact a constitution, thereby giving rise to a new legal order, by revolutionary means or otherwise. But what is the nature of the relation between constituent power and a constitution? In particular, what does an enquiry into the nature of constituent power tell us about constitutions, both descriptively and normatively?

The key to this question lies in the structure and emergence of collective agency, as evoked by the pronoun 'we' in the canonical phrase that inaugurates constitutional preambles, 'We the people...' The exercise of constituent power is held to be the act whereby a manifold of individuals jointly establish the rules by which they are to govern themselves into the future: the constitution. The chapter parses this deceptively straightforward characterization of the relation between constituent power and the constitution into four interconnected issues. The first concerns the kind of *collective agency* implied in the evocation of the 'we' that enacts a constitution. The second pertains to the concept of *constitution*. At issue here is understanding the constitution as a first-person plural concept, namely, as the master rule that structures how a legal collective goes about responding authoritatively to the practical question, 'What ought our joint action to be about?' The third focuses on the *enactment* of a constitution, that is, on the nature of the act of constituent power. The fourth is explicitly normative: what could render *authoritative* the responses to the aforementioned practical question, given that the exercise of constituent power is not itself legally authorized?

I. Authoritative Collective Action

The first step is a model of law that grants pride of place to the first-person plural perspective of a 'we'; I will call this the authoritative collective action model of law (ACA). My view is that law, or more properly a legal order, can best be understood as a species of collective action. I content myself, for the purpose of this chapter, with a bare-bones description of legal order as ACA, beginning with some general remarks about collective action before turning to the concept of authority.

The notion of collective action captures the insight that there is a distinctive first-person plural perspective proper to collective agency, a perspective which is not simply the summation of the first-person singular perspectives of the individuals who compose the group. While there can be no first-person plural perspective without a plurality of

* Hans Lindahl holds the Chair of Legal Philosophy at Tilburg University, the Netherlands.

individuals, and in that sense without a manifold of first-person singular perspectives, the former is not simply an aggregation of the latter. This means, concretely, that judgments, intentions, actions, and responsibility can meaningfully be ascribed to social groups, which groups have an existence irreducible to—although not independent of—the individuals which compose them. This core idea animates a variety of theories of collective action, although I will make no attempt to track the different positions in this subtle and wide-ranging debate.[1] Instead, I would like to briefly suggest several ways in which the concept of collective action, when duly specified, helps us to make sense of legal order.

The first aspect to bear in mind is that collective action gives rise to what Margaret Gilbert calls 'directed' or, following H. L. A. Hart, 'relational' obligations between participant agents.[2] If you and I are taking a walk together, then each of us is entitled to expect that the other act in certain ways (eg calibrating the speed with which we walk, such that we can keep up with each other) and refrain from acts that would hinder or even sabotage our walk. These are *directed* obligations because they hold for certain individuals as a result of their participation in collective action. Moreover, their scope and content flows from the *point* of collective action: our obligations vis-à-vis our fellow participant agents follow from what it is that we are doing together. Finally, they are directed obligations because it is participant agents who have *standing* to demand of other participant agents that they do their bit in contributing to the collective act and to *rebuke* them if they fail to do so. On this reading, legal obligations, as well as the sanctions which may apply to those who fail to discharge their obligations, are a species of directed or relational obligations.

A second aspect concerns the point of joint action. While it often has the form of a purpose, this need not be the case. As Twining aptly puts it with respect to practices, '[p]oint includes purpose, but can refer to any motive, value or reason that can be given to explain or justify [a] practice from the point of view of the actor'.[3] In other words, the point of collective action is what joint action is *about*; that which determines reciprocal expectations between participant agents as to what each of them is to do. Moreover and importantly, the point of joint action need not be and in fact never can be rendered entirely determinate; what it is that we are doing together, and what collective action requires of each of us, need to be sorted out along the way, that is, in the context of our joint action. Hence the content and scope of the directed obligations of collective action, and the relations of reciprocity to which they give rise, are, at any

---

[1] See eg M. Gilbert, *On Social Facts* reprint (Princeton: Princeton University Press, 1992); P. Pettit, *A Theory of Freedom: From the Psychology to the Politics of Agency* (Cambridge: Polity, 2001); M. Bratman, *Faces of Intention: Selected Essays on Intention and Agency* (Cambridge: Cambridge University Press, 1999); J. Searle, 'Collective Intentions and Actions', in P. R. Cohen, J. Morgan, and M.E. Pollack (eds), *Intentions in Communication* (Cambridge, Mass.: MIT Press, 2003), 401–15; R. Tuomela, *The Importance of Us: A Philosophical Study of Basic Social Notions* (Stanford: Stanford University Press, 1995). Scott Shapiro, drawing on Bratman, also argues that collective action plays a key role in making sense of law. See S. Shapiro, *Legality* (Cambridge, Mass.: Belknap Press, 2010).

[2] M. Gilbert, *A Theory of Political Obligation* (Oxford: Oxford University Press, 2008), 40–1; H. L. A. Hart, 'Are There Any Natural Rights?' (1955) 64 *Philosophical Review* 175.

[3] W. Twining, *General Jurisprudence: Understanding Law from a Global Perspective* (Cambridge: Cambridge University Press, 2009), 110.

given moment, a *default setting* of the point of collective action and, as such, more or less amenable to transformation.

Thirdly, collective action opens up a realm of practical possibilities and closes down others. On the one hand, collective action makes available a repertoire of forms of action for participant agents; those acts which are important and relevant to realizing the point of joint action. On the other hand, collective action marginalizes other kinds of action, namely, acts and forms of behaviour which are deemed unimportant and irrelevant to collective action and its point. If collective action is *inclusive*, by dint of incorporating a range of forms of action and participant agents into the first-person plural perspective of a social group, so also this first-person plural perspective is necessarily *exclusive*, because there are things that are irrelevant and unimportant if one is to participate in that group. Trivially, if you and I are going to the movies together, then selecting the movie we want to see is of paramount importance if we are to act jointly, whereas selecting the shoes each of us will wear is not. Likewise, whereas each of us would be entitled to expect of the other that she does what is required such that we can go to the movies together, in principle no such entitlement arises as concerns the shoes each of us will wear. That directed obligations flow from the point of joint action is another way of asserting that social groups cannot include without also excluding. It follows, therefore, that exclusion has, first and foremost, a *positive* significance for social groups, even though, as we shall later see, this does not exhaust its normative significance.

A fourth aspect concerns *identity*. Indeed, if I cut a pie in two, it makes no sense to say that I have included one piece and excluded the other. Inclusion and exclusion are linked to a first-person perspective, whether singular or plural, which is connected in turn to what Paul Ricœur calls identity as selfhood or ipseity, and which he contrasts to identity as sameness.[4] Sameness speaks to numerical or qualitative dimensions of identity, predicated of whatever can be reidentified as remaining one and the same through time (eg a piece of pie, a cloud, a bird, a person, a soccer team, a state). Selfhood, by contrast, speaks to a reflexive dimension of identity, which Philip Pettit describes as follows: 'that an agent is a self means that he can think of himself, or she can think of herself, in the first person as the bearer of certain beliefs and desires and other attitudes and as the author of the action, and perhaps other effects, to which they give rise'.[5] Pettit goes ahead to note that also collectives can be selves, by dint of enjoying a distinct personal perspective whereby their members refer to themselves with indexicals such as 'we', 'our', and 'ours'. In short, the first-person plural perspective of a collective speaks to a dimension or pole of identity through time in which the collective sticks to and can be held accountable for its commitments. A collective remains the same and a self, hence identical through time, to the extent that its members remain committed to acting together with a view to realizing the point of joint action. And in the course of acting together, distinguishing 'ours' from 'theirs', the members of a group engage in recursive acts of collective self-identification

---

[4] P. Ricœur, *Oneself as Another*, K. Blamely (trans) (Chicago: Chicago University Press, 1992).
[5] Pettit, above n 1, 79.

and other-differentiation, that is, in recursive acts of inclusion in and exclusion from the group.

A fifth and final aspect is that acts by participant agents are *ascribed* to a collective, whether by the participant agents or others. It is in each case participant agents who act; but viewing their acts as acts of participants entails viewing them as acts of the collective as a whole, such that the latter, and not (only) its individual actors, can be held responsible for them. By contrast, acts that obstruct or sabotage collective action are acts which we, the group, do not ascribe to ourselves as our own; they are acts we *disown*, refusing to view them as participant acts. Notice that all of this also holds for acts of ascription, to the extent that acts which ascribe or reject the ascription of acts to the collective may be part and parcel of joint action itself.

This last issue brings us into the domain of law. Indeed, there is a form of joint action in which certain participant agents are entrusted with establishing whether or not acts may be ascribed to the collective. More precisely, there is a form of joint action in which the *monitoring* and *enforcement* of collective action is entrusted to certain officials or authorities: legal order. By the 'monitoring' of joint action I mean that, in the course of joint action, certain authorities establish in a binding fashion what is its point and how it can best be achieved, whether in light of the changing context in which joint action unfolds or because conflict about these issues may arise between participant agents. In such circumstances, it is up to authorities to articulate the point of joint action by establishing what will count as the default setting of collective action, and to establish whether an act counts as a *participant* act, hence an act which may be ascribed to the collective as its own act because it is part and parcel of what *we* are doing together. The monitoring of joint action takes place by way of the enactment of general and/or individualized norms, which include but are by no means limited to statutes, administrative acts, and judicial decisions. By the 'enforcement' of joint action I mean that certain authorities are entrusted with establishing whether an obligation has been breached and, if so, what sanctions ought to accrue to the agents who have failed to discharge their obligations under joint action.

This, then, is a bare-bones account of the ACA model of law. While it is extremely abridged and leaves unexamined a number of important questions, some of which will surface later in this chapter, it suffices to show why collective action is the genus of legal order: law involves taking up the first-person plural perspective of a 'we', or more properly, of 'we together', rather than of 'we each', as Gilbert adroitly puts it.[6] The evocation of 'we the people', when enacting a constitution, is one example of this fundamental feature of legal order. But, as I have also suggested, the first-person plural perspective is merely the genus of legal order. Law, on my reading of the matter, is that species of collective action in which specific officials are entrusted with monitoring and enforcing joint action. This entails that legal orders enjoy, at least in principle, a robust identity over time, inasmuch as processes of inclusion in and exclusion from collective action are authoritatively mediated. Notice, to conclude, that this model of law is very broad. While it includes state law, it is by no means limited thereto. Indeed, it suggests that

---

[6] Gilbert, above n 1, 168.

there is no reason to limit the concepts of constitution and constituent power to the enactment of state constitutions. And, as we shall see, it suggests that there is no reason to limit the exercise of constituent power to its revolutionary manifestations.

II. A Functional Concept of a Constitution

It is not difficult to see how a passage can be secured from the ACA model of law to the concept of constituent power. In effect, the model describes the features of a legal order that has *already* been constituted. The analysis of section I speaks to the exercise of *constituted* powers, not of constituent power, which it presupposes without elucidating. But I will postpone addressing this issue till the next section, preferring, for the moment, to examine how the ACA model of law might cast new light on the concept of constitution.

I approach the concept of constitution in the spirit of Hans Kelsen's description thereof: 'the essential function of a constitution consists in governing the organs and the process of general law creation, that is, of legislation'; he adds that constitutions 'may determine the content of future statutes ... in that they prescribe or preclude certain contents'.[7] Mine also will be, initially, a *functional* conceptualization of the constitution, meaning by such an approach that highlights how a constitution structures the authoritative mediation of collective action. To be sure, Kelsen's pure theory of law is premised on the methodological individualism that dissolves the first-person plural perspective of a 'we' in joint action into the summation of a manifold of first-person singular perspectives of individual agents. My aim, to the contrary, is to view a constitution as a first-person plural concept, teasing out its functions with respect to ACA. Assuredly, this functional approach is at a considerable remove from an overtly normative approach to the concept of a constitution. Yet this more modest endeavour has the great advantage of allowing me to highlight a number of key features of constituent power, features which have considerable *normative* implications for constitutionalism, as will transpire in the final section of this chapter.

The functional approach I favour takes its point of departure in an elemental, in the sense of basic, implication of ACA: to the extent that questions arise, in the career of a collective, about the point of joint action and its legal default setting, different—often conflicting—responses about how to carry on may be available to the collective. Thus every legal collective is inevitably confronted with what I will call the 'practical question': *what ought our joint action to be about?* This is not a one-off question which lends itself to a definitive response; to the contrary, it incessantly haunts legal collectives, demanding that it be responded to each time around, whereby not responding is also a response. Here, then, is a preliminary functional characterization of a constitution: it is the master rule that structures how a legal collective goes about responding authoritatively to the practical question. Notice, to repeat an earlier point, that this concept of constitution is very broad and is by no means limited to state constitutions.

---

[7] H. Kelsen, *Introduction to the Problems of Legal Theory*, B. L. Paulson and S. L. Paulson (trans) (Oxford: Clarendon Press, 2002), 64.

This quite abstract characterization of a constitution needs to be fleshed out more fully in various ways. An initial avenue of approach turns on two of the dimensions of the practical question. The first concerns the point of joint action: *what* ought our joint action *to be about*? The second turns on the ascription of action to the collective: what ought *our* joint action to be about? A constitution structures how a collective goes about responding to this question by providing at least some fundamental guidelines for what collective action is about, and to which all default settings thereof must conform, as well as other conditions that must be met, such that participant acts, including authoritative acts of monitoring and enforcing joint action, may be ascribed to the collective. See here, in a different light, the two features that Kelsen assigned to a constitution, namely the regimentation of law-making as concerns its form and its content. Moreover, it would not be difficult to show that the procedural and substantive features of liberal constitutions, including civil and political rights, the division of powers, and elections, are one of the ways in which a constitution can structure how a collective deals authoritatively with the practical question. But constitutions can structure such responses in a host of other ways as well.

Now, to the extent that a constitution lays down how a collective is to respond authoritatively to the practical question, it is also the master rule determining what counts as *legal rationality* for that collective. There is nothing odd in this. As rational behaviour is, in general, behaviour that is or can be grounded or justified, so also legally relevant behaviour in particular, which is grounded or rational from the first-person plural perspective of a legal collective if it is in accordance with the point of joint action and if it meets other conditions such that it can be ascribed to the collective. In other words, behaviour is rational for a legal collective to the extent that it counts as *legal* behaviour, and irrational insofar as it is *illegal*, that is, an act that cannot be grounded because it is neither justifiable in terms of the point of collective action nor ascribable to the collective. Accordingly, to assert that a constitution is the master rule that establishes what counts as legal rationality for a collective is to aver that it is the master rule for authoritatively determining what is to count as legal and illegal behaviour for that collective.

There is yet a further and decisive characterization of a constitution which follows from the ACA model of law. In line with what was noted in section I, ACA opens up a repertoire of forms of behaviour that are made available for participants in ACA. This repertoire obviously includes legal—hence ordered—behaviour; less obviously perhaps, it also includes illegal—hence disordered—behaviour. By opening up a domain of participant agency ACA creates the possibility of behaviour which is in breach of ACA, and which it sanctions in a variety of ways. Accordingly, both legal and illegal behaviour are *included* in ACA as possibilities that can be actualized by participant agents: legal (dis)order. But in the very process of opening up a domain of practical possibilities, ACA also *excludes* other practical possibilities, that is, ways of acting together that are deemed unimportant and irrelevant to the realization of the point of joint action. So, ACA includes a default setting of legal *(dis)order*, while also marginalizing what thereby becomes the domain of the *unordered* for that legal order. For example, a legal order such as the European Union may provide for a legal default setting of a market as a *common* market, thereby establishing what counts as legal (dis)order, while also leaving unordered manifestations of religious life because these are deemed unimportant and irrelevant to market integration. Importantly, the limit between legal (dis)order and the unordered can be shifted. This is what it means to transform the default setting of ACA. Indeed, the practical question asks of a collective that it establish what it deems important and relevant to joint action, and what not. By qualifying new forms of behaviour as legal or illegal, and by declaring illegal what had been legal or vice versa, a collective indirectly shifts the limit between legal (dis)order and the unordered, including in ACA what had been excluded therefrom, or excluding from ACA what had been included therein. So, for example, certain aspects of religious life can come to be regulated by the European Union because they are deemed to impinge on the process of market integration; or certain forms of competition that had been authorized come to be prohibited as being in breach of the commonality of the common market.

I want to say, in light of the foregoing, that a constitution is the master rule for inclusion in and exclusion from ACA. More pointedly, constitutions create practical possibilities in the form of an authorization to certain officials to include new practical possibilities and to exclude existing practical possibilities in the course of monitoring and enforcing the point of joint action. It is in this way that a constitution creates the mechanisms for dealing with the conflicts that arise concerning the proper response to the practical question.

Notice, finally, how all of this ties up with what was said earlier about collective identity. Indeed, recursive acts of inclusion and exclusion are recursive acts whereby a collective seeks to identify itself as the same and as a self through time, thereby distinguishing itself from 'the other', including other collectives. That a constitution is a master rule for inclusion and exclusion entails that it is the master rule for collective self-(re)identification and other-differentiation.

III. Constituent Power

The time is now ripe to introduce the concept and the problem of constituent power into the ACA model of law. In its most elemental formulation, constituent power is the capacity to enact a constitution, by revolutionary means or otherwise, thereby giving rise to a novel legal order. Instead of directly engaging the contemporary debate about the nature and manifestation of constituent power, I have preferred to outline a model of law that could help us cast light on this enigmatic concept in a way that is not generally available to that debate.[8] So, while I will later discuss some aspects of that debate, my aim is to elucidate the concept of constituent power more or less independently thereof, working through the implications and unresolved issues called forth by the ACA model of law. As anticipated in section II, this model suggests why constituent power is a problem which legal theory cannot avoid dealing with. In effect, constituent

---

[8] For a recent contribution to the debate about constituent power, with analyses of normativist, decisionist, and relativist interpretations thereof, see M. Loughlin, 'The Concept of Constituent Power' (2014) *European Journal of Political Theory* 281, available at http://ept.sagepub.com/content/early/2013/05/22/1474885113488766.full.pdf+html. Loughlin's article offers a wealth of bibliographical references for the reader who wishes to pursue the topic further. For an agonistic reading of constituent power, see M. Wenman, *Agonistic Democracy: Constituent Power in the Era of Globalisation* (Cambridge: Cambridge University Press, 2013).

power is shorthand for the general problem concerning the *emergence* of ACA. At least two issues need to be addressed. First, *what* does it mean that constituent power gives rise to the first-person plural perspective of a legal collective? Second, *how* does constituent power contribute to the emergence of a legal 'we'?

The contours of an answer to the first question have already been sketched out in the foregoing sections. If the exercise of constituent power amounts to the enactment of a constitution that gives rise to a new legal order, then, on a functional interpretation of constituent power, its exercise consists in an opening up and a closing down, an inclusion and exclusion, that, indicating what is to be the point of joint action and who is a participant therein, gives rise to the first-person plural perspective of a 'we' in authoritatively mediated joint action. The enactment of a constitution is an opening up, as we have seen, by dint of creating a realm of practical possibilities for participating in joint action. The creation of this realm has the form of an *authorization*, the authorization of a repertoire of acts that henceforth are to count as our own acts, including acts of norm-creation that will themselves authorize practical possibilities. But the exercise of constituent power is also a closing down, a marginalization of practical possibilities, to the extent that by indicating the point of joint action and membership therein, it excludes forms of acting together and of membership that are deemed irrelevant and unimportant with respect to ACA, like when the authorization of a variety of forms of market participation in line with the economic focus of the European Union goes hand in hand with the relegation of manifestations of religious life and of membership in a religious community to the unordered, as the domain of what is unimportant and irrelevant to market integration. This ties into what was said about collective identity. The opening and closure wrought by constituent power interpellates a manifold of individuals, demanding that they act jointly. In other words, constituent power is the inaugural act of collective self-inclusion and other-exclusion. Finally, constituent power lays down a master rule of legal rationality. This means that the exercise of constituent power is itself neither legal nor illegal, rational nor irrational, from the perspective of the collective it institutes. By calling forth a legal 'we', it establishes the conditions under which acts can be viewed as legal or illegal, rational or irrational. Constituent power inaugurates a bounded domain of legal rationality by way of an act that has the structure of a circular reasoning—hence a breach of rationality—insomuch as it presupposes that which it creates.

But in what sense can constituent power be *inaugural*? In other words, in what sense can constituent power bring about something *new*? In contrast to constituted powers, which presuppose a constitution that authorizes them to act, the novelty proper to constituent power suggests a commencement, hence the emergence of a realm of practical possibilities that is irreducible to the realms of practical possibilities made available by extant collectives. But a conundrum becomes apparent. On the one hand, if, by enacting a constitution, constituent power extends an inaugural authorization to a manifold of individuals to engage in authoritatively mediated joint action, then, by definition, this authorizing act cannot itself be legally authorized. On the other, if it is not authorized by law, how can constituent power enact a *constitution*, given that authorizations, if they are to create legal norms, must be derived from the law? The conundrum reappears if we look to the characterization of constituent power as laying down a master rule of legal rationality. For if legal rationality entails that an act is rational (legal) when grounded in the constitution, and irrational (illegal) when not, isn't the act of constituent power that lays down the constitution itself legally groundless? Isn't the ground of the distinction between legality and illegality groundless?[9]

To address this perplexity we need to shift fronts, passing from the question *what* it means that constituent power gives rise to ACA to the question *how* ACA emerges through the exercise of constituent power.

Consider the following passages of the Preamble to the Treaty of Rome and article 1 thereof, whereby a European Economic Community (EEC) was enacted:

> [We, the heads of state of Belgium, Germany, France, Italy, Luxembourg, and the Netherlands]…determined to lay the foundations of an ever closer union among the peoples of Europe…have agreed as follows: Article 1. By this treaty the High Contracting Parties establish among [ourselves] a European Economic Community.[10]

True, I have interpolated the first-person perspective in the citation, whereas the text of the Treaty is formulated in the third person. But this allegedly descriptive, third-person formulation presupposes a first-person plural perspective, without which the parties could neither enter into an agreement with each other nor generate obligations among themselves.

The Treaty illustrates the features germane to the exercise of constituent power, as I have described it. On the one hand, the remainder of the Preamble and article 2 of the Treaty spell out in considerable detail what is the *point* of the EEC. On the other, the Treaty anticipates that this legal collective is open to all European states which are prepared to participate in realizing its point. As such, the Treaty opens up and closes down. It creates a repertoire of practical possibilities in the form of authorizations to officials to monitor and enforce joint action, and to individual agents to participate by way of the famous 'four' freedoms—the free movement of goods, persons, services, and capital—in bringing about a common market, which is the default setting of what the EEC is about, namely promoting 'a harmonious development of economic activities, a continued and balanced expansion, an increase in stability, and accelerated raising of the standard of living and closer relations between the States belonging to it'.[11] Accordingly, the Treaty includes and excludes, not only by virtue of excluding non-Europeans but also by excluding other ways of acting jointly which could lay claim to being European, as witnessed, for example, by those who claim that a European Union predicated on market integration betrays the Christian roots that make of Europe a community of faith. By inviting a manifold of agents to view themselves as participants of a collective, the members of which ought to act together in a certain way, the Treaty inaugurates a collective identity by way of a self-inclusion and other-exclusion. Moreover, it lays down a novel rule of legal rationality. From now on, acts in the framework of the EEC

---

[9] This is the predicament, in a somewhat different guise, that Kelsen encountered when discussing the validity of legal norms, and which he sought to address with the 'basic norm' of a legal order, which is presupposed rather than posited. See Kelsen, above n 7, 56ff.

[10] Treaty Establishing the European Economic Community (Treaty of Rome) (Rome, 25 March 1957, 298 UNTS 3; 4 Eur YB 412).

[11] Ibid, art 1.

are to be viewed as legal, hence rational, to the extent that they are in accordance with its point and are otherwise ascribable to the Community as the acts it owns; and illegal, hence irrational, if in breach of what the European Union is about.

But, it will be objected, can one really speak here of constituent power which gives rise to a *novel* legal order? After all, the Treaty was enacted by six heads of state, each of whom was authorized by their corresponding states to sign the Treaty on their behalf. It seems as though the enactment of the Treaty was very much an authorized act, the act of constituted powers, rather than a legally unauthorized act, as required by the notion of constituent power. But while the heads of states who enacted the Treaty were authorized to sign on behalf of their states, they did more than that: they claimed to represent the *European* community as a whole, even if not all European states entered into the agreement. In effect, the Preamble refers to an 'ever closer union among the peoples of Europe'. But the alleged union of European peoples had not authorized them to enact the EEC on their behalf.

This remarkable situation illustrates what might be called the *paradox of constituent power*. On the one hand, as we have seen, constituent power originates a novel legal order. The founders of the EEC exercise constituent power precisely because theirs is not an act legally authorized by those in whose name they claim to act: the union of European peoples. On the other hand, constituent power claims, when enacting a constitution, that it does no more than *represent* an extant collective, merely giving legal form to what is already—hence originally—a social group. Indeed, the Preamble to the Treaty of Rome claims that there is *already* a union of the peoples of Europe, an extant but thus far de facto union which simply acquires a *de jure* form by way of the EEC. In short, the Preamble takes for granted that while there are European peoples in the plural, there is also a European people *in the singular*, in the sense of a manifold of agents who are already committed to acting together.[12]

What, then, is the nature of the paradox? This: constituent power can only originate a collective if it succeeds in presenting itself as a constituted power that represents the original community, the community we already are, prior to the representational act. In other words, the paradox of constituent power entails that the foundation of a novel legal order can only come about as its *re*-foundation, as the continuation, albeit in a legal guise, of an extant collective. If, at first glance, it seems like the exercise of constituent power can be traced back to a pure here and now, to an absolute spatio-temporal beginning (eg Rome, 25 March 1957), it turns out, on more careful consideration, that the beginning must already have transpired if constituent power is to be a beginning; that sometime (we don't know when) and somewhere (we don't know where) a spatio-temporal closure has come about, spawning the community of European peoples and distinguishing it from the rest of the world.[13]

---

[12] For a more detailed discussion of the paradox of constituent power see H. Lindahl, 'The Paradox of Constituent Power: The Ambiguous Self-Constitution of the European Union' (2007) 20 *Ratio Juris* 485. For general discussions of the paradox see, amongst others, B. van Roermund, *Law, Narrative and Reality: An Essay in Intercepting Politics* (Dordrecht: Kluwer Academic Publishers, 1997), 145ff.; J. Derrida, 'Declarations of Independence' (1986) 15 *New Political Science* 7.

[13] Mark Walters points out in that as a matter of legal theory, the idea of a constitution with no beginning is a powerful one. See Walters in this volume. I fully agree, and would add that the notion of a 'historical constitution' is one of the modes of manifestation of the paradox of representation, which calls into question

Is there really a paradox at work in the emergence of a novel legal order? For, it could be argued, the example we have been examining militates against this. The argument can be made in both directions: as an argument either in defence of constituent power or of constituted power. The former would hold that describing the exercise of constituent power as a paradox collapses rupture into continuity, revolution into reform, novelty into the status quo. By these lights, the Treaty of Rome is thoroughly misleading as an example of constituent power: it is anything but an example of a (revolutionary) beginning. The latter would aver that a theory of the emergence of legal order can dispense with the concept of constituent power altogether because, as the Treaty of Rome shows, the successful enactment of a collective has a necessarily representational structure. If there is to be law, then there can only be constituted powers which are subject, if not to explicit law, then certainly to implicit law. At bottom, what theories of constituent power call the 'emergence' of a novel legal order is no more than the explication of implicit law.

Notice that, despite taking up opposing stances on the contrast between constituent and constituted power, both objections are manifestations of what might be called 'originalism'. The view that constituent power enacts a legal order in an absolute here and now understands constituent power as originating a collective. The view according to which there can only be constituted power because power has a representational structure takes for granted that there is an original community prior to and independent of its representations.

Neither of these objections will work. The defence of constituent power as a purely originating power is blind to one of the cardinal features ACA described in section I, namely, that acts must be *ascribed* to a collective, hence that it is in each case concrete individuals who ascribe an act to the collective by referring, for example, to 'our legislation' or, for that matter, to 'our constitution'. This seemingly trivial fact hides a feature of collective action in general, and of ACA in particular, which is of the greatest importance, and which Bernhard Waldenfels summarizes thus: 'A "we" [cannot] say "we".... A political group only finds its voice by way of spokespersons that speak in its name and represent it as a whole.'[14] The Preamble of the Treaty of Rome illustrates the general point that the unity of a collective, the 'we' in joint action, is always a *represented unity*; a collective is never immediately present to itself as a unity. Precisely because collectives have no direct access to a putative original unity that could determine in advance their identity across time as a self and as the same, they are also always exposed to the practical question—what ought our joint action to be about?—and must respond to it ever again in recursive acts of collective self-reidentification and other-differentiation. For example, the representational structure of constituent power ensures that the European Union is constantly exposed to a twofold question: what renders a market our *common* market? Is the *market* what is common to us? The paradox of constituent power entails

any simply linear reading of time. The further implication of this is, of course, that, contrary to the self-understanding of the common law tradition, 'historical constitutions' have their own constituent moments, even if not in the form of a revolutionary 'big bang', and precisely because constituent power, if successful, appears retrospectively as being no more than the 'augmentation', to borrow Hannah Arendt's beautiful expression, of an already existing community.

[14] B. Waldenfels, *Verfremdung der Moderne: Phänomenologische Grenzgänge* (Essen: Wallstein Verlag, 2001), 140.

that, ontologically speaking, questionability and responsiveness are fundamental features of the mode of existence of legal collectives.

Doesn't the rejection of constituent power as a purely originating act entail conceding victory to the champions of constituted power? Not at all. For they operate with a reductive concept of representation, one which assumes that the task of representation is to render explicit an implicit or latent unity, a unity given prior to and independently of its representation, thus an original unity simply awaiting legal recovery. This second form of originalism is blind to the peculiar retroactivity/proactivity of representation. To borrow a felicitous turn of phrase of my colleague, Bert van Roermund, the representation of unity deploys, if successful, 'a past we can look forward to'. Accordingly, the paradox of constituent power is a specific manifestation of the paradox of representation, namely, that *representation is the creation of what is given*.[15]

To conclude this section, let me briefly examine one of the reasons why I have consistently introduced the conditional 'if it succeeds' when referring to the exercise of constituent power. Indeed, representational acts can misfire; the invitation by a constituent power to its addressees to view themselves as already being a collective, oriented to realizing this or that point, can fall flat. In such cases, the representational act boomerangs back on the alleged representative, who, retrospectively, is no more than a buffoon or, more ominously, a traitor. That the initiative of a would-be constituent power will be carried forward by its addressees cannot be taken for granted; it must succeed in representing these as a group in relations of reciprocity in such a way that this representation is both viable as a future possibility and recognizable to them, albeit retroactively, as articulating what they already (ought to) share. In this sense, constituent power never operates in a void, it is never *ex nihilo*: it is subject to practical constraints, both normative and factual. What André Malraux had to say about artistic creativity also holds for constituent power, which has the form of a 'coherent deformation'.[16]

IV. Legal Authority

I indicated at the outset of this chapter that a conceptual analysis of the relation between constituent power and the constitution must give way to a normative analysis thereof. The reason for this should have become progressively clearer along the way: if a constitution is the master rule that structures how a legal collective goes about responding in an authoritative fashion to the practical question, how can those responses and the constitution itself at all raise a claim to authority, given that the exercise of constituent power is not itself legally authorized? More pointedly, is there a way of advocating a strongly normative conception of *legal authority* if the paradox of constituent power

---

[15] Aharon Barak makes the case for distinguishing between the express and implied meanings of constitutional texts in the context of the broader problem of constitutional interpretation. It is indisputable that judges and scholars involved in processes of legal interpretation conceptualize their interpretation of texts, constitutional or otherwise, as articulating their implicit meaning. See Barak in this volume. In line with the paradox of representation, the trick is to account for this distinction in a way that avoids what I have called originalism: the assumption that there is a meaning that is already there, given prior to and independently of its representation, such that (constitutional) interpretation is nothing more than ex-plicating the im-plicit.

[16] A. Malraux, *La création artistique* (Paris: Skira, 1948), 152, cited by M. Merleau-Ponty, *La prose du monde* (Paris: Gallimard, 1969), 85.

rejects the attempt to separate questions of the genesis of legal order from questions of its validity? This is, admittedly, a very compact formulation of the problem I now want to address, so I begin by unpacking it a bit more before engaging with it in some detail.

Legal order, I have argued, is authoritatively mediated joint action. Authority, on this account, plays a crucial role in explaining the specificity of law. Yet my account of authority has been strictly functional, namely, the monitoring and enforcement of joint action. A functional approach presupposes, without clarifying, how and why authority is a thoroughly normative concept. Indeed, I have focused on the point of joint action and the ascription of acts to the collective, sidelining the normativity of the practical question to which collectives must respond: what *ought* our joint action to be about? The urgency of this question becomes clearer when paraphrased as follows: who and what ought we to include in and exclude from ACA? Surely, whether and how the responses to this question could be binding is the crux of a normative theory of legal authority. A purely functional approach to law cannot be sustained if one is to take seriously the idea that law is *authoritative* collective action. And if a constitution is the master rule that establishes how a collective is to go about responding to this practical question in an authoritative way, then, here also, a purely functional approach is unsustainable.

Now, the line of approach to the problem of legal authority favoured by the wide-ranging line of normative thinking that takes its point of departure in social contract uncouples questions of genesis from questions of validity. The problem of genesis, that is, of the emergence of legal orders, belongs, for contractarians, to the domain of the factual, and can be abandoned, without any normative loss, to legal and political sociology, to political science, and some such. Dealing with the problem of legal validity requires abstracting from all such empirical matters. As the champions of social contract in all its modulations never cease to emphasize, it is an *ideal* model that reveals the criteria that must be met, such that the law can be binding, hence authoritative, and regardless of how a legal order was in fact founded. They readily acknowledge that no order of positive law fully meets the criteria of validity. But, again, that would be to miss the point: the aim of this ideal model is to provide the critical yardstick by which to assess extant legal orders, independently of how they may actually have emerged, and by which to track their progress towards the realization of those criteria.

The sharp distinction between genesis and validity also applies, for contractarians, to the constitution. On the one hand, there are positive—in fact positivistic—conceptions of the constitution, such as that of Kelsen, cited earlier. On the other hand, there are a variety of normative conceptions of a constitution, which seek to lay out what features a constitution must embody if it is to facilitate law-making which could meet the criteria of validity identified in the ideal model. The snag is that if one severs entirely the relation between positivity and validity, to focus only on the latter, one empties ideal normative theory of any practical import. So a connection is re-established between facticity and validity by way of a normative reconstruction of the significance of positive constitutions in constitutional democracies. The core idea here is the equiprimordiality of a constitution and democracy. On the one hand, constitutions structure the process of democratic decision-making, making room for political conflict and its democratic resolution. On the other hand, the normative content of the constitution is itself conflictual, and the object of democratic decision-making.

All of this is well known, and requires no rehashing. It explains, in any case, why contractarian theories, in all their modulations, will have no truck with constituent power: it stands squarely on the side of the factual emergence of a legal order, telling us nothing about the validity of legal orders in general or of constitutions in particular. Constituent power can only distract our attention from what is of paramount practical importance—a theory of legal authority—because it has nothing on offer as concerns the normative criteria by which to respond to the question confronting legal collectives: what *ought* our joint action to be about? Moreover, even if an unauthorized act of inclusion and exclusion is required to kick-start a legal collective, constitutional democracies have, at least in principle, the normative wherewithal to compensate for this, creating conditions of ever-greater inclusiveness. Indeed, complete inclusion is, for contractarians, the *telos* of constitutional democracy; it lends law-making its authoritative character. Moreover, it provides the normative criterion that orients properly *authoritative* responses by constitutional democracies to the practical question noted earlier: our joint action ought to be about securing complete inclusion.

The theory of constituent power I have sketched out fully endorses the central importance of an inclusive legal 'we' and of constitutional institutions oriented to that effect. It acknowledges that precisely because constituent power seizes the initiative to say 'we' on behalf of a legal 'we', this initiative is always *premature* and in need of justification. The concept of constituent power I defend views fundamental rights, the separation of powers, and elections as illustrating some of the ways—but not all—by which constitutions can hold open a space in which the default-setting of legal inclusion and exclusion can be contested and transformed.[17] In other words, the authority of constitutions depends, at least in part, on their acknowledging, albeit indirectly, the unauthorized character of constituent power by putting in place institutions that elicit differing, often conflicting, responses to the practical question. Fundamental rights, the separation of powers and elections, amongst others, are institutions that expose the prematurity of the initiative that says 'we' on behalf of a manifold of individuals and counter it by *deferring* the ascription of a default-setting of legal order to the 'we', hence deferring the authoritative determination of what counts as legal unity, such that the conflict arising from political plurality can become visible with a view to renegotiating the terms of legal reciprocity between the participants in joint action. The deferral of a definitive determination of legal unity also contributes to deferring plurality in the strong form of collective disintegration.[18] Hence the ACA model of legal order encourages the transition from a functional to a normative account of a constitution inasmuch as 'directed' or 'relational' obligations, in a functional interpretation of legal order, presuppose mutual expectations between the participants in joint action, thereby bringing into focus reciprocity as part and parcel of a normative theory of legal authority.[19]

---

[17] It is from this interpretation of the normative concept of a constitution, namely, the deferral of what is to count as *our* joint action, that I read Aileen Kavanagh's thesis that the separation of powers is instrumental to the joint enterprise of governing together. See Kavanagh in this volume.

[18] I am grateful to Thomas Hueglin for drawing my attention to this point.

[19] For a powerful account of the foundational role of reciprocity for the normativity of law in Hobbes's version of social contract, see D. Dyzenhaus, 'The Public Conscience of the Law' (2014) 43 *Netherlands Journal of Legal Philosophy* 115.

But my account of constituent power also suggests that the problem of legal authority is more complex and intractable, normatively speaking, than contractarian theories make it out to be. In particular, it points to at least two problems which these theories have great difficulties in dealing with, and which call into question the very possibility—in principle and not merely in fact—of realizing 'complete inclusion'.

The first turns on the fact that these theories focus overwhelmingly on achieving a greater inclusiveness to accommodate those who are excluded by ACA.[20] As such, they seek to deal with the effects of the unauthorized exclusion to which the foundation of a legal 'we' gives rise. But they are blind to the no less important problem that, more or less against their will, a variable range of individuals and groups may have been *included* by the constituent act; that, despite their opposition, they are deemed to *belong* to the polity. Unauthorized inclusion: 'Not in our name'. A political dilemma confronts those individuals or groups who were included in the collective against their will. On the one hand, they can raise a constitutional claim that, if successful, allows them to obtain political and legal recognition for their distinctness, cultural or otherwise. But the price they must pay for going down this path is to identify themselves as participants in a project with which they do not want to be associated, hence as a minority group within a broader community. On the other, if they oppose their inclusion, refusing to appeal to the constitution's normative possibilities of inclusiveness, they expose themselves to the charge that their acts of contestation need not be accepted as such or even listened to because they are constitutionally 'unreasonable', as per the master rule of legal rationality laid down in the constitution. Succinctly, the challenge to ACA raised by those who have been included against their will is not captured by a response to the practical question— what ought *our* joint action to be about?—precisely because they contest that they belong to that collective. Their democratically secured recognition as equals and members in full standing under a shared constitution is, for them, an act of *domination*.[21]

If the first problem turns on exclusion, the second points to the limits of inclusion. Let me illustrate the nature of the problem with reference to Pettit's argument that radical groups, such as deep environmentalists, should be pragmatic in the claims they raise, if they want to be heard and followed:

> those who are committed to various political causes [should] articulate the concerns they want the state to take up in terms which others can understand and internalize. Unless the devotees of a cause are prepared to do this, they cannot reasonably expect their fellow citizens to listen, let alone to go along.[22]

---

[20] A good example of this is I. M. Young, *Inclusion and Democracy* (Oxford: Oxford University Press, 2000).

[21] See eg the famous *Quebec Secession Reference* of the Canadian Supreme Court, whereby a constitutional stalemate arises between, on the one hand, the Canadian rebuke that the Quebecer secessionists fall prey to a performative contradiction in claiming a unilateral right of secession, and, on the other, the Quebecer objection that Canadians beg the question when they demand that Quebec present its claim as a constitutional claim. *Reference re Secession of Quebec* [1988] 2 SCR 217, 161 DLR (4th) 385. See H. Lindahl, 'Recognition as Domination: Constitutionalism, Reciprocity, and the Problem of Singularity', in N. Walker, S. Tierney, and J. Shaw (eds), *Europe's Constitutional Mosaic* (Oxford: Hart Publishing, 2010), 205–30.

[22] P. Pettit, *Republicanism: A Theory of Freedom and Government* reprint (Oxford: Oxford University Press, 2002), 136.

Pettit's defence of pragmatism is no doubt right as far as it goes, but notice the *petitio principii* to which it gives rise: only those arguments count as 'reasonable' and worthy of being 'listened' to which postulate the rationality of anthropocentrism, which is precisely what radical environmental politics challenges in the first place. Toning down the demands of radical groups amounts to neutralizing and pacifying their challenge to a collective, reformulating it in such a way that it can be viewed as raising the practical question to which a collective can respond: what ought *our* joint action to be about? Demands that radical groups be pragmatic if they want their claims to be recognized and included attest to the circular reasoning that arises when certain normative challenges to a given legal order can only be met by presupposing its point. Now if, as noted earlier, a circular reasoning *inaugurates* a bounded legal rationality, so also it marks the *end* of reason-giving, of justification, of dialogue, of rational grounding. The implication of the fact that constituent power institutes a *bounded* legal rationality is that every collective has a normative blind spot which bursts the reciprocity of the hoary principle of constitutional dialogue: *audi alteram partem*.[23] This blind spot intimates an 'impractical'—or more precisely an *impracticable*—question: that which is *unorderable* for a given collective. If constituent power includes legal (dis)order and excludes the unordered, the domain of the unordered comprises what is orderable and what is unorderable for the collective.

In brief, the ACA model of law and its attendant account of constituent power suggest that collectives are sooner or later confronted with normative challenges which exceed the extant practical possibilities available to that collective, and which it cannot simply brush off as 'unreasonable' or spurious other than by engaging in a form of circular reasoning, that is, by incurring a form of collective self-legitimation. Returning to an ontological characterization of legal collectives, these exist in the mode of a *finite* questionability and a *finite* responsiveness. A normative concept of legal authority has to take account of the fact that there is an irreducible residue of positivity in the law. It is under *these* circumstances, I feel, that claims to legal authority in the course of monitoring and enforcing collective action reveal themselves as fundamentally problematic, circumstances that seem neither articulated nor addressed by social contract theories in all their forms. The problem is this: can legal authority be more than domination in the face of challenges to collective action which resist accommodation within the range of possibilities of reciprocity authorized by a constituent act which is itself neither legally authorized nor ever entirely justifiable *ex post*?

There seem to be two complementary ways in which the ACA model of law and its attendant concept of constituent power might contribute to addressing this vexing problem.

The first appeals to constituent power, which contractarians would happily proscribe from a normative theory of legal authority. I have focused exclusively on the exercise of constituent power that marks the enactment of the 'first' constitution of a legal order—'primary' constituent power. But this by no means exhausts the scope of constituent

---

[23] J. Tully, *Strange Multiplicity: Constitutionalism in an Age of Diversity* (Cambridge: Cambridge University Press, 1995), 115.

power. For if constituent power were limited to the enactment of the 'first' constitution, this would mean that the scope of practical possibilities available to a collective, in the course of responding recursively to the practical question noted above, would be given to it in advance, such that a collective's own possibilities would concern the actualization of practical possibilities that were simply held in reserve until the appropriate moment. Once the 'first' constitution has been enacted, there could be no novelty because the transformation of the default-setting of legal order would be but the explication of possibilities implied in the origin. This would amount to collapsing representation into originalism. Yet 'secondary' constituent power deploys the paradox we have been at pains to describe with respect to 'primary' constituent power, which catches us by surprise because it reveals possibilities as *our* possibilities, yet possibilities we knew nothing about prior to its exercise. 'Secondary' constituent power marks an inaugural moment; it introduces legal possibilities and forms of legal reciprocity that were not legally authorized, projecting possibilities as our own possibilities into the future, such that one moves from the actual to the possible, while also retrojecting these possibilities into our past as possibilities that are already available to us, and which we can now realize.

'Secondary' constituent power can respond in this way to normative challenges that resist accommodation within the extant range of possibilities available to a collective. This is not to say that 'secondary' constituent power operates without constraints, normative and factual. The novel possibilities it opens up must fit coherently into ACA and its normative point, and play into the factual circumstances of ACA which lie beyond the control of constituent power. 'Is' and 'ought' are entwined in the exercise of 'secondary' constituent power, such that a novel response to the normative question, 'what *ought* our joint action to be about?' is also a novel response to the factual question, 'what *is* our joint action about?' No less than 'primary' constituent power, so also 'secondary' constituent power, if it is to be successful, must deploy what Malraux called a 'coherent deformation'. In short, the paradox of constituent power ensures that its exercise is not a one-off event; introducing a rupture with respect to normal politics, 'secondary' constituent power seizes the initiative to authorize forms of legal reciprocity that exceed the extant range of practical possibilities extended by the constitution to participants in ACA.[24]

'Secondary' constituent power takes us part of the way, I think, in dealing authoritatively with normative challenges that exceed the extant range of practical possibilities available to a collective. But it does no more than that because, as noted, the 'deformation' of these possibilities has to be coherent with the normative and factual circumstances in which constituent power is exercised. Can we push a normative account of legal authority any further?

There is, I surmise, a second way of dealing authoritatively with radical challenges to ACA, one which takes us into the domain of 'lawlessness': the exception.

---

[24] A good example of this is the famous *Van Gend & Loos* ruling of the European Court of Justice, which introduced, to everyone's astonishment, the doctrine of direct effect, all the while claiming that this doctrine was simply 'implied' by the Treaty of Rome. The case wonderfully illustrates moreover the circular reasoning proper to constituent power referred to earlier. Case 26/62, *Van Gend & Loos* [1963] ECR 1.

Carl Schmitt accurately captures what is at stake in the exception when noting that it 'is that which cannot be subsumed; [that which] defies the general codification'.[25] Bear in mind that the translation falls short of adequately conveying the German expression with which Schmitt refers to the exception (*die Ausnahme*), namely *sie entzieht sich*, which means that the exception 'defies', 'eludes', and 'exceeds' a legal order, all at once. Phenomenologically speaking, the exception is the mode of appearance of what is *strange* to a collective, and not merely other-than-self. But by assimilating the strange to the enemy, Schmitt levels down the exception to what poses an extreme danger to or imperils the existence of that collective, calling for exceptional measures in the form of a suspension of the constitutional order with a view to neutralizing or destroying the enemy.[26] This amounts to making of the exception a security issue and of exceptional measures the extreme expression of collective self-preservation. But if, as I would argue, enmity is a derivative form of the exception, then another reading of exceptional measures is possible, one which is not out to destroy what is strange but rather precisely the contrary. At stake here, in stark opposition to Schmitt's reading of the political, is a form of *collective self-restraint* in which the suspension or perhaps even the violation of a constitutional order is oriented to *sustaining*, rather than destroying, what radically contests the legal collective. Not collective *self*-preservation but rather the preservation of *the strange* by way of exceptional measures is the kind of respons*a*bility by which a legal collective can take respons*i*bility, albeit indirectly, for the conditions that govern its foundation, namely, that the exercise of constituent power brings about an inclusion in and exclusion from ACA that can never be fully justified. An example of this reading of exceptional measures is, it seems to me, the Canadian Supreme Court's *Quebec Secession Reference*, which determined that the complex rules for the amendment of the Canadian Constitution would be suspended in the event that a clear majority of the inhabitants of Quebec were in favour of secession, thereby giving way to a political process of negotiation concerning the terms of secession.[27]

None of this is an argument against the rule of law in a normatively rich sense of the term.[28] But it does suggest that the price to be paid for the constituent empowerment of joint action under a constitution is a radical disempowerment in the form of a range of practical possibilities which definitively cannot be integrated into the realm of practical possibilities made available by ACA. In such situations, a collective cannot respond to what calls it radically into question with a new legal default-setting of

---

[25] C. Schmitt, *Political Theology: Four Chapters on the Concept of Sovereignty*, G. Schwab (ed trans) (Cambridge, Mass.: MIT Press, 1985), 13 (translation altered).

[26] The political enemy is 'the other, the stranger (*der Fremde*); and it is sufficient for his nature that he is, in a specially intense way, existentially something different and strange, so that in the extreme case conflicts with him are possible'. See C. Schmitt, *The Concept of the Political* expanded edn, G. Schwab (trans) (Chicago: University of Chicago Press, 2007), 27 (translation altered).

[27] *Reference re Secession of Quebec*, above n 21. This argument about the exception and exceptional measures, and more generally the ACA model of legal order, is developed and illustrated at far greater length in H. Lindahl, *Fault Lines of Globalization: Legal Order and the Politics of A-Legality* (Oxford: Oxford University Press, 2013).

[28] While I am in general sympathetic to the account Trevor Allan offers of the rule of law, I believe it falls short of addressing the problems for a normative concept of legal authority called forth by radical challenges to a legal order, even if that order meets the conditions of the rule of law, as he describes it. See Allan in this volume.

the normative point of ACA. Whereas the realm of practical possibilities made available by ACA speaks to power in the most elemental sense of 'we can', namely we can accommodate the normative claim of the other in our legal order, radical challenges to ACA confront a collective with its powerlessness in the no less elemental sense of 'we cannot': we cannot accommodate the other's claim in our legal order. These radical challenges intimate practical possibilities which can only be realized from another first-person plural perspective inaugurated by the exercise of 'primary' constituent power. For this reason, I think that 'lawlessness', when it takes on the form of the exceptional measures by which a collective exercises self-restraint in the face of radical challenges to ACA, is an integral part of the *authority* of law, not its negation. They are the way in which a collective indirectly acknowledges that the enactment of a novel constitution is the expression of constituent power and of constituent powerlessness.

8

Popular Sovereignty and Revolutionary Constitution-Making

Richard Stacey[*]

I. Introduction

Towards the end of 2010 and during 2011, a wave of popular uprisings against long-serving authoritarian rulers swept through the Arab region. Like dominoes, the regimes of Zine el Abidine Ben Ali in Tunisia, Hosni Mubarak in Egypt, Muammar Gaddafi in Libya, and Ali Abdullah Saleh in Yemen fell. In Tunisia and Egypt new constitutions were adopted in early 2014, while constitution-drafting processes in Libya and Yemen have been plagued by ongoing armed conflict. Constitutional reforms were enacted in Morocco in 2011 and in Bahrain in 2012 in efforts to quell popular opposition against the governments in those countries before it spilled over into popular unrest. In Algeria, a constitutional reform package was introduced in May 2014 just after President Abdelaziz Bouteflika's re-election for a fourth term and following his 2011 promise for reform.[1] A bitter civil war continues in Syria despite the drafting and approval at referendum of a new constitution in 2012.

These uprisings have become known as the Arab Spring, and grew from both political and economic roots. If the fuel for the Arab Spring lay in disenchantment with corrupt and kleptocratic rulers, administrative inefficiency in government offices, abuse of power by police and security forces, and dynastic political succession that left no room for the popular election of leaders, its spark was declining economic opportunity, unemployment, and high food prices.[2] In the countries touched by the Arab Spring, significant numbers of people made plain their opposition to the government of the day and to the constitutional system in which that government operated. The cry went up in Tunisia and spread across the region: *Ash-shab yurid isqat an-nizam*, the people want the fall of the regime. In Egypt and Tunisia protests gave way to a constitutional moment, which defined a new constitutional order to replace the hated autocratic

---

[*] Assistant Professor, Faculty of Law, University of Toronto.

[1] 'Algeria leader Bouteflika pledges constitutional reform', *BBC News*, 15 April 2011, http://www.bbc.com/news/world-africa-13102157; P. Markey and L. Chikhi, 'Algeria unveils Bouteflika constitutional reform package', *Reuters*, 16 May 2014, http://www.reuters.com/article/2014/05/16/us-algeria-reforms-idUSBREA4F0PU20140516.

[2] J. Bowen, *The Arab Uprisings* (London: Simon and Schuster, 2012), 5–6. See also T. Gurr, *Why Men Rebel* (Princeton: Princeton University Press, 1970), and the recently updated edition of the book including an examination of the Arab region (T. Gurr, *Why Men Rebel: Fortieth Anniversary Edition* (Boulder: Paradigm, 2011)).

system. The Arab Spring stands as a stirring example of popular sovereignty, of the people expressing a desire for constitutional change and acting to achieve it.

This chapter examines the relationship between popular sovereignty and constitutionalism, in the context of the constitutional moments like those of the Arab Spring. In Egypt, the Supreme Council of the Armed Forces (SCAF) ousted Mubarak and suspended the 1971 Constitution. A handful of 'constitutional declarations' followed, purporting to confer authority on the SCAF to govern until a new constitution could be drawn up, and to manage the process of drafting and adopting the new constitution.[3] But in the vacuum left by the abrogation of the 1971 Constitution—a situation I call the 'constitutional interregnum'—the SCAF's political authority and its exercise of constitution-making power was not based on a constitutional document or an existing constitutional system but on its claim to be exercising popular sovereignty and acting in the name of the Egyptian people. Each of the SCAF's constitutional declarations purports to be a moment at which the people pass the sovereign authority to govern themselves on to a newly constituted power that acts in their name and on their behalf.[4] I see the constitutional interregnum as a laboratory of constitutional theory, a constitutional moment at which our philosophical thoughts about the nature of constitutionalism and popular sovereignty can be observed and interrogated.

One view of this constitutional moment is that it presents the Egyptian people—or indeed the people of any nation which finds itself in a constitutional interregnum—with an opportunity to constitute the political system however they want to, and to confer whatever powers they choose on the governments they establish. On this view, popular sovereignty is unfettered and unbounded during the constitutional moment. Indeed, the SCAF was able to dominate the constitution-writing process while it was in power in Egypt between 2012 and 2014, and reserve significant prerogatives for itself in the text of the 2014 Constitution once it left power. But as the Arab region emerges from a history of autocratic rule clothed in the robes of constitutionalism, this understanding of the constitutional moment sounds a worrying note. The aim of this chapter is to challenge the conception of popular sovereignty as an unbounded power in the hands of constitution-makers. My central claim is that just as a popular constitution constrains and restricts the actions of a government claiming the authority of popular sovereignty, the very nature of popular sovereignty imposes restraints on those who would claim its authority in enacting a new constitution.

My starting point is to reconstruct the architecture of what I refer to as the claim to 'unbounded popular sovereignty', and to consider why we should take this claim seriously. Unbounded popular sovereignty entails the distinction between, on the one

---

[3] See the Supreme Council of the Armed Forces' Constitutional Proclamation of 13 February 2011, 'Egypt's Supreme Council of the Armed Forces: Statements and Key Leaders', *New York Times*, 14 February 2011, http://www.nytimes.com/interactive/2011/02/10/world/middleeast/20110210-egypt-supreme-council.html?_r=0; and the Supreme Council of the Armed Forces Constitutional Declaration 2011.

[4] Hobbes describes the transfer of sovereignty from the multitude of pre-political people to a sovereign as the moment that constitutes them as a people and allows the establishment of civil order. See T. Hobbes, *De Cive*, S. Lamrecht (ed) (New York: Appleton-Century-Croft, 1949), ch VII, para 7; and T. Hobbes, *The Elements of Law Natural and Politic*, F. Tönnies (ed) (London: Simpkin, Marshall and Co, 1889), part II, ch II, para 11.

hand, the exercise of popular sovereignty in a vacuum of constitutional law or in a constitutional interregnum of the kind Egypt experienced, and on the other hand, ordinary, non-exceptional practices of representative politics. In the latter, power is exercised by institutions established by a popular constitution, and in terms of rules set out in that constitution. In circumstances of constitutional interregnum, by contrast, there are no constitutional or political rules to limit or constrain the exercise of popular sovereignty. The idea of unbounded popular sovereignty is rooted in the move from this distinction to the conclusion that the sovereign people are unfettered in the exercise of their sovereignty at the moment at which they define a new legal and political order in the text of a constitution.

And why should we take unbounded popular sovereignty seriously? One reason is that it reframes the debate about constitutionalism and democracy. A common view is that the two positions are opposed: constitutionalism imposes restrictions on the popular will, but for those committed to a particularly majoritarian understanding of democracy, constraints on the exercise of the popular will are undemocratic. On this majoritarian understanding of democracy, the very idea of constitutional democracy is contradictory. If democracy is understood to mean 'popular political self-government— the people of a country deciding for themselves the contents... of the laws that organize and regulate their political associations', and constitutionalism is understood to mean 'the containment of popular political decision-making by a basic law...untouchable by the majoritarian politics it is meant to contain',[5] then tension between the two is inevitable. The counter-majoritarian dilemma emerges as soon as courts enforce the rules or principles of a constitution against the will of the majority.[6] The view of (most of) the people in the present day is not always consonant with the principles that seemed self-evident to the framers of a constitution many years before.

But another way of understanding the debate is to distinguish between two forms of popular sovereignty and to describe constitutionalism and democracy, respectively, as an expression of one or other of these two forms. The exercise of popular sovereignty in the constitutional moment is an expression of the power to constitute an entirely new constitutional order—the constituent power—while the ordinary day-to-day decisions of a government representing the people and acting under the colour of popular sovereignty—the exercise of constituted powers—occur within the limits of a constitutional framework established through the exercise of constituent power.

Reframing the debate like this takes the contradiction out of constitutional democracy: even constitutional limits on the democratic will are rooted in popular sovereignty.[7] The result is that even majoritarian democrats must be committed to some conception of constitutionalism, or at least constituent power. But while I accept that constitutionalism is rooted in popular sovereignty, I question the conclusion that this is indicative of unbounded popular sovereignty. While we already know that a government

[5] F. Michelman, *Brennan and Democracy* (Princeton: Princeton University Press, 1999), 5–6; and M. Walzer, 'Philosophy and Democracy' (1981) *Political Theory* 379, at 383.

[6] A. Bickel, *The Least Dangerous Branch: The Supreme Court at the Bar of Politics* (Binghamton: Bobbs-Merril, 1962).

[7] S. Freeman, 'Constitutional Democracy and the Legitimacy of Judicial Review' (1990–1) 9 *Law and Philosophy* 327.

whose authority is rooted in a constitution is bound to respect the principles and limits imposed by that constitution, I argue that a voluntarist account of popular constitution-making, which sees popular sovereignty as unfettered when exercised to enact a constitution, is an incorrect account of popular sovereignty. The core of my argument against unbounded popular sovereignty flows from a consideration of the rule of law. I argue that just as official adherence to the principles of the rule of law generates the people's 'fidelity to law', an interregnum government's adherence to the inherent principles of popular sovereignty generates 'fidelity to power' and renders the interregnum government's claim to the authority of popular sovereignty more than merely empty rhetoric. The inherent principles of popular sovereignty, in turn, emerge from a consideration of how popular sovereignty actually operates both during periods of ordinary politics and at the constitutional moment. I argue that the claim to popular sovereignty brings with it commitments to the constitutional protection of civil and political rights on the one hand, and to the constitutional prohibition of discrimination—that is, a commitment to equality—on the other. These substantive commitments flowing from the commitment to popular sovereignty belie the claim that the exercise of constitution-making power on the authority of popular sovereignty is unbounded.

II. Popular Sovereignty in Constitutional Theory

A. The people's two bodies

Understanding popular sovereignty as taking one of two forms dispels the contradiction between democracy and constitutionalism. But for popular sovereignty to do this work, it must mean something other than the crude majoritarian principle that the present will of the majority determines political outcomes. Overcoming the view that popular sovereignty and majoritarian nose-counting are the same thing takes some doing, because it makes some intuitive sense that the people's sovereignty translates into a political mechanism by which the majority makes decisions regarding the future of all of the people. Distinguishing popular sovereignty from majoritarianism becomes an important step in distinguishing between two forms of popular sovereignty.

An unmediated or crude form of majoritarianism requires all the business of ordinary government to occur by plebiscite. It is a voluntarist system in which all that matters is the present will of the majority, subject to no constraints and unburdened by pre-existing or independent principles. But politics has to happen through some intermediary mechanism which approximates the majority will, such as a democratically elected representative government. The people that make up Hobbes's multitude cannot rule themselves—they can only appoint a sovereign to govern them. Once they have done so, the people are author of every action taken by the sovereign, and cannot later complain that the sovereign has acted outside of her authority. The multitude does not become a political force until its members have selected a sovereign to represent them, and until the sovereign has been given 'commission to act'.[8]

[8] T. Hobbes, *Leviathan*, E. Curley (ed) (Indianapolis and Cambridge, Mass.: Hackett Publishing, 1994), ch XVI, para 14. See also P. de Marneffe, 'Popular Sovereignty, Original Meaning, and Common Law Constitutionalism' (2004) 23 *Law and Philosophy* 223, at 223.

It makes no sense even to speak of 'the people', or of popular sovereignty, until the people have appointed a sovereign to act on their behalf.

Where popular sovereignty and constitutionalism meet is in the idea that the people do not only appoint the sovereign, but also limit the actions that the sovereign can take. Under a constitution, a representative government acts only according to the commission that the majority has given it, and by exercising only those powers conferred on it by an agreed framework for political conduct. While a system of this kind departs from unmediated majoritarianism, the people (or a majority of them) nevertheless exercise popular sovereignty by charging a representative to act on their behalf within a set of rules they formulate.

Consequently, when a government wins a mandate from the people in a regularly held election, the policymaking and lawmaking that follow carry the stamp of popular approval as long as the government's discharge of its electoral mandate remains within the boundaries of the constitutional framework. Representing the people implies not only a popular mandate, but also that the representative government pursues its mandate by exercising only those powers that the people have agreed it should hold. A new constitution is both constitutive of the political system and regulative of the conduct and functions of the institutions it establishes.[9] Popular sovereignty is exercised both by the constituted powers that represent the people, as well as by the constitution-maker who sets the limits of constituted power. Exercising either form of popular sovereignty involves lawmaking. Representative governments engage in ordinary lawmaking within the framework of regulative principles established during periods of constitutional lawmaking.[10]

On a crude majoritarian understanding of democracy, the idea that some principles of political organization should be beyond the reach of the decision-making power of the people and selected instead by an appeal to philosophy is a symptom of an 'anti-democratic disease' involving an 'invariably esoteric…elitism'.[11] Democracy means that the people ought to be able to decide on 'the laws that organize the institutions of government and set limits to governmental powers'.[12] But in a constitutional moment where the people themselves do decide on these organizational laws and entrench them in a constitution, the commitment to democracy demands adherence to those laws. Although there are serious and irresolvable disagreements on major questions of political morality, it is at least conceivable that the people can reach agreement on the 'laws of lawmaking' that do no more than establish the procedures for further ordinary lawmaking.[13] Even though a legislative majority may make laws that not everyone supports, a law's opponents can accept the institutions and structures by which those laws are made. The principle of constitutional supremacy prohibits the constituted powers

---

[9] On the constitutive and regulative functions of constitutions, see S. Choudhry, 'After the Rights Revolution: Bills of Rights in the Post-Conflict State' (2010) 6 *Annual Review of Law and Social Science* 301; and S. Choudhry, 'Bills of Rights as Instruments of Nation-Building in Multinational States: The Canadian *Charter* and Quebec Nationalism', in J. Kelly and C. Manfredi (eds), *Contested Constitutionalism: Reflections on the Charter of Rights and Freedoms* (Vancouver: University of British Columbia Press, 2009), 233–50.

[10] B. Ackerman, *We the People: Foundations* (Cambridge, Mass.: Belknap Press, 1991), ch 1.

[11] Ibid 12.   [12] Michelman, above n 5, 6.   [13] Ibid 48–9.

from changing organizational laws in the same way that it enacts ordinary laws: the constitution, not the legislature, is supreme.

And where the constitution empowers a court to strike down ordinary laws for reasons of their inconsistency with the organizational laws set out in the constitution, all the court does is ensure that the representative government's discharge of its electoral mandate during periods of ordinary lawmaking remains within the regulative limits set during the period of constitutional lawmaking. Whether a court is entitled to interpret the constitution in this way is contingent on the terms of each constitutional document. Some constitutions may not give the courts this power, but where they do, it is the people themselves, in the exercise of popular sovereignty at a constitutional moment, that establish the power of judicial review.

The majoritarian counter-argument that the legislature should be entitled to change the constitution as it likes can be met by pointing out that where the legislature is itself a product of a moment of constitutional lawmaking, its powers are defined by an expression of popular sovereignty at the constitutional moment, and it would undermine this expression of popular sovereignty if the institutions constituted by the constitution were empowered to change the rules of the system on which they are founded, and in terms of which they function. A commitment to the principle of constitutional supremacy is thus implicit where a constitution claims the imprimatur of popular sovereignty and constitutes a new set of institutions to represent the people.[14] The principle of constitutional supremacy requires that a distinction be drawn between the process for the enactment of ordinary legislation and the process for constitutional amendment.[15]

---

[14] The situation is likely different in cases where the legislature is not constituted by the constitution, or where the constitution takes the form of a collection of fundamental statutes enacted by the legislature as ordinary statutes, as in the United Kingdom and New Zealand, and to an extent in Canada. The Habeas Corpus Acts in the United Kingdom and more recently the Supreme Court Act in Canada (RSC 1985, c S-26) are examples of ordinary statutes with constitutional status. In *Reference re Supreme Court Act, ss 5 and 6* 2014 SCC 21, [2014] 1 SCR 433, the Supreme Court of Canada held that the Supreme Court Act was an ordinary statute that had taken on constitutional status and could not be amended by an ordinary parliamentary majority. It could only be amended through the more onerous procedures set out in the Constitution for constitutional amendment. Even in the United Kingdom the Supreme Court (formerly the House of Lords) has hinted that a form of proto-constitutional supremacy exists in terms of which 'Parliamentary sovereignty is no longer, if it ever was, absolute' (*R (Jackson) v Attorney General* [2005] UKHL 56), and that Parliament's decisions cannot offend 'the basic rights of the individual' (*Secretary of State for the Home Department, ex p Simms* [2000] 2 AC 115, [1999] UKHL 33).

[15] Again, although the UK constitution is not a single, entrenched document, the procedure for making changes to fundamental constitutional statutes is slightly different to the extent that these changes require a 'clear statement' of Parliament's intention to overrule the earlier, fundamental statute. The Human Rights Act 1998, ch 42 (HRA), for example, requires the minister introducing a bill to either attest to the bill's compatibility with the HRA or to clearly indicate the government's intention to proceed with the bill notwithstanding its infringement of rights protected in the HRA (s 19). Sections 3 and 4 of the HRA allow courts to read down Acts of Parliament to render them compatible with the HRA—arguably a challenge to parliamentary supremacy—or to indicate that a statute is incompatible with the HRA, putting pressure on the government to react. Canada's 'notwithstanding' clause (Part I of the *Constitution Act 1982*, s 33, being Schedule B to the *Canada Act 1982* (UK), 1982, c 11) allows Parliament to re-enact a statute notwithstanding a court's declaration that it infringes rights in the Charter of Rights and Freedoms. The political costs of making these clear statements and overruling fundamental constitutional statutes is high, however, and these procedures are rarely relied on in practice (see R. Dixon, 'Weak-Form Judicial Review and American Exceptionalism' (2012) 32 *Oxford Journal of Legal Studies* 487; R. Dixon, 'The Supreme Court of Canada, *Charter* Dialogue, and Deference' (2009) 47 *Osgoode Hall Law Journal* 235; and E. F. Delaney, 'Judiciary Rising: Constitutional Challenge in the United Kingdom' (2014) 108 *Northwestern University Law Review* 543).

Constitutional democracy is not contradictory so much as a combination of these two forms of popular sovereignty. Alongside the popular sovereignty exercised by a political majority identified by elections and by voting in the representative legislature, stands the popular sovereignty exercised in the constitutional decision to establish a political society. And one way that popular sovereignty is exercised to establish a political society is by the people rising up against an existing regime, abrogating an existing constitution and, in the resulting constitutional interregnum, constituting a new set of institutions to represent their will.

On its own, the distinction between two forms of popular sovereignty (or two levels at which it is exercised) is uncontroversial. Moreover, the distinction is attractive to the extent that it more clearly outlines the relationship between constituted powers and the constitution that constitutes them, articulating the principle of constitutional supremacy in systems where the constitution establishes new institutions of representative government. But this distinction opens the door to unbounded popular sovereignty: since constraints on political power arise only once the constituent power has established those constraints, the argument goes that there are no constraints on those who claim constituent power to make a new constitution. The foundations of any new constitution are 'arbitrary, purely factual, based perhaps on the strength of the stronger group(s) able to impose its will'[16] and, like the SCAF in Egypt, able to confer constitution-making authority on itself. In making a new constitution, all that succeeds is success.[17]

B. Constitutional amendment and constitutional replacement

We can distinguish between constitutions made by those whose claim to constitution-making authority is based on strength alone, and constitutions made by those who claim the authority of popular sovereignty to make a constitution. The challenge to which this chapter responds is not presented by the powerful coup-maker who rides roughshod over popular will and opposition to her dictatorship to make a constitution, but by the claim that even those who act under the authority of popular sovereignty are unbounded in making a new constitution. This chapter explores the normative implications of a group of individuals acting as a people to authorize institutions of government to act on behalf of the whole people.

To see the outlines of the challenge of unbounded popular sovereignty, it is useful to consider the difference between constitutional amendment and the replacement of an entire constitutional order. Popular sovereignty must be exercised in order to achieve either amendment or replacement, but the exercise of popular sovereignty to amend a constitution is restrained by the terms of the existing constitution. A constitutional amendment makes changes to the system of ordinary lawmaking, but occurs within the rules that a

---

[16] A. Kalyvas, 'Popular Sovereignty, Democracy, and the Constituent Power' (2005) 12 *Constellations* 223, at 231.

[17] I take the phrase from H. L. A. Hart, who uses it to describe the situation in which a court makes a decision where there are no general legal rules determinative of the outcome (H. L. A. Hart, *The Concept of Law* (New York and London: Oxford University Press, 1961), 149).

constitution has set out for making those changes. These changes are an exercise, by the constituted powers, of constitutionally restrained popular sovereignty rather than an exercise of free and unbounded constitution-making power. It is the same form of limited popular sovereignty that is exercised during periods of ordinary lawmaking. Consequently, the extent of these changes is pre-determined by the rules of the constitution.[18]

Carl Schmitt makes the same point in marking the qualitative difference between constitution-making and constitutional change ('more accurately, revision of individual constitutional provisions'). The power to amend constitutional laws is a 'statutorily regulated competence', and it is in principle limited, constrained, and bounded by the terms of the constitution. The amendment power 'cannot transcend the framework of constitutional regulation on which it rests'.[19] Schmitt argues further, however, that the only way to replace a constitution in its entirety is to step outside the limits of ordinary lawmaking. The German Reich could not have been transformed into an absolute monarchy or a Soviet republic by a two-thirds majority of the Reichstag, and neither could a majority of the English Parliament change England into a Soviet state.[20] Abrogating the constitution in its entirety cannot occur through any rules or procedures that the existing constitution establishes, since any constitutional authority for the exercise of a power of abrogation would dissolve at the moment it is exercised. Where a legislature is established by a constitution, its powers to do anything at all flow from the terms of the constitution. The legislature cannot unmake the constitution from which its power flows.[21] The abrogation of a constitution cannot proceed through the amendment procedure, so the argument goes, because the amendment power that a constitution confers on the constituted powers cannot reach the people's decision to constitute the political system.[22]

Whether Schmitt is correct that fundamental constitutional change or replacement can happen only after some kind of revolution and the abrogation of the existing constitutional order is open to dispute. Hans Kelsen, for example, disagreed with Schmitt and thought that an entire constitution could be replaced by the ordinary amendment procedure.[23] In the situations of constitutional interregnum that I am interested in in

---

[18] Even a change in government that results from rebellion need not disturb the existing constitutional order. For Locke, where the government breaches the obligations it bears to citizens as a party to the social contract, the people hold a right to 'remove or alter the sovereign' (J. Locke, *Second Treatise of Civil Government* (1689), ch XIX, paras 221–2; see also ch IV, para 22). It is better, Locke goes on, that 'the rulers should be sometimes liable to be opposed, when they grow exorbitant in the use of their power, and employ it for the destruction, and not the preservation of the properties of their people' than that 'the people should be always exposed to the boundless will of tyranny'. There is no mischief, Locke concludes, to desire the alteration of the government in these circumstances, even by means of rebellion (J. Locke, *Second Treatise of Civil Government*, ch XIX, paras 229–30).

[19] C. Schmitt, *Constitutional Theory*, J. Seitzer (ed trans) (Durham, N.C.: Duke University Press, 2008), 146.

[20] Ibid 79–80.

[21] See the judgment of the Indian Supreme Court in *Minerva Mills v Union of India* AIR 1980 SC 1789, holding that the Indian Constitution cannot be read to delegate to any constituted political authority the power to destroy the Constitution.

[22] George Lawson, more or less a contemporary of Locke's, described something like constituent power in speaking of 'real majesty' as the 'power to model the state' which includes the 'power to constitute, abolish, alter, reform forms of government' (G. Lawson, *Political Sacra et Civilis*, C. Condren (ed) (Cambridge: Cambridge University Press, 1992), 47).

[23] See the essays in L. Vinx (ed), *The Guardian of the Constitution: Hans Kelsen and Carl Schmitt on the Limits of Constitutional Law* (Cambridge: Cambridge University Press, 2015), especially H. Kelsen, 'Who

this chapter, however, the pre-existing rules for constitutional change—whether pertaining to minor amendments or replacement of the constitution *in toto*—have already been abolished. Whatever constraints on powers of constitutional change existed in terms of the previous constitution, they have been swept away in the abrogation of the previous constitutional order. We are left with the same situation of revolution that Schmitt says is necessary for the replacement of a constitution, and the constitution-maker in this situation is no longer constrained by the rules for amendment that constrained the now-defunct legislature. Whereas the amendment power is cabined within constitutional provisions and within the constitution as a whole, Schmitt describes the constituent power that emerges after the abrogation of the previous constitutional order as unlimited: 'the constitution-making will of the people is an unmediated will. It exists prior to and above every constitutional procedure. No constitutional law, not even a constitution, can confer a constitution-making power and prescribe the form of its initiation.'[24]

Of course, the constituent power that exists in what I call the interregnum already exists for Schmitt in every constitutional system. The defining power of Schmitt's sovereign is that he decides on the circumstances of emergency that would allow an exercise of this constituent power.[25] This is the radical democratic flavour of constitutional theory that Schmitt is known for, and it aligns well with unbounded popular sovereignty. The bearers of constituent power are always free to make or remake the constitution, and the challenge of unbounded popular sovereignty is that constitution-makers in the constitutional interregnum enjoy this unlimited power. If this challenge goes unmet, constitution-makers in Arab Spring Egypt—and anywhere else constitution-makers make a claim to popular sovereignty—are free to remake the constitutional order as they wish.

One way to meet this Schmittian, radical democratic challenge is to focus more closely on the concept of popular sovereignty. If popular sovereignty exercised by the constituted powers at moments of ordinary lawmaking is subject to constraints, then perhaps we can argue that the exercise of popular sovereignty is in principle capable of limitation. On this basis we can then propose that constitution-makers who claim to be acting under the authority of popular sovereignty at the moment of constitutional lawmaking are, in principle, similarly capable of being subjected to constraints.

The task at hand is to describe the constraints on popular sovereignty when it is exercised at the constitutional moment, and to identify the source of these constraints. The route to doing so, I suggest, is in testing the validity of a would-be constitution-maker's claim to popular sovereignty. If there are forms and principles to which a claim to

---

Ought to be the Guardian of the Constitution?', 174–221. There is historical evidence to question Schmitt as well: South Africa's transition from an apartheid state to a constitutional democracy in 1994 was achieved through the passage of the Constitution of the Republic of South Africa Act 200 of 1993 by the existing apartheid legislature. It is hard to think of a more fundamental change to the structure of a political system than South Africa's transition to democracy, but there was no constitutional interregnum or revolutionary overthrow of the existing order, as Schmitt would have us believe there has to be.

[24] Schmitt, above n 19, 132.
[25] C. Schmitt, *Political Theology: Four Chapters on the Concept of Sovereignty*, G. Schwab (trans) (Chicago: University of Chicago Press, 2010), 5.

popular sovereignty must adhere if the people are to accept that their sovereign authority is validly exercised by a group that claims that authority, then the very idea of popular sovereignty imposes restraints on the ends to which it can be put.

III. Fidelity to Power: The Limits of Popular Sovereignty

A. The argument from the rule of law

Say that a constitutional interregnum arises following the revolutionary abrogation of a previous constitution. Assume also that the new revolutionary government eschews might as the source of its authority, and instead claims the imprimatur of popular sovereignty on its exercise of power, including constitution-making power. The SCAF's February 2011 declaration of executive power in Egypt's constitutional interregnum, for example, describes the people as the cornerstone of the nation and points explicitly to the people's own sovereignty as the source of its authority to govern.[26] The thing about popular sovereignty, though, is that it has to be popular if it is to mean anything. In the absence of a formal democratic mandate won by the interregnum government in an election, and without the hypothetical consent of a notional social contract between the people and a Hobbesian sovereign, popular sovereignty remains a source of authority for a revolutionary government only as long as a sufficient number of people continue to accept the government's claim that it actually does act on their behalf.

In stark terms, if a government is to continue to exercise power rooted in popular sovereignty during a constitutional interregnum, it has to keep enough people on its side to eliminate the possibility that some other group will try to overthrow the government because it no longer represents the wishes of the people. Governing on the authority of popular sovereignty alone—without reliance on force—requires fostering and maintaining fidelity to that claim to power. Even though individuals may disagree with specific exercises of power at specific points in time, they continue to respect the government's authority to exercise power over them.

The challenge the revolutionary political system faces here—the challenge of what might be thought of as 'fidelity to power'—is not that different from the challenge that any legal system faces: the law, too, will apply to specific individuals at specific moments in ways they would rather not have it apply to them. If an objective of the law is to order interactions between people by setting rules for conduct, the legal system as a whole has to generate acceptance of the idea that the law is a legitimate means of imposing rules even though individuals may be unhappy with the substance or the application of the rules in specific instances. Where a constitution is in force, there is a set of readily available principles with which the exercise of power and the substance

---

[26] 'Egypt's Supreme Council of the Armed Forces: Statements and Key Leaders', above n 3. Subsequent constitutions in Egypt also make the link between dignity and authority that flows from popular sovereignty. The Preamble to the 2014 Constitution includes the following statement: 'We affirm the right of the people to make their future. They, alone, are the source of authority. Freedom, human dignity, and social justice are a right of every citizen. Sovereignty in a sovereign homeland belongs to us and future generations.'

and application of law must be consistent, and against which each law can be assessed. Governmental acts and decisions that are not justifiable against these constitutional principles are beyond the authority that the constitution confers on the government.[27]

For Lon Fuller, law is not just a technology of government concerned with bringing order to society and directing people how to act. Certainly, the rules of law do impose order on society, and the first seven of Fuller's eight principles of legality are essentially rules for lawmaking setting out the characteristics that laws and the legal system must have if they are to be effective in ordering social interaction.[28] But more than this, Fuller insists that law is 'basically a matter of providing the citizenry with a sound and stable framework for their interactions with one another'.[29] Once the laws and the legal system are in place, the government must comply with its previously declared rules. Fuller's eighth principle of legality, the requirement of congruence, demands that government acts 'within the terms of a previous declaration of general rules'.[30]

Implicit in Fuller's account of the principles of legality is a Kantian conception of human dignity that sees people as rational and autonomous beings making decisions for themselves about how to live their lives within a framework of laws, and demanding rational explanation and justification for exercises of power that affect them. The principles of legality uphold this commitment to human dignity by demanding that government conduct is justifiable to the people to whom they apply. 'To embark on the enterprise of subjecting human conduct to the governance of rules', Fuller claims,

> involves of necessity a commitment to the view that man is, or can become, a responsible agent capable of understanding and following rules, and answerable for his defaults. Every departure from the principles of the law's inner morality is an affront to man's dignity as a responsible agent.[31]

As free and responsible agents, people have a reason to accept a system of laws because it allows each person to make choices about how to act, within the limits of the law, on the understanding that everyone else will do the same (or be prevented from doing differently by law enforcement institutions). Regardless of whether people disagree with the substantive content of specific laws, the system of laws makes it

---

[27] See T. R. S. Allan, 'The Rule of Law as the Rule of Reason: Consent and Constitutionalism' (1999) 115 *Law Quarterly Review* 221, at 231–2. See also the transformation of the South African legal order from the authoritarian apartheid state to a constitutional democracy based on human dignity, equality, and freedom, which Etienne Mureinik describes as the transformation from a culture of authority to a culture of justification: E. Mureinik, 'A Bridge to Where? Introducing the Interim Bill of Rights' (1994) 10 *South African Journal on Human Rights* 31, and D. Dyzenhaus, 'Law as Justification: Etienne Mureinik's Conception of Legal Culture' (1998) 14 *South African Journal on Human Rights* 11.

[28] L. Fuller, *The Morality of Law* revised edn (New Haven and London: Yale University Press, 1969), 46–81. The first seven of Fuller's principles are (i) generality; (ii) publicity; (iii) non-retroactivity; (iv) clarity; (v) coherence; (vi) possibility of compliance; and (vii) constancy over time.

[29] Ibid 210.

[30] Ibid 214. On the distinction between the first seven and the eighth principle of legality, see I. Sánchez-Cuenca, 'Power, Rules, and Compliance', in J. M. Maravall and A. Przeworski (eds), *Democracy and the Rule of Law* (Cambridge: Cambridge University Press, 2003), 62–93, at 69.

[31] Fuller, above n 28, 162.

possible for individuals to live as free and responsible agents. But for individuals to act as free and autonomous agents, government has to act within the terms of its previous declaration of general rules. The rule-of-law principle of congruence demands that government pursue whatever goals it may have within the institutional forms that provide a predictable environment for citizens' own actions. By meeting this demand, government assures each person that her capacity for rational action and autonomy—her dignity—is taken into account at least to the extent that the government will not act outside of the authority that previously declared rules confer on it.[32] As a matter of fact, the government's adherence to previously declared laws generates 'fidelity to law' by ensuring that individuals continue to have a normative basis for accepting the authority of laws.

In an established constitutional democracy the previously declared rules are set out in a constitution. Government conduct such as ordinary lawmaking can be shown to respect citizens' rationality and autonomy if it is congruent with the rules and principles already articulated in the constitution. Fidelity to law depends on the constituted powers' adherence to these previously established rules and principles in making ordinary laws, and on the constituted powers' adherence to ordinary laws once they have been made. As long as the government continues to respect the rule of law, law will retain the fidelity of the people as a mechanism of government.

While fidelity to law in the constitutional setting and fidelity to power in the interregnum both depend on upholding a commitment to human rationality and autonomy, in the interregnum no reliance can be placed on the rules or principles that the people have already set out through a previous exercise of popular sovereignty because there has been no such exercise of popular sovereignty. Fidelity to power must be generated without reference to previously declared rules or principles. Each exercise of power must be shown to be congruent not with rules or principles that have already been articulated, but with the principles that are inherent in the idea of popular sovereignty itself.

Consequently, a constitution made in the interregnum by a government that claims the authority of popular sovereignty must not only respect the principles of popular sovereignty if it is to maintain the fidelity of the people, but must incorporate in its text the substantive commitments implicit in the view that people are bearers of dignity capable of rational and autonomous action.

---

[32] Fuller talks about the 'bond of reciprocity' that develops between citizens who agree to follow rules and the ruler who binds herself to applying only those rules to which citizens agree (ibid 39–41). Jeremy Waldron sees the fidelity to law that results as the 'valuable core' of the rule of law. See J. Waldron, 'Why Law—Efficacy, Freedom, or Fidelity?' (1994) 13 *Law and Philosophy* 259, at 275–80. More generally, the distinction between fidelity to law and fidelity to specific substantive governmental goals is captured in Max Weber's distinction between forms of legitimation that rely on formal legal rationality and those that rely on substantive, goal-oriented leadership or charisma. Weber himself describes formal legal rationality as a 'basic legitimation' or 'inner justification' of power (M. Weber, 'Politics as a Vocation', in H. H. Gerth and C. W. Mills (eds), *From Max Weber* (New York: Oxford University Press, 1958), 78–9; M. Weber, 'Basic Concepts of Sociology', in M. Rheinstein and E. A. Shils (eds), *Max Weber on Law in Economy and Society* (Cambridge, Mass.: Harvard University Press, 1954), at 9). Waldron's account of the rule of law as fidelity to law finds parallels in the constitutional theories of Bruce Ackerman (above n 10, ch 1) and Frank Michelman (above n 5, 48–9).

B. The inherent principles of popular sovereignty: The case for civil and political rights

In a constitutional system where a constitution sets out the rules for lawmaking, ordinary laws can be scrutinized for compliance with both procedural rules for lawmaking and substantive limits on ordinary laws. A law that the government makes without following the formal procedures for lawmaking is unconstitutional.[33] Similarly, an ordinary law that is substantively inconsistent with principles set out in the previously declared constitution will be unconstitutional.

In a constitutional system the constituted powers' conduct and the laws they make can claim the authority of popular sovereignty because mechanisms and procedures have been established to represent the people or allow the people to participate in the lawmaking process. In a constitutional interregnum, however, there are no formal institutions, mechanisms, or procedures for making a new constitution. A constitution-maker cannot claim the authority of popular sovereignty on the basis of the procedure by which the constitution is made, because there are no formal, previously established institutions or procedures for constitution-making. This differs from a new constitution produced by an elected constitutional assembly (or constitutional amendment for that matter) where constitution-making bears the authority of popular sovereignty because the people have had an opportunity to elect their representatives to the constitution-making institution. Whatever the content of that constitution turns out to be, the constitution claims the authority of popular sovereignty because the popular election of representatives to a constitutional assembly imprints popular sovereignty onto the constitution-making process.

In the interregnum, there are no previously established mechanisms that can approximate the popular will, and no process of constitution-making can by itself generate fidelity to power or lend the authority of popular sovereignty to the constitution that emerges from the interregnum. The process by which a constitution is made in the interregnum does not matter to whether the constitution can meaningfully claim the authority of popular sovereignty. Rather, a constitution's claim to popular sovereignty in the interregnum must rest entirely on the substantive content of the constitution.

However, just as there are no previously declared procedures for constitution-making in the interregnum, neither are there previously declared substantive principles with which an interregnum government's acts of power or the content of a new constitution can be shown to be consistent. An interregnum constitution that claims

---

[33] Hart says that we recognize rules as law if they are declared to the public through the procedures that have become accepted as the procedures through which laws must be made—the rule(s) of recognition. A law's validity depends on the manner of its genesis—its source—rather than its content. In apartheid South Africa, for example, the government's attempt to remove 'coloured' people from the voters roll in the 1950s was blocked by the Appellate Division of the Supreme Court because the necessary parliamentary majorities had not been obtained, not because it was a racist law (*Harris v Minister of the Interior* 1952 (2) SA 428 (A) and *Minister of the Interior and Another v Harris and Others* 1952 (4) SA 769 (A)). In post-apartheid South Africa too, the Constitutional Court has held laws invalid because constitutionally required procedures for public consultation had not been followed prior to the enactment and proclamation of the laws (see *Doctors For Life International v Speaker of the National Assembly and Others* 2006 (6) SA 416 (CC) and *Matatiele Municipality and Others v President of the RSA and Others* 2006 (5) SA 47 (CC)).

the authority of popular sovereignty must therefore generate fidelity by ensuring that the content of the constitution remains consistent with the substantive principles that the very claim to popular sovereignty imposes.[34] The claim to popular sovereignty is, after all, the only source of authority on which the purported constitution-maker relies in the interregnum. It should not be surprising that the validity of the constitution that results should be assessed with reference to the basis of the constitution-maker's claim to authority.

What are these inherent principles of popular sovereignty? In thinking about this question it is useful to return to the idea that popular sovereignty takes two forms, in either the constitutional setting or the constitutional interregnum. Where the constituted powers claim the authority of popular sovereignty in the constitutional setting, they are bound both by the mandate they win from the people and by the constitutional limits on how the constituted powers may act in fulfilling that mandate. If a group of people is to exercise their sovereignty and act collectively to confer authority on a government established specifically to represent them, then it is important that each individual who counts herself as one of the group is able to participate in the collective decisions by which the government gets its mandate to represent them— an election, for example. If some individuals over whom the government exercises power are excluded from participating in the election, then the people have not acted collectively and cannot be said to have exercised popular sovereignty in conferring a mandate on the government. Further, if each person's entitlement to participate in a collective decision is to be substantively meaningful, each person's opinion has to be valued just as much as everyone else's. Equality in collective decision-making ensures that everyone's view is taken into account, and that everyone is treated as a rational and autonomous agent.

Before an election takes place, all the members of the group must agree to be bound by the outcome of the collective decision. They would not do this if they believed that certain members of the group were not rational. It would make no sense for individuals to agree to be bound by a decision made by people whose rationality is questionable. The implication, then, is that all individuals who agree to take part in a collective decision recognize and respect the rationality and autonomy of all other individuals in the group. The mutual recognition of each person's equal autonomy to form a view about the mandate to be given to a government is a necessary element of any transfer of sovereignty from the people to a government.

Taking part in the collective decision to confer authority to govern on an institution designed to govern therefore brings with it the reciprocal duty to recognize everyone

---

[34] Hannah Arendt, troubled by the arbitrary and illimitable power of the popular sovereign conceived as constitution-maker, argues that the very act of constitution is limited by principles immanent to the instituting act at the moment of its performance. What saves an act of constitution-making from the arbitrariness of unmediated and unlimited popular sovereignty is the set of principles that the act of constitution-making imposes on itself (H. Arendt, *Between Past and Future: Eight Exercises in Political Thought*, especially the chapter entitled 'What is Freedom?' (New York: Penguin, 1993); H. Arendt, *On Revolution* (New York: Viking Press, 1965); H. Arendt, 'Some Questions of Moral Philosophy' (1994) 61 *Social Research* 739, at 741). See also Kalyvas, above n 16, 234–5.

else as having an equal status as a member of the decision-making collective. No representative democratic institution can claim to represent the people as a political unity, and thereby claim the authority of popular sovereignty, if some persons within the group are treated as less than full and equal participants in the discourse from which the representative government's mandate comes. Every citizen of a constitutional system must have an opportunity commensurate with every other citizen's to participate in and contribute to the formation of the popular will on the authority of which the constituted powers act. Whatever rules are established at the constitutional moment for the determination of the popular will at moments of ordinary politics must treat all individuals as equals in the political process.[35]

In less abstract terms, a claim to popular sovereignty during ordinary lawmaking translates into an obligation to respect civil and political rights at the constitutional level. Each person must be assured that her voice is given as much weight as the next person's in the constituted powers' ordinary law making process. This is usually understood as an obligation to recognize a universal franchise and to confer equal rights to vote and stand for public office. The commitment to popular sovereignty holds substantive implications for both ordinary politics and the constitutional moment. The procedures and process rights that make the claim to popular sovereignty meaningful in periods of ordinary lawmaking and ordinary politics, by ensuring that the rationality and autonomy of each person is respected in these periods, have to be beyond the reach of those ordinary processes of law if they are to continue to make a meaningful claim to popular sovereignty. There may be a number of ways to protect these rights, but where a constitutional document establishes the institutions of politics it makes sense that the same constitutional document would establish the obligation to respect these process rights.[36]

C. The argument for substantive non-discrimination: Schmitt's inadvertent contribution

The argument for civil and political rights relies on the bifurcated understanding of popular sovereignty, and on the implications for constitution-making that the constituted powers' claim to popular sovereignty during periods of ordinary lawmaking holds. The limit of this argument is that the political process must treat everyone equally, and that the law must apply equally to everyone. But H. L. A. Hart's objection to Fuller's inner morality of law would seem to be cogent here too: ordinary laws may be able to carry the imprimatur of popular sovereignty, because everyone is able to

---

[35] See R. Stacey, 'Democratic Jurisprudence and Judicial Review: Waldron's Contribution to Political Positivism' (2010) 30 *Oxford Journal of Legal Studies* 749, at 768–71 (arguing that even in a majoritarian democratic system there must be some guarantee of the process rights that make the practice of radical democratic government possible).

[36] This argument can be distinguished from the argument that whatever principles and norms constitution-makers abide by during the constitution-making process must logically be reflected in the text of the constitution itself. These are the 'implicit presuppositions of constitution-making' that Andreas Kalyvas identifies. See Kalyvas, above n 16, 236.

participate equally in the processes of ordinary lawmaking, yet be morally iniquitous laws.[37] It is conceivable that I could participate in a decision that would deny me an equal status with everyone else in the future, and be bound to accept that reduced status simply because it is an outcome of a political process that treats people as equals. A commitment to equality in the process of lawmaking provides no basis to object to a law that treats people unequally if the process by which it was enacted upheld individual rationality and autonomy equally.

Alongside this argument for process rights stands an argument for a broader principle of substantive non-discrimination as a necessary feature of any constitution that makes a claim to the authority of popular sovereignty. In the same way that a government may be able to claim the authority of popular sovereignty by sticking to the terms of an existing constitution, a government in a constitutional interregnum may be able to do the same by sticking to the basic principles of popular sovereignty. The argument runs along analogous lines to the argument above about the rule of law in established legal systems. Adherence to the rule of law generates fidelity to law as a tool for social order, even where people disagree with the content of the law, because the people know what the law allows and are certain that the government and others will act only in terms of the law. For people to continue to accept the authority of law as the mechanism that orders their social interactions, laws must continue to apply in the same way to everyone to whom they apply. Laws themselves must therefore apply generally to everyone, and must be enforced equally in society by officials. An argument that equality before the law is a necessary feature of a legal system based on a popular constitution comes, somewhat surprisingly, from Carl Schmitt.

Although most of Schmitt's work champions a dictator's unfettered power to define the legal order, especially in exceptional moments, Schmitt argues that a 'merely formal concept of law such as that the law is anything that the lawmaking bodies ordain via the legislative process', reduces a constitution to the 'absolutism of the legislative office'. If this were our understanding of the constitution, Schmitt goes on, the 'multi-headed absolutism of the transitory partisan majority would replace monarchical absolutism' and leave the people no better off than under the tyranny of a supreme despot.[38] Avoiding this view of the constitution requires accepting that the constitution imposes some substantive limits on the lawmaking power of the constituted powers: 'Every constitutional regulation of legislative authorizations *presupposes* a substantive concept of law', Schmitt begins.[39] There are qualities that every rule that claims the status of legal validity must exhibit. He goes on: 'Equality before the law is immanent to the Rechtsstaat concept of the law. In other words, law is that which intrinsically contains equality within the limits of the possible, therefore a general norm.'[40]

---

[37] Hart, above n 17, 202; and J. Raz, 'The Rule of Law and its Virtue', in *The Authority of Law* (Oxford: Oxford University Press, 1979) 224.

[38] Schmitt, above n 19, 191.   [39] Ibid 189.

[40] Ibid 194. I have explored this contradiction in Schmitt's own constitutional theory elsewhere, reading Schmitt against himself in the context of the constitutional transition in Kenya to argue that any exercise of constituent power is bound to recognize at least the substantive principle of equality before the law. See R. Stacey, 'Constituent Power and Carl Schmitt's Theory of Constitution in Kenya's Constitution-making Process' (2011) 9 *International Journal of Constitutional Law* 587, at 606–10.

Schmitt accepts that the law may nevertheless be bad or unjust, but the principle of equality before the law reduces this danger to a minimum and enhances law's protective character.[41] Even Schmitt's constitutional theory recognizes that the exercise of constituent power must lead to a constitution that recognizes the requirement that the law treat people equally. The exercise of constituent power cannot produce a constitutional legal system that discriminates between people in the application of the law—whatever the content of the laws themselves.

But the argument can be taken further than equality merely in the application of the law. We already know from the argument from the rule of law that citizens are unlikely to accept the authority of law if the laws are applied unequally and unpredictably (and especially if they already disagree with its objectives or substance). But the same considerations arise during constitution-making in the constitutional interregnum: fidelity to power requires equality in the act of constitution-making. If constitutional rules are to claim the imprimatur of popular sovereignty, they must ensure that the actions they allow the constituted powers to take respect the rationality and autonomy of all people equally. In contrast to adherence to the rule of law which imposes no substantive commitments on lawmakers, the claim to popular sovereignty—and the fidelity to power that a government relying on that claim must generate—does affect the substance of the law, to the extent that it acts on the constitutional foundations of law rather than merely on official conduct after law is enacted. The people in whose name constitution-making power is claimed and exercised are unlikely to accept the authority of the purported constitution-maker if the constitution that results authorizes the constituted powers to exercise their powers and perform their obligations differently with regard to different individuals or groups in society. A constitution that, for example, does not prohibit the constituted powers from providing benefits to one group of people while withholding them from another, will not be able to make a meaningful claim to the authority of popular sovereignty for the very reason that the failure to treat all of the people as equally rational moral agents compromises fidelity to power. In this event the claim to popular sovereignty is an empty one.

People may disagree over the terms of specific constitutional rules, and they may disagree about the appropriateness of government conduct within those rules. But if the constitutional rules require government to uphold the commitment to equal moral agency and rationality when it makes laws (and not just when it acts in terms of those laws), the people to whom those laws apply will be better able to act as rational and moral agents and will have more reason to remain faithful to the government's claim to the authority of popular sovereignty. While fidelity to law requires equality in the application of law once the lawmaking power has been exercised to enact ordinary laws, fidelity to power requires equality in the application of lawmaking power. And since it is the constitution that constitutes lawmaking power anew as well as regulates it, fidelity to power requires a constitution to prohibit the making of ordinary laws that apply to some people without applying to others. Wherever a constitution that claims the authority of popular sovereignty establishes institutions to make ordinary laws and

---

[41] Schmitt, above n 19, 196. In this regard see also Raz, above n 37, 224.

confers a power to make ordinary laws on them, the claim to the authority of popular sovereignty obliges the constitutional conferral of lawmaking power to prohibit laws that discriminate substantively between people.

IV. Conclusion: The Practical Universality of Liberal Democratic Constitutionalism

The arguments for civil and political rights and for substantive non-discrimination do not suggest that all constitutions are bound to respect civil and political rights and prohibit discrimination. The obligation to recognize civil and political rights and the principle of substantive non-discrimination are not immanent in the act or practice of constitution-making. Rather, it is the claim to popular sovereignty that imposes this obligation. Acts of constitution-making that make no claim to popular sovereignty, or which make a hollow and disingenuous claim to popular sovereignty, may be able to avoid compliance with these principles without sacrificing the basis of its authority to make a constitution. Where a constitution-making body assumes the authority to enact a constitution simply by having defeated all other competitors by force, and is unconcerned with representing the sovereignty of the people, then popular sovereignty is simply not in play and will impose no constraints. There may be other procedural and substantive constraints on constitution-making, but whatever they might be, they will not flow from the claim to popular sovereignty.

The case I make in this chapter is that when a constitution-maker seeks to justify a constitution on the basis of a claim to the authority of popular sovereignty, this implies a meaningful commitment in the text of the constitution to the principles of popular sovereignty. Among these principles, I argue, are included at least the civil and political rights and the prohibition on substantive discrimination that I describe here. To the extent that there are no constitutions in the world that do not claim the authority of popular sovereignty, I am more than happy to accept the implicit conclusion that these liberal democratic commitments are a necessary element of every constitution in the world.

Of course, many of the claims constitution-makers make to popular sovereignty will be disingenuous or meaningless. Where this is the case, the constitution-maker will be as unfettered as a constitution-maker who relies on nothing other than its victory in a civil war for its constitution-making authority. But the focus of this chapter has been to reject the idea that popular sovereignty, where it is meaningfully and honestly exercised, is an unbounded power the exercise of which can give rise to a constitution that says whatever its makers want it to say. My position is rather that the claim to popular sovereignty imposes substantive limitations on constitution-making. The arguments in support of this position should be assiduously pressed against both unbounded popular sovereignty and majoritarian democrats who accept without question what the majority decides, because to accept these alternate views is to invite a return to the kind of constitutional authoritarianism that the Arab Spring sought to overthrow.

9

Constitutional Reason of State

Thomas Poole*

Reason of state is a fundamental dimension of constitutional law, operating as a limit concept, mediating between law and politics, and politics and violence. Although hard to define with precision, reason of state is associated with situations in which state action moves from one register, based on law and right, to another, based on interest and might.[1] The condition for such a move is normally the assertion that a vital interest of the state is at risk. 'The core meaning of the phrase "reason of state" is that public necessity or state interest overrides the legal and ethical restraints that normally apply to human action.'[2] Reason of state's traditional habitat is the apparently marginal activities of the state, war and peace, commerce and empire, diplomacy and interstate relations. I say *apparently* marginal not only because such activities were central to the formation of states,[3] but also because they helped shape the constitutions of those states.[4] As such, reason of state can be understood as a juridical concept or category, and it is this understanding of the term that is explored here.[5]

This chapter defends reason of state as an explanatory category. It begins with an analysis of the law relating to the prerogative (section I), before observing that prerogative cases are much less typical today than an expanding suite of cases involving related matters but where the power in question is sourced in statute or the constitution (section II). The long-term historical narrative towards the constitutionalization of reserve powers can thus be expressed as a move from a princely model of reason of state, epitomized by prerogative, to a polity or law-based model of reason of state, whose characteristic form is statute (section III). Locke's analysis of prerogative is seen as a classic early-modern account of the princely model. Hobbes's state theory provides the basic script of the polity model, but it is in the republican theorists of the same period, notably Harrington, that we see a recognizably modern concern to normalize reason of state through constitutional and institutional design. The chapter then takes issue with modern liberals who follow Hayek in wanting to remove the concept of reason of state from constitutional politics altogether (section IV). Such an approach can only work if the state is itself made to vanish, or if a liberal state disengages from

---

* Professor of Law, London School of Economics and Political Science.
[1] G. Poggi, *The State: Its Nature, Development and Prospects* (Cambridge: Polity, 1990), 84.
[2] J. S. Maloy, *Democratic Statecraft: Political Realism and Popular Power* (Cambridge: Cambridge University Press, 2013), 13.
[3] See eg C. Tilly, *Coercion, Capital, and European States AD 990–1992* (Oxford: Blackwell, 1990).
[4] See eg P. Bobbitt, *The Shield of Achilles: War, Peace, and the Course of History* (New York: Alfred A. Knopf, 2002).
[5] See also C. J. Friedrich, *Constitutional Reason of State* (Providence: Brown University Press, 1957).

interaction with other states. Neither option is plausible. The paper ends with a reflection on the value of the category of reason of state for constitutional theory (section V).

I

Anglophone public lawyers are more familiar with the prerogative than reason of state. Admittedly, prerogative has itself rarely, if ever, been clearly understood, and even the greatest of the common law jurists struggled with the concept. Blackstone characterized prerogative as the despotic power that 'the King hath, over and above all other persons, and out of the ordinary course of the common law, in right of his royal dignity'.[6] Such a power operates in a space beyond the reach of normal law: 'in the exertion of lawful prerogative, the king is and ought to be absolute; that is, so far absolute, that there is no legal authority that can either delay or resist him'.[7] This vision of legally untrammelled executive authority was somehow meant to fit with an equally inflated conception of Parliament as absolute and omnipotent.[8] Dicey defined prerogative as 'nothing else than the residue of discretionary or arbitrary authority, which at any given time is legally left in the hands of the Crown'.[9] This is an attempt to define the category ('prerogative') solely in terms of what it is not ('ordinary law'), hoping that constitutional conventions will somehow square the circle and bring a measure of normality to the otherwise abnormal.[10]

The case law on prerogative is similarly indeterminate. The great sequence of seventeenth-century cases, and the shift in constitutional tectonic plates to which they relate, did clarify certain things. The Bill of Rights 1688 is a constitutional statute one function of which was to exclude a number of 'pretended' prerogative powers, including the power to suspend or dispense with the law and the power to levy money without parliamentary consent. Some relatively clear principles have emerged from this constitutional base. (1) An Act of Parliament passed in an area previously under prerogative authority ousts that prerogative power.[11] (2) The courts have authority to declare the existence and extent of claimed prerogatives: 'the King hath no prerogative, but that which the law of the land allows him'.[12] (3) No new prerogative powers can be created.[13] (However, given that the courts recognize in principle a power to do whatever is 'necessary to meet either an actual or an apprehended threat to the peace'[14] and a power to do

---

[6] W. Blackstone, *Commentaries on the Laws of England, Vol. I*, S. N. Katz (ed) (Chicago: University of Chicago Press, 1979), 232.

[7] Ibid 243.   [8] Ibid 160.

[9] A. V. Dicey, *The Law of the Constitution*, J. W. F. Allison (ed) (Oxford: Oxford University Press, 2013), 188.

[10] Ibid 189: 'The conventions of the constitution are in short rules intended to regulate the exercise of the whole of the remaining discretionary powers of the Crown, whether these powers are exercised by the Queen herself or by the Ministry.'

[11] *Attorney General v De Keyser's Royal Hotel Ltd* [1920] AC 508. That prerogative power cannot subsequently be re-invoked or resurrected: *R v Home Secretary, ex p Fire Brigades Union* [1995] 2 AC 513.

[12] *The Case of Proclamations* (PC 1611) 12 Co Rep 74, at 76.

[13] *Prohibitions del Roy* (1607) 12 Co Rep 63. See also *BBC v Johns* [1965] Ch 32, at 79 (per Diplock LJ): 'It is 350 years and a civil war too late for the Queen's courts to broaden the prerogative.'

[14] *R v Secretary of State for the Home Department, ex p Northumbria Police Authority* [1989] QB 26.

all things necessary in an emergency,[15] this principle is perhaps less restrictive than might be supposed.) (4) No free-floating plea of state necessity will protect anyone accused of an unlawful act.[16] (Although the courts sometimes recognize a 'third source'[17] of authority: that government has the same liberty as an ordinary person to do certain things, such as distribute information and enter into contracts.[18])

But despite the longevity of many of these principles, uncertainty continues to surround the law relating to prerogative. Both Blackstone and Dicey remarked on this lack of clarity which, while it helped to reduce tensions between Crown and Parliament, served to mask the operation of exceptional executive power.[19] The 'powers of Courts are a delicate subject, coming very near to the mystery part of prerogative', William Harrison Moore wrote in his treatise on act of state, paraphrasing James I.[20] And this link between prerogative and *arcana imperii* (secrets of rule) led seventeenth-century judges more often than not to fall in line with the Crown.[21] Similar connotations persist,[22] and judges rarely manage to make it through a prerogative case without referencing Lord Atkin's line about prerogative evoking 'the clanking of mediaeval chains of the ghosts of the past'.[23]

This is not to say that the courts have not tried to normalize the prerogative. The *GCHQ* case decided that exercises of prerogative might in principle be reviewable on ordinary principles.[24] Since then, courts have steadily encroached on what were once 'forbidden areas'[25] of prerogative control. Litigants have brought cases on the prerogative of mercy,[26] the conduct of foreign policy,[27] treaty-making,[28] forced population resettlement,[29] the conduct of the armed forces overseas,[30] even questions of war

---

[15] *Burmah Oil Co Ltd v Lord Advocate* [1965] AC 75, at 101. But Lord Reid, while recognizing such a prerogative, also said the 'mobilization of the industrial and financial resources of the country could not be done without statutory emergency powers. The prerogative is really a relic of a past age, not lost by disuse but only available for a case not covered by statute.' See also *Ex p D. F. Marais* [1902] AC 109.

[16] *Entick v Carrington* 19 State Tr (1765) 1029, at 1066.

[17] B. Harris, 'The "Third Source" of Authority for Government Action' (1992) 108 *Law Quarterly Review* 626.

[18] *Malone v Metropolitan Police Commissioner* [1979] Ch 344; *R (New College London Ltd) v Secretary of State for the Home Department* [2013] UKSC 51. Compare *R v Somerset County Council, ex p Fewings* [1995] 1 All ER 513, at 524, where Laws J said that whereas individuals 'may do anything...which the law does not prohibit', the 'opposite rule' applies to public bodies: anything that they do 'must be justified by positive law'.

[19] Dicey called the prerogative 'a term which has caused more perplexity to students than any other expression referring to the constitution': Dicey, above n 9, 188.

[20] W. H. Moore, *Act of State in English Law* (London: John Murray, 1906), 11.

[21] *Five Knights Case (Darnel's Case)* 3 How St Tr 1 (1627); *The Case of Ship Money (R v Hampden)* 3 How St Tr 825 (1637).

[22] See the House of Commons Public Administration Select Committee Report, 'Taming the Prerogative: Strengthening Ministerial Accountability to Parliament' (March 2004).

[23] *United Australia Ltd v Barclays Bank Ltd* [1941] AC 1, at 29 (per Lord Atkin).

[24] *Council of Civil Service Unions v Minister for the Civil Service* [1985] AC 374. But see also *R v Criminal Injuries Compensation Board, ex p Lain* [1967] 2 QB 864; *Laker Airways Ltd v Department of Trade and Industry* [1977] QB 643.

[25] *R (Abbasi) v Secretary of State for Foreign and Commonwealth Affairs* [2002] EWCA Civ 1598, para 106.

[26] *R v Secretary of State for the Home Department, ex p Bentley* [1994] QB 349.

[27] *Abbasi*, above n 25; *R (Al Rawi) v Secretary of State for Foreign and Commonwealth Affairs* [2006] EWCA Civ 1279.

[28] *R v Secretary of State for Foreign and Commonwealth Affairs, ex p Rees-Mogg* [1994] QB 552.

[29] *R (Bancoult) v Secretary of State for Foreign and Commonwealth Affairs (No. 2)* [2008] UKHL 61.

[30] *Al-Skeini v Secretary of State for Defence* [2007] UKHL 26; *Smith v Ministry of Defence* [2013] UKSC 41 (partly successful claims in negligence as a result of the MoD's failure to provide available equipment and technology to protect servicemen killed in action in Iraq).

and peace.[31] The fact that the judges give a serious hearing to these cases is significant. But it remains the case that few of them result in a decisive judgment in the claimant's favour. Even when they do win, victory is often pyrrhic or abnormal. *Abbasi* is an example of the former. The mother of a British citizen detained in Guantanamo Bay asked the court to compel the Foreign Office to make representations on his behalf to the US government. The court was willing in principle to impose a duty to consider making representations. In practice, though, no such order was made: first, because the Foreign Office had already considered Abbasi's request; second, being a 'delicate time', such an order 'would have an impact on the conduct of foreign policy'.[32] *Bentley* is an example of the latter. In that case, the sister of a man executed for murder successfully challenged the refusal of a posthumous pardon. But no formal order was made. The Home Secretary was instead *invited* to look again at the matter. Cases of this sort underscore the impression that with prerogative we are still dealing with a space unusual in the extent of its legal informality and fuzziness. Despite its continued juridification, prerogative is still governed as much by the logic of *grace* as that of *right*.

II

But as far as reason of state is concerned, the prerogative is only part of the whole. While it once provided the central legal category in which claims of extraordinary executive authority were made and contested, developments led to the gradual displacement of prerogative.[33] The most obvious change was the severing of the direct link between prerogative and kingship as government ministers began to exercise almost all the important prerogatives. In addition, the trend has been for statute to replace prerogative even in areas most associated with special executive discretion. The move was driven by functional needs, since statute is a better form for complicated rule-making. But changing patterns of legitimation also play a role. Examples range from war legislation (eg Defence of the Realm Act 1914) to emergency provisions (eg Civil Contingencies Act 2004) and anti-terrorism laws (eg the PATRIOT Act 2001).

Reserve and special powers were more often than not given constitutional or, more often, statutory form—or at least they were authorized and enabled by statute. Instead of an exceptional category for exceptional authority (prerogative), exceptional claims now operate largely through normal legal forms (statute, delegation, contract) that generate special powers or exemptions, which may create 'carve-outs' from the operation of the normal legal system. Prerogative continues to exist: not only in the concrete sense of providing an operative framework, albeit in a relatively small range of areas,[34] but also as a metaphor, offering a sense of legal shape or a juridical patina to claims for

---

[31] *R (Gentle) v The Prime Minister* [2008] UKHL 20 (unsuccessful attempt by relatives of dead servicemen to claim that ECHR, article 2 required the government to establish an independent public enquiry into all the circumstances surrounding the invasion of Iraq in 2003).

[32] *Abbasi*, above n 25, para 107.

[33] The story was different in respect of the British state's colonial and imperial engagements, where prerogative remained a much more significant legal category.

[34] For a rigorous and careful taxonomy see A. Twomey, 'Pushing the Boundaries of Executive Power—*Pape*, The Prerogative and Nationhood Powers' (2010) 34 *Melbourne University Law Review* 313.

otherwise inchoate or legally shapeless extraordinary authority to act for the safety of the people (*salus populi*).[35] In this second sense, and to paraphrase Dicey, prerogative provides the residue of a residual category.

By way of illustration, let us consider some recent cases. Only the first is a prerogative case. The others involve claims of the sort that once would have fallen under prerogative but now implicate different legal categories.

1. *Bancoult (No. 2)* involved a challenge against the British government's refusal to repatriate inhabitants of the Chagos Islands, a British Indian Overseas Territory.[36] The inhabitants had been removed to make way for a US naval base on the main island, Diego Garcia. A court had previously ruled the expulsion to be unlawful.[37] The decision not to resettle was defended on the basis of an adverse feasibility study and because the US government was concerned that it might compromise the security of the base. All relevant decisions were taken under the prerogative, here retaining its prominent status within colonial governance. The court decided, by a majority, that the decision not to repatriate was lawful. Historically, such prerogative legislation was 'apt to confer plenary law-making authority'.[38] Legally, the court should not interfere with 'what is essentially a political judgment'.[39]

2. *Corner House* involved a challenge to a decision to suspend an investigation into allegations that British Aerospace had bribed Saudi Arabian officials while negotiating the sale of aircraft.[40] The Saudi government threatened to withdraw cooperation with the United Kingdom in countering terrorism if the investigation was not stopped. After consultation with government officials at the highest level, the Director of the Serious Fraud Office stopped the investigation. Challenged by an NGO, Corner House, the Law Lords held that national security and the risk to British lives was a relevant consideration in the exercise of the Director's discretion, and that it was lawful for the Director to defer to the government on the nature of the risk.

3. *Charkaoui v Canada (Citizenship and Immigration)*[41] concerned provisions of an Act[42] which allowed specified government ministers to issue a certificate of inadmissibility declaring that a foreign national or permanent resident may not enter Canadian territory on grounds inter alia of national security, leading in most cases to the detention of the person named in the certificate. Although certification and detention were subject to judicial review, the process might deprive the

---

[35] *Chandler v Director of Public Prosecutions* [1964] AC 763; *Secretary of State for the Home Department v Rehman* [2001] UKHL 47; *R (Lord Carlile of Berriew) v Secretary of State for the Home Department* [2014] UKSC 60.
[36] *Bancoult (No. 2)*, above n 49. For analysis of the historical background, and the complex multi-leveled litigation that is still ongoing see S. Allen, *The Chagos Islanders and International Law* (Oxford: Hart Publishing, 2014).
[37] *R (Bancoult) v Secretary of State for Foreign and Commonwealth Affairs* [2001] QB 1067.
[38] Ibid para 50 (per Lord Hoffmann).   [39] Ibid para 130 (per Lord Carswell).
[40] *R (Corner House Research) v Director of the Serious Fraud Office* [2008] UKHL 60.
[41] 2007 SCC 9. The case has strong echoes of the Belmarsh case that had gone through British courts a few years previously: *A v Secretary of State for the Home Department* [2004] UKHL 56.
[42] Immigration and Refugee Protection Act SC 2001, c 27, ss 77–84.

named person of some or all of the information on the basis of which the certification was made. Once a certificate was confirmed, a foreign national could not
apply for review for another 120 days (whereas detention of a permanent resident
had to be reviewed within 48 hours). The Supreme Court of Canada found the
certification process to violate section 7 of the Charter (fair process protections
associated with the right to life, liberty, and security), specifically because it failed
to afford the named person an opportunity to meet the case against him or her.[43]
The provision for the extended detention of foreign nationals also violated the
guarantee of freedom from arbitrary detention contained within section 9 of the
Charter.[44] The remedy for these violations was rather unusual. The Court issued
a declaration that the procedure for judicial approval of certificates was inconsistent with the Charter and hence unlawful, suspended for one year from the date of
judgment in order to give Parliament time to amend the law.[45]

4. *Pape v Commissioner of Taxation of the Commonwealth of Australia* was a challenge to the constitutionality of the stimulus package devised by the Australian
government in response to the global financial crisis of 2007–8.[46] The High
Court of Australia, by a majority, held that the Act was valid, supported by
section 51 of the Constitution as being incidental to the exercise by the government of its executive power under section 61 of the Constitution.[47] The Court
decided this either on the basis (per French CJ) of an inherent and inchoate
authority 'derived partly from the Royal Prerogative and probably even more
from the necessities of a modern national government' which exists so as 'to
be capable of serving the proper purposes of a national government';[48] or (per
Gummow, Crennan, and Bell JJ) because the power of the executive 'involves
much more than the enjoyment of the benefit of those preferences, immunities
and exceptions which are…commonly identified with "the prerogative", so
as to enable 'the undertaking of action appropriate to the position of the Commonwealth as a polity created by the Constitution and having regard to the spheres
of responsibility vested in it'.[49]

In each case, we see the government making a claim of special authority to do something they couldn't otherwise do lawfully. This claim comes in harness with another,
more specifically jurisdictional claim: namely, that the government is better placed
than the courts to assess (and so to warrant) that the situation in question necessi-
tates the special authority that is claimed. We see, then, the same juridical structure as
the old prerogative, played out in similar domains. But the legal form it takes tends to

---

[43] Ibid para 55.   [44] Ibid para 93.   [45] Ibid paras 139–40.
[46] Tax Bonus for Working Australians Act (No. 2) 2009 (Cth).
[47] (2009) 238 CLR 1; [2009] HCA 23.   [48] Ibid paras 127–8.
[49] Ibid para 214. See analogously *Quake Outcasts v Ministry for Canterbury Earthquake Recovery* [2015]
NZSC 27, where the New Zealand government defended its decision to announce a 'red zone' in post-
earthquake Christchurch where rebuilding would not occur, and to offer purchase of properties in that zone
(at comparatively low rates), on the basis that it was made under the Crown's power to enter into contracts
as a natural person (at para 112). The Supreme Court held, on the contrary, that the Canterbury Earthquake
Recovery Act 2011 'covered the field' and that procedures specified by that Act should have applied. The
Court did say, however, that a residual power was recognized, as long as it was not displaced by statute.

be different. *Bancoult* now seems the anomaly—although even here the normalizing dimensions of the judgment are apparent—the others typical, whether questioning the exercise of statutory discretion in *Corner House* or challenging executive authority on constitutional grounds as in *Charkaoui* and *Pape*.

Some commentators continue to find value in talking about such cases in the old way. For instance, when Judith Butler talks about the 'resurgent prerogative', which she sees in post-9/11 developments in security politics, she uses the word in a metaphorical sense, aware that most of the developments she refers to take a different legal form.[50] While this use of the term is acceptable, I prefer to talk about this domain of constitutional politics, which covers public emergency (*Belmarsh*), the suspension of the normal operation of law (*Corner House*), neo-colonial prerogative cases (*Bancoult*), and also the standing practice of diplomacy (*Abbasi*), under the umbrella of reason of state. The term, like prerogative, has considerable pedigree. But, unlike prerogative, its history is not so restricted in time, jurisdiction, or form. Reason of state takes us closer to the heart of the matter, in that it picks up what is perhaps most important about the category in question, namely a certain type of authority claim that normally includes a plea for special measures, grounded in a principle (*salus populi*) that invokes the state's capacity as protective agent. Reason of state thus draws our attention directly to what is perhaps most distinctive about the political idea to which it relates, which is the state acting in the persona of *custos*, as guardian or protector of the constitution. Inevitably, this type of claim involves dimensions of power and politics, and in fact these are often acute. But for all that, it remains a claim in public law—and not, for instance, purely an assertion of force. This is evidenced by the fact that the plea is generally made through normal (or near normal) legal channels—consent is asked of legislatures and courts and, through them, the public. And, if consented to, the special measures will operate for the most part under a regime that may be different in quality but still functions according to legal criteria.

Thinking in terms of the prerogative is outmoded, but also risks obscuring an important element of modern constitutional politics. A defining feature of prerogative was that it was arbitrary, as Dicey observed, in the sense that it was unstructured by law. Prerogative expresses the irreducibly personal aspect of the power and the sacerdotal element that it kept from medieval notions of kingship. But modern reason of state works through dense legal networks. This is not to say that personality no longer matters in politics—the opposite may be true in this area of state affairs, where the appeal of charismatic politics persists. But we have moved from a context in which the king and a few favourites can determine the affairs of state and decide questions of war and peace. More typical today is an expansive web of government departments, committees, and agencies, each of which acts as a miniature legal order, complete with a bespoke regulatory structure and supervisory institutions. Reason of state is rarely now in the formal sense non-arbitrary. It largely mirrors the humdrum realities and bureaucratic shape of the administrative state and has, as such, lost much of its exceptional form.

---

[50] J. Butler, *Precarious Life: The Power of Mourning and Violence* (London: Verso, 2006).

Reason of state has become normalized then, at least to the extent that the exceptional is commonly camouflaged in standard administrative-state khaki. This does not mean that it is not *exercised* in a substantively arbitrary way, in a peremptory or draconian manner, for instance. Nor does it mean that these institutionalized reason of state practices are fully public and transparent. Reason of state retains much of its old connection with *arcana imperii*.[51] As Jack Goldsmith observes, older conceptions of prerogative based on Lockean ideas of executive action in defiance of law are 'no longer part of [an executive's] justificatory tool kit'. The real danger is secrecy, Goldsmith argues, specifically the 'executive auto-interpretation of executive authorities, and in particular *secret executive branch interpretation of law*'.[52] We see echoes of this concern in our illustrative cases. *Bancoult, Abbasi*, and *Corner House* all involve matters that were withheld from the court[53] or were at the very limits of the courts' cognitive abilities, such as diplomatic relations and security risk assessments.

Developments to increase the transparency and accountability of decision-making of the state's reason of state activities have taken place on a number of fronts. In the legal arena, the rise of judicial review and the willingness of courts to enter territory previously reserved for governments has led to the widespread acceptance of the need for such activities to be authorized by law. The result is that while we probably don't know all the state's 'dirty little secrets',[54] we probably have a fairer idea about what it is up to than ever before. It seems far less common for the state to seek to operate within extra-legal scenarios—or 'legal black holes', in the vernacular. That is not to say that secrecy and pockets of executive discretion do not exist,[55] only that there are fewer sustained attempts to define those spaces as existing outside the law.[56] In Donald Rumsfeld's taxonomy, the primary juridical problem today is not so much the unknown unknowns—or, more likely, the half-guessed-at unknowns of state interest prosecution. What is perhaps more symptomatic is 'grey hole' secrecy: that is, a world of relatively 'known unknowns' typified by government attempts to carve out for itself various safe (or safer) spaces within the jurisdiction of the law.[57]

At the core of this process of normalizing reason of state is the move away from extra-legal action, which is necessarily secret in that it operates in a zone of silence outside the apparatus of lawful action and public reason that is the normal life of the state, to a heightened demand for secrecy for the most part within the interstices of the law. In some institutions dominated by reason of state matters, such as the Foreign Intelligence

[51] See eg Blackstone, above n 6, 230–1.
[52] J. Goldsmith, 'The Irrelevance of Prerogative Power, and the Evils of Secret Legal Interpretation', in C. Fatovic and B. A. Kleinerman (eds), *Extra-Legal Power and Legitimacy: Perspective on Prerogative* (New York: Oxford University Press, 2013), 214–32.
[53] *R (Binyam Mohamed) v Secretary of State for Foreign and Commonwealth Affairs* [2010] EWCA Civ 158.
[54] G. Greenwald, *No Place to Hide: Edward Snowden, the NSA and the Surveillance State* (London: Hamish Hamilton, 2014), discussing the 'ubiquitous, secretive system of suspicionless surveillance' that may be the enduring legacy of the 'war on terror' (ibid 5).
[55] G. L. Neuman, 'Anomalous Zones' (1996) 48 *Stanford Law Review* 1197.
[56] For a juridical map of this terrain see J. M. Balkin, 'The Constitution in the National Surveillance State' (2008) 93 *Minnesota Law Review* 1.
[57] D. Dyzenhaus, 'Are States of Emergency Inside or Outside the Legal Order?' (2006) 27 *Cardozo Law Review* 2005, at 2026: 'grey holes are more harmful to the rule of law than black holes'.

Surveillance Act (FISA) court in the United States or the UK's Investigatory Powers Tribunal, secrecy is the norm. But even in the ordinary courts, there has been more recourse to abnormal or secret proceedings. In the United Kingdom, the Justice and Security Act 2013 extended what had been specific provision for the inclusion of secret elements ('closed material proceedings') to any civil case where 'sensitive material' the disclosure of which would be damaging to the interests of national security is in issue.[58] The Act gives statutory authorization to a process that the Supreme Court had judged to be at odds with the common law principle of open and natural justice.[59]

While reason of state may not look formally all that exceptional, it remains substantively distinctive. Not only on account of the exceptional quality of the powers usually claimed, which often include carve-outs from the normal law, secrecy in proceedings, special powers, and exemptions, but also by virtue of what might be called its jurisdictional component. That is, reason of state is a claim for extra power that also involves a claim for special jurisdiction: that the wielder of power is, for the time being, in a stronger position to judge on whether the power is exercised legitimately. This jurisdictional element may in fact be the more distinctive feature of rule of law claims, in that it is this element that seeks more directly to deny the application of the normal logic of public reason. The essential claim is that this logic be superseded in whole or in part by the logic of reason of state, often on the basis that the matters at stake are so important or complex that the jurisdiction of 'ordinary' law is to be replaced by the 'special' jurisdiction of interest. To an extent, then, reason of state claims operate like ouster or privative clauses, which seek to shield particular government decisions from judicial oversight.[60] There is every reason for courts[61] and other actors[62] to treat reason of state claims with the same scepticism they show ouster clauses, a point that is developed later.

III

We return to contemporary matters shortly, but not before deepening the historical and conceptual analysis. Reviewing the argument so far, we might be tempted to conclude that there has been a historical move from prerogative to reason of state. That is, a general shift over time from older, quasi-sacerdotal notions of an exceptional, arbitrary, and legally inchoate capacity vested in 'the Prince' or 'the Crown' for use in times of turmoil, to a normalized, formally non-arbitrary, and more heavily institutionalized reservoir of special executive authority. There is perhaps some truth to this reading.

---

[58] E. Nanopoulos, 'European Human Rights Law and the Normalisation of the "Closed Material Procedure": Limit or Source?' (forthcoming, 2016) 79 *Modern Law Review*.

[59] *Al Rawi v The Security Service* [2011] UKSC 34.

[60] The classic case in English law on ouster clauses, *Anisminic v Foreign Compensation Commission* [1969] 2 AC 147, can be seen as a reason of state case, since it concerned claims arising from the appropriation of the property of British companies in the wake of the Suez Crisis.

[61] The High Court of Australia has been particularly active on this front: see *Plaintiff S157/2002 v Commonwealth of Australia* (2003) 211 CLR 476; *Kirk v Industrial Relations Commission* (2010) 239 CLR 531.

[62] For an account of the successful political opposition to a proposed ouster clause to restrict legal challenges to asylum decisions see R. Rawlings, 'Review, Revenge, Retreat' (2005) 68 *Modern Law Review* 378.

But, on balance, it is better to understand the course of development as a move from one mode of reason of state to another. We might say that the first phase corresponds to a model of 'princely' reason of state while the second is structured according to a 'polity' model of reason of state. Whereas the juristic category of prerogative is a natural fit within, perhaps even intrinsic to, the former, to the latter it is anomalous. This perspective allows us to identify a family of practices ('reason of state') and to isolate what is continuous and contingent within it. It also avoids two potential anachronisms. Given that the terminology of reason of state and its synonyms (*raison d'état, ragione di stato, Staatsraison*) does not post-date prerogative,[63] it is odd to suggest that the defining move in this area has been from the latter to the former.[64] And, as we have seen, the fact that some states still use prerogative indicates that the category is not entirely redundant.

But what does the shift from princely to polity modes of reason of state involve? We can take Locke's theory of king's prerogative as a paradigmatic expression of princely reason of state.[65] This is not to say that it offers an accurate account of contemporary juridical realities. Seventeenth-century practice in this area was both more confused and contested,[66] and also more intensely *legal* than Locke seems to allow.[67] Jurists were also more inclined to speak in terms of specific prerogative *powers* rather than one open-ended prerogative power.[68] Locke's theory nonetheless offers a clear account of the princely model, one moreover that is written from a liberal perspective. Strangely given his politics,[69] Locke retains much of the older conceptual structure of prerogative. While insisting that government ought to be exercised both through and under established laws,[70] he also acknowledges the existence of extraordinary powers. These are discretionary powers, existing beyond the realm of ordinary law, to be exercised by the king for the public good. They operate *extra et contra legem*. As such, prerogative is on this account beyond classification in two key senses. It has no juridical shape or structure of its own, but takes shape *against* the normal system of civil law. And, unlike other exercises of lawful authority, prerogative is invested in a *person* as much as an *office*—that is, the king (man) as well as the King (Crown).[71]

---

[63] The classic work remains F. Meinecke, *Machiavellism: The Doctrine of Raison d'État and Its Place in Modern History*, W. Stark (trans) (New Brunswick: Transaction Publishers, 1998).

[64] M. McGlynn, *The Royal Prerogative and the Learning of the Inns of Court* (Cambridge: Cambridge University Press, 2003).

[65] J. Locke, 'Second Treatise of Government', in J. Locke, *Two Treatises of Government*, P. Laslett (ed) (Cambridge: Cambridge University Press, 1988), ch XIV.

[66] G. Burgess, *The Politics of the Ancient Constitution: An Introduction to English Political Thought, 1603-1642* (London: Macmillan, 1992).

[67] Although the late Stuart period in which Locke wrote the *Two Treatises* saw perhaps the highpoint of 'princely' prerogative as recognized by the courts: see *Godden v Hales* 2 Shower 475 (1686); *East India Company v Sandys* 1 Vern 127 (1683).

[68] M. Hale, *The Prerogatives of the King*, D. E. C. Yale (ed) (London: Selden Society, 1976).

[69] R. Ashcraft, *Revolutionary Politics and Locke's Two Treatises of Government* (Princeton: Princeton University Press, 1986).

[70] Locke, above n 65, para 131 (353): 'And so whoever has the Legislative or Supream Power of any Common-wealth, is bound to govern by establish'd *standing Laws*, promulgated and known to the People, and not by Extemporary Decrees.'

[71] C. Fatovic, *Outside the Law: Emergency and Executive Power* (Baltimore: Johns Hopkins University Press, 2009), 65.

We must be careful when discussing the legally unbound quality of the princely mode of reason of state. The Prince in the exercise of his prerogative may be unbound by the law in the sense of being unaccountable for his actions to any earthly authority. But he was not in all senses unbound by Law. For Locke as much as for his contemporaries, the Prince remained subject to natural law and, as such, answerable to God. Indeed, we might go further by saying that it was precisely the juridical thinness of prerogative that made the Prince acting in respect of prerogative so very close to God. But Locke gave the familiar account a Machiavellian twist (or at least made explicit what had previously been implied). He linked the king's exercise of prerogative purportedly for the good of the public to the people's right to rebel against illegitimate rulers. Princely prerogative now has its plebeian mirror image in the right of rebellion. When a political actor endeavours to set up absolute power or their own arbitrary will 'as the law of society', Locke wrote, 'they put themselves into a state of war with the people'. The latter 'are thereupon absolved from any farther obedience' to that actor.[72] On this account, prerogative becomes a site of contestation, a normatively unstable and legally unanchored space in which the most basic authority claims are made and tested. In that sense, prerogative is both post- but also pre-political, in that it both assumes the existence of an existing framework of authority but also moves beyond it in a way that opens it up to contestation and potential subversion. Prerogative is intimately connected, on this account, to death and rebirth of constitutional orders, hence the immanence of God in the resolution of conflict over prerogative:

> But if the prince, or whoever they be in the administration, decline that way of determination, the appeal then lies no where but to heaven; force between either persons, who have no known superior on earth, or which permits no appeal to a judge on earth, being properly a state of war, wherein the appeal lies only to heaven; and in that state the injured party must judge for himself, when he will think fit to make use of that appeal, and put himself upon it.[73]

The normative open-endedness of the prerogative zone in Locke's theory, its emphasis on sovereignty and trials of political strength had precursors, not least Machiavelli's advocacy of the Roman model of dictatorship,[74] and successors, notably Carl Schmitt's work on 'the exception'.[75] But it became increasingly a minority approach, its princely aspects and assumptions gradually displaced in favour of a more integrative and polity-based approach to exceptional executive powers. On this front, it was some of Locke's contemporaries who showed the way forward. Perhaps the greatest work of political philosophy in that period, Hobbes's *Leviathan*, does not mention 'prerogative'. Nonetheless, it can be read as an attempt to repudiate fashionable reason of state thinking.[76]

---

[72] Locke, above n 65, paras 151, 222.

[73] Ibid para 242. On the theological aspects of Locke's political theory see J. Waldron, *God, Locke, and Equality: Christian Foundations in Locke's Political Thought* (Cambridge: Cambridge University Press, 2002).

[74] N. Machiavelli, *The Discourses*, B. Crick (ed) (Harmondsworth: Penguin, 1983), I.34.

[75] C. Schmitt, *Political Theology: Four Chapters on the Concept of Sovereignty*, G. Schwab (trans) (Chicago: University of Chicago Press, 1985).

[76] N. Malcolm, *Reason of State, Propaganda, and the Thirty Years' War: An Unknown Translation by Thomas Hobbes* (Oxford: Oxford University Press, 2007), 119.

The argument seems to be this. It is true that authority ('Law') rests on untrammelled power ('sovereignty'). This means that there must be an open-ended reservoir of power underlying law, which the sovereign may in principle tap into as it sees fit.[77] (In his more applied writings, Hobbes elaborates on the extent of these prerogatives. His analysis in the *Dialogue* puts him on the far royalist end of the spectrum when it comes to what the king is allowed to do through prerogative.[78]) Law needs prerogative for its actualization; but prerogative threatens the stability of a regime of law and is, as such, a threat to peace. So how does Hobbes square the circle? If you follow the postulates of Hobbesian 'civil science', a central feature of which is the replacement of open-ended discretionary and personal authority (the Prince) by an architectonic structure of legal rule (the commonwealth or state) which acts with the full authorization of each subject, the only rational thing for the sovereign to do is to exercise its power through law. This rule by law structure has its own formal requirements, such as rules relating to the promulgation of legislation, and systemic constraints, such as the obligation on judges to interpret law against standards sourced in natural law or equity. Moreover, in foreign affairs—the sphere in which prerogative is most frequently invoked—the Hobbesian commonwealth is not expansionary and seeks to avoid conflict.[79] The net result is that the sovereign (which is rational and whose overriding priority is to seek peace) will consistently rule through law and not prerogative. In fact, Hobbes pushes the point, or flips it: it is precisely the existence of an unqualified and unquestioned reservoir of exceptional authority that makes recourse to it unnecessary, other perhaps than at moments of true crisis.

Hobbes may have written its basic script, but it was the English republicans, Locke's fellow travellers, who provided most of the contours and colouring of the polity model of reason of state, at least as far as Anglophone constitutional theory is concerned. It was they who filled in two important dimensions of the model about which Hobbes was either lukewarm or hostile: liberty and constitutional design. The consideration given these topics in the work of writers such as Marchamont Nedham, Algernon Sidney, and James Harrington makes them closer to modern sensibilities than Hobbes, at least when stripped of their profound, pervasive religiosity and militarism. They built from the core of Hobbesian state theory, while antagonistic to many of Hobbes's prescriptions. They went further than Hobbes in sketching the demands made of law within the commonwealth.[80] And they were far more vigorous about the need to control and disperse power through strategies of separation and rotation.

[77] T. Hobbes, *Leviathan*, R. Tuck (ed) (Cambridge: Cambridge University Press, 1996), 153.
[78] T. Hobbes, 'A Dialogue Between a Philosopher and a Student, of the Common Laws of England', in T. Hobbes, *Writings on Common Law and Hereditary Right*, A. Cromartie and Q. Skinner (eds) (Oxford: Oxford University Press, 2008), 18, 22, 55, 91, 127–9.
[79] N. Malcolm, 'Hobbes's Theory of International Relations', in N. Malcolm, *Aspects of Hobbes* (Oxford: Oxford University Press, 2002).
[80] See eg A. Sidney, *Discourses Concerning Government*, T. G. West (ed) (Indianapolis: Liberty Press, 1990), 225, 394: (1) Magistrates possess no original authority: there is 'no such thing as a right universally belonging to a name; but everyone enjoys that which the laws, by which he is, confer upon him. The law that gives the power, regulates it.' (2) Magistrates have no extra-legal authority: 'They are under the law, and the law is not under them; their letters or commands are not to be regarded: In the administration of justice, the question is not what pleases them, but what the law declares to be right.'

Like Hobbes, who wrote that the state 'does not want to take anything away from the citizen in underhanded ways, and yet is willing to take everything from him in an open fashion',[81] the republicans sought a political solution in which openness and honesty trumped secrecy and scheming. Unlike Hobbes, though, they were troubled about extensive executive authority, whether vested in kings like the Stuarts or popular autocrats like Cromwell. As such, reason of state was a central concern. Republicans were swingeing in their criticism of the *ragione di stato* practices of contemporary European princes.[82] But for all this, their plan was not so much to wish reason of state into non-existence, but to transform and suborn it. With the arrival of a republic, the interest of government will align with interest of the nation, they claimed, as princely reason of state is replaced by polity reason of state. Harrington, as so often, was the most astute of republican writers here. The essence of republican government, he insisted, was the substitution of private interest government, whether monarchical or aristocratic or (as under Cromwell) authoritarian democratic, with public interest government. He distinguishes between private reason ('the interest of the private man'), 'reason of state' (the interest of the ruler or rulers), and 'that reason which is the interest of mankind or of the whole'—'right reason' or what we might call public reason: 'if reason be nothing else but interest, and the interest of mankind be the right interest, then the reason of mankind must be right reason. Now compute well, for if the interest of popular government come the nearest unto the interest of mankind, then the reason of popular government must come the nearest unto right reason.'[83] A move from monarchy to popular government is good precisely because it represents a shift from private interest to public interest government and thus a move in the direction of justice and right reason.[84]

Whereas Hobbes in his more theoretical works tended to avoid the language of prerogative, Harrington went further. Previously reserved for kings and princes, the term is now reserved for the *people*. Sovereignty in the republic resides with 'King People', where the people are transformed into the 'prerogative tribe'[85] wielding two main 'prerogative powers': the legislative power and the power of judicature. The executive is firmly under the law, officials being 'answerable unto the people that his execution be according unto the law; by which Leviathan may see that the hand or sword that executeth the law is in it, not above it'.[86] But what appears to be the simple equation of reason of state with government in the private interest turns out to be rather more complicated. One reason why this is so relates to the republicans' belligerent stance on foreign policy. They recognized that private interest has most often arisen in reason of

---

[81] T. Hobbes, *On the Citizen*, R. Tuck and M. Silverthorne (eds) (Cambridge: Cambridge University Press, 1998), 86. Compare Jonathan Scott's interpretation of Harrington: 'Nobody is autonomous in Oceana, for everyone is enslaved to the state.' J. Scott, 'The Rapture of Motion: James Harrington's Republicanism', in N. Phillipson and Q. Skinner (eds), *Political Discourse in Early Modern Britain* (Cambridge: Cambridge University Press, 1993), 139–63, at 150–1.

[82] M. Nedham, *The Excellencie of a Free State: Or, The Right Constitution of a Commonwealth*, B. Worden (ed) (Indianapolis: Liberty Fund, 2011), 105–6 said that reason of state was a 'strange pocus' which 'can rant as a Souldier, complement as a Monsieur, trick as a Juggler, strut it as a States man, and is changable as the Moon, in the variety of her apperances'.

[83] J. Harrington, 'Oceana', in J. G. A Pocock (ed), *The Commonwealth of Oceana and A System of Politics* (Cambridge: Cambridge University Press, 1992), 1–266, at 22.

[84] Ibid 61.   [85] Ibid 147.   [86] Ibid 25.

state context, especially international affairs (including war and empire), but argued, in contrast to Hobbes, in favour of a 'republic for expansion' on a scale and with an intensity that would have made even Machiavelli blanch.[87] The republicans claimed as a result that reason of state did not cease to exist with the coming of the republic as it was a function of every state, but argued that it varied according to each state's constitution. What is essentially a good thing when practised by a republic is problematic when used by governments geared to private interest, where 'that which is reason of state with them is directly opposite to that which is truly so'.[88]

How, in practice, republican government was to avoid degenerating into private interest rule was a matter on which republican writers differed. Some believed that it was necessary to cultivate virtuous citizens (Milton, Sidney), while others emphasized institutional solutions (Nedham, Harrington).[89] But all paid real attention to reason of state, seeing it as a potential blind spot within the republican constitution. They carried the logic of republican constitutionalism, with its strategies of diffusion and rotation of power and its attachment to accountability and the rule of law, into the prerogative zone: right, that is, into what had been the holy of holies of the princely state. This process was advanced on two levels, the constitutional and institutional. At the constitutional level, republicans insisted on the completeness and sanctity of the constitution, understood as an expression of public reason, and denied (contra Locke) the existence of any real executive power outside the laws. As Sidney wrote, magistrates have 'no other power but what is so conferred on them' by the constitution and 'are to exercise those powers according to the proportion and the ends to which they were given'.[90] This is the Leviathan state, given a strong republican twist.

The institutional level saw, if anything, even greater innovation, the republicans here pursuing Machiavelli's principle, a rider to his defence of Roman dictatorship, that '[n]o republic is ever perfect unless by its laws it has provided for all contingencies, and for every eventuality has provided a remedy and determined the method of applying it.'[91] All executive actions were accountable to the law and to the popular assembly, naturally. But republican writers gave considerable thought as to how this could be institutionally finessed. Nedham, for instance, distinguished two categories of reason of state, 'Acts of State' (*Acta Imperii*) and 'Secrets of State' (*Arcana Imperii*). The former, involving general matters of strategy and common sense, he made subject to the legislative assembly in the ordinary way. The people were best placed to decide such matters, as they 'best know where the shooe pinches them'. The latter should be delegated, he argued, to 'Peoples Trustees', small groups of assemblymen who had permission to operate (for the time being) in secret but remained at all points accountable to the

---

[87] Not least because for the English republicans expansion was not just a necessity—the best form of defence—but also a moral (and religious) obligation. Just as Rome in confirming her liberty propagated her empire, so too must Oceana, Harrington insisted, become 'an holy asylum unto the distressed world', acting as 'a minister of God upon earth': ibid 221.

[88] Harrington, above n 83, ch X.

[89] Republicans of this period all believed, taking their cue from Machiavelli, that an armed citizenry was essential for the maintenance of liberty.

[90] Sidney, above n 80, 99 (and yet scholars keep recycling the claim that proportionality has its origins in Prussian administrative law!).

[91] Ibid I.34 (195).

assembly. This body of Trustees should not be thought of as a standing senate. Ideally, it should operate on a temporary and ad hoc basis, its members returning to the ranks of legislators once their particular task was finished.[92] Harrington's disciple Henry Neville came up with a proposal for the creation of special parliamentary committees to integrate reason of state matters within a constitutional structure. The plan involved splintering the royal prerogative into four categories of 'state-affairs': foreign affairs (peace and war, treaties, and alliance); police (armies, militia, and the 'country force'); the appointment of officials; and fiscal management. In relation to each, the king ought to be required to act through the agency of a bespoke parliamentary committee, the members of which are subject to quick rotation (a third of members to be replaced each year) and answerable to Parliament.[93]

The detail is important, not necessarily on account of its later influence, but because it illustrates the move out of the old world of princely reason of state, still dominated by prerogative, to the new world of polity-based reason of state. In this respect, Hobbes and the other early-modern state theorists provided the hardware, that is, the foundational logic of the polity model. The republicans and those they influenced accepted much of this structure, but provided a much clearer blueprint of the constitutional and institutional software that over time came to shape thinking about exceptional power in liberal constitutional orders. Whereas Hobbes's basic script could lead in a variety of directions, including both authoritarianism and liberalism, the republicans were concerned with the design of one type of polity, a rule-bound state where government was for the interest of the public and where the interests of government and governed were aligned through sophisticated constitutional techniques. Although they worked on different aspects of the problem, both Hobbes and the republicans sought to fold reason of state into the juridical structure of the polity. The point was to eradicate if at all possible the freewheeling or open-ended prerogative. This move was at once constitutionalizing and secularizing. There was no space in the modern constitution for the prerogative operating in the Lockean style as a kind of *deus ex machina*,[94] popping up like a superhero to save the people, or else to test their faith to destruction (and possible rebirth).

---

[92] Nedham, above n 82, 55–6: the authority of the Peoples Trustees continues 'of right, no longer than meer Necessity requires, for their [the people's] own redress and safety; which being provided for, they [the Trustees] are to return into a condition of Subjection and Obedience, with the rest of the people, to such Laws and Government as themselves have erected.'

[93] H. Neville, 'Plato Redivivus, or A Dialogue Concerning Government', in C. Robbins (ed), *Two English Republican Tracts* (Cambridge: Cambridge University Press, 1969), 61–200, at 184–90. Problematically, the plan allows the king to retain a free hand in imperial and mercantile matters. The same dialogue also contains a clear exposition of what (moderate) republicans saw as a basic fault in late-Stuart England, namely the 'inexecution of our laws'—or the insidious nature of princely discretion through the misuse of prerogative: 'Now when you have thought well what it should be that gives the king a liberty to choose whether any part of the law shall be current or no; you will, that it is the great power the king enjoys in the government: when the parliament has discovered this, they will no doubt demand of his majesty an abatement of his royal prerogative in those matters only which concern our enjoyment of our all, that is our lives, liberties and estates' (184–5).

[94] This does not mean that, at least on the initial formulations of this model, there was any less room for God. It was precisely the point of the law-bound and public interest-based conception of the polity advanced by republicans that the result would be a more moral, that is, more Godly, commonwealth.

The examples in the previous section can now be seen as illustrations of a structural shift from a princely (or prerogative-based) to a polity (or law-based) model
of reason of state. Analyses of reason of state that pay too much attention to the
arbitrary or extralegal character of reason of state—'the exception', in Schmitt's
formulation—miss these constitutionalizing dynamics,[95] which involve a series
of developments: the juridification of governmental action; the transfer of reserve
powers from kings (prerogative) to government ministers (executive powers); the
depersonalization of exceptional activity; a profound and dispersed institutionaliza-
tion of reason of state, in part a result of the expansion in the range of state activities;
the subjection of reserve powers to a variety of forms of legislative oversight; and
constitutional architecture—notably (outside the United Kingdom) written constitutions, policed by constitutional and supreme courts, which structure and can limit
reason of state and emergency action. These are not just lawyers' structures and processes. They reflect and serve in turn to structure our expectations as citizens about
the practical operation of reason of state.

IV

The move from princely to modern models does not mean that reason of state has
disappeared either as a practical or a juridical problem. In fact, it is possible to argue
that such problems have become if anything more pronounced. For one thing, the
same state-building dynamics that led to the domestication of reason of state also
enabled the state to operate effectively on a hitherto unknown scale, vastly increasing its capacity to operate in spheres of activity traditionally occupied by reason
of state, including war and international competition.[96] For another, the increase
in the number of legal and political avenues through which to oversee executive
action, and the increased effectiveness of such scrutiny, is likely to drive an increase
in reason of state cases. So, as we saw earlier, the rise in judicial review would seem
to entail both more frequent and more significant reason of state cases. Problematic
instances connected with reason of state thus now more commonly occur *within*
the interstices of law, as opposed to targeting directly the boundary between law
and power.

There is some uncertainty about what the best liberal response is to this scenario.
Some seem to think that the best strategy is one of avoidance. Wojciech Sadurski argues
that the concept of reason of state is either otiose in that it can be subsumed within
the more familiar and less tarnished framework of public reason as modelled by John
Rawls, or it is pernicious: understood as applying to the security and survival of the

---

[95] An alternative perspective, branded as 'Schmittian' but not so in my view, accepts the importance of
many of these trends, but argues that the constraints on executive power coming from the legislative and
judicial branches is all but redundant, leaving the executive unbound by these institutions but checked
internally through the complexity of its own multifarious operations and externally by the popular will
as exercised in periodic elections. See E. A. Posner and A. Vermeule, *The Executive Unbound: After the
Madisonian Republic* (New York: Oxford University Press, 2010). In my view, the authors vastly overstate
the weaknesses of legislative and judicial checks on executive power.
[96] This was entirely in line with early-modern republican thinking, which as we have seen favoured both
liberty at home *and* expansion overseas.

state and 'based on the insight that, "if the political order is assumed to an essential condition of free moral existence, the survival of this order becomes crucial", reason of state fails to provide a useful working concept since it is not 'something that people of diverse viewpoints and ideologies may agree on'.[97] There is something initially attractive about this argument, in that it seems to hold out the prospect of the eradication of what has always been a problematic category. The problem is, as I explain in the remainder of this section, that it secures the purity of liberal theory at the expense of descriptive accuracy and normative plausibility. To develop the argument, I turn to Friedrich Hayek, who provided a sophisticated version of this argument.

Hayek's response to the pathologies of the modern administrative state, with its creeping bureaucratization and interest-driven mass politics, was to level it. He sought in particular to foreclose any sites of sovereignty, and his constitutional analysis can be seen as a systematic attempt to do away with reason of state altogether. The image of common law as the epitome of law understood as *nomos* (the law of liberty) is crucial, for it demonstrates how 'rules that have never been deliberately invented but have grown through a gradual process of trial and error in which the experience of successive generations has helped to make them what they are'.[98] The common law shows how an order of laws can develop largely in the absence of design. Seen as a collective intelligence device, a vast system of trial and error on matters of law and coordination, it is a near-perfect way, so Hayek argues, of aggregating experience and of transmitting accumulated stock of knowledge through time.

Reason of state, from Hayek's perspective, is doubly flawed. First, conceived as the reflection of the reason of the individual or small group who happen to control the state, it is necessarily limited, certainly when set against the accumulated knowledge gains of generations embodied in the evolved law (*nomos*). It is even more limited than the law of legislation (*thesis*), which is at least refracted through a series of institutions (ie more and larger groups) before becoming law. Second, reason of state is often presented as in a sense operating outside time. The moment of decision interrupts the normal flow of social intercourse and development. The sort of intelligence that this kind of action presupposes is antithetical to Hayek: 'any attempt to use reason to control or direct the social process threatens not only to impede the development of our powers of reason but also to bring the growth of knowledge to a halt'.[99] The exception, understood as a kind of caesura in constitutional time threatens, for Hayek, the evolution of the spontaneous order of freedom and is deeply problematic.

Hayek's interpretation of the maxim *salus populi suprema lex esto* is also illuminating. The maxim links to reason of state, as we have seen, providing a justification for agents of government to act on their own initiative outside and sometimes against the requirements of the law. Hayek turns the usual reading of the maxim on its head. Correctly understood, he argues, *salus populi* 'means that the end of the law ought to be the welfare of the people, that the general rules should be so designed as to serve

---

[97] W. Sadurski, 'Reason of State and Public Reason' (2014) 27 *Ratio Juris* 21, at 26–7, quoting C. J. Friedrich, *Constitutional Reason of State* (Providence: Brown University Press, 1957), 6.

[98] F. A. Hayek, *The Constitution of Liberty* (London: Routledge, 2010), 138.

[99] C. Kukathas, *Hayek and Modern Liberalism* (Oxford: Oxford University Press, 1989), 61.

it, but *not* that any conception of a particular social end should provide a justification for breaking those general rules'.[100] There is nothing either special or mysterious about the state—it is just the structure through which social cooperation under rules tends to take place. So there is no cause to personify the state, and no justification for imbuing it with any special notion of agency. The rules that are contained within the state's legal order (or, perhaps better, the rules that as a system define the state) ought to serve the welfare of the people, and should do so where law-making operates as *nomos*. Breaking these rules is unlikely to benefit the public, as opposed to a powerful group within it.

This conception of state and law is remarkable for the extent to which it seeks to deny agency on the part of the state or its officials. But the escape from reason of state is not complete. Hayek recognizes that the laws may have to be suspended when the preservation of a society is threatened:

> Though normally the individuals need be concerned only with their own concrete aims, and in pursuing them will best serve the common welfare, there may temporarily arise circumstances when the preservation of the overall order becomes the overruling common purpose, and when in consequence the spontaneous order, on a local or national scale, must for a time be converted into an organization'[101]

This way of conceptualizing emergency action is unconvincing. The shift in register from *nomos* to reason of state is presented as a natural phenomenon, like 'a wounded animal in flight from mortal danger'. Elsewhere, Hayek is critical of the application of animistic imagery to describe political action. Developed societies are complex and do not correspond to a model of intimate fellowship.[102] Hayek steps here into Schmitt's territory, even adopting the conceptual logic of 'the exception'. But whereas Schmitt had extensively laid the groundwork for this position, Hayek has done the opposite, denying the conditions that make the Schmittian exception possible. For Hayek, there is no sovereign, little by way of individual or small-group political agency, and only an attenuated role for the state. As Renato Cristi observes, what Hayek reveals in his account of emergency constitutionalism is a failure to supersede Schmitt's position. He ends up instead providing the exact counterpart of that theory. 'What generally happens when one proceeds in this manner is that the position one is attacking is not transcended but tends to be preserved as an obverted mirror-image. Something like this has happened to Hayek.'[103]

Hayek's failure to incorporate a plausible account of reason of state into his constitutional theory is instructive and warns against taking the path that seeks to be rid of the concept altogether. Such an approach blinds us towards some of the defining and perennial juridical questions of the modern state. Unfortunately for liberals, more liberalism does not correlate to a simple reduction in reason of state, let alone the eradication

---

[100] Hayek, above n 98, 139.

[101] F. A. Hayek, *Law, Legislation and Liberty: A New Statement of the Liberal Principles of Justice and Political Economy Vol. I: Rules and Order* (London: Routledge, 1982), 124.

[102] F. A. Hayek, *The Fatal Conceit: The Errors of Socialism* (Chicago: University of Chicago Press, 1988), 113.

[103] F. R. Cristi, 'Hayek and Schmitt on the Rule of Law' (1984) 17 *Canadian Journal of Political Science* 521, at 523.

of the practice. In a sense, the opposite might be true, as the liberal constitution tends to see more reason of state matters appear before supervisory institutions and also to present more frequently as juridical questions. The constitutional dynamics that ensue, in which there is an undeniable risk that normal law and legal process might become contaminated or even cannibalized by reason of state practices, is nonetheless part of a now very old liberal tradition that aspires to see the more questionable and marginal of state actions brought within and hopefully tamed by the piecemeal extension of law's domain. This approach is realistic at least to the extent that it recognizes that even if the state were to model itself on pure Rawlsian principles, reason of state questions would still arise. Unless the state cut itself off from the outside world, which is not an option for a liberal state,[104] it would still have to engage with other polities, including less perfectly liberal and illiberal states. Even if conflict or problematic entanglements with those states were avoided, the liberal state would still engage in some diplomatic and intelligence-gathering activities. But even these are best understood as 'standing' or 'ordinary' reason of state practices to which legal principles can never straightforwardly apply.

V

This chapter has offered an articulation and partial defence of the concept of reason of state. It has argued that reason of state provides an explanatory category through which a vital but troublesome dimension of state action can be analysed. That dimension is otherwise glimpsed through a disparate variety of forms and scenarios: prerogative, emergency, exception, necessity, national security, and so on. Reason of state provides a framework in which many of these claims can be bundled into a coherent whole. But its explanatory strength derives from the fact that it highlights what is most germane about the category from the jurist's perspective, namely the claim made by an agent of the state to be recognized as having special jurisdiction over a sensitive area of activity or special authority over a particular problem, authority that the law in the normal course of things would not provide.

This bare definition was elaborated by way of a historical argument, a principal feature of which was the steady transformation of the sort of 'arbitrary' power that most troubled jurists from Coke to Dicey: legally unlimited, personal power sourced in reserve powers and prerogatives. But when combined with the increase in state activities, that process of transformation, which normalized reason of state through the establishment of constitutional principles, reintroduced a not altogether dissimilar problem: wide reserve powers, containing broad discretionary authority, not so much now as an exception to the law—outside and against the law, in Locke's phrase—but within the interstices of the law and its institutional processes.

Layered into this analysis was a more normative argument that takes a stance against liberal dreamers like Hayek, who were read as aiming at the eradication of reason of state. But they do not—I would say cannot—escape the problem, since their solution

---

[104] J. Rawls, *The Law of Peoples* (Cambridge, Mass.: Harvard University Press, 2001).

(more liberalism, more law) is a variation on an old story. True, we might hope to tame the excesses associated with the invocation of reason of state in this way. But it will hardly serve to remove the concept from constitutional politics—in fact the opposite seems more likely to be true. The only possible way of escaping from reason of state altogether would be to rid ourselves of the state (and any similar political structure). Hayek sometimes seems tempted to think in such terms.[105] Irrespective of the plausibility of such a move, this scenario is outside the scope of constitutional law and the boundaries of this study.

But focusing on reason of state has wider theoretical benefits. The concept reflects, for better or worse, the 'unpurged relic of lordship' within the modern state.[106] As such, it draws our attention to what might be called the imperial dimension of constitutional law. 'Imperial' not just because of the historical connection between reason of state and the imperial expansion of the state both outside and within its own borders, but also because of the relatively stark connection between reason of state and authority (*imperium*). This is a side of constitutional politics that jurists often overlook. Lawyers tend to focus on the negative or constraining function of the constitution,[107] especially checking institutions such as the legislature (as opposed to the executive), constitutional rights (as opposed to the enabling provisions of constitutions), and judicial review (as opposed to administrative action). This tendency is perhaps even stronger among constitutional theorists. The constitutional politics surrounding reason of state certainly brings into play these institutions—in fact, reason of state can be seen as a particularly hard testing ground for the idea of checks and balances. But to focus too much attention on the constraining side of constitutions is to leave an incomplete and unreal impression. Reason of state is a fairly immediate reminder that constitutions are as much about how power is sourced and operationalized as they are about how power is checked and constrained. It also shows us that law's empire is often a motley affair. Normal law normally includes exceptional powers. Or, better, normalizing the exception is a process whose goal is never reached.

---

[105] See C. Kukathas, 'Hayek's Theory of the State' in D. Dyzenhaus and T. Poole, *Law, Liberty and State* (Cambridge: Cambridge University Press, 2015), 281–94.

[106] M. Oakeshott, *On Human Conduct* (Oxford: Oxford University Press, 1975), 268.

[107] S. Holmes, *Passions and Constraint: On the Theory of Liberal Democracy* (Chicago: University of Chicago Press, 1995).

PART III

CONSTITUTIONAL FUNDAMENTALS

10

The Rule of Law

T. R. S. Allan*

I. Introduction

Central to our aspirations for liberty and justice is the political ideal of the rule of law. We can make sense of the rule of law as a legal or constitutional principle only by studying the underlying political ideal; and that ideal in turn invokes a distinctive concept of law, which philosophical reflection can help to elucidate. We confront, initially, a conflict between two contrasting images of law, which encapsulate divergent understandings of its characteristic or primary nature and functions. In one prominent image, law is an instrument for the effective implementation of government policy by rules or requirements that carry a mark of state authority.[1] Presenting a danger to individual liberty, even when intended to serve the public interest, the law must be harnessed to a framework that limits its potential for arbitrariness. The *rule of law*, accordingly, requires state coercion to be limited and regulated by published or promulgated and determinate rules, issued or enacted according to settled public procedures for making law.[2]

A contrasting image of law, however, emphasizes its role in resolving disputes in accordance with standards of justice or fairness.[3] The special authority of law is derived, in large part, from the efforts of judges and officials to conform their decisions to sound moral principles and customary expectations or understandings. Courts of law are primarily *courts of justice*, at least in the sense that the administration of law is supposed to reflect the moral rights and duties of the litigants—having due regard, of course, to the social and political context in which those rights and duties are necessarily asserted or denied. From this perspective, there is more to legality than compliance with whatever rules and regulations exhibit the requisite signs of official state endorsement. There is a duty on private citizens and public officials alike to comply with standards of just conduct, as determined by reasoned elaboration of a shared legal and constitutional tradition. There must be dutiful submission to final judicial decisions, as regards the content of the pertinent rights and duties; public authorities, like private citizens, must bow to

* Professor of Jurisprudence and Public Law, University of Cambridge. The helpful comments of the editors and workshop participants on earlier drafts of this chapter are very gratefully acknowledged.
[1] In H. L. A. Hart's account, law is distinguished from other sources of obligation by the derivation of its authority from a 'rule of recognition', consisting in the settled conduct and attitudes of officials: see H. L. A. Hart, *The Concept of Law* 2nd edn (Oxford: Clarendon Press, 1994), 100–10.
[2] See eg J. Raz, *The Authority of Law: Essays on Law and Morality* (Oxford: Clarendon Press, 1979), ch 11.
[3] Compare with S. R. Perry, 'Judicial Obligation, Precedent and the Common Law' (1987) 7 *Oxford Journal of Legal Studies* 215, at 215–18.

judicial orders intended to enforce the law. But such judicial orders and decisions borrow their authority, as precedent, from the reasons they invoke in support; and because judges possess no monopoly of reason their rulings must be vulnerable to inspection, criticism, and (in due course) reassessment and overruling.[4]

The image of law as a corpus of readily ascertainable rules corresponds to a largely formal conception of the rule of law. When legal rules are reasonably clear and non-contradictory, duly published or promulgated, and have prospective effect (retroactive rules being reserved for remedying special cases of unforeseen injustice or injury) it is possible for the citizen to comply with the law. Not only are governmental objectives more securely attained, but also rule by or through law safeguards the citizen's freedom in the sense of *independence*.[5] Being better able to predict the incidence of governmental interference, she can arrange her affairs in the manner best suited to her own aims or interests. Strict adherence to published rules—or at least publicly acknowledged standards of judgment, defining and limiting any relevant criteria of 'public interest'—safeguards independence by granting each person an inviolable domain of action. She can organize her affairs without fear of unforeseen intervention by officials: she is not at the mercy of official *discretion* unfettered by previously published rules. The citizen enjoys the protection of the rule of law in the sense that provided she takes care to comply with readily ascertainable rules or standards, she is otherwise free to act as she pleases—she need not fear the displeasure of officials who may deplore her opinions and censure her conduct.

When state officials are bound to comply with the published rules in the same manner as ordinary persons—answerable to independent and impartial courts for breaches of the rules that harm people's interests—the rule of law exists as a bulwark against arbitrary power. Power exercised in breach of the rules, or at least in conflict with the policies or purposes publicly acknowledged as their proper ends or purposes, is arbitrary in the sense that there is no applicable standard of judgment. An actor who oversteps the limits of his powers, as these are defined by the pertinent public rules, ceases in substance to be a *public* official: he displaces the standards of law by his own personal opinions or private interests, which makes any citizen affected an unwitting tool at another's disposal.

In this account of the rule of law—or legality—there are, however, no implications for the substance of law: the pertinent rules (or officially acknowledged public policy criteria) may have any content, as long as they are consistently and faithfully applied. The rule of law does not bind the legislature, whose rules constitute the principal source of whatever rights and duties the legal system enforces. Indeed, legality is largely conceived as a matter of conformity to enacted rules: it looks to written instruments, whether a formally entrenched constitution or parliamentary legislation duly enacted, to mark out the division between law and custom, or between law and politics. The rule

---

[4] Ronald Dworkin draws a similar distinction between the 'rule-book' and 'rights' conceptions of the rule of law, that latter conception being 'the ideal of rule by an accurate public conception of individual rights': R. Dworkin, *A Matter of Principle* (Oxford: Clarendon Press, 1986), 11–12.

[5] Compare with N. Simmonds, *Law as a Moral Idea* (Oxford: Oxford University Press, 2007), 101–4, 141–3.

of law is consistent with a simple, majoritarian conception of democracy: there must be full and faithful adherence to whatever scheme of regulation has been endorsed by a majority of the people or their duly elected representatives.

The contrasting image of law as a means for the resolution of disputes in accordance with justice suggests a more ambitious, more substantive conception of the rule of law. On this view, the rule of law requires more than the fair and impartial *administration of law*, whatever its content. It demands, in addition, that the law should embody a coherent and consistent scheme of justice, treating all alike according to the standards of that scheme. Formal equality before the law—the equal subjection of all, regardless of rank or status, to general rules—is underpinned by a deeper conception of equal citizenship: there must be equal protection of the law in the sense that rights or benefits enjoyed by some cannot be *unfairly* denied to others. While laws or public policies inevitably discriminate between persons, according to their specific purposes, they must nevertheless do so on defensible grounds. The relevant distinctions must not violate general principles of good governance, acknowledged by both government and governed as intrinsic to a just constitution. Now all branches of government are made subject to law: their powers are inherently limited by principles that express a vision of constitutional justice, according each citizen the same standing and dignity as an equal member of the political community.[6]

Admittedly, the defence of a substantive conception of the rule of law invites the objection that the separate ideals of legality and justice are being conflated and confused.[7] We generally suppose that there is a difference between acting justly and acting within the law: an unjust enactment or decision may nonetheless be lawfully made. The objection has force in the limited sense that the rule of law is, no doubt, compatible with a variety of arrangements for the orderly conduct of civil society and legitimate governance. It is a moral ideal to which different regimes approximate in contrasting ways; and it is the task of the lawmakers in each jurisdiction to choose those rules most suited to the people's welfare in the particular circumstances of time and place. The governing ideal of liberty—liberty in the sense of independence—nonetheless imposes limits on legislative discretion. The familiar features of liberal democracy, including the judicial protection of fundamental human or constitutional rights, may be understood as reinforcing the security provided by the rule of law in its more formal instantiation. There are principles of respect for persons that limit the scope of the legislative power within any polity governed in accordance with the rule of law.

If the law is intended to be a bulwark against arbitrary power, providing a shield against domination by powerful private interests or public officials, its content must embody the same ideal that underpins the requirement of fair and impartial application of determinate rules. The security of freedom—its guarantee against encroachment at

---

[6] This is the vision I have tried to articulate in my books, T. R. S. Allan, *Constitutional Justice: A Liberal Theory of the Rule of Law* (Oxford: Oxford University Press, 2001); T. R. S. Allan, *The Sovereignty of Law: Freedom, Constitution, and Common Law* (Oxford: Oxford University Press, 2013).

[7] See eg J. Raz, above n 2, ch 11. According to Raz, the rule of law should not 'be confused with democracy, justice, equality (before the law or otherwise), human rights of any kind or respect for persons or for the dignity of man' (ibid 211). For a more nuanced view, however, see J. Raz, *Ethics in the Public Domain: Essays in the Morality of Law and Politics* (Oxford: Clarendon Press, 1994), ch 16.

the hands of misguided or hostile officials—requires the assurance that legal rules will be formulated, interpreted, and changed only in ways that respect the fundamental interest of each individual in leading his own life, according to his own aims and convictions. The law must preserve a sphere of independent decision and action, securing as far as possible an equal freedom for all. Such familiar constitutional freedoms as those of conscience, speech, association, and personal liberty supplement the protections for person and property in the ordinary civil law: they identify stable elements of a larger scheme of justice intended to reconcile each person's freedom with the similar freedom of others. While the rule of law is compatible with different accounts of those basic freedoms, reconciling their potentially conflicting demands in divergent ways, it forges a fundamental unity of constitutional governance. Observance of the rule of law confers legitimacy on systems of government by preserving the conditions that honour each person's dignity as an independent agent, responsible for the shape and character of her own life—answerable to her own convictions about what gives life its point and value.[8]

Interpreted in this way, the rule of law corresponds to the German *Rechtsstaat*, which requires all governmental power to be asserted in accordance with law: there are no 'sovereign' or prerogative powers immune from judicial review for compliance with basic constitutional law.[9] In Kantian terms, political authority is consistent with liberty, understood as independence, when it secures the rightful civil condition under which each person is free to pursue his own ends compatibly with the equal freedom of others. Independence requires adherence to the Universal Principle of Right, which states that 'any action is *right* if it can coexist with everyone's freedom in accordance with a universal law, or if on its maxim the freedom of choice of each can coexist with everyone's freedom in accordance with a universal law'.[10] While the innate right of humanity, or equal independence, encompasses such fundamental rights as freedoms of conscience and expression, there is a role for positive law in giving them specific practical content. Equal citizenship implies democratic lawmaking; but the lawmakers are charged with establishing and maintaining a rightful condition, preserving liberty as independence.[11]

While the rule of law, correctly interpreted, embraces both form and substance—transcending the contrasting images of law with which we began—it identifies a specific understanding of *law*. In its central meaning, underlying the ideal of legality, law is fundamentally non-instrumental. Law provides the conditions in which each person's freedom as independence can be secured: its primary task is to define individual

---

[8] See further Allan, 2013, above n 6, ch 3.

[9] Both *Rechtsstaat* and rule of law have been subject to formal and substantive interpretations, demonstrating a high degree of convergence: see R. Grote, 'The German *Rechtsstaat* in a Comparative Perspective', in J. R. Silkenat, J. E. Hickey Jr, and P. D. Barenboim (eds), *The Legal Doctrines of the Rule of Law and the Legal State (Rechtsstaat)* (London: Springer, 2014), ch 13.

[10] I. Kant, *The Metaphysics of Morals: The Doctrine of Right*, in M. J. Gregor (ed trans), *Practical Philosophy* (Cambridge: Cambridge University Press, 1996), 6:230 (in the German edition), 387 (in the English translation).

[11] Compare with A. Ripstein, *Force and Freedom: Kant's Legal and Political Philosophy* (Cambridge, Mass.: Harvard University Press, 2009). As Ripstein explains, 'Kantian independence can only be compromised by the deeds of others. It is not a good to be promoted; it is a constraint on the conduct of others, imposed by the fact that each person is entitled to be his or her own master' (ibid 15).

domains of liberty, protected from coercive interference both by governmental authorities, on the one hand, and other individuals or organizations, on the other. The rule of law preserves the sovereignty of individual choice and action by allowing each person to pursue his own purposes, free from domination either by state officials or overbearing fellow citizens.[12]

II. Law, Liberty, and Equality

Compliance by parliament or executive government with the various precepts of the formal conception of the rule of law is an important feature of constitutionalism. It makes the law a bulwark of liberty rather than a threat to its enjoyment. When the laws are framed as published and prospective general rules, which are capable of being obeyed and are faithfully applied by officials, they serve to insulate the citizen from arbitrary state action—action that lacks any clear basis in powers or duties previously conferred or declared. Liberty is not best understood as an immunity from legal duties or restrictions, but rather as a domain of independence marked out by law: 'freedom of men under government is to have a standing rule to live by, common to every one of that society, and made by the legislative power erected in it'. John Locke celebrates freedom as the 'liberty to follow my own will in all things where that rule prescribes not, not to be subject to the inconstant, uncertain, unknown, arbitrary will of another man'.[13] There is no subjection to any 'absolute, arbitrary, despotical power', characteristic of slavery, because even the 'legislative or supreme power of any commonwealth' must govern by 'established standing laws promulgated and known to the people, and not by extemporary decrees'.[14] Such published general rules must be applied by 'indifferent and upright judges', whose decisions will be duly governed by established law.

The contrast drawn between free man and slave is characteristic of the 'republican' or neo-Roman conception of liberty, defining liberty as independence or freedom from domination.[15] Liberty is denied, on this view, not only by actual interference, unregulated by pre-existing legal rules, but by the mere *threat* of such interference. A person who must constantly beware of provoking disapproval and coercive intervention in his affairs is akin to a slave, at all times beholden to his master for his current enjoyment of whatever freedom is conceded. A person who lives under the protection of the rule of law, by contrast, may act as he pleases, subject only to the requirements of the general law. His freedom is genuine, even if sharply constrained by specified conditions or restrictions, because within whatever limits are clearly established he may act as he sees fit, disregarding (if he wishes) the disapproval or dislike of other citizens or officials. A citizen—by contrast with a slave—may have few choices available in practice, but he

---

[12] For a sustained critique of an instrumental account of law, distinct from the moral value of 'rule of law', see Simmonds, above n 5, especially 44–56. Compare with J. Waldron, 'The Concept and the Rule of Law' (2008–9) 43 *Georgia Law Review* 1, especially 10–13, 44–7.

[13] J. Locke, *Two Treatises of Government* (London: Dent, Everyman, 1924), vol II, para 22.

[14] Ibid para 131.

[15] See Q. Skinner, *Liberty before Liberalism* (Cambridge: Cambridge University Press, 1998); compare with P. Pettit, *Republicanism: A Theory of Freedom and Government* (Oxford: Clarendon Press, 1997).

is free to 'shape his course of action in accordance with his present intentions', not being subject to another person's will.[16]

This conception of liberty as independence provides a basis for Lon Fuller's claim that the various canons of formal legality he identified—governance by general rules, which are published, clear, prospective, not constantly changing or self-contradictory or impossible to obey, and accurately administered in practice—amount to a moral ideal.[17] Objections that such precepts are merely matters of technical efficiency, making the law a more effective instrument of social policy, overlook the manner in which adherence to Fuller's 'inner morality of law' protects individual freedom. If, as Fuller observes, every departure from these principles of formal legality 'is an affront to man's dignity as a responsible agent', it is so because only a high degree of governmental compliance can give him the necessary security for making plans and pursuing self-chosen ends.[18] When the law is unpublished or contradictory or retrospective or subject to unpredictable change or rarely applied in particular cases, there is little opportunity to lead a purposeful life: people are reduced to the playthings of powerful officials. The mere threat of interference destroys individual freedom in the sense of independence.

Defending Fuller's claims for the moral status of the rule of law, Nigel Simmonds contends that we should understand the various desiderata of formal legality as features of an abstract archetype—the archetype of law, to which legal systems will approximate according to their degree of compliance with the rule of law. Governmental adherence to legality is not best explained as a matter of instrumental efficiency, but rather 'by reference to a concern to maintain an intrinsically valuable form of moral association', embodied in the rule of law.[19] That form of moral association consists in the protection of liberty as independence, preserving domains of freedom independent of the will of others:

> Even if we restrict our account of law's nature to the relatively austere and formal conditions set out in Fuller's eight *desiderata*, the conditions for liberty as independence will necessarily be realized.... If the government restricts its use of violence to circumstances where a rule has been breached (Fuller's requirement of 'congruence between declared rule and official action'), and if the rules are possible to comply with..., there will of necessity be zones of conduct where more than one option will be permissible.[20]

It is important to observe, however, that there is great scope for refining the archetype. Taken too literally, its image of law as enacted rules would call into question the status of the common law; yet we should resist the implication that common law principles, developed by extrapolation from judicial precedent, represent a threat to liberty. We can form a bridge between formal and more substantive accounts of the rule of law, holding out the promise of reconciliation. As Simmonds observes, the requirements of law may be *knowable* even if no rule is published in advance of our actions. We

---

[16] F. A. Hayek, *The Constitution of Liberty* (London: Routledge & Kegan Paul, 1960), 13.

[17] L. L. Fuller, *The Morality of Law* rev edn (New Haven: Yale University Press, 1969), ch 2.

[18] 'To judge his actions by unpublished or retrospective laws, or to order him to do an act that is impossible, is to convey to him your indifference to his powers of self-determination' (ibid 162).

[19] Simmonds, above n 5, 64–6.   [20] Ibid 142.

may be able to rely on a grasp of relevant case law or, instead, on our understanding of settled practices and widely shared values. Moreover, even a body of explicit rules, satisfying Fuller's desiderata, may prove quite impractical as a basis for legitimate governance: they may fail to express an intelligible and viable way of life that anyone could be persuaded to follow.[21]

These considerations suggest that, while a formal account of the rule of law exhibits the difference between law, correctly so called, and the exercise of will or power, a satisfactory account must be more complex and demanding. Liberty, understood as independence, is enhanced when the rules enacted reflect a coherent scheme of principle, enabling people to interpret them appropriately in a manner that the courts may be expected, if necessary, to confirm. The development and application of legal principle serve to give unity to the legal order, providing a shared moral foundation for the ascertainment of people's rights and duties—the legal rules being illuminated by their reasoned application in particular cases. In common law jurisdictions, judicial precedent provides a basis for interpretation by linking legal rules with the general principles that inform and justify them, making their scope and application sensitive to the requirements of those principles in different contexts or conditions. Formal equality before the law, ensured by the consistent application of legal rules to everyone, whatever his social rank or official status, becomes a more substantive ideal of equal citizenship.[22]

The rule of law requires governmental adherence to a unified *scheme of justice*, which treats people equally in the sense that both departures from the general rule in particular cases and the divergent treatment of different groups of persons must be properly justified. Distinctions between persons or groups must bear an appropriate relationship to avowed state objectives; and those objectives must be legitimate ones—consistent with recognition of the equal dignity and worth of persons as individual bearers of the same basic constitutional rights. Insofar as these requirements lead to the judicial invalidation of enacted rules, or even to an interpretation that departs significantly from 'ordinary meaning', there is an undeniable risk of uncertainty. But the demands of legal certainty may be better served overall by adherence to settled legal and constitutional principle: the risks of being misled by taking enacted rules at face value are offset by the greater assurance that acknowledged principles of justice will be reliably upheld.[23]

Liberty as independence is preserved, in part, by the maintenance of a coherent and comprehensible scheme of governance, which assists people both to predict the incidence of state coercion and to criticize officials whose conduct violates that general scheme. Liberty is further protected, however, by the conformity of that general scheme to an arrangement of rights and duties that secures for everyone a domain of independent thought and action. The traditional civil and political liberties represent fixed points

---

[21] Ibid 160–3.

[22] Compare with R. Dworkin, *Law's Empire* (London: Fontana, 1986), defending a conception of law as 'integrity', which 'requires government to speak with one voice, to act in a principled and coherent manner toward all its citizens, to extend to everyone the substantive standards of justice or fairness it uses for some' (ibid 165). See also J. Waldron, above n 12, 32–6.

[23] For discussion of the interpretation of statutes in accordance with the rule of law, see Allan, 2013, above n 6, especially ch 5.

within any legitimate constitution, marking the essential conditions in which people can lead independent lives, cooperating and collaborating with others as they choose. Basic freedoms of conscience, speech, association, personal liberty, and movement, for example, serve to guarantee political conditions favourable to the independent formation and pursuit of private plans and purposes. The state is the servant of the people, viewed as individual moral agents, responsible for the direction and character of their own lives: people cannot be made the instruments of collective state purposes antithetical to their own commitments and convictions.

We can acknowledge the existence of law and legality—the minimal condition of rule by law—even in tyrannical regimes, where the legal rules, though accurately and reliably administered, may express an intolerant ideology, curtailing individual freedom or routinely distinguishing between persons on racial, religious, sexual, or other dubious grounds. Such regimes, however, may be understood to exhibit a deficient or deviant conception of the rule of law, falling well short of the ideal of law implicit in the concept of legality.[24] If we value adherence to law as a safeguard of liberty as independence, we must recognize the equal status of persons with respect to that value: equality before the law provides independence for all. The civil and political liberties characteristic of liberal or social democracy may be understood to serve the same basic ideal: they broaden the security of each person's domain of liberty against unjustified state interference. Embedded within the formal account of the rule of law, accordingly, is a larger, nobler ideal: public authorities govern by law when they provide and maintain the conditions under which everyone enjoys the maximum freedom (understood as independence) compatible with a similar freedom for all. The familiar civil and political rights, central to liberal constitutional theory, honour the equal entitlement of persons to form and follow their own ends, free from domination by powerful individuals or public officials.

At the heart of the ideal of the rule of law is the regular and reliable enforcement of the ordinary civil and criminal law, affording essential security against domination.[25] As F. A. Hayek explains, people can 'use their own knowledge in the pursuit of their own ends without colliding with each other only if clear boundaries can be drawn between their respective domains of free action', and such domains are constituted, in part, by rules that govern the possession and use of property: 'Law, liberty, and property are an inseparable trinity. There can be no law in the sense of universal rules of conduct which does not determine boundaries of the domains of freedom by laying down rules that enable each to ascertain where he is free to act.'[26] There is no perfect blueprint for the just society; solutions must be found to new problems by making adjustments that develop and improve the existing order of rules, on which legitimate expectations depend.[27]

---

[24] Compare with D. Dyzenhaus, *Hard Cases in Wicked Legal Systems: Pathologies of Legality* 2nd edn (Oxford: Oxford University Press, 2010), exploring the pathologies of law and legality in South Africa under apartheid. Dyzenhaus shows how departures from the moral principles of the rule of law, especially that of equality, result in a form of arbitrary power that lacks the primary characteristics of law or legality.

[25] See further T. R. S. Allan, 'The Rule of Law as the Rule of Private Law', in L. M. Austin and D. Klimchuk (eds), *Private Law and the Rule of Law* (Oxford: Oxford University Press, 2014), 41–66.

[26] F. A. Hayek, *Law, Legislation and Liberty* (London: Routledge & Kegan Paul, 1982), vol I, 107.

[27] Ibid ch 5.

The first principle of the rule of law, as regards executive public authorities, is the requirement of compliance with the civil and criminal law. Any grant of administrative powers must be tightly construed by reference to the relevant statutory purposes; there must be a burden placed on the public authority, if challenged, to establish any necessary exemption from the general duty to act in accordance with the ordinary law binding on private citizens. A.V. Dicey made the subjection of public officials to the 'ordinary law of the realm', administered by the 'ordinary tribunals', an essential element of his defence of the rule of law.[28] Central to his account of the English conception of legality was the critical role of private law as the measure of legitimate state action against individuals: 'the principles of private law have with us been by the action of the Courts and Parliament so extended as to determine the position of the Crown and of its servants; thus the constitution is the result of the ordinary law of the land'.[29]

Public law is supplementary to private law in the sense that it operates to prevent the abuse of special powers—powers that enable public officials to use coercion in (what would otherwise be) a breach of the civil or criminal law. Public law imposes strict standards of due process, which require such officials to justify their coercive interference by reference to legitimate public ends, suitably qualified in recognition of the countervailing demands of individual freedom. The rule of law is satisfied, on this account, only when both enactment and administration of law conform to settled standards of constitutional propriety: the ordinary civil and criminal law, regulating interaction between private citizens, must be supplemented by the fundamental rights that affirm and protect the ideal of independence. Freedoms of speech, conscience, and association, for example, are the foundation of anyone's attempt to live a life in accordance with his own considered aspirations and convictions. Much the same can be said of most of the 'natural and imprescriptible rights' affirmed in the French Declaration of the Rights of Man and Citizen 1789, and echoed in the Universal Declaration of Human Rights 1948. There is scope for different interpretations of these basic rights and freedoms; but the rule of law demands the consistent application, without fear or favour, of a coherent overall account—the account embodied in, and exemplified by, settled constitutional practice and tradition.

In the absence of an enacted code of rights, the 'ordinary' law in a system of common law can be interpreted as a scheme of constitutional justice. When the legal order prizes individual liberty, as an implicit demand of human dignity, judicial precedent can be understood as the reasoned elaboration of principle, guided by the ideal of the rule of law. What, then, began as a search for the rule of law by study of the requisite form of legislation has deepened into reflection on the nature of law as the safeguard of liberty; and statute law has been placed in its broader context, being subject to interpretation in the light of legal and constitutional principle. The idea of legality associated with law's form, giving assurance of formal equality before the law, has flowered into a deeper, more substantive conception. The rule of law means the subjection of public

---

[28] A. V. Dicey, *Lectures Introductory to the Study of the Law of the Constitution*, in J. W. F. Allison (ed), *Oxford Edition of Dicey*, vol I (Oxford: Oxford University Press, 2013), 100.

[29] Ibid 119. Freedom of the press was, in England, an application of 'the general principle, that no man is punishable except for a distinct breach of the law' (ibid 142).

power to standards of justice or fairness rooted in legal and constitutional tradition, underpinned by the guiding ideal of independence and supplementing the scheme of equal liberty embodied in private law. The formal equality of all before the law—public official and private citizen alike—engages a more substantive equality of justice. Like cases should be treated alike, according to public and defensible criteria of likeness; the distinctions between persons or groups, made by public authorities, must be open to critical scrutiny by reference to such criteria.[30]

The absence of any convincing justification for distinguishing between nationals and foreigners, as regards the preventative detention of suspected terrorists, was the ground on which the House of Lords denied the legality of the British government's actions in response to perceived threats to national security.[31] The Anti-terrorism, Crime and Security Act 2001 provided for the detention of an alien whom the Home Secretary suspected of being a terrorist but who could not (without breach of the European Convention on Human Rights) be deported. A purported derogation from the detainees' rights to liberty (under article 5 of the Convention) on grounds of public emergency (article 15) was held unlawful: the measures taken were not 'strictly required' to meet any such emergency, as the Convention stipulated. Draconian measures, apparently unnecessary to meet an admittedly similar threat from British nationals, could scarcely be shown to be necessary in the case of non-nationals.[32] Lord Bingham quoted Justice Jackson's celebrated denunciation of unequal laws:

> The framers of the Constitution knew...that there is no more effective practical guaranty against arbitrary and unreasonable government than to require that the principles of law which officials would impose upon a minority must be imposed generally. Conversely, nothing opens the door to arbitrary action so effectively as to allow those officials to pick and choose only a few to whom they will apply legislation and thus to escape the political retribution that might be visited upon them if larger numbers were affected. Courts can take no better measure to assure that laws will be just than to require that laws be equal in operation.[33]

Jackson's dictum has the merit of showing how law and politics combine into a unified system of protection. Formal equality leads to political equality when the generality of legal rules is open to judicial scrutiny. There must be a close and convincing connection between a defensible public purpose, on the one hand, and the rationality of the

---

[30] Everyone bears a moral responsibility to seek general compliance with the acknowledged scheme of public and private law, though there is also a continuing duty to question the entitlement of that scheme (as it evolves) to his or her allegiance: see Allan, 2013, above n 6, ch 4. Compare with G. J. Postema, 'Law's Rule: Reflexivity, Mutual Accountability, and the Rule of Law', in Z. Xiaobo and M. Quinn (eds), *Bentham's Theory of Law and Public Opinion* (Cambridge: Cambridge University Press, 2014) 7–39; and G. J. Postema, 'Fidelity in Law's Commonwealth', in Austin and Klimchuk, above n 25, 17–40.

[31] *A v Secretary of State for the Home Dept* [2004] UKHL 56.

[32] It is a separate question whether preventative detention could have been legitimately imposed on citizens, dependent on rigorous appraisal of the nature of any 'public emergency' (an appraisal lacking in the majority judgments). See D. Dyzenhaus, *The Constitution of Law: Legality in a Time of Emergency* (Cambridge: Cambridge University Press, 2006), 175–90.

[33] *Railway Express Agency Inc v New York* 336 US 106 (1949), 112–13.

means adopted to achieve it, on the other. Arbitrary discrimination, in breach of constitutional rights, consists in the weakness or implausibility of that connection.

III. The Separation of Powers

The doctrine of separation of powers is an implicit feature of the rule of law. Our insistence on the derivation of the law's content from general rules and principles, which should determine its administration in particular cases—whether by judges or other public officials—makes sense only on the assumption that the lawmakers cannot themselves be charged with the law's application. The citizen's freedom as independence depends on the division between legislature, executive, and judiciary.[34] If an executive official may exercise coercive powers against him, it is only in the circumstances specified by the general law; and any doubts about the extent of such powers must be settled by an independent court, detached from the policymaking and public interest orientation of the other branches of government. The law can rule, in contradistinction to the shifting demands of public policy, only when the courts can enforce a boundary between law and the current governmental agenda. The citizen may be compelled to cooperate only within the limits of previously articulated general rules, or else within the judicially determined limits of an official discretion, closely circumscribed and qualified by requirements of rationality and due process.

The connections between law, liberty, and the separation of powers are clearly identified by Hayek:

> The [pertinent] conception of freedom under the law...rests on the contention that when we obey laws, in the sense of general abstract rules laid down irrespective of their application to us, we are not subject to another man's will and are therefore free. It is because the lawgiver does not know the particular cases to which his rules will apply, and it is because the judge who applies them has no choice in drawing the conclusions that follow from the existing body of rules and the particular facts of the case, that it can be said that laws and not men rule.[35]

The rule of law is flouted when legislative and judicial powers are confused, allowing the legislature to determine the fate of identifiable individuals, whose conduct may have provoked popular hatred or contempt, or permitting judges to make new law, retrospectively, to govern particular cases arising for decision. Arbitrary discrimination between persons—rules that make distinctions that lack any reasonable justification, consonant with equal dignity—can be avoided only if laws are general in form, applying to all those (and only those) whose conduct needs to be regulated in the public interest. Such general rules must then be fairly applied by judges or other officials, steering a defensible line between rigid adherence to statutory purpose, on the one hand, and sensitivity to the particularities of marginal cases, on the other. In that way the law is administered with equity, reconciling public purposes and private rights or interests, as far as possible, at levels of both lawmaking and application.

---

[34] Compare with Kant, above n 10, 6:313–18.   [35] Hayek, above n 16, 153.

The paradigm case of violation of the rule of law—the clearest instance of a *measure* that fails to meet the necessary conceptual conditions of *law*—is the bill of attainder, by which the legislature asserts the guilt of the victim and specifies the punishment. Parliament thereby claims authority as legislator, judge, and jury, dispensing with the basic constitutional requirements of generality and due process: the victim is deprived of the ordinary safeguards of a fair trial on charges of having breached a previously specified criminal law.[36] Even when parliament permits the court to conduct a trial to determine guilt or innocence, there is a similar violation of the rule of law if the judges are directed to apply a measure specially tailored to meet the circumstances of the defendant's case, or if the ordinary rules of procedure and evidence are set aside to guarantee a conviction. In *Liyanage*, the court struck down a special enactment intended to punish government opponents by creation of a new offence, *ex post facto*, with minimum sentences attached and temporary changes to rules of procedure and evidence.[37] A legislative plan to 'secure the conviction and enhance the punishment' of particular persons was held to breach the separation of powers, implicit in the constitution, which included a Charter of Justice vesting the administration of justice exclusively in the courts it established.[38]

If we were to accept a view of the *common law*, characteristic of legal positivism, that permitted judges to act as lawmakers—applying new rules retrospectively to resolve contentious legal issues—we should have to acknowledge that common law adjudication involved systematic infringement of the rule of law.[39] If judges exercise *discretion* in developing the common law, imposing their own political choices whenever there is room for argument over the proper interpretation of precedent, the litigants in doubtful cases are denied the protection of the rule of law: they are subject, instead, to the rule of judges.[40] When we embrace the larger, more substantive conception of the rule of law, however, we can reasonably insist that any judicial ruling must always be subject to critical scrutiny by reference to genuine legal principles, independent of judicial whim or predilection. Courts are required to proceed on the working assumption that the corpus of legal rules amounts to a scheme of justice, developed by interpretation of a distinctive constitutional tradition. A new common law rule is only the byproduct of the decision in a particular case—a decision made by analysis of general principles, drawn from a study of that tradition. Competent lawyers may disagree about the correct answer; but they typically agree that there is a correct answer to find and that only certain kinds of reason—reasons consonant with legal tradition—are eligible grounds for their divergent conclusions.

---

[36] See Allan, 2001, above n 6, 148–57, 244–6, 251–2; Allan, 2013, above n 6, 93–4, 140–1.

[37] *Liyanage v R* [1967] 1 AC 259 (Judicial Committee of the Privy Council); Allan, 2001, above n 6, 233–4, 238–9, 254; Allan, 2013, above n 6, 297–301.

[38] The constitution of Ceylon (Sri Lanka) was derived chiefly from the Ceylon Independence Act 1947 and the Ceylon (Constitution) Order in Council 1946.

[39] Emphasizing the 'open texture' of legal rules, Hart attributed to courts a marginal 'rule-producing function' analogous to that of administrative bodies in 'the elaboration of variable standards': Hart, above n 1, 135–6; see also *Postscript*, ibid 272–6.

[40] For Dworkin's critique of Hart's invocation of judicial discretion, in the strong sense of being free from binding legal standards, see R. Dworkin, *Taking Rights Seriously* (Cambridge, Mass.: Harvard University Press, 1977; London: Duckworth, 1978), 31–9.

Hayek rightly denies that a judge may exercise 'discretion' in the sense of 'authority to follow his own will to pursue particular concrete aims', observing that his interpretation of law is usually subject to review by a higher court: 'The task of the judge is to discover the implications contained in the spirit of the whole system of valid rules of law or to express as a general rule, when necessary, what was not explicitly stated previously in a court of law or by the legislator.'[41] In a similar vein, Ronald Dworkin contends that a judge must resolve a particular case by giving appropriate weight, according to the circumstances, to those principles that together provide the best moral justification of the explicit substantive and institutional rules of his jurisdiction.[42] Dworkin's principle of 'integrity' displaces conflicting views about justice by the requirement of adherence to a single, coherent, and comprehensive set of principles of political morality, treating all alike according to those principles. The law may impose genuine obligations, on this view, even when it fails to match the true requirements of justice; its obligations may be associative in nature, grounded in fraternity: the community's practices of asserting and acknowledging responsibilities must 'display a pervasive mutual concern that fits a plausible conception of equal concern'.[43]

Insofar as the citizen is subject to coercive discretionary powers—his legal rights dependent on an official's view of the needs of the wider public interest, as these are assessed from time to time—his freedom as independence is plainly threatened. The blurring of the separation of powers places the ideal of legality in jeopardy, making private rights and interests subservient to official aims or goals that are not (or not clearly) defined by prior legislation. Hayek was adamantly opposed to the exercise of coercive discretionary powers, observing that under the rule of law 'the private citizen and his property are not an object of administration by the government' or a means of pursuing its purposes.[44] Hayek's antipathy to administrative discretion was shared by Dicey, who contrasted the rule of law with 'the exercise by persons in authority of wide, arbitrary, or discretionary powers of constraint', insisting that in England 'no man is punishable or can be lawfully made to suffer in body or goods except for a distinct breach of law established in the ordinary legal manner before the ordinary Courts of the land'.[45] Dicey's reference to the ordinary courts underlined his disapproval of administrative tribunals, whose place at the intersection of judicial and executive powers threatened the purity of the division between law and public policy.

If, however, administrative discretion must be embraced as a necessary, or even desirable, feature of the modern welfare-regulatory state, it does not follow (as sometimes supposed) that the rule of law may be *overridden*, sacrificing individual liberty for reasons of material equality. Instead, the rule of law must be maintained by rigorous application of principles of *due process*, ensuring that discretionary powers are employed only for legitimate purposes and in a manner that satisfies demanding standards of

---

[41] Hayek, above n 16, 212.   [42] Dworkin, above n 40, 66.
[43] Dworkin, above n 22, 201. Dworkin stresses, however, that the requirements of justice play an important role in the constructive interpretation of legal sources that integrity demands.
[44] Hayek, above n 16, 213.   [45] Dicey, above n 28, 97.

fairness and reasonableness.[46] Even the application of a general rule invokes analogous principles of fair procedure: the relevant facts must be ascertained by recourse to admissible evidence, and there must be proper opportunity to challenge the scope and content of the rule if its application to the facts is a matter of reasonable controversy. Proceedings before an administrative tribunal need not meet the demanding standards of a criminal trial: there is normally less at stake for those involved. Nor should public administration be hampered by legalistic constraints, hostile to legitimate political programmes; but judicial control of administrative discretion safeguards the integrity of legislative scheme and constitutional principle alike.[47]

In Hayek's view, administrative discretion undermined the *Rechtsstaat* ideal because it made individuals subject to official coercion beyond the limits of any generally applicable rule. An administrative decision affecting a person's private sphere of action should not 'be affected by any special knowledge possessed by the government or by its momentary purposes and the particular values it attaches to different concrete aims, including the preferences it may have concerning the effects on different people'.[48] The rule of law was secure only if such decisions were deducible from rules of law, whose correct application could be checked by an independent court. When we insist, however, that all coercive decisions should be made in accordance with consistent and relevant *criteria*—even if such criteria are determined by the administrative agency itself in furtherance of its public functions—we can closely approach the ideal of legality. There is then an analogy with common law precedent, distinguishing between cases only on closely reasoned grounds available for public scrutiny.[49]

Moreover, Hayek's objection to 'administrative courts' concerns only the 'quasi-judicial bodies inside the administrative machinery', intended rather to supervise the execution of state law than to protect individual liberty. Provided that such courts are independent of the executive and able to hold public agencies to their own *general criteria*, if not always to formally enacted rules, the rule of law is substantially maintained. Any intrusions into a person's private sphere will be strictly controlled by pre-existing standards of judgment and subject to impartial judicial review. While we may sometimes fall short of perfect compliance with the ideal of the rule of law—the tension between law and official discretion remains a challenge—we can adjust the requirements of due process to meet the gravity of the threat to individual liberty. The more important the particular rights or liberties at stake, within our constitutional practice, or the more serious the threatened infringement, the closer our standards of administrative propriety must come to those of judicial rectitude. When, in particular, executive bodies perform quasi-judicial functions, in which the deserts or entitlements of

[46] The ordinary standards of administrative legality, imposed on official agencies by the common law and enforced by judicial review, are as much a feature of the rule of law as the canons of legislative propriety that lie at the heart of a formal conception of legality: see Allan, 2013, above n 6, 110–14, 212–31.
[47] Herein lies the basis of the English principle of ultra vires, which attributes the pertinent principles of administrative legality to a 'legislative intent', premised on the assumption that adherence to a public authority's statutory mandate entails compliance with the various requirements of the rule of law: see Allan, 2013, above n 6, ch 6.
[48] Hayek, above n 16, 214.   [49] See Allan, 2001, above n 6, 127–33.

specific persons are of central concern, they should be held to the standards of impartiality and fairness characteristic of judicial proceedings.[50]

We bring administrative discretion within the purview of the rule of law, accordingly, by rejecting any sharp division between procedure and substance. The demands of *due process* extend from principles of procedural fairness, such as those that require public authorities to listen to the representations of persons affected by their decisions, to more substantive obligations of fair treatment and respect for constitutional rights.[51] If, in principle, public agencies are obliged in their decision-making to have regard only to strictly relevant criteria, as judged by independent courts of law, they must be similarly obliged to give such criteria a defensible *weight* in all the circumstances. The proper scope of official discretion must be sensitive to the constitutional context, allowing the courts to exercise independent oversight of any administrative jurisdiction capable of injuring important individual rights and interests. Any restrictions or constraints on the enjoyment of constitutional rights must be proportionate to the anticipated public benefit: they must be shown to be both *necessary*, in the sense that no less intrusive state action could achieve the public end in view, and *legitimate*, in the sense that the limitation of rights is not so serious as to challenge their status as pillars of the constitutional framework.[52]

IV. Sovereignty and the Rule of Law

The twin concepts of the rule of law and sovereignty are closely aligned, narrower and broader conceptions of the former corresponding, respectively, to stronger and weaker versions of the latter. When the rule of law is conceived as a formal or procedural principle, there are no implicit legal limits to the scope of coercive state authority. Leviathan must assert his will by means of promulgated, published, and (mainly) prospective rules; but that will may have any content, reflecting an unfettered official appraisal of the demands of the public interest. Understood, however, as a substantive principle of legitimate governance, affirming human dignity and the equal status of persons, the rule of law divides and limits sovereignty: Leviathan may not trample on the fundamental rights and freedoms of the governed. Instead of sovereignty being enjoyed by a monarch or an assembly—an unelected or elected dictator—it is distributed between the various institutions of the state so as to guarantee as far as possible that *law* rules, rather than prominent men or women.[53] Parliamentary sovereignty, taken at face value, asserts the priority of the legislative will over any constraints of law.

---

[50] Ibid 140–8; and Allan, 2013, above n 6, 188–91.   [51] Allan, 2013, above n 6, ch 7.
[52] An exclusion of homosexuals from the armed forces, curtailing rights of privacy and personhood, could not for example be justified by marginal and speculative gains to national security: *Smith and Grady v United Kingdom* (1999) 29 EHRR 493; Allan, 2013, above n 6, 244–9.
[53] Accountable only to God and not to his people, Hobbes's sovereign was not constrained by civil (as opposed to natural) law. To set the law above the sovereign was only to make a new sovereign to judge and punish him, to 'the Confusion, and Dissolution of the Commonwealth': see T. Hobbes, *Leviathan* (Harmondsworth: Penguin, 1968), ch 29. Hobbes thought it an error to suppose that the sovereign power might be divided: division meant dissolution, 'for Powers divided mutually destroy each other'. For radical reassessment of Hobbes, however, see Dyzenhaus, above n 24, 205–17 (emphasizing the central place in Hobbes's theory of the laws of nature).

But in a constitutional or liberal democracy it must be understood as a doctrine of *legislative supremacy*: the supreme legislator, even when representing the people at large, must at all times honour the demands of the rule of law, both formal and substantive.[54]

The absolutist doctrine of sovereignty is sometimes invoked in English law alongside a 'principle of legality', purporting to acknowledge basic constitutional rights. There is a common law presumption that even the most general words of an enactment are 'intended to be subject to the basic rights of the individual'; yet the presumption is usually held to yield to 'express language or necessary implication to the contrary'.[55] On that account, parliamentary sovereignty 'means that Parliament can, if it chooses, legislate contrary to fundamental principles of human rights': the rule of law surrenders in the final analysis to sovereign power, any limitations on that power being 'ultimately political, not legal'.[56] Confronted, however, by the full implications of such stark doctrine, judges are tempted to threaten something akin to political retaliation, so that 'an exorbitant assertion of government power', by resort to a complaisant parliamentary majority, would be likely to 'test the relative merits of strict legalism and constitutional legal principle in the courts at the most fundamental level'.[57] There is implicit here, however, a dubious separation of law and fundamental principle, or legality and constitutionalism. Strict legality, correctly conceived, entails compliance with constitutional principle by both courts and legislature, excluding any assertion of exorbitant or arbitrary powers.

The underlying assumption, apparently, is that in the absence of a written or codified constitution, formally placing fundamental rights beyond ordinary legislative interference, Parliament must enjoy unfettered legislative authority. That assumption accompanies the largely instrumental concept of law characteristic of legal positivism, which identifies law and legal obligation by reference to their conventionally established sources. When, however, we make the conceptual connection between law and liberty, in the manner of the constitutional ideal of the rule of law, we can interpret an unwritten constitution as a framework of fundamental law (akin to the *Rechtsstaat* or Kant's account of the Principle of Right). Not every measure formally enacted by ordinary procedure counts as *law*, correctly understood. A genuine law must, in the first place, be a *general rule* rather than an *ad hominem* command: it must not be a *measure* directed at particular persons, whose conduct or character has aroused popular or official hostility and condemnation. A bill of attainder (as I have argued above) is not a valid law in the only sense in which we could acknowledge Parliament's power to *make law*, consistently with the principle of the rule of law. Legislative authority, moreover, is further constrained by other essential elements of the rule of law. Parliament could not legitimately undermine the separation of powers by conferring sweeping powers of lawmaking on executive officials (as opposed to the grant of more narrowly delineated delegated legislative powers for specific purposes). Nor could Parliament be permitted to insulate the exercise of powers conferred on public authorities from all judicial

---

[54] See further Allan, 2013, above n 6, chs 4 and 5.
[55] *R v Secretary of State for the Home Dept, ex p Simms* [2000] 2 AC 115, 131 (per Lord Hoffmann).
[56] Ibid.   [57] *R (Jackson) v Attorney General* [2005] UKHL 56, para 101 (per Lord Steyn).

oversight, granting what would be in effect arbitrary powers of action immune from legal challenge.[58]

In Hayek's view, notions of parliamentary omnipotence are connected with an erroneous conception of popular sovereignty, attributing unqualified authority to majority decisions. Such an outlook, dependent on the assumption that there must always be an ultimate source of unlimited power, was the product of a 'false constructivistic interpretation of the formation of human institutions which attempts to trace them all to an original designer or some other deliberate act of will'.[59] Social order rests not on a deliberate decision to adopt certain common rules, but rather 'the existence among the people of certain opinions of what is right and wrong'. Until modern democracy inherited an earlier tradition of absolutism, 'the conception was still kept alive that legitimacy rested in the last resort on the approval by the people at large of certain fundamental principles underlying and limiting all government, and not on their consent to particular measures'.[60] While Parliament's claim to sovereignty initially meant only that it recognized no superior will, it gradually came to mean that it enjoyed unfettered power.[61]

The idea of the rule of law has been obscured, in Hayek's view, by the dual function of the representative assembly. In addition to its primary task of articulating and approving general rules of just conduct, comprising the ordinary civil and criminal law, the assembly is typically involved in the direction of governmental administration, authorizing the exercise of coercive powers for particular purposes. Authorizations of the latter sort do not amount to 'law' in the sense in which the rule of law invokes that idea as a bastion of liberty.[62] Hayek distinguishes between laws (correctly so called) regulating the interactions between persons, on the one hand, and 'so-called laws', on the other, which are merely 'instructions issued by the state to its servants concerning the manner in which they are to direct the apparatus of government and the means which are at their disposal'.[63] The rule of law means adherence, by both citizen and official, to the requirements of law in its primary sense of rules of just conduct, defining the citizen's protected domain of liberty.[64]

Parliament's legislative authority proceeds from its primary function of maintaining and improving those rules of civil and criminal law on which the successful interaction of free and equal citizens depends. What initially seems to be a merely formal requirement in Hayek's scheme—the enactment of general rules, applicable to unknown persons on innumerable future occasions—has substantive implications for human freedom. Since such general rules are intended only to regulate the relations between independent individuals, enabling each to pursue his own aims and interests with or without the voluntary cooperation of other persons, they cannot properly prohibit whatever the majority may currently disapprove. It is inherent in the ideal of the rule of law that people may live according to their own ethical values, provided that their

---

[58] See *Anisminic Ltd v Foreign Compensation Commission* [1969] 2 AC 147; Allan, 2013, above n 6, 214–15, 219–20, 230–1.

[59] Hayek, above n 26, vol III, 33.   [60] Ibid 35.   [61] Ibid 4.   [62] Ibid 20–31.

[63] Hayek, above n 16, 207.

[64] Hayek emphasizes the distinction between *ius* and *lex*, *droit* and *loi*, *Recht* and *Gesetz*: Hayek, above n 26, vol I, 94.

actions are compatible with others having the same freedom. In Kantian terms, parliament's authority proceeds from its duty to secure a rightful civil condition, which guarantees the equal independence of persons—their entitlement to set their own purposes and pursue them with whatever means they legitimately control, avoiding the wrongful coercion of others.

It follows that, in addition to the various requirements of formality inherent in the idea of governance by legal rule, there are substantive constraints on the scope of legislative supremacy. While parliament may exercise wide authority in its efforts to reform or clarify the civil and criminal law, and in conferring powers on officials for public purposes, it cannot legitimately infringe individual rights intrinsic to fundamental constitutional freedom. Freedoms of speech, conscience, religion, association, and assembly, for example, are essential requirements of independence, allowing each person to make informed decisions and choices: their integrity is a necessary condition of any valid assertion of state authority, however important the public purposes in view. Insofar as officials exercise coercive powers, they must obey the ordinary rules of civil and criminal law; or if certain functions demand some qualification of these general rules of just conduct, the special powers conferred must not violate basic constitutional rights. Any limitation or qualification of such rights must be both *necessary* for legitimate public purposes and consistent, having regard to the special urgency of the public need, with the underlying rationale of these rights in the protection of human dignity and independence.

V. Conclusion

I have argued that the principle of the rule of law can be fully understood only in connection with a certain view of the related ideals of human dignity and individual liberty. While the various formal precepts of Fuller's 'inner morality' of law play an important role in curbing the risk of arbitrary legislative power, they are only part of a larger, more complex conception of legality. In safeguarding freedom as independence, the canons of formal legality contribute to a scheme of governance that, in all its aspects, renders state coercion legitimate by adherence to fundamental constraints. The rule of law permits coercion only to secure the conditions in which each person's liberty can be exercised compatibly with a like liberty for all; and liberty is to be understood as the sense in which each individual is sovereign in setting and pursuing his own ends, consistently with others having the same freedom. Properly understood, the rule of law is not a shield against the abuse of *law*, as it is sometimes portrayed. It is the moral ideal of governance according to *law in its primary sense*—the sense in which it enforces a scheme of rights and duties that provides for each individual a domain of liberty, secure from the threat of domination either by public officials or powerful private interests.

Of equal importance to compliance with the precepts of formal legality, applicable to legislation, is adherence to the requirements of procedural fairness and due process as regards the application of law to particular cases. There must be a separation of powers between parliament, government, and judiciary, enabling the courts to act impartially and independently. Only under those conditions can the law be fairly applied in accordance with its true meaning, which may differ (in any particular instance) from the expectations of certain legislators or the preferences of other public officials. And the demands of due process are inextricably bound up, in practice, with the law's permissible content: the exercise of administrative discretion must respect the citizen's fundamental rights and the limits of legitimate government. No powers can be lawfully conferred on a public agency that would violate constitutional rights; a statutory mandate must always be interpreted in the light of the proper limits of state authority.

There can be no restriction of the central freedoms of thought, speech, conscience, and association that would curtail a person's ability to form and pursue her own ethical ideals. She cannot surrender the responsibility for choosing the purposes and projects that best fulfil her ambitions for her own life; and she cannot therefore properly accede to rules designed to fetter that responsibility. Individual independence is not threatened by an equal freedom to hear and express competing views about the nature of a good life: the rule of law, accordingly, forbids censorship of unorthodox or unpopular opinion. Freedoms of conscience and religion are central aspects of legality, when the rule of law is understood in the light of the general principle of freedom as independence: no governmental action can be properly justified on the basis of religious doctrine, even if such doctrine currently evokes a broad consensus. Moreover, there are limits to the legitimate regulation of private and family life: the criminal law may not reflect a moral paternalism, grounded on disapproval of people's choices of lifestyle or character. It is an affront to people's dignity to deny them liberty to conduct their own lives in accordance with their convictions, assuming that they do not impede an equal liberty enjoyed by others.[65]

Speech may, of course, be constrained by protections against defamation or fraud or incitement to crime; in these cases the speaker's right is qualified in deference to the conflicting rights of other persons. The ideal of the rule of law, however, treats these various rights as components of a larger, integrated account of independence; while the details may vary between jurisdictions, the basic structure of intersecting rights is common to all genuine instances of the *Rechtsstaat*.[66] That is the basis of our assumption that a court of law has no discretion, in the sense that it must settle each case arising in accordance with pre-existing law. Our confidence that there is always law to find, if necessary by recourse to general principle, rests on the conviction that we do not need to choose in an arbitrary fashion between incommensurable values.[67] A court of law must interpret the official legal record as an effort to lend precision to a structure of constitutional rights, which when correctly understood preserves individual independence

---

[65] Compare with R. Dworkin, *Justice for Hedgehogs* (Cambridge, Mass.: Harvard University Press, 2011), chs 9 and 17, defending a principle of ethical independence as a requirement of the authenticity demanded by respect for human dignity.

[66] In Kant's account, the most important rights are implicit in the individual's innate right to freedom; and state coercion is legitimate only insofar as it is consistent with innate rights. Positive legislation must be 'a law that free persons could impose on themselves, where the test of the possible imposition is their rightful capacity to bind themselves, that is, consistency with their rightful honour': Ripstein, above n 11, 213.

[67] Compare with Dworkin, above n 65, 90–6, 118–20, challenging common assumptions about the indeterminacy and incommensurability of fundamental values.

as the basic demand of human dignity. We can envisage a seamless transition from study of the domestic legal regime, specific to a single jurisdiction, to deeper exploration of the underlying philosophy of right: the former is underpinned and inspired by the latter. Legal rights and duties are genuine—provoking legitimate state force in their defence—only when they are features of a scheme of governance that, correctly interpreted, accords each individual the freedom that his human dignity demands.

exercise only a discrete set of powers to the exclusion of the other branches, the Nation would be ungovernable.[6] Many argue that some 'intermixture' of functions is both necessary and desirable.[7]

There is a second (related) line of criticism stemming from this concern about the strictness of the separation. If the ideal of the separation of powers requires us to maximize the independence and separation of the three branches of government, is this undermined by a system of checks and balances? After all, a scheme of checks and balances involves a degree of mutual supervision between the branches of government and, therefore, a degree of interference by one branch into the functions and tasks of the other.[8] As Geoffrey Marshall pointed out, it is unclear whether a scheme of checks and balances 'is part of, or a departure from, separation of powers theory'.[9]

A third argument is that the classic tripartite separation of powers articulated in the eighteenth century is archaic and anachronistic, because it fails to account for other sources of power in the modern state, most notably, the 'fourth branch' of the 'administrative state'.[10] Since administrative agencies combine adjudicatory, rule-making, and executive functions, they are 'abhorred by separation of powers traditionalists'.[11] Moreover, although the United States is sometimes heralded as an archetypal 'separation of powers system', there is a perennial worry that the institutional separation between the legislative and executive branch under the US Constitution leads to gridlock and ineffective government.[12] Little wonder, then, that US scholars question whether the separation of powers is a principle worth preserving in modern times.[13]

There are also conceptual problems. Many theorists argue that the separation of powers is bedevilled by indeterminacy and confusion.[14] The ideas of legislative, executive, and judicial powers have not proved capable of precise definition.[15] And there is considerable disagreement about which values underpin the doctrine.[16] For some, the purpose of the separation of powers is to curb abuse of power, partly by preventing its concentration in the hands of one person or body. For others, its purpose is to protect liberty and the rule of law.[17] Still others argue that the central value of the separation of powers is that it ensures 'efficiency' in government, where efficiency is understood as 'the matching of tasks

---

[6] R. Pierce, 'Separation of Powers and the Limits of Independence' (1989) 30 *William & Mary Law Review* 365; Vile, above n 4, 318.

[7] See Carolan, above n 4.   [8] Vile, above n 4, 18; Carolan, above n 4, 32.

[9] G. Marshall, *Constitutional Theory* (Oxford: Clarendon Press, 1971), 103; C. Munro, *Studies in Constitutional Law* 2nd edn (Oxford: Oxford University Press, 2005), 307.

[10] P. Strauss, 'The Place of Agencies in Government: Separation of Powers and the Fourth Branch' (1984) 84 *Columbia Law Review* 573, at 581; Carolan, above n 4, 42ff.

[11] Marshall, above n 9, 118; A. Vermeule, 'Optimal Abuse of Power' (2015) 109 *Northwestern University Law Review* 673, at 680.

[12] R. Albert, 'The Fusion of Presidentialism and Parliamentarism' (2009) 57 *The American Journal of Comparative Law* 531, at 562.

[13] See eg R. Goldwin and A. Kaufman (eds), *Separation of Powers—Does It Still Work?* (Washington, D.C.: AEI Press, 1986); E. Posner and A. Vermeule, *The Executive Unbound: After the Madisonian Republic* (Oxford: Oxford University Press, 2010).

[14] Marshall, above n 9, 97, 124.   [15] Ibid 124.

[16] Carolan, above n 4, 27; W. B. Gwyn, *The Meaning of the Separation of Powers* (The Hague: Martinus Nijhoff, 1965), 127.

[17] T. R. S. Allan, *Law, Liberty and Justice: The Legal Foundations of British Constitutionalism* (Oxford: Oxford University Press, 1994), ch 3.

11

The Constitutional Separation of Powers

*Aileen Kavanagh**

In the panoply of principles regulating constitutional government, the separation of powers occupies a position of deep ambivalence. On the one hand, all constitutional democracies rest on some form of division between three distinct branches of government—the legislature, executive, and judiciary. Moreover, within these countries, the separation of powers is invoked as an *ideal*, that is as a standard (or, perhaps, set of standards) to which the legal and constitutional arrangements of a modern state ought to conform. The assumption is that the separation of powers is an ideal worth having and that we gain something valuable by conforming to it. Indeed, this assumption has had a long pedigree in the canonical literature on constitutional theory. In the eighteenth century, the separation of powers was hailed as a bulwark against the abuse of state power and the threat of tyranny. Montesquieu wrote that without a separation of powers, there would be 'no liberty'.[1] The French Declaration of the Rights of Man in 1789 went so far as to suggest that 'Any society in which the safeguarding of rights is not assured, and the separation of powers is not established, has no constitution.'[2] Right up to the present day, theorists argue that the separation of powers is the very 'essence of constitutionalism'[3] and 'a universal criterion of constitutional government'.[4]

However, despite being a pervasive feature of constitutional democracies, there are deep reservations about the separation of powers in contemporary times. The first line of common criticism concerns the perceived stringency of the separation requirement. If what is required is a complete separation of three mutually exclusive functions carried out by three branches of government hermetically sealed from each other, then this has never been instantiated in any modern state.[5] Indeed, as one commentator observed, 'if powers truly were separated so that each branch of government could

* Associate Professor, Faculty of Law, University of Oxford and Fellow of St Edmund Hall, Oxford. I would like to thank all the participants at the conference for this volume at the University of Toronto in May 2014 for extremely helpful comments on an earlier version of this paper. Thanks also go to Nick Barber, Adrian Briggs, Richard Ekins, and Simon Whittaker for illuminating discussions on the separation of powers. The final version of this paper was written with support from the British Academy.

[1] C. Montesquieu, *The Spirit of the Laws* (1748), bk 11, ch 6.   [2] Art 16.
[3] E. Barendt, 'Is there a UK Constitution?' (1997) 17 *Oxford Journal of Legal Studies* 137; E. Barendt, 'Separation of Powers and Constitutional Government' (1995) *Public Law* 599.
[4] M. J. C. Vile, *Constitutionalism and the Separation of Powers* (Oxford: Oxford University Press, 1967), 97; E. Carolan, *The New Separation of Powers: A Theory of the Modern State* (Oxford: Oxford University Press, 2009), 18.
[5] Carolan, above n 4, 18; V. Nourse, 'The Vertical Separation of Powers' (1999) 49 *Duke Law Journal* 749, at 754; C. Mollers, *The Three Branches: A Comparative Model of Separation of Powers* (Oxford: Oxford University Press, 2013), 8.

to those bodies best suited to execute them'.[18] Perhaps if we could disentangle the various values served by the separation of powers, this would help us to assess intelligently what counts as achieving the ideal, and what is at stake in various possible violations.

The aim of this chapter is to do some of this disentangling work. It will proceed in the following way. Section I will examine 'the pure view' of the separation of powers which is premised on a triad of mutually exclusive functions. I argue that this account of the separation of powers is flawed, but that an appreciation of its flaws points us in the right direction. Section II presents a reconstructed view which seeks to meet the criticisms levelled at the orthodox or pure account. I argue that the separation of powers requires a division of power and labour, rather than a strict separation of functions. In section III, I argue that the separation of powers is not exhausted by division-of-labour considerations. It must be supplemented by the dimension of checks and balances. Section IV brings these dual dimensions together, arguing that they are both underpinned by the value of 'coordinated institutional effort between branches of government' in the service of good government.[19] There is no denying that this argument has an air of paradox about it. How can a doctrine which urges us to *separate* powers be underpinned by the value of institutional coordination in a *joint* enterprise? Part of the task of section IV will be to explain this apparent paradox, before dissolving it.

I. Separation of Powers: The Pure View

Throughout its history, the 'separation of powers' has received effusive praise and vitriolic opprobrium in equal measure.[20] But what does it require? This is harder to answer than one might think because the term 'separation of powers' is fraught with ambiguity. The first source of ambiguity concerns the word 'powers', which could refer either to institutions (as in 'powers in the land') or to the legal authority to do certain acts or, alternatively, to the functions of legislating, executing, or judging.[21] The second source of ambiguity concerns the word 'separation'. Separation can vary in form and degree. It can be absolute or partial—and partial separation can allow for some interconnection. Given these ambiguities, the phrase 'separation of powers' has been used to refer to a wide array of different ideas (not all of which are compatible), including: a triad of mutually exclusive functions; a prohibition on plural office-holding; the isolation, immunity, or independence of one branch of government from interference from another; or a scheme of interlocking checks and balances.[22] How do we navigate between these ideas?

---

[18] N. Barber, 'Prelude to the Separation of Powers' (2001) 60 *Cambridge Law Journal* 59; J. Manning, 'Separation of Powers as Ordinary Interpretation' (2011) 124 *Harvard Law Review* 1939, at 1994.

[19] D. Kyritsis, 'What is Good about Legal Conventionalism?' (2008) 14 *Legal Theory* 135, at 154; D. Kyritsis, 'Constitutional Review in a Representative Democracy' (2012) 32 *Oxford Journal of Legal Studies* 297, at 303; see also Carolan, above n 4, 186.

[20] For an in-depth historical account of the 'pattern of attraction and repulsion' to the idea of the separation of powers, see Vile, above n 4, 3ff.

[21] J. Finnis, 'Separation of Powers in the Australian Constitution: Some Preliminary Considerations' (1967) 3 *Adelaide Law Review* 159; Vile, above n 4, 12; Marshall, above n 9.

[22] Marshall, above n 9, 100.

A useful place to start is Maurice Vile's influential articulation of 'the pure doctrine of the separation of powers'.[23] According to the pure doctrine, the separation of powers requires that:

> the government should be divided into three branches or departments, the legislature, the executive, and the judiciary. To each of these branches, there is a corresponding identifiable function of government, legislative, executive, or judicial. Each branch of the government must be confined to the exercise of its own function and not allowed to encroach upon the functions of the other branches. Furthermore, the persons who compose these three agencies of government must be kept separate and distinct, no individual being allowed to be at the same time a member of more than one branch. In this way each of the branches will be a check to the others and no single group of people will be able to control the machinery of the State.[24]

Though Vile conceded that the separation of powers has 'rarely been held in this extreme form, and even more rarely been put into practice',[25] the pure doctrine is widely invoked as an ideal-type or a benchmark against which alternative conceptions of the separation of powers are assessed.[26] Indeed, with its emphasis on a distinction between three different types of function, the pure doctrine is often thought to encapsulate 'the traditional understanding that governmental activities can be classified under three functional headings—legislative, executive, or judicial—with each function associated with one of the three branches of government'.[27] A strict separation along functional lines is thought to lie at the heart of 'the classic doctrine of the separation of powers'.[28]

Interestingly, the pure doctrine is often associated with Montesquieu,[29] despite the fact that Montesquieu never clearly articulated a theory of functional separation and specialization in its pure form.[30] Moreover, Montesquieu's tripartite distinction has been widely criticized as overly simplistic, even in the eighteenth century.[31] Nonetheless, it is now commonplace to think of the classic theory of the separation of powers as a

---

[23] Vile, above n 4, 13.   [24] Ibid.   [25] Ibid.

[26] K. Malleson, 'The Rehabilitation of Separation of Powers in the UK', in L. de Groot-van Leeuwen and W. Rombouts (eds), *Separation of Powers in Theory and Practice: An International Perspective* (Nijmegen: Wolf Publishing, 2010), 99–122, at 115.

[27] T. Merrill, 'The Constitutional Principle of Separation of Powers' (1991) *Supreme Court Review* 225, at 231; see also G. Brennan and A. Hamlin, 'A Revisionist View of the Separation of Powers' (1994) 6 *Journal of Theoretical Politics* 345, at 351; Barendt, 1995, above n 3, 601 (describing the pure doctrine as the 'classic' formulation); B. Manin, 'Checks, Balances and Boundaries: The Separation of Powers in the Constitutional Debate of 1787', in B. Fontana (ed), *The Invention of the Modern Republic* (Cambridge: Cambridge University Press, 1994), 27–62, at 30; M. Hansen, 'The Mixed Constitution versus the Separation of Powers: Monarchical and Aristocratic Aspects of Modern Democracy' (2010) 31 *History of Political Thought* 509, at 510.

[28] Brennan and Hamlin, above n 27, 351; Barendt, 1995, above n 3, 601; M. E. Magill, 'Beyond Powers and Branches in Separation of Powers Law' (2001) 150 *University of Pennsylvania Law Review* 603, at 608.

[29] See A. Tomkins, *Public Law* (Oxford: Clarendon Press, 2003), 36; Hansen, above n 27, 511, 517; L. N. Cutler, 'Now is the Time for All Good Men...' (1989) 30 *William & Mary Law Review* 387.

[30] Vile, above n 4, 90. As Manin observes, 'the question here is not whether or not Montesquieu himself advocated this pure version of the theory of the separation of powers. The fact is that for decades if not centuries, most legal experts and political actors (with the notable exception of the American Federalists) believed and proclaimed that he did' (Manin, above n 27, 30).

[31] See further L. Claus, 'Montesquieu's Mistakes and the True Meaning of Separation of Powers' (2005) 25 *Oxford Journal of Legal Studies* 419; D. Kyritsis, *Shared Authority* (Oxford: Hart Publishing, 2015), 107.

'theory about division between three different functions'[32] inspired by Montesquieu and that the principle prohibits any intermixture of functions.[33] Whatever the truth of its intellectual provenance,[34] the 'pure doctrine' has had an enduring influence on our thinking about what the separation of powers requires.[35] It has become the orthodox understanding of what the principle requires. Therefore, we should subject this idea to some close analysis.

The pure view has three central components: a separation of *institutions*, a separation of *functions*, and a separation of *personnel*. I will address the issue of separation of personnel later in the chapter. Here, I will focus on the requirement of functional separation since this idea lies at the heart of the pure view. Two features of that requirement bear emphasis at the outset. The first is that the pure doctrine of functional separation seems to posit a 'one-to-one correlation'[36] between the three branches of government and their respective functions. To each branch, there is an identifiable function which, in turn, gives the branch its name. We could call this the '*one branch—one function*' view.[37] The second feature is the requirement that each branch must be confined to the exercise of its own (single) function and should not encroach upon the functions of the other branches. For it to assume any other function would be ultra vires. We can call this the '*separation as confinement*' view.

Both of these ideas—the 'one branch—one function' view and the 'separation as confinement' requirement—are deeply problematic. Let us start with the 'one branch—one function' idea. The claim that there is a one-to-one correlation between function and branch is impossible to sustain in any modern state. As is well known, the executive typically carries out a significant legislative function in the form of 'delegated legislation'. Indeed, in many countries, the executive has a predominant role in primary legislation as well. Executive power is strikingly multifunctional.[38]

Even if we set aside the executive, serious problems arise with respect to the courts and legislatures as well. When we look at the courts, we can see that the judicial branch has to keep order in the court and manage court facilities (thus carrying out executive functions). The courts also exercise legislative functions when they make rules governing court procedures and the costs of litigation. Many people also argue that in settling disputes about what legal rules require, the courts also make new law, albeit within certain limits.[39] Certainly in common law systems, there is a widespread recognition

---

[32] Hansen, above n 27, 523; W. Heun, *The Constitution of Germany: A Contextual Analysis* (Oxford: Hart Publishing, 2011), 86.

[33] Vermeule, above n 11, 680.

[34] Dicey argued that the separation of powers as understood in France and the United States in the eighteenth century was based on a misunderstanding of Montesquieu. See A. V. Dicey, *Introduction to the Study of the Law of the Constitution* 8th edn (London: Macmillan, 1915).

[35] E. Corwin, *Constitution of the United States of America: Analysis and Interpretation* (Washington, D.C.: United States Printing Office, 1953), 9–10.

[36] D. Kyritsis, 'Principles, Policies and the Power of Courts' (2007) 20 *Canadian Journal of Law and Jurisprudence* 379, at 386; Merrill, above n 27, 231.

[37] See Merrill, above n 27, 231.

[38] W. B. Gwyn, 'The Indeterminacy of the Separation of Powers in the Age of the Framers' (1989) 30 *William & Mary Law Review* 263, at 266.

[39] Of course, whether the creative aspect of the judicial role is aptly characterized as 'making law' is an ongoing matter of dispute in legal theory. See further R. Dworkin, *A Matter of Principle* (Cambridge,

that 'law-making—within certain limits—is an inevitable and legitimate element of the judge's role'.[40] Moreover, in those jurisdictions where courts have the power to strike down legislation for non-compliance with constitutional rights, the idea that the judicial function is exclusively to apply the law looks strained, at best. When we turn to the legislature, a similarly multifunctional picture emerges. The legislative branch needs to keep order in the legislature, administering the process for voting on bills (an executive task) and it also needs to resolve disputes over contempt and breach of privilege (arguably a judicial function).[41]

Clearly, the strict 'one branch—one function' view cannot be sustained as a descriptive matter, because all three branches exercise all three functions to some degree. In order for each branch to be well organized for its own tasks, they must all carry out executive, legislative, and judicial tasks.[42] This multifunctionality casts doubt on the explanatory power of the pure doctrine. With its monolithic insistence that each branch perform one single function and no other, it seems to present a theory of what distinguishes the branches of government which does not capture the complicated institutional realities of modern states.[43] Little wonder, then, that 'the problem of distinguishing the three functions of government has long been, and continues to be, one of the most intractable puzzles in constitutional law'.[44]

Is there any way of rescuing the functional classification which is widely believed to lie at the very heart of the separation of powers? One solution is to relax the stringency of the 'one branch—one function' requirement and accept that it is a matter of degree. On this view, we could say that each branch of government has a primary or core function, even though it may sometimes perform other functions at the periphery. In this way, we can preserve some correlation between branch and function, whilst not requiring a strict one-to-one correlation entailed by the pure doctrine.[45]

Clearly, this 'core functions' approach to the separation of powers is much more promising, both as a descriptive and as a normative matter. By accommodating a degree of multifunctionality, it rescues the separation of powers from claims of being irrelevant as a theory for modern government. It also avoids the mistake of thinking that just because two things cannot always be distinguished clearly, that therefore there is no distinction between them. But whilst it deflects some of the more obvious critiques of the so-called pure account of the separation of powers, it does not solve all the problems with the orthodox understanding. First, it continues to cash out the distinctness between the branches in terms of one single function—albeit in terms of a primary, rather than exclusive one. This is problematic because we know that the overlap

---

Mass.: Harvard University Press, 1985), 48; J. Gardner, 'Legal Positivism: 5½ Myths', in J. Gardner, *Law as a Leap of Faith* (Oxford: Oxford University Press, 2012); and Dyzenhaus in this volume.

[40] Lord Irvine, 'Activism and Restraint: Human Rights and the Interpretative Process' (1999) 4 *European Human Rights Law Review* 350, at 352; Lord Reid, 'The Judge as Lawmaker' (1972) 12 *Journal of Public Teachers of Law* 22.

[41] Strauss, above n 10, 573.

[42] T. Endicott, *Administrative Law* 2nd edn (Oxford: Oxford University Press, 2011), 15.

[43] G. Lawson, 'The Rise and Rise of the Administrative State' (1994) 107 *Harvard Law Review* 1231; see further M. E. Magill, 'The Real Separation in the Separation of Powers' (2000) 86 *Virginia Law Review* 1127, at 1136–47.

[44] Lawson, above n 43, 1142.   [45] Barendt, 1995, above n 3; Carolan, above n 4, 21.

of function is not just at the peripheries of the various functions, but is significant, pervasive, and unavoidable. As Victoria Nourse observed, it is an 'open secret that the departments all perform the functions of other departments'.[46]

Second, even those who advance a 'core functions' approach face the formidable challenge of identifying—and then describing—what the core branch functions are. Take, for example, the executive. In most modern states, we would resist the conclusion that its core function is to execute or give effect to policy, with other functions relegated to a secondary or peripheral role. In many countries, we think of the executive as the body which initiates—rather than executes—policy. What is the 'core' function of the courts? Is it to adjudicate individual disputes, or apply the law, or uphold the rule of law, or to hold the other branches to account? The task of identifying the core function of legislatures fares no better. Though it is certainly tempting to say that the core task of the legislature is to legislate, this is widely disputed by political scientists who argue that legislatures typically carry out a multiplicity of functions and it is by no means a foregone conclusion that lawmaking is the most important amongst them.[47] For many, the main role of the legislature is not to make law, but to scrutinize and pass judgment on legislative proposals made by the executive.[48] The main role of the legislature is, thus, to legitimate rather than legislate. It follows that softening the rigours of the pure doctrine by allowing for branches to exercise peripheral or non-core functions does not escape entirely the 'intractable puzzles'[49] posed by the pure doctrine.

Let us turn now to the idea of 'separation as confinement'. Clearly, if the import of this idea is to urge each branch to confine itself to the exercise of one, single function, then this will be vulnerable to some of the same problems encountered by the 'one branch—one function' view. After all, if each branch exercises more than one function (indeed, if it is both inevitable and desirable that they should), then the 'separation as confinement' view will seem like a misguided prescription. However, it runs up against further difficulties. For when we look at how each branch carries out its respective tasks, we can see that the idea of institutional 'confinement' fails to capture a crucial feature of the institutional practice. This is the interdependence of—and interaction between—the three branches of government when carrying out their respective roles in the constitutional order.

Consider, for example, the role of the legislature. When the legislature enacts a statute, it has a number of legislative tools at its disposal. One such tool is to rely on *vague* terms in the statutory text, such as 'reasonable care', 'offensive behaviour', or 'within a reasonable time'. [50] When the legislature relies on such terms, the legislation sets out the general legal framework, leaving it to other bodies (often the courts) to fill in the gaps and work out how it should be applied in individual cases.[51] This is an example of what Joseph Raz has called 'directed powers', that is, where the legislature gives

[46] Nourse, above n 5, 758, 760, 782, 789.
[47] P. Norton, *Parliament in British Politics* 2nd edn (Basingstoke: Palgrave Macmillan, 2013), 9ff.
[48] Ibid 7.   [49] Lawson, above n 43.
[50] Vague language is not exceptional, but is rather a 'pervasive legislative tool' and is ineliminable in the law. See T. Endicott, 'The Impossibility of the Rule of Law' (1999) 19 *Oxford Journal of Legal Studies* 1, at 5.
[51] J. Raz, *The Authority of Law* (Oxford: Oxford University Press, 1979), 194.

other institutional actors (either ministers or subordinate administrative bodies or the courts) discretion to decide what the law requires, subject to the ends which must be served by the exercise of those powers.[52] And, as Raz points out, 'the general function of directed powers is to introduce and maintain a certain division of power and of labour between various authorities'.[53]

The prevalence of various kinds of directed powers in legislation illustrates some of the limitations of the 'separation as confinement' view. When deciding how to legislate, the legislator does not confine itself to its own function viewed in isolation. On the contrary, it is an integral part of the legislative role that the legislature has to make decisions about the appropriate division of labour between various state institutions, assessing the relative institutional competence of each, and to take account of the role those other organs can play. This should not surprise us since the legislature is often dependent on the courts and other actors to implement and give effect to the legislation it enacts.

The same kind of interaction and interdependence is manifest when we look at the same situation from the point of view of the courts. In fact, from this point of view, the interdependence of the branches of government seems even more pronounced, since the courts' dependence on the legislature is a defining feature of the courts' institutional role, since judges must apply the law enacted by the legislature. However, despite this applicative role, it would be a mistake to think of the judicial role as entirely passive. The legislation may contain 'directed powers', thus directing them to develop the law in ways unregulated by the statute, albeit constrained by the framework set out by it.[54] Moreover, when the courts are dealing with an area of the law which is regulated partly by statute and partly by judge-made law, the courts have to integrate legislation with doctrine and to ensure that there is overall coherence in the law, so that the legislation and doctrine can work well together.[55]

Therefore, it is unhelpful to say that the branches of government should confine themselves to their own function if by that it is meant that they make their decisions in isolation from, or oblivious to, the actions and decisions of the other branches of government. As Aharon Barak has put it, the branches of government are not '*latifundia* that have no connection between them'.[56] In order to carry out their respective roles, each branch must take account of the role and responsibilities of the other branches. The 'separation as confinement' view fails to capture the interactive and interdependent nature of the way in which each branch carries out its respective tasks.

Given the shortcomings of the 'one branch—one function' and 'separation as confinement' ideas which lie at the core of the pure doctrine, it might be tempting to dismiss the separation of powers outright as a meaningful constitutional ideal. That was the route taken by many British scholars throughout the nineteenth and twentieth

---

[52] J. Raz, *Ethics in the Public Domain* (Oxford: Clarendon Press, 1994), 249.   [53] Ibid 243.

[54] Gardner, above n 39; A. Kavanagh, 'The Elusive Divide between Interpretation and Legislation under the Human Rights Act 1998' (2004) 24 *Oxford Journal of Legal Studies* 259, at 270–4.

[55] Raz, above n 52, 377; P. Sales, 'Judges and Legislature: Values into Law' (2012) 71 *Cambridge Law Journal* 287, at 296.

[56] A. Barak, *The Judge in a Democracy* (Princeton: Princeton University Press, 2006), 36.

centuries. Bemoaning the 'facile alignment'[57] between function and institution pre-supposed by the pure or orthodox account, many scholars dismissed the separation of powers as a complete irrelevance for British constitutional law.[58] In the United States, too, the rigid and formalistic prescriptions of the 'one branch—one function' view has prompted leading scholars to call for the abandonment of the separation of powers as an outmoded ideal for modern government.[59]

However, whilst we should certainly reject the pure doctrine, this does not mean that we should abandon the principle of the separation of powers altogether. On the contrary, the flaws of the pure doctrine should stimulate us to develop a more plausible conception of the separation of powers—one which does not fall prey to the shortcomings of the pure doctrine. Such an account faces two challenges. The first is to provide a meaningful way of accounting for the distinctness of the branches of government in a way which does not collapse into an implausible essentialism about function which has bedeviled the pure doctrine since its inception.[60] We can call this the *desideratum of distinctness*.[61] The second challenge is to develop a conception of the separation of powers which can accommodate the interaction and interdependence between the branches. We can call this the *desideratum of interaction*. With both of these desiderata in place as points of guidance, we can now embark on the reconstructive effort.

II. Separation of Powers: The Reconstructed View

Let us start by posing a basic question: *why* separate power between different branches of government? Nobody wants a return to unified authority under one single ruler empowered to make all governmental decisions. But why not? What do we gain by separating powers between different branches of government? The classic eighteenth-century answer to this question was that the separation of powers helps us to avert the risk of tyranny and potential abuse of power. As Montesquieu warned, 'constant experience shows us that every man interested with power is apt to abuse it, and to carry his authority as far it will go'.[62] The solution was to divide power amongst distinct organs of government, so as to ensure that no single body was omnipotent, whilst simultaneously allowing them to check and sanction each other when that was required. Right up to the present day, curbing abuse of power and preventing its concentration is regarded as the primary purpose of the separation of powers.[63]

But this overlooks the sound intuition which lies at the heart of the 'one branch—one function' view, namely, that there must be some meaningful correlation between the nature of particular institutions on the one hand, and the tasks we assign to them on the other.[64] If the sole purpose of the separation of powers is to prevent a concentration

---

[57] J. Griffith, 'A Pilgrim's Progress' (1995) 22 *Journal of Law and Society* 410, at 411; I. Jennings, *The Law and the Constitution* 5th edn (London: University of London Press, 1959), 281–2, 303.
[58] S. de Smith and R. Brazier, *Constitutional and Administrative Law* 8th edn (London: Penguin, 1998).
[59] Posner and Vermeule, above n 13.   [60] Nourse, above n 5.
[61] Kyritsis, above n 36.   [62] Vile, above n 4, 78.
[63] R. Albert, 'Presidential Values in Parliamentary Democracies' (2010) 8 *International Journal of Constitutional Law* 207; Magill, above n 43.
[64] Magill, above n 28, 606.

of power in one person or body, then we could fulfil that purpose by dispersing pow-ers randomly amongst a variety of bodies. If concentration of power is the problem, then dispersal of power is an obvious solution, no matter what form the dispersal takes. Similarly, if the sole purpose is to ensure that powers are checked and monitored, then we can satisfy this goal by putting institutional checks in place, without worrying about the basis of the original power-allocation.

But from a constitutional point of view, we are extremely reluctant to accept that powers should be allocated to different branches on a random basis. We think it mat-ters a great deal who gets to decide what in constitutional law. Not only do we want to ensure that the right decisions are made by the institutions which govern us, we also care about whether the right decisions have been made by the right body.[65] In other words, our constitutional thinking is sensitive to jurisdictional concerns which are a crucial determinant of political legitimacy. Therefore, we need a positive justification for allocating powers to particular branches, beyond the negative reasons of seeking to avoid a concentration of power. Can such a justification be found?

One possible justification is rooted in the nature of governing and the multitasking which this requires.[66] Responsible government in any complex society comprises a mul-tiplicity of different tasks. Every country needs an executive body to initiate and make policy decisions. But beyond this, responsible government needs a means of making clear, open, prospective, stable, general rules for the community. And, as H. L. A. Hart pointed out, any complex legal system needs a means of resolving disputes about the rules and their application.[67] But there is no 'one-size-fits-all' decision-making process which would be appropriate for all the tasks the State must carry out. Typically, we need an *independent body* (the courts) to resolve disputes about the rules required in indi-vidual cases; and we need a *deliberative and representative body* (a legislative assembly) to make general rules for the community which can be deliberately made and changed.

Here we have the seeds of a division of labour between the three branches of govern-ment. It shows that the point of separating power is not just to disperse power randomly amongst various bodies, but to create two particular branches of government—the courts and the legislature—which are distinct from the executive branch, and to which the executive will be accountable.[68] Note that, on this understanding, the separation of powers is motivated by two basic concerns of institutional design. The first is to allocate power and assign tasks to those bodies best suited to carry them out. In the literature on the separation of powers, this is sometimes referred to as the value of 'efficiency'.[69] The second is to put mechanisms in place to correct for potential abuse of power and jurisdictional overreach.

---

[65] Thus, the justification of judicial review is a (second-order) question about the relative institutional competence and legitimacy of the courts vis-à-vis the executive and legislature to make decisions about rights, rather than a first-order debate about what rights require. See J. Waldron, 'A Right-Based Critique of Constitutional Rights' (1993) 13 *Oxford Journal of Legal Studies* 18; Compare with A. Kavanagh, 'Participation and Judicial Review: A Reply to Jeremy Waldron' (2003) 22 *Law and Philosophy* 451.

[66] L. Green, 'The Duty to Govern' (2007) 13 *Legal Theory* 165.

[67] H. L. A. Hart, *The Concept of Law* 3rd edn, L. Green (ed) (Oxford: Clarendon Press, 2012).

[68] Endicott, above n 42, 15.   [69] Barber, above n 18.

How do we work out how to allocate power to different branches? Typically, we assess whether an institution is well equipped to carry out certain tasks, in part, by virtue of various procedural features the institution may possess, such as its composition, decision-making process, resources, access to information, and the skills and expertise of the people who work within these institutions.[70] Understanding an institution requires that we should attend to the reasons for choosing and maintaining that institution.[71] This means that in order to work out which tasks to assign to which institutions, we need to relate those tasks to the appropriate decision-making processes and the values which the various institutional roles are meant to serve. In short, we must relate substantive tasks to decision-making processes.[72]

For example, in order to have an effective organ for making clear, open, prospective, stable rules for the community, we need a legislative assembly which is structured so that it can deliberate on legislative proposals and enact and change law in response to all the reasons that bear on such decisions. The fact that the legislature is accountable to the electorate gives it a range of institutional incentives. Most obviously, its decisions will be responsive to the wishes of the electorate in various ways. This is also a way of ensuring that there is sufficient support and cooperation amongst the general populace and that there is input on legislative proposals from a wide range of perspectives. Moreover, its connection to the electorate gives it political legitimacy to make public policy decisions on behalf of the community.

Similarly, in order to have an effective adjudicative body for resolving disputes about what the law requires, we need a body which is independent (both from the executive and legislature, and from the individual parties). Being independent helps the courts to adjudicate fairly and even-handedly between opposing parties, by applying the law faithfully to the dispute in question.[73] The independence of the courts ensures that they will not become the mere instrument of the executive or legislative branch when adjudicating disputes about what the law requires. It enables them to resist pressure from those other branches, thus strengthening their ability to uphold the rule of law.[74]

How does this division of labour differ from the pure doctrine which advocated a tight one-to-one correlation between branch and function? The main difference is that rather than trying to distinguish the branches of government in terms of single mutually exclusive functions, the approach adopted here cashes out the separation of powers in terms of a division of labour between distinct organs of government, where each organ performs a different institutional role.[75] Note that the distinction between the institutional roles of the courts and the legislature does not map directly onto a distinction between the function of making law and the function of applying it. In fact, it cuts

[70] Kyritsis, 2012, above n 19; Vile, above n 4; Carolan, above n 4.
[71] T. Nagel, 'Due Process', in J. Pennock and J. Chapman (eds), *Due Process: Nomos XVIII* (New York: New York University Press, 1977), 93–125.
[72] Kyritsis, 2008, above n 19.
[73] R. Ekins, 'Statutory Interpretation and the Separation of Powers', draft working paper (on file with author), at 8.
[74] For this reason, many scholars argue that the separation of judicial power from the legislature and executive is a necessary precondition for the rule of law. See Allan, above n 17, and in this volume.
[75] J. Raz, 'The Institutional Nature of Law', in Raz, above n 51, 106; Claus, above n 31, 445.

across that distinction, because institutional roles can encompass a number of different functions. On the view advanced here, separate institutions can share powers and functions, whilst performing different roles in the joint enterprise of governing.[76]

But once we admit some sharing and overlap of function, the worry arises that this account of the separation of powers flouts the *desideratum of distinctness*. For example, if both the courts and the legislature make law, how can we distinguish between them? The answer is that whilst both institutions make law, they do so in different ways—ways which are informed by their different roles in the constitutional scheme. That is, there is an important qualitative difference between legislative lawmaking on the one hand, and judicial lawmaking on the other.[77]

In general, the ability and power of the courts to make new law is generally more limited than that of the legislators, since courts typically make law by filling in gaps in existing legal frameworks, extending existing doctrines incrementally on a case-by-case basis, adjusting them to changing circumstances, etc. Judicial lawmaking powers tend to be piecemeal and incremental[78] and the courts must reason according to law, even when developing it. By contrast, legislators have the power to make radical, broad-ranging changes in the law, which are not based on existing legal norms. Thus, as John Gardner observed:

> What is really morally important under the heading of the separation of powers is not the separation of law-making powers from law-applying powers, but rather the separation of legislative powers of law-making (ie powers to make legally unprecedented laws) from judicial powers of law-making (ie powers to develop the law gradually using existing legal resources).[79]

Of course, there is sometimes an overlap in the lawmaking tasks both institutions carry out. Some legislative lawmaking is incremental and interstitial, and some judicial lawmaking can have wide-ranging effects.[80] Nonetheless, both branches are subject to different institutional constraints and incentives—constraints which arise from, and inform, the scope and limits of their constitutional role.[81]

One final question arises from the *desideratum of distinctness*. This is the question of whether the separation of *powers* requires a separation of *personnel*. Clearly, some separation of persons between the branches is advisable as a general matter. There are some tasks which would be difficult to carry out if performed by only one person or body. For example, it may be difficult for one body to make decisions and then review

---

[76] See generally Kyritsis, above n 31; R. Neustadt, *Presidential Power and the Modern Presidents: The Politics of Leadership from Roosevelt to Reagan* (New York: The Free Press, 1990), 101.
[77] For a more detailed account of the distinction between legislative and judicial lawmaking, see Kavanagh, above n 54, 270–4; Gardner, above n 39, 37–47; Raz, above n 51, 194–201.
[78] Kavanagh, above n 54, 270–4.   [79] Gardner, above n 39, 41.
[80] For the view that judicial lawmaking is nonetheless typically piecemeal and incremental (despite occasionally having wide-ranging effects), see A. Kavanagh, 'The Idea of a Living Constitution' (2003) 16 *Canadian Journal of Law and Jurisprudence* 55, at 73–9.
[81] To clarify: the distinction between the judicial and legislative roles is not that between constrained and unconstrained decision-making. Rather, it lies in the nature and extent of the constraints. See further J. Raz, 'The Authority and Interpretation of Constitutions', in L. Alexander (ed), *Constitutionalism: Philosophical Foundations* (Cambridge: Cambridge University Press, 1998), 152–93, at 153.

or check them, since the body might become susceptible to various forms of bias and self-interest which will prevent it checking the original decision in any meaningful way. In fact, this is a common way of showing that a separation of powers (and persons) is required by the rule of law. On this view, the very idea of government subject to law requires that the law is upheld and enforced (against the government and/or the legislature) by independent courts.[82]

However, the desirability of some separation of personnel does not mean that we must take an absolutist position on this question, since we are familiar with the possibility of one person or body 'wearing two hats' in a way which is conducive overall to good government.[83] These are exactly the kinds of arguments which were used in the United Kingdom to support the fact that judges were members of the upper chamber of the legislature (the House of Lords). There, it was argued that judges could contribute legal knowledge and judicial expertise to the legislative process, whilst nonetheless preserving their judicial independence when deciding cases. The separation of roles was maintained largely due to the observance of constitutional conventions to ensure that the relevant actors exercised self-restraint.[84] Here is not the place to rehearse or evaluate the arguments for and against these arrangements. It is merely to suggest that such overlaps are not necessarily precluded by the principle of the separation of powers (at least on the reconstructed view advanced here), as long as a 'separation in thought' is observed.

III. Combining Separation and Supervision

Thus far, I have argued that the separation of powers requires a division of labour between the branches of government, such that they each play a distinct role in the constitutional scheme. But we have not yet said anything about checks and balances. This may seem like a grave omission since the contemporary literature on the separation of powers—especially that which is focused on the US system—emphasizes the central importance of checks and balances. Indeed, there are many who argue that such checks are the very 'essence'[85] of the separation of powers. In this section, I will argue that division-of-labour considerations do not exhaust the meaning or rationale of the separation of powers. In order to curb abuse of power (an important concern of institutional design), it is necessary to supplement division of labour with checks and balances. In short, we need to combine separation with supervision.

In thinking about this issue, it is useful to recall James Madison's canonical account of the value of checks and balances within a constitutional separation of powers. Writing in *The Federalist Papers*, Madison argued that the first task for the separation of powers was to make some 'division of the government into distinct and separate departments',[86] where each department must have a 'will of its own'.[87] But then 'the

---

[82] Allan, above n 17.

[83] See J. Waldron, 'Separation of Powers in Thought and Practice' (2013) 54 *Boston College Law Review* 433, at 433ff.

[84] See eg Sales, above n 55, 292.   [85] Barendt, 1995, above n 3.

[86] J. Madison, 'No. 51', in C. Rossiter (ed), *The Federalist Papers* (New York: Penguin Putnam, 1999), 288–93.

[87] Ibid.

next and most difficult task is to provide some *practical security* for each, against the invasion of the others'.[88] Madison contended that it was not 'sufficient to mark, with precision, the boundaries of these departments [of government], and to trust to the parchment barriers against the encroaching spirit of power'. In order to avert the risk of abuse of power we must 'so contriv[e] the interior structure of the government as that its several constituent parts may, by their mutual relations, be the means of keeping each other in their proper places'.[89]

In this way, checks and balances are required by the separation of powers in order to prevent one branch of government usurping another and to provide each branch with the 'necessary constitutional means' to resist such usurpation and prevent it occurring. Checks and balances help to protect the separation, as well as helping to ensure that each branch does not overstep its role in the constitutional scheme. This follows from the normal precepts of institutional design. When setting up institutions, we should structure institutions so that they can play to their institutional strengths. But we also need to consider how to mitigate any of their attendant risks.[90] This is why the separation of powers includes both a division-of-labour and checks-and-balances component. Implementing the separation of powers is a 'two-sided exercise',[91] involving both the identification of the valuable role each institution can play, as well as an appreciation of their attendant risks.

Viewed in this way, the separation of powers has both a positive and negative dimension. On the positive side, it gives us a principled starting point for thinking about how to allocate power to different institutions. The positive dimension of the separation of powers explains why it plays a fundamental role in constitutional formation. After all, the first (positive) role of constitutions is to *constitute* government—to set up the institutional framework for organizing government, setting forth the powers and procedures of the various institutions and the basic structure of the legal system.[92] But a good governmental structure will also require that there are mechanisms in place to curb potential abuse of power and provide reassurance and security that each branch of government will observe its limitations when carrying out its role. Therefore, the separation of powers also fulfils the negative virtue of curbing, limiting, and checking government power. As Christoph Mollers put it the 'separation of powers should not be understood as a pure instrument of restraining political power. It is also an instrument that constitutes this power'.[93] It embodies what Vile described as the dual values of *coordination* and *control*.[94]

IV. Governing Together in a Joint Enterprise

Thus far, I have argued that the separation of powers comprises both a division-of labour component and checks-and-balances component. The task of this section is to

[88] J. Madison, 'No. 48', in Rossiter, above n 86, 276–81; see also Allan, above n 17, 53.
[89] Madison, above n 86.   [90] Kyritsis, 2012, above n 19, 303.   [91] Ibid.
[92] L. Alexander, 'What Are Constitutions, and What Should (and Can) They Do?' (2011) 28 *Social Philosophy and Policy* 1, at 2.
[93] Mollers, above n 5, 10.   [94] Vile, above n 4, ch 12.

show that both of these elements are underpinned by the deeper value of coordinated institutional effort between branches of government in the service of good government.[95] I will call this the 'joint enterprise of governing' for short. At first blush, this argument has an air of paradox about it. How can the *separation* of powers be underpinned by the value of *coordinated* institutional action as part of a *joint* enterprise?

The paradox is dissolved once we see that there are different forms and degrees of separation, not all of which preclude coordination or joint action between the separated bodies. If we support the pure doctrine, we will think of the branches as completely separated—isolated and insulated from the other branches. However, on the reconstructed view, we will think of the branches—not as solitary entities confined to one single function—but as constituent parts of a joint enterprise, each with their own role to play. Though distinct, these parts have to work together. Though they are independent from one another, they are also interdependent in various, subtle ways. The US Supreme Court captured this idea of separate but interconnected branches when it observed that:

> While the Constitution diffuses power the better to secure liberty, it also contemplates that practice will integrate the dispersed powers into a workable government. It enjoins upon its branches separateness but interdependence, autonomy but reciprocity.[96]

Some of that interdependence came into view when we considered the tasks of legislating and adjudicating. There, we saw that the branches of government must take account of the acts and decisions of the other branches when carrying out their own tasks. No one branch can carry out all the tasks of governing. Therefore, each branch makes a (necessarily) partial contribution to the joint enterprise. The legislature may enact the general rules and provide the statutory framework, but the courts must decide what those general rules mean and require in particular cases, which may involve resolving indeterminacy in meaning, filling in gaps in the framework, and integrating particular statutory provisions into the broader fabric of legal principle. Here we see lawmaking as a collaborative enterprise, where each branch contributes different elements in ways which reflect their particular institutional structures, skills, competence, and legitimacy. Thus, when making decisions as part of the scheme of governance, each branch must recognize what Jeremy Waldron called 'the collective action structure'[97] of the problems they face and the decisions they have to make. On this view, the separation of powers is not just a principle which informs the distribution of power and the division of labour, but also the *relationships* between the three branches when carrying out their distinct roles as part of a joint enterprise.

One central feature of that joint action is the requirement of *inter-institutional comity*.[98] Inter-institutional comity is 'that respect which one great organ of the State owes to another'.[99] As the House of Lords (now UK Supreme Court) put it in *Jackson v*

[95] Kyritsis, 2008, above n 19; Kyritsis, 2012, above n 19; see also Carolan, above n 4, 186.

[96] *Youngstown Co v Sawyer* 343 US 579 (1952), 635 (per Jackson J). —

[97] J. Waldron, 'Authority for Officials', in L. Meyer, S. Paulson, and T. Pogge (eds), *Rights, Culture, and the Law: Themes from the Legal and Political Philosophy of Joseph Raz* (Oxford: Oxford University Press, 2003) 45–70.

[98] J. King, 'Institutional Approaches to Judicial Restraint' (2008) 28 *Oxford Journal of Legal Studies* 409, at 428.

[99] *Buckley v Attorney General* [1950] Irish Reports 67, 80 (per O'Byrne J); see further A. Kavanagh, 'Deference or Defiance? The Limits of the Judicial Role in Constitutional Adjudication', in G. Huscroft (ed),

Attorney General, 'the delicate balance between the various institutions... is maintained to a large degree by the *mutual respect* which each institution has for the other'.[100] This is by no means a peculiar feature of the separation of powers in the United Kingdom. The requirement of reciprocal respect between the institutional actors is a generalizable feature of any constitutional system based on the separation of powers.

How do the various branches of government show respect for decisions of the other branches as contributions to the joint enterprise of good government? This will vary depending on the institution and its interrelationship with other institutions. But, in broad terms, it involves both a *leeway requirement* and a *mutual support requirement*. Comity requires each institution to give the other institutions leeway to carry out their own tasks and functions (the *leeway requirement*). They should respect the jurisdiction of other institutions and be alert to the fact that other institutions may be better placed to carry out a certain task. As the UK Supreme Court put it, both the courts and legislature must recognize that each institution has 'their own particular role to play in our constitution, and that each must be careful to respect the sphere of action of the other'.[101]

All the institutions must exercise some self-restraint when appropriate—both to ensure that they keep within their own jurisdiction, and to ensure that they do not trespass into the jurisdiction of another institution. Self-restraint may also be required in the sense of refraining from criticizing the decisions of the other branches, when to do so would undermine the ability of that branch to do its job well. Beyond this self-restraint, each branch of government may be required to actively support the decisions of the other branches, either by implementing those decisions or interpreting them in a way which respects the underlying substantive and institutional choices or in allocating to other institutions tasks which they are well placed to carry out well (the *mutual support requirement*). They must support each other in the general promotion of good government.[102]

The idea that the value underpinning the separation of powers is coordinated institutional effort in the joint enterprise of governing may seem jarring, given the strong hold of the pure doctrine over our understanding of the separation of powers. But the idea of the branches being both independent *and* interdependent—distinct but interconnected—also has some pedigree in the canonical literature. After all, one of Madison's central insights was that we should not conceive of the legislative, executive, and judicial power as 'wholly unconnected with each other'.[103] Indeed, Madison viewed the branches of government as 'constituent parts' of the overall scheme of government and it was 'their mutual relations' which would provide 'the means of keeping each other in their proper places'.[104]

Expounding the Constitution (Cambridge: Cambridge University Press, 2008), 184–216, at 187ff; Endicott, above n 42, ch XV, 17.

[100] [2005] UKHL 56, [2005] 3 WLR 733 [125] (emphasis added).
[101] *AXA General Insurance Ltd & Ors v Lord Advocate & Ors (Scotland)* [2011] UKSC 46, [2012] 1 AC 868 [148].
[102] Ibid.   [103] Madison, above n 88.   [104] Madison, above n 86.

It is often thought that by recommending checks and balances, Madison introduced a relational or inter-institutional dimension to the more traditional understandings of the separation of powers. That is correct. However, on the view advanced here, the relational dimension goes far beyond the existence of checks and balances. It includes more positive forms of inter-institutional interaction where the branches must take account of each other's actions and work together in partnership. Mutual supervision takes place against the broader backdrop of mutual respect and support. In this way, the reconstructed view honours the *desideratum of interaction*, not only by accepting the need for checks and balances, but also by acknowledging the wider context of the constitutional relations between the branches. In some contexts, the interaction between the branches will be supervisory, where the goal is to check, review, and hold the other to account. At other times, the interaction will be a form of cooperative engagement where the branches have to support each other's role in the joint endeavour.[105]

V. Conclusion

This chapter has argued that we should abandon the pure doctrine in favour of a reconstructed view underpinned by the value of coordinated institutional effort in the joint enterprise of governing. The argument presented here marks a departure from traditional accounts of the separation of powers in two main ways. First, instead of distinguishing the branches in terms of three mutually exclusive functions, we should think of the separation of powers as requiring a division of labour where each branch plays a distinct role in the constitutional scheme. Though the labour is divided, functions may be shared.

Second, instead of conceptualizing the branches of government as isolated or compartmentalized bodies with 'high walls'[106] between them, the view advanced here emphasizes the necessary interdependence, interaction, and interconnections between the branches. The actions of each branch take effect in a complex interactive setting, where the branches take account of—and coordinate with—the actions of the other branches. They have to work together in the joint enterprise of governing.

There is no denying that this understanding of the separation of powers posits a less strict or rigid separation between the branches than the orthodox account would allow. But the strictures of the pure view are not observed anywhere. In every constitutional democracy, the dogma of a strict separation of functions 'contrasts sharply with the actual constitutional distribution of powers as well as constitutional practice and reality'.[107] Some intermixture of function is both unavoidable and desirable. But if this is so, what explains the stubborn appeal of the pure doctrine over centuries?

Some commentators have suggested that the key to 'the global diffusion' of the pure doctrine is its seductive simplicity.[108] After all, the pure view provides a clear and simple way of distinguishing between the branches, and it provides a neat answer to the

---

[105] Malleson, above n 26, 119.
[106] *Plaut v Spendthrift Farms Inc* 514 US 211 (1995) (per Scalia J).
[107] Heun, above n 32, 86.   [108] Carolan, above n 4, 22.

sound intuition that there must be some meaningful correlation between the nature of each institution and the tasks allocated to it.

However, it must also be remembered that the separation of powers was forged as a foundational principle of constitutional government at a time when the prevailing concern was to limit power and curb its abuse. Viewed in the context of the 'tyrannophobia'[109] of the eighteenth century, the separation of powers was wielded as a slogan requiring a strict separation on functional lines and/or a system of checks and balances conceived as powerful 'sanctioning devices'.[110] Both of these views rested on distrust of political power and both were conceived as a way of keeping each branch of government within strict bounds.[111] Since the aim was to ward off tyranny and prevent the abuse of power, the very strictness of the classic and formal tripartite distinction became a 'voice of assurance'[112] that the limits of power would be observed.

As is often the case when a political ideal captures the imagination of large numbers of people and is wielded in political struggles, its main tenets become simplified slogans which bear little relation to the original ideas which animated it.[113] This is what happened with the separation of powers in the eighteenth century, where the seductively simple 'one branch—one function' idea became a popular shorthand for the much more complex, nuanced, and interactive division of labour between the branches which existed in constitutional practice.[114] If taken as a descriptive assertion, the 'one branch—one function' view was unsustainable. But if viewed prescriptively as an abbreviated way of expressing the injunction to all three branches of government to ensure that they do not stray beyond their proper constitutional role, then its appeal can be seen more clearly.[115] The lure of the strict 'one branch—one function' view is that it seems to hold out what Peter Strauss calls the 'promise of containment of government function'.[116]

The problem is that the pure view cannot deliver on this promise, largely because it is radically detached from the practice of contemporary constitutional government. Despite its persistent appeal, the descriptive and normative inadequacies of the pure view have also led to widespread disillusion with the separation of powers, thus accounting for the deep ambivalence surrounding the principle right up to the present day. Not only does the pure view posit an impossibly tight connection between each institution and its corresponding function, it obscures the necessary and desirable interconnections, interdependence, and interactions between the branches of government. In fact, it goes further by casting a presumptively negative light on such interactions.

The account of the separation of powers presented in this chapter embraces institutional interaction and collaboration as part and parcel of the ideal of the separation

---

[109] Posner and Vermeule, above n 13.

[110] P. Pettit, *Republicanism: A Theory of Freedom and Government* (Oxford: Oxford University Press, 1997).

[111] Vile, above n 4, 335.

[112] P. Strauss, 'Formal and Functional Approaches to Separation of Powers Questions: A Foolish Inconsistency' (1987) 72 *Cornell Law Review* 488, at 513. Bernard Manin argues that this was an important driver of the Anti-Federalist position in the American Founding era (Manin, above n 27, 44ff).

[113] J. Raz, 'The Rule of Law and its Virtue', in Raz, above n 51.   [114] Claus, above n 31, 445.

[115] See further J. Finnis, 'The Fairy-Tale's Moral' (1999) 115 *Law Quarterly Review* 170, at 172–4.

[116] Strauss, above n 112, 526.

of powers, rather than being antithetical to its basic requirements. It emphasizes that lawmaking, law-applying, and law-executing are collaborative tasks where each organ of government must cooperate with the other organs in an interactive setting.[117] We should reject the rigidities of the pure doctrine, together with the implausible essentialism about function on which it rests. Freed from its strictures, we can consider the possibility of a sharing of functions and power amongst the branches of government where each has a distinct role in the joint enterprise of governing.

---

[117] W. Eskridge and P. Frickey, 'Foreword: Law as Equilibrium' (1994) 108 *Harvard Law Review* 26, at 28–9.

12

The Framework Model
and Constitutional Interpretation

*Jack M. Balkin**

I. Constitutional Construction and
the Constitution-in-Practice

A standard way of thinking about constitutions is that they are sets of basic legal norms that do not change over time (except through amendment) but are successively applied to new cases. It follows that constitutional interpretation is the art of applying a fixed constitution to changing circumstances. This familiar portrait, however, conceals more than it reveals. In fact, constitutional interpretation is a process of *legitimate change* within an *evolving* constitutional order. Rather than a device for preventing change, a working constitution in a political order is always changing, even (and especially) if the written text of a constitution rarely changes.

How can this be? First, much of what people usually call 'interpretation' does not involve ascertaining the meaning of the constitutional text. Rather, it is a process of *constitutional construction*—the building out of the constitutional system over time through doctrinal development, legislation, administration, institution building (and reform), and the creation and evolution of conventions. As the political branches develop the state, form or alter conventions, and construct new institutions and state capacities, judges decide constitutional controversies that arise from what political actors have done. Judges produce decisions and doctrines that build out constitutional law over time. That law, in turn, shapes the way that future state-building occurs, and so on.

Constitutional construction, in other words, is a dialectical process: the political branches act based on their assertions about what the constitution permits them to do. Often different parts of the political system will offer competing claims: the legislative and executive branches, national and local governments, or opposing political parties may disagree about what the constitution means in practice. Judges respond by hearing disputes, creating doctrines and distinctions that apply and flesh out the constitution, shaping, channeling—and sometimes provoking—later attempts at state-building. Thus, judges operate in a larger system of constitutional construction. They do not simply settle questions of constitutional meaning; they also legitimate state-building by the political branches, police constitutional norms, provoke responses in politics, and present new questions for dispute.

* Knight Professor of Constitutional Law and the First Amendment, Yale Law School.

At any point in time there will be a configuration of institutions, conventions, practices, and doctrines whose contours are partially disputed. We might call that configuration the *constitution-in-practice*. The constitution-in-practice is how the constitution considered as an ongoing institution operates at any point in time. We should distinguish the constitution-in-practice from the text of the constitution, on the one hand, and from what an individual believes to be the best or ideal reading of the constitution, on the other. Thus, even if the text does not change, conventions, institutions, and legal doctrines can change. And even if people in a political community disagree about the best interpretation of their constitution, all of them can recognize that the constitution-in-practice conforms to their preferred views only to a certain extent.

The constitution-in-practice is open ended; its shape and content is only partly determined at any point in time. First, changes in ordinary law and state-building are continuous, creating new problems. Second, some questions have not been raised or settled in the courts. (Indeed, depending on the constitutional system, some constitutional questions are never settled by courts.) Third, disagreements about the constitution may persist among legal officials—including judges—and among the general public.

We can now better understand the claim that constitutional interpretation is a process of legitimate change within a constitutional order. Even if the written text of a constitution does not change, constitutional construction by the political branches and the judiciary is ongoing, and the constitution-in-practice changes as a result. Interpretation does not so much preserve the constitution-in-practice as add to or alter it. Change occurs not only when a constitution is misinterpreted; it also occurs when participants attempt to apply it faithfully—for example, to new statutes or practices, or in light of new technologies. Because a working constitution is always being interpreted (and fought over) in practice, it is always changing. Or more precisely, because *constitutional construction* is always ongoing, the *constitution-in-practice* is always changing. To paraphrase Heraclitus, one cannot step into the same constitution twice.

II. Constitutions Make Politics Possible

This account of constitutional interpretation rests on a more general theory of what constitutions are and how they work. A familiar account of constitutions is that they are pre-commitment devices that seek to limit discretion and prevent later actors from making unwise decisions. Many constitutional *provisions* are designed precisely for this purpose. Nevertheless, this is not the best general account of constitutions as a whole or of constitutionalism.

Constitutions as a whole are not designed to prevent political decision-making— they are designed to enable it. Constitutions are not so much *pre-commitment* devices as *coordination* devices.[1] They allow people who may have very different interests and

---

[1] For examples of this general approach, see A. Sabl, *Hume's Politics: Coordination and Crisis in the History of England* (Princeton: Princeton University Press, 2012); R. Hardin, *Liberalism, Constitutionalism, and Democracy* (Oxford: Oxford University Press, 1999).

goals to coordinate their efforts and engage in political action. They structure reciprocal relations of authority and allegiance and thereby help states operate as going concerns. Even when people oppose each other in a constitutional system, one of the central goals of a constitution is to get them to engage with each other in certain ways (mobilization, argument, politics) rather than in others (violence, anarchy, civil war). Successful constitutions give people reasons not to turn to violence to settle questions of power and successions to power; instead, constitutions allow more subtle and ramified exercises of power through setting out rules of succession, creating institutions, dividing powers, setting institutions in competition with each other, and imposing norms that channel government action.

Constitutions are designed, in other words, to make politics possible. Constitutions serve as basic platforms that help constitute a political order and allow people engaged in politics to do things within that order. To achieve this function, however, constitutions must be open-ended. By facilitating politics, they also allow political activity to build new institutions, practices, and norms atop them. To make politics possible, constitutions must also make constitutional politics possible; and they inevitably generate a constitution-in-practice that changes over time.

III. Constitutions as Frameworks and Skyscrapers

Contrast two different idealized models of a constitution: the constitution as *skyscraper* and the constitution as *framework*.[2] Each model has a contrasting view of interpretation, of the role of judges (to the extent that the system recognizes judicial review), of political struggle within a constitution, and of constituent power—the public's ability to change the constitution. If, as I have argued above, the point of constitutions is to make politics possible, the framework model is the better way to understand modern written constitutions.

According to the skyscraper model of a constitution, an adopted constitution is like a completed building. A constitution is a finished product, although always subject to further amendment or to a new constitutional convention. People live within the constitution as they would live within a building. Just as finished buildings provide walls that shelter inhabitants and create spaces for them to live and work, the constitution-as-skyscraper sets boundaries on ordinary politics and creates a space for ordinary politics and lawmaking. But this lawmaking is not constitutional construction; it does not alter the constitution. Rather, it is ordinary law that is permissible within the boundaries set by the constitution. Similarly, constitutional interpretations—whether by members of the judiciary or by others—do not change the constitution, at least if the interpretations are correct. Rather, correct interpretations simply implement or apply the constitution to new situations.

The skyscraper model has little use for the concepts of constitutional construction or of a constitution-in-practice. It sharply distinguishes ordinary politics from

---

[2] The argument that follows is drawn from J. M. Balkin, *Living Originalism* (Cambridge, Mass.: Belknap Press, 2011), 21–3 (distinguishing between framework and skyscraper models of fidelity to original meaning).

constitutional politics. The only way to change a constitution is through amendment or by replacing the constitution with a new one. Politics outside the amendment or adoption process is not constitutional politics and it cannot legitimately change the proper interpretation of the constitution. Thus, once a constitution is adopted, the skyscraper model offers relatively limited opportunities for constituent power. Constituent power is exercised rarely: it occurs only through amendment, a new convention, or the dissolution of the constitution and the formation of a new regime.

The framework model, by contrast, views a constitution as always unfinished. It is an initial framework for governance, a platform that enables future political development. The constitution sets politics in motion and it must be filled out over time through constitutional construction. To be sure, when a new constitution replaces the constitution of an older regime, political actors may bring with them many expectations, assumptions, institutions, and laws from the prior regime. The new constitution may borrow language from previous versions. Even so, a new constitution requires further consolidation, adjustment, and development, precisely because there has been a transition to a new regime.

In the skyscraper model, adoption completes a constitution. In the framework model, adoption is only the beginning of the job. Subsequent actors must implement the constitution-in-practice. Constitutional construction both by the political branches and by the judiciary is crucial to this process. Under the framework model, when people interpret the constitution, they are not simply applying content already known and fixed. Rather, they are building the constitution-in-practice.

Because it emphasizes the role of constitutional construction, the framework model does not sharply distinguish between constitutional politics and ordinary politics. Although there may be obvious examples of each type of politics, the boundaries between them are not always clear, and the two forms tend to fade into each other in practice. Long-term changes in constitutional practices may arise from incremental moves in ordinary politics. Mobilizations for policy change often have constitutional overtones, or they may seek legal and institutional changes that generate new constitutional constructions. In the United States the women's movement sought a constitutional amendment to guarantee sex equality; but the movement's supporters also sought new statutes, administrative regulations, and judicial decisions, not to mention changes in social, economic, and cultural practices. Through these efforts, the women's movement eventually transformed the constitution-in-practice, even though an Equal Rights Amendment explicitly banning sex discrimination was never ratified.[3] Government programmes created by ordinary legislation may create new state capacities and new expectations about government power. These changes may alter constitutional understandings among legal professionals, later confirmed by judicial constructions.

The skyscraper model and the framework model of constitutions offer contrasting accounts of democratic legitimacy, judicial review, and constituent power. In the

---

[3] See R. B. Siegel, 'Constitutional Culture, Social Movement Conflict and Constitutional Change: The Case of the de facto ERA' (2006) 94 *California Law Review* 1323.

skyscraper model, democratic legitimacy occurs through engaging in ordinary politics permitted by the completed constitutional edifice. Judicial review is consistent with democracy to the extent that it enforces the constitution already in place; its job is to police the constitutional bargain and preserve the space for ordinary politics created by the constitution. Otherwise, judges must leave ordinary politics alone. (If, as in some systems, the judiciary is permitted to pass on the validity of new amendments, it must do so according to the rules and doctrines already laid down.)

The framework model sees the relationship between democratic legitimacy, judicial review, and constituent power quite differently. Constitutional construction is a dialectical process: the political branches and the judiciary work together to build out the constitution over time. Both the political branches *and* the judiciary inevitably reflect and respond to changing social demands and changing social mores. Nevertheless, the judiciary and the political branches play very different roles within the basic framework. Their authority to engage in constitutional construction comes from respecting their respective roles within the framework and their joint responsiveness to public opinion over long stretches of time.

In the framework model, constituent power continues throughout the life of a constitution; it is exercised through all of the modes and methods of politics and legal argument that result in constitutional constructions. In particular, social and political mobilizations may exercise constituent power to the extent that they change public opinion and influence constitutional constructions by the political branches or by the judiciary.

One might object that—unlike constitutional adoption or constitutional amendments—these forms of constituent power are not genuine. That is because constitutional construction is perpetually mediated by institutions and practices like legislation, administrative regulation, and judicial decision-making. But constituent power is always mediated by institutions, even if they are not the same institutions employed in ordinary lawmaking. In order to adopt a new amendment or a new constitution, the people must still act through institutions, which provide representation, create agendas, and structure participation. Indeed, even popular uprisings need organizational forms to succeed; and they must eventually turn to institutions to amend the constitution or establish a new constitutional order.

The difference between the kinds of constituent power recognized in the framework model and more traditional examples is not that the power of the people is mediated in the former and unmediated in the latter. Rather, the difference is that in the framework model, there are simply many more ways that 'the people' can be heard and can exercise constituent power through a wide range of practices and institutions. Some of these institutions and practices, in fact, may arise from previous acts of constitutional construction.[4] The framework model does

---

[4] B.A. Ackerman's model of dualist democracy, for example, argues that public participation at key moments in history self-consciously alters the methods of legitimate constitutional change. B. A. Ackerman, *We the People: Foundations* (Cambridge, Mass.: Belknap Press, 1991), 1. See also Balkin, above n 2, chs 13 and 14 (critiquing Ackerman and providing an alternative account of constitutional change through constitutional construction).

not de-emphasize the role of constituent power outside of ordinary lawmaking—it merely asserts that constituent power also exists within an ongoing constitutional order. The framework model contests the view that the public is essentially shut out of constitution-making except during relatively brief episodes of adopting a constitution or amending it.

Finally, the skyscraper and framework models suggest two different models of proper judicial behaviour and judicial interpretation. According to the skyscraper model, judges are constrained by the constitutional bargain in the finished constitution and must use the appropriate methodology for ascertaining the constitution's meaning. To the extent that judges fail to do this, they are unconstrained and the danger is that they are merely imposing their own political beliefs and policy preferences. Hence the skyscraper model cares greatly about discovering and applying the correct interpretive methodology. Judges must apply that proper methodology to limit their temptation to foist their personal values on an unsuspecting public. Therefore judges and commentators must devote considerable efforts to ascertain what the correct methodology is and to make sure that all judges follow it all the time.

The framework model sees things differently. Judges are obligated to enforce the constitutional framework and they may not vary from it. Nevertheless, by definition that framework is unfinished, offering an economy of delegation and constraint to future actors, including judges. By itself the basic framework will not be sufficient to decide many if not most constitutional controversies that arise over time. Therefore good judging requires constitutional construction within the basic framework. Judges must build constitutional doctrines that best serve constitutional functions and purposes, and they must apply them to ever-new situations, leading to further constructions. Judicial constructions of the constitution will operate in dialectical conversation with constitutional constructions by the political branches; both kinds of constructions will inevitably be indirectly influenced by long-term shifts in public opinion.

Consensus on a single correct interpretive methodology is less urgent in the framework model than in the skyscraper model. Judges and lawyers will often disagree not only on the best interpretation, but also on the best interpretive methodology. Because judicial construction has a dialectical relationship to politics in an evolving state, the course of constitutional doctrine may have many complicated and path-dependent influences and effects. Constitutional law may not always feature a smooth course of development; depending on what the political branches do, it may change significantly in relatively short periods of time.[5]

Indeed, it is possible that there may be no single correct method or approach that can plausibly and reliably direct judicial interpretation as the state develops. From the perspective of the framework model, however, that is not a serious problem. Judicial behaviour is disciplined by a combination of professional, cultural, social, institutional, and political constraints.

---

[5] See Ackerman, above n 4.

IV. Constraints on Judges

Legal scholars often argue—or assume—that judges must follow the correct interpretive theory because this will keep judges faithful to the constitution. But we should distinguish what theories do—giving advice to judges or offering criticisms of judicial practice—from what actually constrains judicial behaviour. Theories of constitutional interpretation may be useful ways of *critiquing* or *legitimating* particular judicial decisions, but that is not the same thing as saying that they are good at *constraining* judges.

Theories of interpretation probably do very little to constrain judges in practice. Most judges are not constitutional theorists, and their assimilation of constitutional theory is likely to be quite haphazard. On a multi-member court, each judge may have a different view, so the court as a whole will have no guiding constitutional theory. There is no way of ensuring that judges apply a theory of constitutional interpretation correctly or consistently, and any single judge's attempt to apply a theory will inevitably require compromises with other judges.

What actually constrains judicial behaviour, then? Constraints come from many different features of the constitutional and political system. We might divide them into social, cultural, institutional, and political constraints.

Social constraints include the audience for judges—that is, the people before whom judges 'perform' and whose good opinion they seek to maintain and cultivate.[6] This includes influences and opinions by family, friends, social acquaintances, and media organizations. Because judges are often drawn from elites, social constraints may include elite opinion, or that part of elite opinion that judges regularly encounter.[7] Social constraints may also include the influences and opinions of the organizations that judges join and the professional subcultures in which judges live and work.[8]

Cultural constraints include the legal culture in which judges are educated, the forms of argument they routinely employ, and the professional norms that they inculcate both through their legal education and through their interactions with other lawyers and judges. Viewed from this perspective, we can see how debates over interpretive methodology might contribute to professional cultural constraints. If certain interpretive methods become part of what judges understand to be accepted professional norms, these methods will shape how they do their jobs, and this would be true even if judges do not adopt a uniform method.[9]

Institutional constraints concern how judges are selected, the length of judicial terms, the scope of the courts' jurisdiction, and the structure of judicial institutions.

---

[6] L. Baum, *Judges and Their Audiences: A Perspective on Judicial Behavior* (Princeton: Princeton University Press, 2006).

[7] See L. Baum and N. Devins, 'Why the Supreme Court Cares About Elites, Not the American People' (2010) 98 *William & Mary Law Review* 1515; M. A. Graber, 'The Coming Constitutional Yo-Yo? Elite Opinion, Polarization, and the Direction of Judicial Decision Making' (2013) 56 *Howard Law Journal* 661.

[8] See A. Hollis-Brusky, *Ideas with Consequences: The Federalist Society and the Conservative Counterrevolution* (New York: Oxford University Press, 2015) (showing how conservative organizations like the Federalist Society have created a new audience and reference group for conservative judges in the United States).

[9] See ibid.

Examples of relevant institutional structures might include whether there is a separate constitutional court, whether constitutional courts sit in multi-member panels, the length of judicial terms, limits on the kinds of cases courts may hear, whether the system permits abstract judicial review or requires concrete controversies, and so on.

Finally, political constraints include the political branches' powers of appointment, removal and impeachment, their ability to change the length of judicial terms (including renewals), and the available forms of political response to what judges do.

V. Interpretation versus Amendment: 'Off-the-Wall' and 'on-the-Wall' Interpretation

If interpretation produces change, what is the relationship between interpretation and amendment? One important difference is that constitutional amendment produces changes in the constitutional text, while construction does not. Nevertheless, some constitutional constructions may produce changes similar to those that would be produced by changing the text. As noted above, constitutional guarantees of sex equality in the United States might have been achieved through ratifying an Equal Rights Amendment to the Constitution; instead, sex equality was achieved through a series of constitutional constructions by the courts and the political branches.

The kinds of change that can be achieved through constitutional amendment and constitutional interpretation often overlap, and this chapter offers a number of reasons why that is so. Nevertheless, amendment and interpretation are not the same process, and not everything that can be done through one method can be done through the other.

At any point in time in a constitution's history, some constitutional interpretations are simply not plausible. If people want to achieve certain kinds of change, they must amend the constitution or ratify a new constitution. Put differently, at any point in time, some proposed interpretations are 'off-the-wall', while others are plausible or 'on-the-wall', even if they are not necessarily the best interpretation.[10]

Nevertheless, the concepts of 'off-the-wall' and 'on-the-wall' are not fixed or stable properties of interpretations. First, within the political community there may be disagreements about what kinds of interpretations are 'on-the-wall' and 'off-the-wall'. Conservatives may think that certain interpretations are perfectly plausible—and even correct—while liberals disagree. Second, the boundary between what people regard as reasonable and unreasonable is not fixed; it can change as a result of legal discussion and political mobilization. Some positions that at one point in history were deemed 'off-the-wall' can become 'on-the-wall' later on; in fact, they can move from plausible to persuasive and even orthodox, while the former, widely accepted interpretation may itself become 'off-the-wall'. Norm entrepreneurs—including legal intellectuals, social and political movements, politicians, and political parties—can work assiduously to shift the boundaries of the reasonable and the unreasonable. Through media

---

[10] On the concepts of 'off-the-wall' and 'on-the-wall', see J. M. Balkin, *Constitutional Redemption: Political Faith in an Unjust World* (Cambridge, Mass.: Harvard University Press, 2011), 179–83.

campaigns, legal argument, cultural persuasion, and political protest, they can reshape people's constitutional common sense, and turn previously marginal or unthinkable claims about the constitution into plausible or even dominant positions.

The gay rights movement in the United States offers an example of how social processes shape the plausibility of constitutional interpretations. When the social movement for gay rights began in earnest in the late 1960s, arguments that gays and lesbians had constitutional rights to engage in same-sex relationships, much less to marry, were 'off-the-wall', at least in the eyes of most legal professionals. However, gays and lesbians mobilized, gathered political allies, and slowly pushed these claims about the American constitution from 'off-the-wall' to 'on-the-wall'. They did so through changing the facts on the ground, thus presenting their fellow citizens with a new reality. They also did so through acts of protest and persuasion, and through multiple interventions in culture and cultural norms.

Gays and lesbians increasingly came out to their family and friends, altering how others perceived them; gay and lesbian couples quietly began to adopt children in low-publicity proceedings in family courts, thus undermining assumptions that gays and lesbians could not form stable families. Lawyers working on behalf of gays and lesbians began strategic waves of litigation in state and federal courts, attempting to change the law bit by bit. In so doing they worked assiduously to devise novel claims and strategies and offer creative interpretations of many different kinds of laws in many different areas. Advocates sought anti-discrimination ordinances in state and local governments around the country, and the repeal or modification of hostile laws. In the public sphere, advocates for gay and lesbian rights made legal and policy arguments for reform, and produced books, plays, movies, songs, and television shows portraying gays and lesbians in a sympathetic light.

All of these changes—factual, legal, social, and cultural—altered what legal professionals thought were reasonable and unreasonable claims about the meaning of the Constitution. By 2003, the US Supreme Court held that the Constitution protected same-sex relationships from criminalization. But this was only one moment in an ongoing dialectic between the judiciary and the political branches. The 2003 decision was followed by Congress overturning a ban on gays and lesbians serving openly in the military, a presidential Executive Order prohibiting discrimination in federal employment and contracting, and a series of decisions in state and federal courts on same-sex marriage that led to a 2015 Supreme Court decision guaranteeing the right of same-sex couples to marry.[11]

This example shows how processes of constitutional change operate on many different levels simultaneously, incorporating contributions from non-constitutional bodies of law as well as from mobilizations in civil society, and informal mechanisms of cultural change and social persuasion. When I say that these processes cumulatively change the constitution in practice, I do not mean to suggest that they are official acts of constitutional lawmaking (although some may involve changes in other kinds of law). Indeed, none of these factors changes constitutional law *officially*; none by itself

---

[11] *Obergefell v Hodges* 576 US—, 135 S Ct 2584 (2015).

actually alters doctrine, much less the text of the constitution. Rather, together they change the world in which constitutional interpretation occurs. They lead increasing numbers of legal professionals—including especially judges—to see things as plausible and reasonable that they had not before. Those changes may bear fruit in constructions by the political branches that are upheld by the courts, or in new decisions of the courts altering doctrine. These new political constructions and judicial doctrines, in turn, also affect professional judgments of plausibility and reasonableness, and shape the possibilities for future construction.

When we view constitutional interpretation as a social process rather than as isolated acts of opinion-writing by individual judges, we recognize mechanisms of social influence that produce the felt sense of where the law is and must go. Shelley famously remarked that poets are the unacknowledged legislators of the world; he might have added that the members of society, in their various institutional configurations, are the unacknowledged interpreters of a constitution.

The mutability of constitutional interpretation, nevertheless, is constrained. Not everything that can be done through amendment can also be done through interpretation. Some positions cannot be made plausible in a given interpretive community at a given point in history despite copious amounts of effort.

Rather the point of the distinction between what is 'off-the-wall' and 'on-the-wall' in interpretation is to emphasize that what is plausible and reasonable to a legal audience is produced over time through intellectual and political work. The boundary between what can be done through interpretation and what must be done through amendment is produced, reinforced, *and* altered through constitutional politics.

As the example of gay rights suggests, constitutional argument—and therefore constitutional development—occurs within a larger legal and political culture. The work of judges is only the tip of the iceberg; although it serves as the official manifestation of constitutional law, it is nourished by larger forces. Constitutions, as political conventions, depend for their efficacy on social, cultural, and professional systems of mutual influence and persuasion. Mutual influence and persuasion among political and legal elites and among the general public shapes what is thinkable and unthinkable—and what people regard as reasonable and unreasonable—in political and constitutional discourse. Systems of mutual influence and persuasion both produce change and police the boundaries of possible change.

VI. How Constitutional Language Invites Constitutional Construction

Constitutional construction is an inevitable feature of a working constitution. In fact, constitutional language invites constitutional construction. Through using different kinds of constitutional norms, constitutions allow participants to build out the state over time—through doctrinal development, through the evolution of political conventions, and through the construction of institutions. Thus, as part of their role as frameworks for governance, constitutions are also elaborate *economies of delegation and constraint* to future generations. We can see how this economy operates by considering the different types of legal norms that most constitutions employ.

Rules are legal norms that require relatively little practical or evaluative judgment to apply to concrete situations. An example is article I, section 3 of the US Constitution: 'The Senate of the United States shall be composed of two Senators from each State.' Rules tend to require (or permit) the least amount of constitutional construction. Nevertheless, construction may be permissible or even necessary where rules conflict with other provisions or lead to absurd results.

Standards are legal norms that require considerable practical or evaluative judgment to apply to concrete situations because they contain vague terms or terms that involve questions of degree. These norms generally require constitutional construction. The Fourth Amendment, for example, provides that 'The right of the people to be secure in their persons, houses, papers, and effects, against unreasonable searches and seizures, shall not be violated.' Whether a search or seizure is 'reasonable' requires judgment, which may be fact-specific.

Rules and standards exist along a continuum. The more rule-like a legal norm is, the less discretion it offers, and the less practical judgment it requires to apply. The more standard-like a legal norm is, the more discretion it offers and the more practical judgment it requires to apply. For this reason, standards normally require (and invite) more construction than rules; hence they involve a greater degree of delegation to future decision-makers.

Principles are a third kind of legal norm. When rules and standards apply to a situation, they are normally conclusive in deciding a legal question (although decision-makers may be able to make various exceptions and adjustments given the legal culture's canons and techniques of construction). Principles, by contrast, are norms that, when relevant, are not conclusive but must be considered in reaching a decision. Decision-makers may balance them against other considerations, and sometimes the principle does not prevail.[12] Here is an example from the Fourteenth Amendment: 'No state shall ... deny to any person within its jurisdiction the equal protection of the laws.'

Principles generally require constitutional construction for two reasons. First, principles often contain vague—and often highly abstract—language that must be cashed out in practice through subsidiary rules, standards, and principles. Second, even when principles apply to situations, they are not conclusive but must be balanced against competing considerations. The constitutional guarantee of equal protection, for example, does not require equality in all respects. Constitutional construction is necessary to decide what kinds of equality are required and when the constitutional value of equality must be balanced against other concerns. Many rights-conferring provisions in constitutions are principles, especially those enforced through proportionality review.

Adopters can limit the discretion afforded by standards and principles by making them *historical* standards and principles. For example, a constitutional provision might provide that 'freedom of speech as secured at the time of this constitution shall not be abridged'. This provision requires later interpreters to apply the free speech principle as it would have been understood and applied in the past. Nevertheless, most rights-protecting provisions are not written in this way.

---

[12] See eg R. Dworkin, *Taking Rights Seriously* (Cambridge, Mass.: Harvard University Press, 1978), 26–7; R. Alexy, *A Theory of Constitutional Rights*, J. Rivers (trans) (Oxford: Oxford University Press, 2002), 47–8.

Rules, standards, and principles may also contain *ambiguous* terms or phrases that require interpretation. A term is ambiguous if it might refer to more than one concept. By contrast, a term is vague if the reach of its application is unclear or indefinite. 'Meet me at the bank by the river' is ambiguous; it could refer to a riverbank or a financial institution near a river. 'Meet me near the river' is vague; it is not clear where to meet. Rules with ambiguous terms may require interpretation to resolve the ambiguity, but thereafter offer relatively little discretion (and therefore very little need for constitutional construction). Because standards and principles have vague terms and/or require balancing, they may still offer considerable discretion even after all ambiguous terms are clarified.

Rules, standards, and principles may also contain legal terms of art whose boundaries must be specified through further legal construction. Take the example of the Fourth Amendment quoted above. Almost all of the key terms—'persons, papers, and effects', 'searches', and 'seizures'—have unclear boundaries that require construction. Moreover, even when the reach of a term or phrase seems relatively stable, technological changes can upset expectations and require further construction.

Constitutional adopters choose different kinds of language for different purposes. For example, adopters are likely to use fixed rules when they want to limit the discretion of future actors. Thus the American Constitution specifies that the President's term is four years; a term lasting for 'a reasonable period of time' would be unworkable in a presidential system. Constitutional adopters may use standards and principles because they want to channel politics through key concepts and institutions but delegate the details to later decision-makers.

Why would constitution-makers deliberately include standards and principles, or use abstract or vague terms in a constitution? First, it may be impossible to specify certain kinds of norms—for example, certain kinds of rights guarantees—through 'hard-wired' rules. Second, too much specification may split political coalitions for constitutional reform and prevent adoption. If constitutions or constitutional amendments require supermajority support, using abstract or vague language may be a matter of political necessity. Abstract and vague language allows supporters of constitutional reform to agree to disagree, obtaining the benefits of political union or constitutional reform, while allowing the remaining constitutional questions to be worked out later in politics or in the courts.

Sometimes constitutional adopters are completely silent on an issue. There are several reasons why this might occur. Adopters may not have contemplated a particular problem; or they may have assumed that certain matters would go without saying given existing political understandings or conventions. Finally, adopters may have been unable to agree on language and therefore left the question open to be worked out (or fought out) in the future.

Taken together, the combination of the different kinds of norms (and silences) in a written constitution creates an economy of constraint and delegation to the future.[13]

---

[13] Scott Shapiro points out that this is true of all laws, not just constitutions. See S. Shapiro, *Legality* (Cambridge, Mass.: Harvard University Press, 2011).

This economy of constraint and delegation limits construction in certain ways, while permitting or even requiring it in others.

In sum, constitutional language—and the interpretation of constitutional language—does not simply block power; it shapes, channels, and produces power. Both structural and rights provisions should be seen in this light. They channel the exercise of political power in certain ways rather than others. They shape political relations and structure the kinds of actions that people can take towards each other. They make certain types of claims and certain kinds of strategies possible and efficacious in politics. A president, for example, can threaten a veto as a bargaining chip only because the constitution creates the possibility of such a move. Thus, both structural and rights provisions in constitutions *produce* forms of political power as much as they limit them.

Many structural provisions, for example, create institutions that are then expected to compete with each other, shaping constitutional development and conventions of political behaviour over time. One of the most interesting features of modern states is how such states, although seemingly limited by constitutions, have thereby been enabled to exercise new forms of power, engage in collective projects, and regulate behaviour in increasingly elaborate ways that earlier forms of social organization could never have dreamed of.

Rights provisions are often expressed in terms of standards and principles. By their nature, such provisions cannot constrain behaviour in the same way as hard-wired rules. But this does not make them mere 'parchment barriers', as James Madison once described them.[14] Rather, they channel and discipline politics; they announce a key set of values and commitments that shape the beliefs and behaviour of political actors, and that political actors can invoke both in politics and in law. Rights-conferring provisions also articulate ideals and goals for governance. They can become rallying points for political action and mobilization, shaping the conventions of politics.

VII. Constructions by Courts and the Political Branches

What is the relationship between constitutional *construction* and *interpreting* the constitutional *text*? Sometimes constitutional disputes really are just disputes about the meanings of words and phrases in the text, or about what framers and adopters meant when they employed particular words. But most controversial cases require something more. Judges must *give effect* to constitutional provisions by creating and elaborating doctrines, applying existing doctrinal tests, filling in gaps, and so on, given the history of previous decisions and constructions both by the judiciary and the political branches. The language of construction seeks to capture this fact about constitutional interpretation—that it is a process of implementing and building out the constitution based on what is already in place.

To be sure, people often speak of constitutional interpretation as deciding what the constitution *means*. But that very expression—'what the constitution means'—reveals

---

[14] See J. Madison, 'No. 48', in C. Rossiter (ed), *The Federalist Papers* (New York: Penguin Putnam, 1999), 276–81.

a crucial ambiguity in the term 'meaning' itself. 'Meaning' may refer to the communicative content of a phrase or expression ('what does this sentence mean in English?'). But the word 'meaning' has many other meanings: it may refer to intentions or purposes ('I didn't mean to hurt you'). It may refer to the point of an activity ('what is the meaning of life?'). It may refer to personal or cultural associations ('what does the Statue of Liberty mean to me?'). Finally, it may refer to practical application or effect ('what does this mean in practice?'). When people debate what a constitution 'means', they often refer to many of these ideas simultaneously. When lawyers and judges argue about what the constitution 'means', they may be interested in the meaning of words or phrases, or the purpose or point of the constitution. But above all, they are interested in application—the practical effect of the constitution in specific controversies. Debates about constitutional 'meaning', therefore are usually also debates about constitutional construction.

Doctrinal tools—like the proportionality review used in many different constitutional systems, or the system of scrutiny rules employed in the United States—are familiar examples of constitutional constructions. They give effect to constitutional provisions and, in turn, often produce new constitutional constructions in the form of precedents. When constitutional courts use proportionality analysis to resolve constitutional controversies, it is common to say that they are engaged in constitutional interpretation, but they are actually engaged in constitutional construction. They are using tools created by previous judges and designed to give effect to constitutional provisions in order to generate constitutional decisions. Over time, constitutional decisions can create an elaborate network of constructions; the study of these constructions, to a very large extent, fills out the constitutional law of a country.

When people think about constitutional interpretation, they generally think first of judges, and of lawyers arguing in front of judges. That is hardly surprising. Judges play important roles in the constitutional enterprise. After all, judges write the opinions and create the doctrines that create the official law of the constitution; these are the materials that lawyers and politicians use, invoke, and sometimes criticize in promoting their own projects. Moreover, unlike popular opinions, judicial opinions about the constitution are backed up by the coercive power of the state. Even in systems without strong judicial review, judicial constructions of the constitution may affect the interpretations of statutes, or otherwise shape what the political branches do.

Nevertheless, many different people in the constitutional system besides judges—including politicians, political parties, civil society organizations, interest groups, social movements, and individuals—also make claims about the constitution. Perhaps equally important, judicial decisions and judicial doctrine are not the only kinds of constitutional constructions. Many interpretations of a constitution arise either directly or indirectly through acts of *state-building*. People and institutions may develop, contest, or apply constitutional conventions. Political actors may pass statutes, issue regulations, or build or modify institutions to carry out constitutional functions and purposes. All of these activities either assert or presume how the constitution should be correctly interpreted. Moreover, they may create new realities on the ground about how the government functions and what kinds of things governments do. We might call all of these activities in politics and law *state-building constructions*.[15] Judges repeatedly must consider how best to interpret the constitution in light of these changed conditions of governance. Judicial constructions are in continual conversation with constructions by the political branches. Examples of state-building constructions in the American context include the building of various government departments and agencies with different functions, the creation and expansion of the administrative and regulatory state, and the development of institutions for national security.

The idea of state-building constructions is not limited to actions that *increase* the size of government. The constitution-in-practice changes by *subtraction* as well as by addition. One of the most important features of late twentieth-century state-building in many countries was privatization of previously governmental functions, often raising a host of constitutional problems. Nor does the idea of state-building constructions presume that the institutions of government are bare-bones or underdeveloped whenever a new constitution is adopted, and that the state has to be built out from scratch. Quite the contrary: most constitutions come into being in the context of a previous regime with laws, practices, and institutions. Many constitutional controversies arise precisely out of the need for the political branches and the courts to synthesize political and legal decisions from the old order with the new constitution.

State-building constructions—and judicial responses to them—are a key source of constitutional change outside of official amendment. The text of the American Constitution did not substantially change as the country became a modern administrative, regulatory, and welfare state in the middle of the twentieth century. The passage of new statutes and the creation of new institutions altered the way government worked and it changed expectations about what government could properly do. The constitution-in-practice changed radically as a result. Understandings about foundational concepts like liberty, federalism, and the separation of powers were drastically altered. Judges confirmed these changes with a series of landmark opinions, sweeping away decades of previous precedents in a relatively short period of time. Yet one would not be able to tell all of this merely from inspecting the constitutional text, which barely changed at all, and even then not about subjects directly related to these transformations.[16]

Between 1990 and 2015 the United States invested billions of dollars in technologies and institutions for foreign and domestic surveillance complete with enormous investments of time and money in infrastructure, bureaucracy, and operational practices. That set of institutions—the national surveillance state—was built on the premise that its operations were lawful and consistent with the Constitution. To be sure, the political branches may change some features out of constitutional concerns. Judges may hold some aspects of the national surveillance state unconstitutional or subject to judicial supervision.[17] It is likely, however, that judges will leave most elements in place.

---

[15] Balkin, above n 2, 5.

[16] See B. A. Ackerman, 'The Living Constitution' (2007) 120 *Harvard Law Review* 1737.

[17] On some of the constitutional problems, see J. M. Balkin and S. Levinson, 'The Processes of Constitutional Change: From Partisan Entrenchment to the National Surveillance State' (2006) 75 *Fordham Law Review* 489; J. M. Balkin, 'The Constitution in the National Surveillance State' (2008) 93 *Minnesota Law Review* 1.

Moreover, some, perhaps most, elements of this system will never be subject to judicial review. These new institutions and the constitutional theories that justify and limit them will become part of the constitution-in-practice. They will influence how future judges, lawyers, and political actors understand what is reasonable and unreasonable in the interpretation and application of the American constitution.

Like the creation of the administrative and regulatory state—and like the gay rights movement described earlier in this chapter—the construction of the national surveillance state did more than advance new constitutional claims. It also created new social realities. Even if some aspects of the national surveillance state are later declared unconstitutional by courts, many of the basic bureaucratic, legal, and technological structures will likely remain as aspects of political governance. After all, the administrative and regulatory state that arose in the twentieth century has not disappeared simply because courts began to impose constitutional limits on its actions. If anything, the administrative and regulatory state has tended to grow in symbiosis with judicial review.

One of the most important functions of constitutional courts is legitimating and rationalizing constitutional constructions by the other branches of government. First, courts provide reasons why political constructions are faithful (or not faithful) to the constitution. Second, courts subject political constructions to judicial doctrines that will guide and legitimate political constructions in the future. Thus, judicial construction blesses or limits what other actors have already done and it sets ground rules for further political activity. Legitimation is Janus-faced: it establishes what government can do by establishing what the government cannot do. Thus, even when the judiciary strikes down parts of what the other branches of government do, it implicitly legitimates other actions as within the constitution.

In short, much judicial construction of a constitution is a response to constitutional constructions by other actors. In the process, courts create new doctrines that shape future political action. Through this interaction between political and judicial constructions, the constitutional system evolves and the state is built out.

VIII. The Framework Model and Law as Integrity

At this point we might compare the framework model of constitutions offered in this chapter with Ronald Dworkin's famous argument that legal interpretation should aim at producing and preserving legal integrity.[18] The two models are not necessarily inconsistent: almost everything in the framework model might be translated into Dworkin's perspective. Moreover, as a leading advocate of a 'living Constitution' in the United States, Dworkin was certainly not averse to the notion that the application of constitutional provisions might change—and change significantly—over time. Indeed, much of Dworkin's work in constitutional theory seems designed to explain and justify the transformations in constitutional law that came with the American civil rights movement and the rights revolution of the 1960s and 1970s.

[18] R. Dworkin, *Law's Empire* (Cambridge, Mass.: Belknap Press, 1986); see also R. Dworkin, *Freedom's Law: The Moral Reading of the Constitution* (Cambridge, Mass.: Harvard University Press, 1996).

Nevertheless, the framework model looks at the processes of change quite differently from Dworkin's account and it focuses on different questions. When we re-describe the framework model in Dworkin's terms, important elements are missing or at the very least distorted.

Dworkin's primary concern is judges and judicial behaviour, and he treats citizen interpretation as a special case of judicial interpretation. He does not focus on state-building as an important feature of constitutional interpretation. Although Dworkin believes that individual citizens can interpret the constitution for themselves, he is not especially interested in constitutional claims by social and political movements. By contrast, the framework model treats these claims as central to constitutional development.

Dworkin's model of constitutional change is based on the traditions of common-law decision-making by judges; it analogizes constitutional interpretation to the writing of a chain novel that seeks to maintain continuity with the judicial decisions of the past. The framework model argues that constitutional change is driven not by the internal logic of the common law but by waves of political mobilizations and counter-mobilizations and by repeated exercises of state-building. As a result, courts often discard significant parts of previous jurisprudence when they legitimate new constitutional orders. (The development of the American administrative and regulatory state in the 1930s and 1940s is a good example.) From the standpoint of the framework model, Dworkin's focus on common law judging obscures the actual drivers of constitutional change and smooths over discontinuous or revolutionary features of constitutional development.

Dworkin famously describes courts as the 'forum of principle';[19] he generally views ordinary politics as a domain of compromise. Or he views politics as infected by passion and political will that wise and principled judges must restrain and correct. The framework model, by contrast, argues that these implicit oppositions are misguided. Politics may also be driven by principle. Many constitutional principles later promulgated by judges originally emerged out of constitutional politics. Conversely, judicial decision-making that presents itself as principled may involve unstated or implicit compromises.

The framework model emphasizes how judges and other parts of the political process interact as state institutions and state power develop over time. In Dworkin's model, this interaction is either flattened out or entirely missing. What the framework model calls constitutional construction by the political branches becomes, in Dworkin's theory, just data for judges to ponder. It is an aspect of the 'fit' with the existing body of legal materials that judges should consider in deciding cases according to principle; it is not in and of itself part of the process of constitutional interpretation.

The framework model emphasizes how the political branches and social and political mobilizations change social realities and affect contemporary notions of what is reasonable and unreasonable, generating a back-and-forth relationship with judicial constructions of the constitution. These features of social influence on the judiciary are not particularly relevant to Dworkin's model; they matter, if at all, only in the question of how well judicial interpretations fit with the existing body of legal materials at a particular point in time.

[19] R. Dworkin, 'The Forum of Principle' (1981) 56 *New York University Law Review* 469.

Dworkin's model of law as integrity insists that 'judicial decision be a matter of principle, not compromise or strategy or political accommodation'.[20] He is also famous for his assertion that judges lack discretion in deciding cases and that there is usually a single right answer to hard questions of law. It follows that no matter how the state is built out, there is (usually) a single correct way for judges to interpret the constitution, given the constraints of fit with existing legal materials (which include state-building by the political branches) and justification according to the best available moral and political philosophy. If judges truly understood the existing set of laws and practices in place and their interrelationships; truly understood the relevant facts before them—including the nature and function of state institutions—and truly understood the best available moral and political philosophy, they would have no choice in how to proceed. There would be a single best way for judges to engage in constitutional construction.

Dworkin freely admits that only an ideal judge, whom he calls Hercules, would have the wisdom and the ability to perform the necessary calculations to match the requirements of fit and justification. Nevertheless, he offers Hercules as a normative ideal towards which judges should strive. Thus, it does not matter whether we say that judges 'add' or 'create' doctrines and distinctions in constitutional law as long as they do so with integrity and without discretion.

Indeed, in Dworkin's model the only discretion in the constitutional system consists in how the political branches build out the state and how social and political mobilizations influence constitutional construction by the political branches. Although these groups may act based on their views about the constitution, they are not judges, and therefore they are not bound by obligations of fit with previous laws or norms of judicial integrity (although Dworkin argues that they have independent moral obligations of *political* integrity). Courts must respond with constitutional interpretations that seek to achieve integrity through the proper balance of fit and justification. There is no dialectical give and take between judges and other political actors. Instead, at each step in the process, there is a single correct way for judges to engage in constitutional construction—assuming, of course, that judges possessed the relevant knowledge and skill.

The framework model, by contrast, does not insist that there must always be a single best way to engage in constitutional construction, although it does not deny that this could be the case in any particular situation. Construction is concerned above all with successful (1) *implementation* and *application* of constitutional norms (2) *over time* (3) *in ongoing relationships to other actors* in the political system. This focus leads to different concerns than Dworkin's demand that judges reason only through principle, and that they must not engage in political accommodation, compromise, or strategic decision-making.

To implement a constitutional norm like freedom of speech, federalism, or equal protection of the laws, judges are likely to be faced with a complex set of practical considerations. Should judges employ rules or standards to implement constitutional values? Should they employ bright-line distinctions or multifactor tests? Should they engage in

---

[20] Dworkin, 1996, above n 18, 83.

a proportionality-style balancing of interests to protect constitutional rights or create clear constitutional privileges and obligations? If they engage in balancing, what degree of deference should they offer to factual and moral judgments by the other branches? Should judges' statements of the law be broad or narrow? Should they proceed one step at a time in building their doctrines, waiting to see what the political branches do in response, or should they articulate their views with full clarity and depth at the outset?[21] Should they attempt to predict the political reaction from the political branches and adjust or temporize accordingly, or should they ignore how their decisions will be received—and whether their best intentions will be frustrated by political resistance? Should they employ what Alexander Bickel once called the 'passive virtues' and use various procedural and jurisdictional devices to delay articulation of constitutional norms, or should they push forward as soon as a genuine constitutional question is properly raised?[22] Should they adopt doctrines that will be difficult for the political branches to evade but that may not fully protect the constitutional interests at stake, or should they choose more capacious doctrines that will require considerable buy-in or cooperation from the other branches to be effective?

These, and other questions like them, are implicit in the notion of constitutional construction. Each of them asks how to implement constitutional norms in practice through making decisions and creating legal tools that other people will use or react to. Some of these questions—about what form doctrine should take—are mostly elided in Dworkin's model. Other questions fit only awkwardly with his approach, because they depend on considerations of prudence, judgments about timing, and predictions about the future. They concern path-dependent effects and the results of interactions with other institutions that not even Hercules himself could know with certainty—unless he also counted clairvoyance among his many abilities. Still other features of constitutional construction seem squarely in conflict with Dworkin's insistence that judges not engage in compromise, strategic thinking, political accommodation, or judgments of policy. By contrast, none of these features of constitutional construction pose a special problem for the framework model, because it assumes that judges are constantly engaged in an interactive relationship with the other branches of government and with the public.

IX. Justifying Interpretations: The Modalities of Constitutional Argument

Generally speaking people justify constitutional constructions through a set of standard forms of argument. Philip Bobbitt has famously called them the modalities of constitutional interpretation.[23] These modalities of argument act like *topoi* in classical rhetoric.

---

[21] See C. R. Sunstein, *One Case at a Time: Judicial Minimalism on the Supreme Court* (Cambridge, Mass.: Harvard University Press, 1999).

[22] See A. M. Bickel, 'Foreword: The Passive Virtues' (1961) 75 *Harvard Law Review* 40.

[23] See P. C. Bobbitt, *Constitutional Interpretation* (Oxford: Basil Blackwell, 1991); P. C. Bobbitt, *Constitutional Fate: Theory of the Constitution* (New York: Oxford University Press, 1982); R. H. Fallon, Jr, 'A Constructivist Coherence Theory of Constitutional Interpretation' (1987) 100 *Harvard Law Review* 1189.

They give the participants within a shared culture common cultural tools to characterize the situation before them, diagnose and solve problems, and persuade others.

The modalities of constitutional argument are cultural forms that emerge from the
history of rhetoric and from its use in politics and in law. For this reason the list of permissible modalities of constitutional argument may vary somewhat from legal culture
to legal culture. Nevertheless there is still considerable overlap in the legal cultures of
countries with enforceable written constitutions.

Modalities of argument are forms of justification. They offer reasons why we
should accept one constitutional construction rather than another. Each modality
of argument is premised on an implicit theory of legal justification; each presumes
a theory of why arguments of that type are valid and should persuade others. For
example, arguments from constitutional structure assert that an interpretation is
correct because it will cause the various parts of the constitution or the constitution
as a whole to function properly; conversely, constructions that produce constitutional dysfunction or are inconsistent with the way the constitution is supposed to
work in practice are bad interpretations. Arguments from judicial precedent presume that interpretations of the constitution should be consistent with rule of law
values. Arguments from consequences are premised on the notion that where the
constitutional text is unclear, we should adopt the reading that produces the best
consequences and the least injustice.

Here is a list of the most familiar modalities of constitutional argument, classified by
the kinds of justificatory reasons they offer.[24]

An interpretation or construction is the best one because it:

1. elucidates the meaning of the text, for example, by using standard canons of statutory construction or by comparing parts of the constitutional text with each other
   or with other important legal texts (*arguments from text*);

2. is most consistent with the proper function or structural logic underlying the
   constitutional system (*arguments from structure*);

3. is most consistent with the underlying purposes, principles, or point behind the
   constitution or some part of the constitution (*arguments from purpose*);

4. best resolves gaps, conflicts, vagueness, or ambiguity by choosing the interpretation that has the best consequences or is otherwise most just (*arguments from
   consequences*);

5. shows how previous judicial precedents require a particular result (*arguments
   from judicial precedent*);

6. appeals to existing political settlements or conventions among political actors
   and institutions (*arguments from political convention*);

7. appeals to the public's customs and lived experience (*arguments from custom*);

8. appeals to natural law or natural rights (*arguments from natural law*);

---

[24] This list is taken from J. M. Balkin, 'The New Originalism and the Uses of History' (2013) 82 *Fordham
Law Review* 641. For reasons described in that article, it is more elaborate than Bobbitt's or Fallon's lists.

9. appeals to important and widely honoured values of the nation and its political culture (*arguments from national ethos*);

10. appeals to national political traditions and to the normative meaning of important events and narratives in the nation's cultural memory, including both events that are honoured or worthy of emulation and events that are dishonoured or should never be repeated (*arguments from political tradition*); or

11. appeals to the values, beliefs, and examples of national culture heroes (*arguments from honoured authority*).

This list is not intended to be exhaustive. Not all constitutional cultures feature all of these forms of argument, and the forms of argument may be slightly different in different cultures. Here are two examples. First, in some constitutional cultures arguments from political tradition may primarily treat history as a negative example rather than as a positive source of value. They may emphasize 'aversive history', deriving the point or purpose of the constitution from unhappy or unjust features of a nation's past that the constitution is designed to prevent in the future.[25] Second, in some constitutional cultures, appeals to religious scriptures, doctrines, or authority are a permissible form of constitutional argument.[26]

Many constitutional theorists assume that appeals to history constitute a separate kind of constitutional argument, and therefore a distinct modality of interpretation. Bobbitt himself identified the historical modality with arguments from the original intentions of a constitution's framers.[27] Not all arguments from history, however, are appeals to framers' intentions. For example, arguments from consequences and structure may appeal to 'the lessons of history', which may be drawn from the history of many different nations and times.

Even appeals to constitutional framers or ratifiers might fall into several different modalities. For example, people might invoke constitutional founders to make arguments about the original meaning of the constitutional text, about structure, about purpose; or to make appeals about political tradition or national ethos. In the United States many 'originalist' arguments are also arguments from honoured authority, because the framers and ratifiers of the American Constitution are widely regarded as culture heroes.[28]

Rather than being a distinctive form of argument, people use history to support virtually all of the different modalities of argument, and the way that history is used is different for each modality. For example, arguments from precedent or political convention use history differently than arguments from constitutional structure. They may consider different kinds of facts salient or use the same facts in very different ways. An

---

[25] See K. L. Scheppele, 'Aspirational and Aversive Constitutionalism: The Case for Studying Cross-Constitutional Influence through Negative Models' (2003) 1 *International Journal of Constitutional Law* 296.

[26] See R. Hirschl, *Constitutional Theocracy* (Cambridge, Mass.: Harvard University Press, 2010).

[27] See eg Bobbitt, 1991, above n 23, 13 ('A historical modality may be attributed to constitutional arguments that claim that the framers and ratifiers [of a constitutional provision] intended, or did not intend…'); Fallon, above n 23, 1244, 1254 (identifying '[a]rguments of historical intent' with 'the intent of the framers').

[28] See Balkin, above n 24.

argument from precedent or convention is interested in the history of particular decisions and courses of action. An argument from structure, by contrast, uses history to
explain why a particular institutional arrangement functions properly or badly.

Modalities of argument are important for four reasons.

First, constitutional modalities of argument provide a common language for all
members of the political community. Because the modalities are available to everyone
in the legal culture, they enable constitutional interpretations by non-judicial actors,
which, as we have seen, are important drivers of constitutional development and constitutional change. To be sure, lawyers and judges will probably be most proficient at
making arguments from doctrine and judicial precedent. Indeed, lawyers may tend to
conflate constitutional argument with arguments from doctrine and judicial precedent
because of their professional training. They have a natural interest in monopolizing the
task of constitutional interpretation by maintaining that it is only for those who are
professionally credentialled. But that is precisely why noting the multiple modalities of
argument is important.

Second, the modalities of argument are simultaneously vehicles of creativity and
constraint. The forms of argument allow participants to express a wide variety of opinions about the proper construction of the constitution. Even so, it is not the case that
'anything goes' in constitutional interpretation. Constitutional interpretation is a social
practice that provides participants with certain resources for argument. Constitutional
modalities offer a toolkit for understanding situations and persuading other members
of the community. Nevertheless, like other resources, these resources of argument have
limits, and the tools in the toolkit cannot be used equally well to justify any possible
result. At any point in time, some arguments using the modalities will be more plausible than others in the interpretive community. Thus, as noted previously, some constitutional positions will be 'off-the-wall', while others will be 'on-the-wall'. The use of
common modalities of argument shapes what people consider thinkable and reasonable in a constitutional culture; this helps us to understand why the indeterminacy of
constitutional construction is always a constrained indeterminacy.

Nevertheless, as I have also noted previously, what is 'off-the-wall' and what is
'on-the-wall' in constitutional argument can change over time as the result of sustained
political mobilizations and other forms of social change. With sufficient time and effort,
people may find new ways to use common modalities of argument and draw on common cultural resources to persuade others. As constitutional common sense and political imagination change, so too will the boundaries of what people regard as reasonable
and unreasonable in constitutional argument.

Third, because there are multiple modalities, constitutional argument is likely to be
eclectic. Different people will be drawn to different modalities to express their ideas
about the constitution. Members of the community may often disagree about which
modality should prevail in case of a conflict among them.[29]

---

[29] For example, my own view is that when it is clear, we should follow the 'original communicative content' of the text—that is, the original semantic meaning of the words of the text, taking into account any
legal terms of art and any implications from background context that are necessary to understand the text.
J. M. Balkin, 'Must We Be Faithful to Original Meaning?' (2013) 7 *Jerusalem Review of Legal Studies* 57, at
61. But not everyone in American legal culture agrees.

Fourth, the modalities remind us how much constitutional development depends on mutual influence and persuasion, both in the courts and in the larger society that surrounds them. There is no guarantee that a developing system of constitutional understandings will progress towards justice; but to the extent that justice results from constitutional rhetoric, it will likely have to travel through common tools of political and legal argument.

X. Conclusion: Who Interprets?

Who engages in constitutional interpretation? Pretty much everyone in the political community. That does not mean that all members have the same institutional role, of course. When popular mobilizations pronounce what the constitution means, they are often reacting to the work of judges or addressing themselves to the judiciary as well as their fellow citizens. Indeed, when mobilizations claim that the 'true' constitution has been hijacked or betrayed, they are often either looking to the courts for assistance against the political branches or denouncing the previous work of judges.

Even so, as we have seen in this chapter, the judicial power to issue official opinions about the constitution does not exhaust the role of constitutional interpretation in a complex political system. Judicial interpretation is just a special case of constitutional interpretation in an ongoing constitutional order.[30]

Even without judicial review, controversies about the constitution's meaning and application will inevitably arise. For example, until after the Civil War, many if not most of the key constitutional controversies in the United States were debated and resolved by politicians making explicitly constitutional arguments about countless questions of policy and state-building, ranging from tariffs to treaties to territorial acquisition. (Slavery was, of course, the most heated question in the antebellum period, and it was usually discussed in explicitly constitutional terms.) The federal judiciary only achieved its present prominence in American constitutional interpretation over time, through evolutionary processes of constitutional construction.

In some constitutional systems, to be sure, people may avoid arguing in constitutional terms and prefer to focus on arguments of policy, while in other systems, like that of the antebellum United States, people may find constitutional overtones in virtually every important political controversy. But that is not because of the presence or absence of judicial review; it is because of the history of the particular country and its constitutional evolution.

Adding judicial review to a constitutional system does not eliminate the multiplicity of constitutional interpreters. People and institutions will continue to make constitutional arguments and generate constitutional constructions. Government officials of all types and at all levels of government will still assert constitutional claims; so too will politicians, parties, political and social movements, interest groups, members of the media, civil society organizations, and ordinary individuals.

---

[30] See S. Levinson, *Constitutional Faith* 2nd edn (Princeton: Princeton University Press, 2012) (offering a theory of 'protestant constitutionalism').

What judicial review adds is an additional layer of institutional complexity in interpretative debates. First, non-judicial actors will often address their arguments to courts and criticize courts when they fail to interpret the constitution the 'right way'—that is, according to their favoured position. Second, political and social movements may invest more in lawyers to conduct litigation campaigns in order to achieve policy goals through judicial interpretation of the constitution.

Third, in systems with judicial review, politicians may rely on courts to further certain policy goals through constitutional interpretation.[31] Fourth, politicians may be happy to throw the responsibility for some unpopular or coalition-splitting decisions to the courts. They may find that they can avoid taking unpopular positions on certain questions by announcing that the courts have spoken and that they will defer to that judgment.[32] Fifth, and conversely, politicians and social movements can sometimes gain political advantage by attacking court decisions. Judicial decision-making offers political actors a convenient foil that allows them to mobilize support and advocate for change.[33] Sixth, in some systems with judicial review, the method of judicial appointments may become particularly important to constitutional politics. Political actors and social and political movements may organize to influence judicial appointments in order to influence how constitutional disputes get resolved.

These institutional features suggest why, even if many different actors interpret the constitution, judicial interpretations may tend to dominate the legal imagination over time. This is essentially what happened in the United States, especially following the Civil War. Politicians may find judicial review a useful institution, and therefore normally defer to it, even when their favoured position is not always vindicated in the courts.[34] Because constitutional interpretations may have significant policy consequences or may alter the relative power and wealth of groups in society, interested actors will seek to control or influence the courts and they will mobilize in response to or in support of judicial interpretations of the constitution. These political efforts may help make judicial interpretations especially important, and make winning judicial confirmation of one's position a particularly valuable prize in politics.

As people increasingly organize their political strategies around judicial interpretations of the constitution, judicial review may begin to look a lot like judicial supremacy. But appearances can be deceiving. Judges are part of a larger system of politics, social influence, and persuasion. Although they may appear to have the last word on constitutional interpretation at any point in time, they often turn out to be far more responsive to the constitutional views of other actors when their work is considered over long periods of time.

---

[31] K. E. Whittington, *Political Foundations of Judicial Supremacy: The Presidency, the Supreme Court, and Constitutional Leadership in U.S. History* (Princeton: Princeton University Press, 2007).

[32] See M. A. Graber, 'The Nonmajoritarian Difficulty: Legislative Deference to the Judiciary' (1993) 7 *Studies in American Political Development* 35.

[33] R. C. Post and R. B. Siegel, '*Roe* Rage: Democratic Constitutionalism and Backlash' (2007) 42 *Harvard Civil Rights–Civil Liberties Law Review* 373.

[34] Whittington, above n 31.

13

Philosophical Foundations of Judicial Review

*Cristina Lafont**

I. Introduction

Most philosophical debates concerning judicial review stem from the problem of indeterminacy—and the disagreements it generates. Even written constitutions contain abstract and open-textured provisions that require further specification when applied to specific cases and in the face of societal changes. The inherent indeterminacy of many constitutional provisions makes *constitutional review both unavoidable and problematic*. In a democratic society the practice of constitutional review raises questions about who should conduct such a review while also tacitly acknowledging the difficulty of justifying any such delegation by bestowing final authority upon a specific actor or institution at the expense of others. Philosophical debates on judicial review therefore cannot simply focus upon narrow issues of jurisprudential methodology (eg the correct theory of constitutional interpretation). Instead they must address two more fundamental questions. First, what is the proper understanding of constitutional review? Here the main issue is how to reconcile constitutionalism with the democratic ideal of self-government. Answers to this question vary widely depending on one's conception of democracy.[1] This variation gives rise to sharply different answers to the second fundamental question, namely, whether it is legitimate to delegate the task of constitutional review to the judicial branch of government in particular, that is, to the courts. Here the main divide is between those who question the legitimacy of judicial review (eg Waldron, Kramer, Bellamy, Tushnet)[2] and those who endorse it (eg Ely, Dworkin, Eisgruber, Rawls, Habermas, Sunstein).[3] However,

---

* Professor of Philosophy, Northwestern University. I thank Karen Alter for helpful comments on an earlier version of this chapter.

[1] For a good overview see C. Zurn, 'Deliberative Democracy and Constitutional Review' (2002) 21 *Law and Philosophy* 467, at 467–542, and *Deliberative Democracy and the Institutions of Judicial Review* (Cambridge: Cambridge University Press, 2007).

[2] See eg J. Waldron, 'The Core of the Case Against Judicial Review' (2006) 115 *Yale Law Journal* 1346, at 1346–1406, also 'Constitutionalism: A Skeptical View', *Philip A. Hart Memorial Lecture* 4 (2010), available at http://scholarship.law.georgetown.edu./hartlecture/4, and *Law and Disagreement* (Oxford: Oxford University Press, 1999); L. D. Kramer, *The People Themselves: Popular Constitutionalism and Judicial Review* (Oxford: Oxford University Press, 2004); R. Bellamy, *Political Constitutionalism* (Cambridge: Cambridge University Press, 2007); M. Tushnet, *Taking the Constitution Away from the Courts* (Princeton: Princeton University Press, 1999); M. Tushnet, *Weak Courts, Strong Rights: Judicial Review and Social Welfare Rights in Comparative Constitutional Law* (Princeton: Princeton University Press, 2008).

[3] See eg J. H. Ely, *Democracy and Distrust. A Theory of Judicial Review* (Cambridge, Mass.: Harvard University Press, 1981); R. Dworkin, *A Matter of Principle* (Cambridge, Mass.: Harvard University Press, 1985); R. Dworkin, *Law's Empire* (Cambridge, Mass.: Harvard University Press, 1986); R. Dworkin, *Freedom's Law: The Moral Reading of the Constitution* (Cambridge, Mass.: Harvard University Press, 1996); C. L. Eisgruber, *Constitutional Self-Government* (Cambridge, Mass.: Harvard University Press, 2001);

within both camps there are also important differences among the positive proposals that each author makes regarding the specific form that constitutional review should take in order to be legitimate.

In spite of such disagreement most critics of the legitimacy of judicial review and even many of its defenders agree that it is an undemocratic practice. They see judicial review as the result of a compromise between two potentially incompatible normative goals: protection of minority rights and democratic self-government.[4] This is what Bickel famously referred to as 'the counter-majoritarian difficulty'. He explains this difficulty as follows: 'judicial review is a counter-majoritarian force in our system … When *the Supreme Court* declares unconstitutional a legislative act … it thwarts the will of representatives *of the actual people* of the here and now'.[5] From this perspective, the question is whether or not judicial review is necessary for the protection of rights. What is unquestioned is the tacit assumption that a loss in democratic self-government is simply the price we have to pay for the institutions of judicial review. For those who think democratic procedures possess merely instrumental value the price is not high at all, so long as judicial review delivers the expected outcome of improved rights protections.[6] By contrast, those who ascribe intrinsic value to democratic procedures tend to see this price as prohibitively high, especially since there is no guarantee that the courts will always deliver the right decisions. Waldron's staunch opposition to judicial review exemplifies the latter position.[7] On his view, the effectiveness of judicial review at protecting rights is at best mixed, so the outcome-related reasons in favour of it are rather weak. However, since the loss in democratic self-government is an inevitable part of judicial review, so the argument goes, this gives us very strong process-related reasons against the practice.[8] Therefore, from a normative perspective, there is a compelling argument against the practice and, consequently, its introduction in a particular society should be considered only in light of the presence of specific institutional pathologies.[9]

I would like to question that view. In my opinion, judicial review fulfils some key democratic functions and, to the extent that it does, it should be considered democratically legitimate.[10] My aim is to articulate a compelling normative argument in favour

J. Rawls, *A Theory of Justice* (Cambridge, Mass.: Harvard University Press, 1971); J. Rawls, *Political Liberalism* (Cambridge, Mass.: Harvard University Press, 1993); J. Habermas, *Between Facts and Norms* (Cambridge, Mass.: MIT Press, 1998); C. Sunstein, *One Case at a Time: Judicial Minimalism on the Supreme Court* (Cambridge, Mass.: Harvard University Press, 2001).

[4] For defences of judicial review that challenge the claim that it is an inherently undemocratic practice see eg Dworkin, 1996, above n 3; Eisgruber, 2001, above n 3; L. Sager, *Justice in Plainclothes: A Theory of American Constitutional Practice* (New Haven: Yale University Press, 2004); W. J. Waluchow, 'Judicial Review' (2007) 2 *Philosophy Compass* 258, at 258–66. Although I agree with their criticism of Waldron's purely majoritarian conception of democracy, their defences of the legitimacy of judicial review fail to highlight the role of citizens in the practice and its democratic significance. This is what I aim to explore here.

[5] A. Bickel, *The Least Dangerous Branch: The Supreme Court at the Bar of Politics* (New Haven: Yale University Press, 1986), 16–17 (emphasis added).

[6] See eg J. Raz, 'Disagreement in Politics' (1998) 43 *American Journal of Jurisprudence* 45, at 45.

[7] See Waldron, 1999, above n 2; Waldron, 2006, above n 2; J. Waldron, *Torture, Terror, and Trade-Offs: Philosophy for the White House* (Oxford: Oxford University Press, 2010).

[8] Waldron, 2006, above n 2, 1375–6.   [9] Ibid 1386.

[10] This is a normative claim. It is therefore compatible with a variety of empirical circumstances that may make the institution of judicial review democratically illegitimate in the context of a given country. The same, of course, holds for institutions within other branches of government. The normative argument

of the practice that is based on democratic considerations. However, I do not defend the view that strong judicial review is preferable to weaker forms or that, from a democratic perspective, no other institutional solution could be superior to such weaker forms.[11] The answer to that question depends in large measure on empirical aspects of specific societies and their historical circumstances. Consequently, it makes little sense to assume that there is a single right answer. Rather, my more modest task in articulating the democratic case in favour of judicial review is to question the assumptions behind the framework within which the question of the legitimacy of judicial review is usually debated and which fuel the impression that, other things being equal, the democratic default speaks against judicial review, as its critics claim.[12]

II. Framing the Philosophical Debate on the Legitimacy of Judicial Review

As indicated above, philosophical debate on the legitimacy of judicial review is structured by several framing assumptions, which create the impression that, all other things being equal, constitutional democracies with judicial review of legislation are less democratic *for that reason alone*. Participants in this debate often adopt a narrow *juricentric* perspective that exclusively focuses on the internal workings of courts without paying sufficient attention to the political system within which the courts operate and where they play their specific institutional role.[13] Moreover, this narrowness is not only institutional but temporal as well: participants often adopt a *synchronic* perspective that exclusively focuses on how the courts can uphold or strike down a piece of legislation as unconstitutional at a particular point in time. This perspective is too short-sighted. The full significance and implications of judicial review can only be appreciated from a *diachronic* perspective. For, when institutional and temporal narrowness are combined, *the role of citizens* in the process of constitutional review drops out of the picture entirely. The only choice citizens are left with is to delegate the task of constitutional review to either the judiciary or the legislature. Either way, the citizenry plays a rather

---

aims to answer the question of whether a specific institution serves some key democratic functions and is therefore required for democratic reasons. Once it is determined that an institution (eg judicial review, democratic parliament, etc.) is indeed so needed, this opens up the empirical question regarding how we can ensure that the institution works as it is intended, how to best avoid its potential anti-democratic drawbacks, and so on.

[11] For an overview of stronger and weaker forms of judicial review that are adopted in different countries see Waldron, 2006, above n 2, 1354–7; see also M. Tushnet, 'Alternative Forms of Judicial Review' (2003) 101 *Michigan Law Review* 2781, at 2781–802. In my view, it would be wrong to claim that strong judicial review is always preferable over its alternatives. But the reason this claim is wrong is not because strong judicial review is democratically illegitimate, as critics like Waldron would have it. Rather, this claim is wrong for the simple reason that constitutional democracies with weak judicial review (eg Canada) or without judicial review (eg the United Kingdom, at least before the adoption of the Human Rights Act 1998) may also be democratically legitimate. Whether weaker or stronger forms of judicial review should be preferable from a democratic perspective is an empirical question that can be answered in different ways depending on the historical, social, and political circumstances of each specific country.

[12] Given this aim, the analysis that follows will focus on judicial review of democratic legislation and will not address issues concerning judicial review of executive action or administrative decision-making.

[13] For a complaint along these lines see R. Post and R. Siegel, '*Roe* Rage: Democratic Constitutionalism and Backlash' (2007) 42 *Harvard Civil Rights–Civil Liberties Law Review* 373, at 373–433.

marginal role in the process of constitutional review of legislation. Even defenders of popular constitutionalism who oppose the marginalization of the citizenry within processes of constitutional review seem to share these framing assumptions.[14] For they assume that the practice of judicial review is incompatible with citizens taking ownership over their constitution.[15]

Now, regardless of the particular conception of democracy that one endorses, a central element of the democratic ideal of self-government is that citizens must be able to see themselves as not only subject to the law but also as authors of the laws that they are bound by. They must be able to take ownership over the law and see that it tracks their interests and ideas.[16] This core feature of the democratic ideal suggests that constitutional review cannot be permanently delegated. Rather, it must be a process in which all sources of legitimate power, including the constituent power of citizens, can be genuinely engaged. However, there is no reason to accept the widespread assumption that citizens cannot take ownership over constitutional review such that once it is set up they can only become passive recipients who play no relevant role in the process. In order to frame the question of the legitimacy of judicial review in the right way we need to ask a broader question, namely, which set of institutional arrangements give us the best assurance that the citizenry as a whole can be actively engaged in developing the meaning of their own constitution over time?

III. Juricentric versus Holistic Perspective

As already mentioned, most participants in the debate on the legitimacy of judicial review adopt a *juricentric* perspective. Their analysis focuses on the internal workings of the court, the role that judges' beliefs play in their decisions, and the pros and cons of judicial versus legislative supremacy. When this last issue is addressed the perspective typically gets broadened so as to include the different branches of government. Nevertheless, the perspective of the citizenry is largely missing. This absence is striking since, for the most part, judicial review is a process that is triggered by citizens' right to legal contestation. Thus, when evaluating the legitimacy of judicial review it seems important to consider the rationale and the justification for this practice *as understood by the citizens who are supposed to make use of it*. From that perspective, judicial review can be seen as an institution of democratic control to the extent that its justification partly derives from the right of affected citizens to effectively contest the political decisions to which they are subject. As Pettit puts it, it is essential to democracy that citizens 'are able to contest decisions at will and, if the contestation establishes a mismatch with their relevant interests or opinions to force an amendment'.[17] The fact that judicial

---

[14] See Kramer, above n 2; Bellamy, above n 2; Tushnet, 1999, above n 2.

[15] For an interesting exception to this trend see Post and Siegel's defence of 'democratic constitutionalism' in Post and Siegel, above n 13, and 'Popular Constitutionalism, Departmentalism and Judicial Supremacy' (2004) 92 *California Law Review* 1027.

[16] I take this expression from P. Pettit, *Republicanism: A Theory of Freedom and Government* (Oxford: Oxford University Press, 1997), 185.

[17] Ibid 186. I agree with Pettit's emphasis on the importance of the right to legal contestation in democratic societies, but I disagree with many aspects of his interpretation. I discuss some of the differences in what follows.

review can be justified in this way does not mean that it is the only institution that could satisfy such a right. Other types of institutions may do so as well and perhaps even more effectively. The point is not to claim that judicial review is uniquely legitimate, but simply that whether or not it is should be judged from the perspective of whether it is one of the institutions needed to secure a right of citizens that essentially amounts to a form of democratic control. If it can be shown that judicial review is necessary for securing such a right, then the claim that it is an anti-democratic institution becomes doubtful. As we saw in Bickel's influential characterization of 'the counter-majoritarian difficulty' noted above, the 'difficulty' is portrayed as a disagreement between the court's belief in the unconstitutionality of a given statute, on the one side, and the beliefs of the democratically elected legislature that enacted it, on the other. Seen from this perspective a question immediately arises: why should the beliefs of a few judges have any more moral authority than those of the people?

However, this way of looking at the issue disregards the relevant fact that citizens who bring cases to the court are the initiators of the process. This means that these *citizens* believe that a certain contested statute is unconstitutional. Since these citizens certainly belong to the people, it is quite misleading to portray the issue as one that concerns a disagreement between a few judges, on the one hand, and 'the people' on the other. Granted, the observation that the disagreement about the constitutionality of a statute is a disagreement among citizens does not justify judicial review as the best way to (temporarily) settle the disagreement. Additional arguments would be needed. However, this shift in perspective reveals the inadequacy of approaches that start by framing judicial review as a disagreement between the courts and the people and then, without further argument, go on to claim that it is a democratically illegitimate practice. Judicial review does indeed harbour 'a counter-majoritarian difficulty', but it is important to keep in mind that this difficulty concerns a disagreement *among the people*. So, Bickel is right to claim the Supreme Court thwarts the will of representatives of the people when it declares a legislative act unconstitutional, but this is not the same as claiming that it thwarts the will of the people—unless, for some incomprehensible reason, the citizens the Court agrees with are not supposed to be part of 'the people'.[18]

However, even authors like Pettit who interpret and justify legal contestation as a form of democratic control still conceptualize this contestation as an apolitical affair, as a depoliticized venue that removes the issue from political debate among citizens.[19] Legal contestation is portrayed as an apolitical mechanism that individuals have at their disposal in order to counteract the tyranny of the majority. This is precisely what justifies judicial review over legislative supremacy, according to this view. As Pettit notes, the legal complaints of individuals 'should be heard away from the tumult of

---

[18] In the present context, it would be embarrassingly circular to claim that only the acts of the legislature express the will of the people even when they are in tension with those of other political venues (eg the executive, the judiciary, citizen initiatives, referenda, etc.). Even Waldron acknowledges that commitment to the validity of majority rule is compatible with believing that 'minorities are entitled to a degree of support, recognition and insulation that is not necessarily guaranteed by their numbers or by their political weight' (Waldron, 2006, above n 2, 1364).

[19] See Pettit, above n 16, and 'Depoliticizing Democracy', in S. Besson and J. L. Martí (eds), *Deliberative Democracy and its Discontents* (Aldershot: Ashgate, 2006), 93–106.

popular discussion and away, even, from the theater of parliamentary debate'.[20]In this same vein, Dworkin characterizes judicial review as an apolitical process and ties the legitimacy of the institution to the fact that it enables reasoned debate on issues of principle that are 'removed from ordinary politics'.[21] Unsurprisingly, this picture of judicial review immediately raises the anti-democratic objection. Indeed, if the purpose of judicial review were to successfully isolate the revision of democratic legislation from public political debate it would jeopardize the equal political rights *of the rest of the citizenry* to engage and shape the process of constitutional review.[22] If this picture were accurate, then Waldron would be right to characterize such a legal practice as 'a mode of citizen involvement that is undisciplined by the principles of political equality'.[23]

IV. Judicial Review as Conversation Initiator

There is no obvious reason why individuals or groups who make use of the right to legal contestation should merely be taken in their role as private persons subject to the law, and not *also* in their role as citizens who are co-authors of the law.[24] On such a limited perspective the act of questioning the constitutionality of legislation is not politically significant. Even Waldron questions the view (although with a different argumentative aim) that citizens who utilize their right to legal contestation are simply exercising a private right as individual persons and not a political right as citizens. As he notes,

> plaintiffs or petitioners are selected by advocacy groups precisely in order to embody the abstract characteristics that the groups want to emphasize as part of a general public policy argument. The particular idiosyncrasies of the individual litigants have usually dropped out of sight by the time the U.S. Supreme Court addresses the issue, and the Court almost always addresses the issue in general terms.[25]

Given that the aim of the process is to review the constitutionality of a piece of legislation, it is hardly surprising that litigants see the process as one that concerns not just their specific private interests—as in other forms of litigation—but one that is

---

[20] Pettit explains: 'There are a variety of contestations where popular debate would give the worst possible sort of hearing to the complaints involved. In these cases, the requirement of contestatory democracy is that the complaints should be depoliticized and should be heard away from the tumult of popular discussion and away, even, from the theater of parliamentary debate. In such instances, democracy requires recourse to the relative quiet of the parliamentary, cross-party committee, or the standing appeals board or the quasi-judicial tribunal, or the autonomous, professionalized body. It is only in that sort of quiet … that the contestations in question can receive a decent hearing' (Pettit, above n 16, 196).

[21] Dworkin, 1996, above n 3, 30.

[22] The democratic antidote for the illicit politicization of constitutional questions is not *isolation from political debate* but rather the *constitutionalization of political debate*. As I argue in what follows, judicial review plays a key role in facilitating this process and, to the extent that it does, it serves a genuinely democratic function.

[23] Waldron, 2006, above n 2, 1395.

[24] I do not mean to deny the standing that litigants have before the court, which makes them subject to the law, or the possibility that litigants might pursue purely private goals. Instead, my point is simply to question the view that it is democratically illegitimate for litigants to pursue judicial review with genuinely political aims. This remains the case for litigants who are not citizens. But, since I will not focus on the specifics of this particular case, I speak of citizens throughout for the sake of simplicity.

[25] Waldron, 2006, above n 2, 1380.

essentially about the appropriateness of some general public policy. This observation can only be seen as an objection to judicial review or an embarrassment for its defenders if we assume, as authors across both camps commonly do, that initiating the legal process of constitutional review is not a task to be undertaken by *citizens* with political aims, but rather a task to be delegated to the courts that is triggered by private subjects pursuing exclusively personal aims. However, once legal contestation is seen as a political form of citizen involvement, Waldron's characterization of the process as 'a mode of citizen involvement that is undisciplined by the principles of political equality'[26] doesn't seem quite right. Waldron portrays citizens' use of legal contestation as an attempt to obtain an unfair advantage over other citizens who limit their participation to the normal political process. The idea is that citizens are political equals to the extent that they have an equal right to vote, and that those who look to judicial review after having been outvoted in the political process are simply trying to get 'greater weight for their opinions than electoral politics will give them'. Therefore, 'the attitudes towards one's fellow citizens that judicial review conveys are not respectable'.[27]

There are several problems with this picture.[28] First of all, citizens have equal rights to legal contestation. From a purely process-related perspective, exercising the right to legal contestation is not obviously 'undisciplined by the principles of political equality'. The path to legal contestation is in principle open to all citizens.[29] The mere fact that certain citizens initiate a legal process to contest a piece of legislation does not preclude other citizens from litigating their cases, presenting their own legal arguments, picking their preferred venues, and so forth. Even after the process has reached a final verdict in the Supreme Court, nothing prevents citizens from mobilizing for a referendum on an amendment proposal or similar political measures. More to the point, the reference to political equality in Waldron's characterization of judicial review suggests a misleading analogy between the right to legal contestation and the right to vote. Whereas the latter gives citizens decision-making authority, the former does not give citizens any such right. The right to legal contestation does not give citizens any right whatsoever to *decide* a case. What it gives them is the power to request a fair review of a case on the basis of reasoned arguments. The right to legal contestation is a right to a fair hearing of arguments and objections against a statute that purportedly violates the constitution. It gives citizens the opportunity to try to convince the court and other citizens of the merits of their case. But precisely because the process is driven by the merits, there is no sense in which the litigants are getting some extra or unfair political influence.[30] By

---

[26] Ibid 1395.   [27] Ibid.

[28] Here I am focusing only on the difficulties of Waldron's conception of political equality as it bears on the question of judicial review. For insightful criticisms of Waldron's conception of political equality in general see T. Christiano, 'Waldron on Law and Disagreement' (2000) 19 *Law and Philosophy* 513, at 513–43; and D. Estlund, 'Jeremy Waldron on Law and Disagreement' (2000) 99 *Philosophical Studies* 111, at 111–28.

[29] But see next note.

[30] Just in case some readers may get impatient at this point, let me note that we cannot address the issue of whether the judges are getting an unfair political influence without begging the question. Whether or not the judges' influence is unfair depends in part on whether citizens should have a right to legal contestation in the first place, which is what we are trying to figure out. Other readers may worry that wealthier citizens are likely to get an unfair political advantage due to the easier access to the courts that wealth provides. This is indeed worrisome. However, as an empirical matter, the worry equally extends to the easier access that wealth provides to all branches of government and not just to the courts. These empirical questions fall

using the legal venue, litigants do not acquire any power to make their views and arguments any more or less convincing than they actually are. The right to legal contestation is more modest. It gives citizens a right to be listened to, to open or reopen a conversation based on arguments about the constitutionality of a statute, so that explicit and reasoned justifications for and against the statute in question become available for public deliberation.

Granted, the political process also allows for that kind of reasoned deliberation in both the legislature and the public sphere. However, it cannot guarantee it. Even with minimally complex pieces of legislation it is not possible to anticipate all the repercussions and differential impacts that they may have on the fundamental rights of different citizens and groups as a result of their application under changing social and historical circumstances. Statutes and policies often do not wear their potential unconstitutionality on their sleeves, so to speak. Consequently, there is no way to guarantee that, for each piece of legislation, the political process will reliably identify all potential collisions with the fundamental rights of different citizens and groups, such that they can be pre-emptively subjected to proper political deliberation and ruled out with convincing arguments. Indeed, as Waldron himself recognizes, those citizens directly affected by the contested statutes or policies are more likely to detect the specific ways in which they infringe upon their rights than other citizens or politicians. Moreover, since there are bound to be disagreements among citizens regarding whether or not the statute in question violates rights, it is unlikely that those who fail to see any merits in the case will engage in a reasoned revision of their own accord, since, from their perspective, there is nothing in particular to deliberate about or revise.[31]

While Waldron recognizes this point, he treats it as a purely outcome-related consideration. He conceptualizes the instrumental value of judicial review from an epistemic perspective that sees those affected as more reliable at identifying potential rights violations, and he recognizes that 'it is useful to have a mechanism that allows citizens to bring these issues to everyone's attention as they arise'.[32] However, he argues that there are other mechanisms that can fulfil this same epistemic function such as charging the attorney general with a 'duty to scrutinize legislative proposals and publicly identify any issues of rights that they raise'.[33] From a purely epistemic perspective, such an alternative procedure has major weaknesses: rights issues may become visible only after the subsequent application of the law, and they may only be 'visible' to the affected individuals while the rest of the citizenry continues to be blind to them. However, leaving these weaknesses aside, the main problem with assessing the right to legal contestation

outside the scope of a normative analysis of the legitimacy of the institutions in question, since the latter must operate under the assumption that these institutions are equally capable of doing what they are set up to do if it is to avoid begging the question.

[31] It is noticeable that Waldron's argument relies on examples of issues that have already become constitutional issues, such as abortion, affirmative action, or capital punishment. However, such examples are not particularly helpful for the question under discussion, since what we are asking is what set of institutions would be most conducive to ensure that questions of fundamental rights are reliably *identified* as such in spite of deep moral and political disagreements among citizens. In order to assess the relative contribution that different institutions may make to *that* task we need to adopt a *prospective* perspective that does not assume the task in question has already been accomplished.

[32] Waldron, 2006, above n 2, 1370.   [33] Ibid.

from a purely instrumental perspective is that it fails to recognize the right's intrinsic political value.

Perhaps the best way to highlight this intrinsic political value is by thinking of a case where *per hypothesis* we can rule out any instrumental value. Let's imagine a small group of citizens is convinced that a particular statute violates some of their fundamental rights, but that the rest of the citizenry cannot see any merit in the case at all. Since the constitutionality of statutes is often difficult to discern and disagreements are pervasive in politics, chances are that a contested statute is constitutional if an overwhelming majority of citizens think that it is. In such an imagined scenario, the citizenry is very unlikely to engage in a thorough and reasoned debate where all the necessary evidence and arguments are provided so as to convincingly rebut the opinion of the dissenting group of citizens. But this does not have to be an indication that they do not care about rights or that they are acting in bad faith. After all, there are only so many wrong views that citizens can devote time and energy towards trying to disprove by collecting the needed evidence, providing suitable reasons and justifications, responding to all kinds of counterarguments, and so on. Surely it cannot be the obligation of citizens or the legislature to address every complaint that citizens might have regardless of how plausible it appears. But this is precisely the kind of obligation that the courts are well suited to discharge.

What the political process cannot possibly *guarantee*, the legal process typically does: the individual right to a fair hearing in which explicit, reasoned justifications for and against a contested statute become publicly available for political deliberation. In the hypothetical situation just considered, the right to legal contestation did not have any instrumental value from an outcome-related perspective. It was not useful at all since *per hypothesis* the statute did not violate the rights of the litigants and, consequently, their political equality had in fact been preserved alongside the political equality of the rest of the citizenry. But even if the litigants lost their case, exercising their right to legal contestation had the intrinsic, expressive value of reinforcing the political community's commitment to treating all citizens as free and equal. Given the ubiquity of political disagreement in democratic societies, it is not enough that a political community does not in fact violate the fundamental rights of its citizens. It must also be willing to show that it respects them when challenged by citizens' objections to the contrary. The right to legal contestation guarantees that all citizens can, on their own initiative, open or reopen a deliberative process in which reasons and justifications in support of the contested statute are made publicly available, such that they can be inspected and challenged with counterarguments that may eventually lead to a change in public opinion. If citizens owe one another justifications for the laws they collectively impose on one another,[34] then it seems to be a necessary component

---

[34] I take this formulation from A. Gutmann and D. Thompson, *Why Deliberative Democracy?* (Princeton: Princeton University Press, 2004), 133. For similar defences of mutual justifiability as a criterion of democratic legitimacy, see eg Rawls, 1993, above n 3, 217–20; Habermas, above n 3, 107–11; J. Cohen, *Philosophy, Politics, Democracy: Selected Essays* (Cambridge, Mass.: Harvard University Press, 2009), ch 10, 330; I offer a specific interpretation and defence of this criterion of democratic legitimacy in C. Lafont, 'Is the Ideal of Deliberative Democracy Coherent?', in Besson and Martí, above n 19, 3–26.

of legislative legitimacy that citizens have the ability to initiate the process of publicly reasoned justification when they believe their fundamental rights are violated by some statute or policy.

From this perspective, the right to legal contestation guarantees all citizens that their communicative power, their ability to trigger political deliberation on issues of fundamental rights, won't fall below some acceptable minimum regardless of how implausible, unpopular, or idiosyncratic their beliefs may happen to be.[35] If citizens are strongly convinced that their rights are violated, then they have the power to make themselves heard, to reignite the conversation, and to receive upon request proper answers to their argumentative challenges independently of the epistemic merits of their views *as judged by other citizens*. As indicated above, the political process cannot guarantee such a communicative minimum in the same way that legal venues can, but this has nothing to do with *pathological* circumstances that may afflict the legislature and impede its proper functioning. It simply follows from the 'circumstances of politics' that Waldron himself highlights.[36]

A. The fact of disagreement and its predictable consequences

Given the majoritarian mechanism of political decision-making and the enduring presence of disagreement it is inevitable that majoritarian decisions on particular statutes or policies will align with the views of some citizens but not with those of others. Electoral politics will predictably give citizens 'greater weight for their opinions' if their views happen to align with those of the decisional majority. Indeed, the more unpopular the views the less weight they will have in the electoral process. Thus, when it comes to highly idiosyncratic views, it is perfectly possible that the weight of these opinions falls below some minimal threshold within the electoral process. Again, this predictable circumstance has nothing to do with a majority that either does not care about rights or is acting in bad faith. It is simply a consequence of the fact that (1) ordinary citizens as well as politicians have strong moral and political disagreements, (2) they are supposed to judge the appropriateness of legislation strictly on its merits, and (3) they cannot have the obligation to properly address and debunk every idiosyncratic belief that each individual citizen or group may have. Given these predictable circumstances, the right to legal contestation helps ensure the fair value of the right to political equality for all citizens.[37] It makes sure that their communicative power won't fall below an acceptable minimum—as it might, if it were made to exclusively depend upon the substantive merits of their opinions *as judged by other citizens*. Judges have a legal obligation to examine the complaints of litigants, to listen to their arguments, and to provide a reasoned answer even if they ultimately find that the opinion in question has little

---

[35] On the notion of communicative power see Habermas, above n 3, 151–67.

[36] Adapting Rawls's discussion of the 'circumstances of justice', Waldron defines the 'circumstances of politics' as 'the felt need among the members of a certain group for a common framework or decision or course of action on some matter, even in the face of disagreement about what that framework, decision or action should be' (Waldron, 1999, above n 2, 102).

[37] On the notion of securing the fair value of political rights and liberties see Rawls, 1993, above n 3, 5.

merit and they therefore rule against the litigants. Citizens cannot know in advance whether decisional majorities will tend to agree with their views about fundamental rights or whether their views will be seen as marginal and idiosyncratic. They therefore have good *prospective* reasons to insist upon an equal right to legal contestation that assures each citizen will have a minimum level of communicative power whenever questions of fundamental rights are at stake. Such a right provides the power to make oneself heard and to influence public opinion, to have the opposing majority listen to one's counterarguments, and to have them addressed. Even if they lose, the process of reasoned debate allows litigants to examine the specific reasoning behind the decision, so that if they continue to disagree they can look for counterarguments and gather factual evidence that might lead to a change of public opinion in the future.[38] Granted, the argument for a right to legal contestation does not address the question of whether we should prefer weaker or stronger forms of judicial review. But it should cast some serious doubt upon the view that democratic concerns about political equality speak against any form of judicial review. If we broaden the perspective from the individual citizen to the political system as a whole we can identify additional reasons to doubt such a view.

V. The Democratic Significance of the Forum of Principle

When I surveyed the arguments in favour of judicial review offered by authors such as Dworkin and Pettit I rejected their characterization of the process as being non-political. I did so from the perspective of citizens who make use of the institution. However, these authors highlight an important difference between the legal and the political processes that needs to be taken into consideration. In his defence of the legitimacy of judicial review Dworkin draws an important distinction between the judicial and the political process. Whereas the former takes place in the 'forum of principle' the latter is a majoritarian process that 'encourages compromises that may subordinate important issues of principle'.[39] Waldron criticizes this contrast by arguing that it presupposes pathological circumstances and that it therefore has no place in a normative theory about the normal functioning of the judicial and legislative branches of government within democratic societies. The legitimacy of judicial review must be judged under the normative assumption that all branches of government are equally capable of doing what they are set up to do. Since the legislature is supposed to take the constitutionality of the legislation it passes into account, it should be as concerned about protecting rights as any other branch of government. Therefore, it would beg the question to characterize the judiciary as the only branch of government that is properly sensitive to principle and to dismiss the legislature as incapable of meeting its own obligations. A legislature in a society under particularly pathological circumstances might be unable to meet these obligations and therefore setting up special institutions to compensate for such pathologies might be an appropriate step. But this hypothetical scenario is not

---

[38] See the text surrounding n 48 below.   [39] Dworkin, 1985, above n 3, 30.

a normative argument in favour of judicial review that would apply to societies without such pathologies or in societies attempting to set up new democracies.

Waldron's argument suggests that, based on what they are ideally set up to do, the judiciary and the legislature are both equally 'forums of principle'. However, this assumption seems to give no consideration to the obvious fact that each of these institutions is set up to do very different things. It is hard to deny that the political process encourages compromises as part of what it is set up to do, namely, to reach agreements among different parties in order to achieve specific political goals. Passing legislation requires a good faith effort to reach fair compromises across different political parties, interests, and views. Now, if statutes and policies do not wear their potential unconstitutionality 'on their sleeves', so to speak, then it won't always be clear in advance whether the outcomes of political compromises are problematic. It is always possible that some of these compromises may have subordinated important issues of principle. This is so, not because legislatures are more susceptible to pathologies than other institutions, but rather because they are in charge of making all kinds of political decisions—most of which are not matters of principle. Indeed, if political compromises among different parties are needed in order to achieve important political goals for a community, then it would be quite harmful if parties treated every political decision as a matter of principle. The legislature should not be the forum of principle because *per design* it should be a genuinely political forum. Similarly, the public sphere should not simply be a forum of principle, since a great deal of political deliberation is not about matters of principle, but rather about the various kinds of political goals that the political community would like to achieve, the most efficient ways to reach them, etc. And, since it is often not obvious which political decisions may have constitutional implications, political deliberation *in general* should not be conceived of on the model of a forum of principle.[40] By contrast, an institution in charge of checking the constitutionality of statutes is *per design* a forum of principle. But this is only possible precisely because *per design* it is not an institution in charge of making political decisions of all kinds like legislatures. This has nothing to do with the moral character of their respective members, but with an institutional division of labour. From this perspective, Dworkin's observation that 'the majoritarian process encourages compromises that may subordinate important issues of principle'[41] should not be read as commentary on the pathological character of politicians, but instead as an obvious consequence of the fact that there is no way to know in advance all the potential issues of principle (eg the infringement of some fundamental right) that any piece of legislation may bring about. However, this fact does not undermine the legitimacy of a democratic political system, so long as citizens in that system have the right to legal contestation, that is, the right to receive a fair examination of their claim that a specific statute or policy infringes upon their fundamental rights. As long as citizens may question the constitutionality of any statute by initiating a legal challenge, they can *structure* public debate on the statute in question as a debate about

---

[40] This is not to deny that the public sphere ought to become a forum of principle when political deliberation focuses on policies or statutes that touch upon fundamental rights and issues of basic justice. I discuss this issue in the next section.

[41] Dworkin, 1985, above n 3, 30.

fundamental rights, and therefore a debate in which the priority of public reasons (to use Rawlsian terms) must be respected. [42] From this perspective the political significance of the process of judicial review is that it functions as a *conversation initiator* on the constitutionality of any specific policy or statute. In so doing, it facilitates the constitutionalization of political debate in the public sphere.

VI. Citizens in Robes: The Public Sphere as a Forum of Principle

The right to legal contestation allows citizens to structure the public debate on a particular statute or policy as one about fundamental rights—even if other citizens or the legislature had not framed the debate in those terms or had failed to foresee the impact of the statute on the fundamental rights of certain citizens. This in turn has important implications for the question of political equality. Given the fact of pluralism, citizens are bound to disagree about the right way to frame a political debate. However, other things being equal, democratic societies should err on the side of making sure that fundamental rights are not violated. But how can this be achieved? How can political debate be bent in such a way without giving preferential treatment or superior authority to anyone's views or beliefs? If participants in political debate are supposed to judge the issues on their merits, that is, on the basis of their own convictions, there is no particular reason to assume that unfettered political debate would allow citizens with unpopular or idiosyncratic beliefs to structure the debate in a way that goes against what the majority of citizens genuinely find persuasive. If this analysis is correct, then an extra device would be needed in order to *err* on the side of making sure that those who believe that some fundamental rights are violated have their claims properly scrutinized and appropriately answered, even if most people are convinced that such claims are wrong on their merits. The right to legal contestation allows citizens to structure the public political debate in such a way that priority is given to the question of whether or not a contested statute violates some fundamental right, even if such structuring does not seem antecedently plausible to the rest of the citizenry. In that sense, we can say with Waldron that these citizens are trying to get 'greater weight for their opinions than electoral politics will give them'. However, we need to be more specific about the *aspect* of their opinions that is getting greater weight by virtue of their right to legal contestation. The 'greater weight' in question is not about *getting the outcome* that they think is right. If we assume that a democratic system is functioning normally, then there is nothing they can do to force judges to rule in their favour. Rather, the 'greater weight' they are seeking is about *receiving the kind of scrutiny* that they think is appropriate and we all agree they deserve, as free and equal citizens, even if we think that they are plainly wrong about the particular case. [43] Indeed, the claim that the contested statute

---

[42] See J. Rawls, 'The Idea of Public Reason', in Rawls, 1993, above n 3, 212–54; and J. Rawls, 'The Idea of Public Reason Revisited', in J. Rawls, *The Law of Peoples* (Cambridge, Mass.: Harvard University Press, 1999), 129–80.

[43] This argument points to a tension between Waldron's assumption that, in the ideal normative case under consideration, there is a strong and general commitment to *protecting rights* in society (Waldron, 2006, above n 2, 1364) and that political equality requires *giving equal weight to all opinions* (ibid 1364). It

violates a fundamental right may turn out to be wrong, and litigants may not be able to change public opinion. But even in such a case they still have the right to receive an explicit reasoned justification about why the statute does not in fact violate their rights and is therefore compatible with treating them as free and equal.

Moreover, for those who continue to disagree, this reasoned justification in turn highlights the reasons, arguments, and evidence that they would need to more effectively undermine in order to change public opinion on the matter. Although examples are always problematic, the debate on same-sex marriage in the United States offers a good illustration here. For decades the issue was treated in public debate as turning on the meaning of marriage. On that question, there was widespread agreement that marriage is between a man and a woman.[44] However, once political initiatives for state constitutional amendments to ban same-sex marriage became part of the political agenda, and citizens legally contested such initiatives in the courts, the focus of public deliberation switched from an ethical and religious debate on the meaning of marriage to a constitutional debate on equal treatment and fundamental rights.[45] Judicial review on the constitutionality of state bans on same-sex marriage led public debate to treat the issue as a matter of principle or, to use Rawls's expression, as a matter of constitutional essentials. Quite surprisingly, once the debate became structured in that way, an astonishing switch in public opinion took place in favour of same-sex marriage.[46]

Although this development is a complex empirical issue, it is hard to avoid the impression that once the debate became a constitutional debate, many of the citizens who were against same-sex marriage on the basis of their religious or ethical views about the meaning of marriage could not find convincing reasons to justify unequal treatment under the law, and that they therefore changed their minds about *whether it should be legal*.[47] Given the astonishingly short period of time within which that change in public opinion has taken place, there is no reason to assume that the majority of citizens who initially opposed same-sex marriage were all acting in bad faith or

---

is not clear how the first assumption could find practical or institutional expression without any deviation from the second assumption.

[44] Indeed, in 1996 the US Congress passed the Defense of Marriage Act (DOMA), which President Bill Clinton subsequently signed. For federal purposes, section 3 of DOMA defines marriage as the union of a man and a woman. Needless to say, the 'widespread agreement' on the meaning of marriage was not shared among members of the LGTB minority. See n 48.

[45] In 1998 Hawaii and Alaska became the first US states to pass constitutional amendments against same-sex marriage. Other US states followed suit and passed similar amendments in the following years, reaching a peak of thirty-one in 2012. In June 2015 the US Supreme Court ruled that the US Constitution guarantees all citizens the right to enter into same-sex marriages.

[46] According to Pew Research polling', in 2001, Americans opposed same-sex marriage by a 57% to 35% margin. Since then, support for same-sex marriage has steadily grown. Based on polling in 2015, a majority of Americans (55%) support same-sex marriage, compared with 39% who oppose it.' Data available at http://www.pewforum.org/2015/07/29/graphics-slideshow-changing-attitudes-on-gay-marriage/.

[47] Given the short period of time under consideration, the changes in attitude are only partly due to generational change. As the Pew Research data shows, older generations have consistently become more supportive of same-sex marriage in recent years. It is also interesting to notice that the change in attitude concerns the narrow question of whether same-sex marriage should be legal and not necessarily the ethical or religious beliefs concerning homosexuality (eg 49 per cent of Americans believe that engaging in homosexual behaviour is a sin). See data available at http://www.pewforum.org/2015/07/29/graphics-slideshow-changing-attitudes-on-gay-marriage/.

that they were unconcerned about rights and not attending to reasons. Under such an assumption it would be hard to explain why they changed their minds. However, there are good reasons to assume that, without the extra power that the right to legal contestation granted litigants such that they could *structure* the political debate as a constitutional debate about fundamental rights, the 'unfettered' political debate in the public sphere would have continued to turn on religious and ethical questions about which citizens strongly disagree.[48] As a consequence, the religious and ethical views of the majority about the meaning of marriage would have continued to dictate policy. By contrast, once the public debate became framed in constitutional terms the standards of scrutiny characteristic of judicial review (eg identifying the relevant government interests, investigating the proportionality of the means, weighting the empirical evidence, etc.) allowed litigants to get traction within and ultimately transform the views of the majority.

Indeed, whereas it is unclear what standard of scrutiny could be used to resolve debates over the meaning of marriage amongst citizens holding different religious and ethical views, it is quite clear that the standards of scrutiny appropriate for a constitutional debate about fundamental rights gives rise to forms of argumentative entanglement that allow citizens to call each other to account, gather and weight factual evidence 'for' and 'against' proposals, and transform one another's views over time as a consequence. In the example of the debate over same-sex marriage, the review process required its opponents to identify the specific government interests that justify the ban. Once such interests were publicly identified (eg protecting the health and welfare of children, fostering procreation within a marital setting, etc.) the debate began to turn on questions for which factual evidence could be decisive in settling the answer (eg statistical evidence about the welfare of children raised in same-sex couple households, the existence of married couples unable to procreate, etc.).

If we focus on the political empowerment that the right to legal contestation gives to citizens, we can see the politically significant sense in which the courts can play the institutional role of *conversation initiators*. As Bickel points out 'virtually all important decisions of the Supreme Court are the beginnings of conversations between the Court and the people and their representatives'.[49] This is certainly true in many cases, but it is important to pay attention to the specific sense in which it is true. It is not that the courts begin the conversation on their own initiative or that they lead the debate because judges have superior moral insight or are more sensitive to principle. This juricentric perspective mischaracterizes the actual dynamics of political debate on important and highly contested issues. More often than not, conversations surrounding

[48] *Baehr v Lewin* 74 Hawaii 530 (1993) was the first lawsuit seeking to have the ban on same-sex marriages declared unconstitutional that led to a positive ruling on the question. The Supreme Court of the US state of Hawaii ruled that, under the state's equal protection clause, denying marriage licences to same-sex couples constituted discrimination based on sex that the state needed to justify under the standard known as strict scrutiny, that is, by demonstrating that it 'furthers compelling state interests and is narrowly drawn to avoid unnecessary abridgments of constitutional rights'. This finding prompted Congress to pass the Defense of Marriage Act (DOMA) and many states to pass constitutional amendments to ban same-sex marriages. See nn 44 and 45.

[49] A. M. Bickel, *The Supreme Court and the Idea of Progress* (New Haven: Yale University Press, 1978), 91.

contested political issues have been present within the public sphere long before such issues are legally contested. But conversations that had been structured in a variety of disparate ways become *constitutional* conversations by (at the latest) the time they reach the Supreme Court precisely in virtue of citizens' right to submit contested issues to the sluices of judicial review.[50]

If this account is plausible, then the normative contribution of the institution of judicial review is not, as Dworkin and Pettit suggest, that it makes it possible to answer questions about the constitutionality of a contested statute or policy in isolation from political debate. To the contrary, the important contribution of the courts—which are indeed 'depoliticized' in the sense of being a forum of principle (ie a forum that *per design* specifically focuses on the question of the constitutionality of statutes)—has nothing to do with isolating their decisions from the political debate among all citizens in the public sphere. Indeed, the fact that relevant contributions to the debate from external parties can be included through filing of *amicus curiae* briefs speaks against this isolationist view. Most importantly, as Dworkin mentions in passing, if the issue under consideration is important enough 'it can be expected to be elaborated, expanded, contracted or even reversed by future decisions, a sustained national debate begins, in newspapers and other media, in law schools and classrooms, in public meetings and around dinner tables'.[51] From a holistic and diachronic perspective, the democratic contribution of judicial review is not that the courts undertake constitutional review in isolation from the political debate in the public sphere, as if justice needs to be in robes in order to properly attend to matters of principle.[52] To the contrary, from a democratic perspective, the main contribution of the institution is that it empowers citizens to call the rest of the citizenry to put on their robes in order to publicly debate rights-related constitutional issues as matters of principle.[53]

[50] Dworkin points at this idea when he claims that judicial review 'forces political debate to include argument over principle, not only when a case comes to the Court but also long before and long after' (Dworkin, 1985, above n 3, 70).
[51] Dworkin, 1996, above n 3, 345.
[52] See R. Dworkin, *Justice in Robes* (Cambridge, Mass.: Harvard University Press, 2006).
[53] I offer a detailed articulation of this view in C. Lafont, 'Religious Pluralism in a Deliberative Democracy', in F. Requejo and C. Ungureanu (eds), *Democracy, Law and Religious Pluralism in Europe* (London: Routledge, 2014), 46–60.

PART IV

CONSTITUTIONAL RIGHTS AND THEIR LIMITATION

14

Equality Rights and Stereotypes

*Sophia Moreau**

Equality rights seem to be fundamental to the very idea of a democratic constitution. Perhaps this is partly because the value of equality is so intimately connected with political legitimacy. No government or public authority can claim legitimacy if it does not treat people, in some important sense, *as equals*. This may be because it is a deep moral truth about us that we are all, in fact, of equal value. Or, more modestly, we may prefer to claim only that a democratic state must, for political purposes, assume that the people that it governs are all of equal value and hence are deserving of equal respect. Either way, political legitimacy seems to require that the state acknowledge that it stands under an obligation to treat those whom it governs as equals.

In this respect, equality arguably differs from many of the values that ground other kinds of rights that are commonly given constitutional protection, such as mobility rights or rights to freedom of expression, association, or religion. One can imagine a democratic society that simply chooses not to give constitutional protection to one of these other kinds of rights. We might criticize this society's decision on a number of different grounds: for instance, that it fails to acknowledge the full moral importance of these interests; that it is unjust; or that it is illiberal. But most theories of political legitimacy, whether procedural or substantive, would not imply that such a government was thereby rendered illegitimate. By contrast, a democratic government that refused to recognize a constitutional obligation to treat individuals as equals would seem illegitimate, on most plausible conceptions of political legitimacy.

One might argue that, although this is true, it does not show that a constitution needs to recognize a special kind of right called an 'equality right'. Taking Peter Westen's view of equality, one might suggest that all that follows from these reflections on legitimacy is that whatever constitutional rights a government ought to give to citizens, these rights must be given, equally, to every person.[1] On this view, there is no need for a further constitutional right to equality: all that a government is required to do, in order to treat people as equals, is to ensure that each person is given the same (or a morally equivalent) bundle of rights.

But interestingly, this is not what most democratic countries seem to believe. Most of them seem to believe that governments do have a special constitutional obligation to treat those whom they govern as equals, in some sense that goes above and beyond simply giving them all an equal bundle of rights. For most democratic constitutions

---

* Associate Professor, Faculty of Law and Department of Philosophy, University of Toronto.
[1] P. Westen, 'The Empty Idea of Equality' (1982) 95 *Harvard Law Review* 7, at 537.

do include an additional and very explicit right to equality, either within a section of a written constitution, such as the American Fourteenth Amendment or section 15 of Canada's *Charter of Rights and Freedoms*, or through legislation such as the United Kingdom's 2010 *Equality Act*. These laws place the state under obligations of non-discrimination, requiring it to avoid discriminating against individuals on the basis of certain personal traits, such as race, sex, sexual orientation, religion, age, and disability. They do not, however, explicitly define 'discrimination' or explain when and why it is unjustified. And so they raise an important set of questions. What is it about treating some people differently on the basis of certain kinds of characteristics—such as race, sex, or religion—that denies these people's status as equals? And why do we think that denying people this status is different from, and from a moral standpoint, probably even more serious than simply failing to respect another constitutional right of theirs, such as a mobility right? In other words, how can we make sense of what discrimination involves, in a way that might explain why we require constitutional protection from it by means of a distinctive right to equality?

My aim in this chapter is not to settle these questions so much as to point us in the direction of where the debate should be. And I want to do this by exploring a view of discrimination that has recently gained popularity, partly within the United States in the context of litigation over sex discrimination, and even more prominently within Canadian constitutional law as the dominant view of what makes discrimination on the basis of *any* protected trait wrongful. This view holds that when discrimination is not motivated by prejudice or malice, what makes it wrongful or unfair is the presence of tacit *stereotyping*—that is, reliance on a generalization about a group and the traits that its members have by virtue of membership in that group. I shall argue that this view is mistaken: the mere fact that a law embodies or relies on a stereotype is not, on its own, sufficient to make that law unfairly discriminatory. But this view is so plausible, I think, partly because the idea of a stereotype seems to offer us a number of compelling explanations of why we need to give special constitutional protection to equality rights. That is, the idea of a stereotype seems to capture some of the particularly outrageous ways in which the state can fail to treat us as equals, even if it meticulously grants us many other important constitutional rights. I shall try to show, however, that what does the real moral work in these explanations is not any intrinsic feature of a stereotype qua stereotype, but rather certain harmful effects that particular stereotypes involving traits such as race, sex, and religion have on members of these groups, given the histories of maltreatment and exclusion of these groups in our societies. Such stereotypes often deprive individuals from already underprivileged groups of important opportunities, thereby undermining their freedom or their autonomy, they sometimes carry demeaning messages about these groups, suggesting that they are less than fully human, and they can reinforce or implicitly sanction long-standing prejudices in the mind of the public. I shall argue that it is harmful effects such as these that we ought to think of as central to a law's failure to treat people as equals; and I shall suggest that we need to think further about whether it is just one of these effects, or a combination of them, that equality rights are best understood as protecting us against. But if this is correct, then we do not need to appeal to the concept of a stereotype in order to make sense of discrimination. The concept of a stereotype turns out to be pedagogically useful in pointing us to the terrain where the debate about the purpose of equality rights should take place; but it does not itself need to be used, either as evidence of discrimination or as part of an explanation of why it is wrong. Instead, we need to ask which harmful effects are relevant to the unfairness of discrimination, and whether all of those harms that seem relevant can coherently be brought into a single unitary theory of discrimination or whether a pluralistic theory seems more appropriate.

This chapter is in five sections. I begin with two very brief discussions: section I looks at the concept of a stereotype and section II presents some of the ways in which stereotypes have been regarded as central to racial and sex discrimination in American constitutional law and as central to all forms of discrimination in Canadian constitutional law. Section III tests the idea that stereotypes can explain what is unfair about cases of wrongful discrimination. Here, I draw out a number of different possible explanations of why stereotyping renders discriminatory acts unfair, and I argue that it is actually not anything about stereotypes per se that explains this, but rather certain harmful effects that stereotypes based on prohibited grounds of discrimination can have in certain situations. Section IV presents a number of cases in which there appears to be unfair discrimination without stereotyping. These cases cast doubt on the idea that claimants should have to provide evidence of stereotyping in order to support a claim of unfair discrimination. Finally, section V of the chapter appeals to the various harmful effects that were laid out in section III, in order to argue that we need to refocus our debates about the purpose of equality rights directly on these harms. It is here, and not in the idea of a stereotype, that we will find our answers to the question of why we need special equality rights in our constitutions.

I. What Is a Stereotype?

Like many of the abstract nouns in our language, which conceal in their etymologies metaphors based on very tangible things or processes,[2] the word 'stereotype' hides a metaphor, one based on eighteenth-century printmaking. In the eighteenth century, metal plates called 'stereotypes' were cast from moulds of the original wooden blocks set with letters, and these stereotypes allowed printers to make multiple copies of a page without having constantly to reset the letters on the wooden block. The term acquired its abstract meaning of today largely through the writings of the American journalist and political commentator Walter Lippmann.[3] He used the phrase 'cultural stereotype' to describe the way in which people tend to generalize about others before observing them: he noted that, rather than observing first and then generalizing, people tend to filter all of their observations about others through certain preconceived notions.[4]

---

[2] Think of 'spirit', whose Latin root means 'breath'; or 'expression', which literally means 'to squeeze out'. For a beautiful discussion of the metaphors concealed in many abstract terms, see O. Barfield, *The Rediscovery of Meaning and Other Essays* (Middletown, Conn.: Wesleyan University Press, 1977).

[3] W. Lippmann, *Public Opinion* (New York: Harcourt, 1922).

[4] For further discussion of Lippmann's use of the term, see R. Cook and S. Cusack, *Gender Stereotyping: Transnational Legal Perspectives* (Philadelphia: University of Pennsylvania Press, 2010); and C. Franklin, 'The Anti-Stereotyping Principle in Constitutional Sex Discrimination Law' (2010) 1 *New York University Law Review* 85, at 101.

Over time, the term 'stereotype' has come to mean any generalization about a group of people that treats them as though they are identical copies. Interestingly, just as the eighteenth-century printer's stereotype enabled him to make copies, not directly from the original wooden block, but from a *copy* of it, so our figurative 'stereotypes' are generalizations about people that are not directly based on observation of the actual individuals in the group, but are instead based upon a preconceived notion.

There is no explicit or agreed-upon legal definition of a 'stereotype', perhaps because most courts and legal scholars seem to assume that the meaning of the term is self-evident. But the definition offered by Cook and Cusack in the context of gender stereotyping in international law seems to capture a number of the features that we commonly associate with stereotypes, and so provides a good starting point for us. Cook and Cusack define a stereotype as: 'a generalized view or preconception of the attributes or characteristics possessed by, or the roles that are or should be performed by, members of a particular group'; and they add that it is usually assumed that members of the stereotyped group possess the trait or are suitable for the role in question *because* they are members of this group—for instance, that women are nurturers because they are women and this is something that comes naturally to women, rather than because each of them independently chooses to become good at nurturing.[5] Note that this definition is neutral as to the truth-value of stereotypes: they may be complete myths or falsehoods, or they may be statistically true in the sense that most group members do have the trait in question, even though a few do not. This definition allows that stereotypes may be overbroad (or may not); and of course it suggests that they are used as a substitute for consideration of particular individuals' real abilities or circumstances. It also suggests that stereotypes may harm people's autonomy by implying that the activities they should engage in, or the roles they should occupy, are set by certain allegedly natural abilities or inabilities, rather than shaped by their choices. But beyond this, this definition of a stereotype does not fully lay out the harmful effects that stereotypes may have upon the individuals who are stereotyped, or on the group as a whole. So we will have to look at particular examples of discrimination involving stereotyping in order to understand why exactly stereotyping is supposed to render particular cases of discrimination unfair. I shall consider a number of different possibilities in section III; but before that, I want to turn to the claims that have been made in American and Canadian constitutional law about the role of stereotypes in our understanding of discrimination.

II. Stereotypes in American and Canadian Constitutional Law

It is easy to see, from Cook and Cusack's definition of a stereotype, how the persistence of stereotypes about particular groups in our laws and our shared political discourse could help to *cause* discrimination. When members of a certain group are assumed to possess certain traits, or be fit for certain roles, simply by virtue of their membership in that group (when for instance, members of certain ethnic minorities are assumed to

[5] Cook and Cusack, above n 4, 9, 12.

have a propensity toward aggressive behaviour or criminality, because 'people like that just do', or every woman is assumed to want to stay at home as a caregiver, because 'of course that is what they really want') then it is more likely that we will continue to treat these groups differently and to leave in place policies or structures that systematically disadvantage them. It is also more likely that distinctions between 'people like that' and 'us' will continue to be thought of as natural and relevant instead of being questioned. Indeed, that stereotypes help to cause discrimination has been publicly recognized by a number of international human rights enforcement bodies, particularly in the context of gender-based discrimination.[6]

But courts in the United States and Canada have posited an even stronger connection between stereotypes and discrimination. They have suggested that stereotyping is not just one among many causes of discrimination, but is in some cases *what makes it unfair*. During the civil rights movement and the fight against the Jim Crow laws, American litigators suggested that it was a violation of the Fourteenth Amendment for the state to act in ways that reinforced stereotypical assumptions about the relative abilities and proper social roles of blacks and whites. Similar arguments were made in cases of gender-based discrimination in the United States beginning in the 1970s, with a focus on the ways in which stereotypes about women as possessing inferior abilities, and as being fit only for subservient roles or undervalued jobs, contributed to their unequal treatment relative to their male counterparts.[7] And recently, the 'anti-stereotyping principle' in American equal protection law has been invoked in cases involving discrimination on the ground of sexual orientation, as part of the argument that institutions such as marriage, when restricted to heterosexual couples, inappropriately reinforce stereotypes about gays and lesbians as unable to enter into long-term committed relationships and unable to raise children.

Canada is the country that has gone the farthest in asserting a connection between discrimination and stereotypes. Recently, in the 2008–9 Canadian cases of *R v. Kapp* and *Ermineskin Indian Band and Nation v. Canada*, the Supreme Court of Canada distanced itself from its own earlier expansive interpretation of discrimination as 'a violation of dignity' and suggested that the best test for wrongful discrimination under

---

[6] For instance, CEDAW has explicitly stated that state parties have, as part of their obligation to eliminate discrimination, a duty 'to address prevailing gender relations and the persistence of gender-based stereotypes that affect women...in law, and in legal and societal structures and institutions'. Committee for the Elimination of Discrimination Against Women (CEDAW) (New York City, 3 September 1981, A/59/38, General Recommendation No. 25), 4. Similarly, The Convention on the Rights of Persons with Disabilities contains a provision requiring state parties 'to combat stereotypes, prejudices and harmful practices'—see Convention on the Rights of Persons with Disabilities (UN General Assembly, 13 December 2006, art 8.1.b). And a report commissioned by the Office of the High Commissioner for Human Rights in 2013 recommended that more work be done generally 'to prioritize stereotypes and stereotyping as a human rights concern'. See *Gender Stereotyping as a Human Rights Violation* (OHCHR Commissioned Report, 2013), available at http://www.ohchr.org/EN/Issues/Women/WRGS/Pages/GenderStereotypes.aspx.

[7] Franklin offers an excellent discussion of the history of the American courts' use of an 'anti-stereotyping principle', and also argues that the current American Supreme Court could make more use of this principle in cases involving gender-based discrimination, in 'The Anti-Stereotyping Principle in Constitutional Sex Discrimination Law', above n 4. See also C. Franklin, 'Justice Ginsburg's Advocacy and the Future of Equal Protection' (2013) 122 *Yale Law Journal Online* 227; and N. S. Siegel and R. B. Siegel, 'Pregnancy and Sex-Role Stereotyping: From *Struck* to *Carhart*' (2009) 4 *Ohio State Law Journal* 70, at 1095.

section 15(1) of the *Canadian Charter of Rights and Freedoms* is whether a law or action 'perpetuates prejudice and stereotyping'.[8] As I understand the Court's view, it conceives of unfair discrimination as being primarily of two kinds. There are cases in which the government's intent is prejudicial or stereotyped: a policy is adopted out of contempt for a particular group or on the basis of a stereotyped view of their needs or capacities. And there are cases in which, even though the government is not itself prejudiced or engaged in stereotyping, nevertheless its policy seems to embody or reinforce a stereotype, either because the policy is easily justified in terms of a common stereotype or because it functions, in practice, to reinforce that stereotype. On the current Canadian approach to discrimination, then, in order to count as unfair discrimination, policies must either emanate from a prejudicial or stereotyped intent, or they must be justified by, or have the effect of perpetuating, stereotypes.[9]

In this chapter, I shall try to show that it is a mistake to focus so heavily on stereotypes as the source of the unfairness of discrimination. I shall argue that the concept of a stereotype is somewhat helpful, insofar as it points us in the direction of a number of ways in which the state can fail to treat us as equals, above and beyond simply denying us other constitutional rights. But, as I shall explain, none of these plausible explanations of why certain laws are unfairly discriminatory relies essentially on the fact that they involve *stereotypes*. The explanations appeal either to (i) certain features of stereotypes qua *generalizations*, which are features even of some non-stereotypical generalizations, and which in any case cannot on their own explain why a law fails to treat us as equals in some special or interesting sense; or they appeal to (ii) certain harmful *effects* of stereotypes involving race, sex, or other prohibited traits, which effects can also result from laws that don't involve such stereotypes. I shall try thereby to show that it would be much clearer and more productive simply to focus directly on these harmful effects and to ask which of them, or which combination of them, explains why discrimination is unfair.

III. Why Might Stereotypes Seem Relevant?

The Supreme Court of Canada has not explicitly stated why, in its view, stereotyping renders certain laws unfairly discriminatory. But if we look at certain cases of discrimination, cases in which Canadian or American courts have found discrimination

---

[8] *R v. Kapp* [2008] 2 SCR 483; and *Ermineskin Indian Band and Nation v. Canada* [2009] 1 SCR 222.

[9] Some Canadian legal scholars have suggested that the Supreme Court has stepped back slightly from this view in recent decisions such as *Withler v. Canada (Attorney General)* [2011] 1 SCR 396; and *Quebec (Attorney General) v. A* [2013] 1 SCR 61. Some members of the Court have mentioned in these cases that prejudice and stereotyping should really be treated just as 'useful guides' to cases of unfair discrimination. However, in these and other recent cases, the Court has had nothing concrete to say about what else, other than prejudice and stereotyping, might explain wrongful discrimination—except what the Court calls 'perpetuation of disadvantage'. Since all laws disadvantage some groups, and some laws disadvantage groups on the basis of protected traits without thereby amounting to wrongful discrimination, the concept of mere disadvantage does not, on its own, offer a helpful alternative explanation of why some cases of discrimination are unfair. And so, in practice, claimants in recent Canadian equality rights cases have been left with the hurdle of having to show that the governmental act that excluded them was either prejudiced or in some way expressed or perpetuated a stereotype.

on the basis of a stereotype and cases where many would agree that there is some kind of discrimination and that it seems to involve a stereotype, then I think we can see a number of very different ways in which stereotypes might be thought relevant. It will be helpful to group these into two broad categories: those cases in which the stereotype seems problematic because of some fact about it or its use as a generalization (its falsity; its over-inclusiveness; its substitution for individual consideration), and those cases in which the stereotype seems problematic because of its harmful effects on the individuals excluded and the group as a whole.

A. What's wrong with stereotypes, as generalizations?

1. Stereotypes can be false

Sometimes, stereotypes express myths about the capacities of a certain group: members of a group are alleged to be incapable of doing certain things, and hence of occupying certain roles or belonging to certain institutions, but in fact the members of this group do not possess this incapacity to any greater extent than does any random sample of the population. Among the cases in which Canadian courts have found violations of the constitutional equality rights in section 15(1), a high number seem to be of this type: that is, they involve laws that are justifiable only by appealing to a stereotype that falsely ascribes certain incapacities to all members of a group. For instance, the exclusion of same-sex couples from the institution of marriage was found by Canadian courts to be a violation of equality rights, and seemed to the courts to be based on myths such as 'same-sex couples are incapable of raising children' or 'same-sex couples are incapable of lasting relationships'.[10] In an earlier Canadian equality rights case, the exclusion of non-citizens from the practice of law was found to violate their equality rights partly because it was based on a stereotype about non-citizens being less knowledgeable about Canada and less trustworthy than Canadian citizens.[11] In the American context, the Jim Crow laws and many of the sex-discrimination cases of the 1970s involved this type of stereotype: just as the Jim Crow laws were found to violate the Fourteenth Amendment because they reinforced false stereotypes about the relative abilities of whites and blacks, so many of the sex-discrimination cases of the 1970s involved laws that depended upon false stereotypes about women's inability to perform particular roles.

2. Stereotypes are used as substitutes for individual assessments

Not all stereotypes that are involved in discriminatory laws express myths or falsehoods about the group in question. Some stereotypes ascribe a trait to members of a group and that trait is in fact possessed by the majority of the group's members, perhaps

---

[10] See for instance *Halpern v. Canada (Attorney General)* (2003), 225 DLR (4th) 529; *Hendricks v. Québec (Procureur général)* (2002) RJQ 2506; and *Barbeau v. British Columbia (Attorney General)* (2003) 225 DLR (4th) 472.
[11] See *Andrews v. Law Society of British Columbia* [1989] 1 SCR 143.

even possessed by them *because* they are members of that group. For instance, it is true that the elderly tend to suffer from declining mental acuity and loss of physical stamina, and true that they are more likely to suffer from this than are younger people, because of their advanced age. But when a group is excluded from some opportunity or benefit on the basis of a true stereotype, they may nevertheless object to the use of that stereotype, claiming that fairness requires that each of them be given an individual assessment. This seems to be the best way to understand the objection of claimants in contentious mandatory retirement cases. They are objecting, not to the truth-status of the stereotype, but to its use in the first place as a substitute for individualized consideration. This way of understanding what is problematic about the use of certain stereotypes of course appeals to a very basic feature of stereotypes that Lippmann highlighted in his early article and that is noted in Cook and Cusack's definition as well: namely, that they are preconceived ideas about particular groups, which we invoke precisely in order to avoid having to take the time and resources to look directly at their real abilities and circumstances.

3. Stereotypes are over-inclusive

In other cases, we may recognize that an individual assessment for each member of a group is impractical. Yet we may think that a more nuanced generalization is required as a substitute for individual consideration. If people are denied a benefit on the basis of a generalization that is over-inclusive, in circumstances where the government could have used a generalization that was more narrowly tailored to its objective, then a law may seem discriminatory. A very recent example of such a case in Canada involved a challenge to Canada's prohibition on assisted suicide.[12] A number of people with degenerative diseases argued that the prohibition on assisted suicide violated their constitutional equality rights in part because it rested on a stereotype about people with significant disabilities: namely, that they are vulnerable and unable to make a free and responsible decision to end their lives. The claimants argued that although this may be true of some members of this class, it is not true of all of them, and it is unfair to deny all of them the chance to end their lives with dignity on the basis of such an overbroad generalization.[13]

I have now considered three features of stereotypes, as generalizations: they can be false, they are substitutes for individual assessments, and they can be over-inclusive. I have suggested that these features seem to play a role in our thought about certain cases of discrimination. However, I now want to argue that none of these features of a stereotype is, on its own, capable of explaining the unfairness involved in these cases; and, more importantly, that none of them could offer the kind of explanation

---

[12] *Carter v. Canada (Attorney General)* [2015] 1 SCR 331.

[13] The Supreme Court of Canada agreed with this claim about overbreadth but chose to discuss it as part of an analysis of the claimant's section 7 rights to life, liberty, and security under the *Canadian Charter of Rights and Freedoms*. I shall argue later in this section that concerns about overbreadth do not help us to explain the distinctive unfairness of discriminatory acts, in a way that makes it clear why they are failing to treat people as equals. This is perhaps reflected in the fact that the Canadian Supreme Court felt it could deal with this concern under section 7 and did not need to engage in a section 15(1) equality rights analysis.

that might make it clear why, in cases of unfair discrimination, people are being denied equal standing in some interesting and special sense.

What is unfair about excluding certain groups from privileges on the basis of a false stereotype is not just that people will be denied a benefit on the basis of a falsehood. It seems likely that a good number of our laws are based in part on false claims about the needs or circumstances of particular groups. Yet we do not thereby think that all of these people are being treated unfairly. On the contrary, we accept that it is inevitable that large governments trying to represent and protect many different interests of many different groups will make some mistakes. What seems particularly problematic in cases like the same-sex marriage cases or the Jim Crow laws is rather that, because these false generalizations are about groups that have historically faced misunderstanding, stigmatization, and disadvantage, continued reliance on false stereotypes will have certain harmful effects on these groups. For instance, it will likely perpetuate prejudices against them; it will continue to undermine their autonomy; and it will demean them. In other words, if we think that the falsity of the generalizations matters here, I think this is only because of particular facts about the groups that are being stereotyped in these cases, and particular facts about the harmful effects of these stereotypes on them. The same is true in cases of discrimination where the over-inclusiveness of a particular generalization, or its substitution for individualized assessment, seems to result in unfairness. As Frederick Schauer has argued at length, there is nothing intrinsically unfair either about a lack of individual assessment or about over-inclusiveness.[14] Many branches of the government (tax, customs, police) could not function unless they were permitted to rely sometimes on generalizations instead of conducting individual assessments of everyone under their purview. And there is no such thing as a perfectly tailored generalization: all generalizations are over-inclusive and under-inclusive to some degree. In each context, we need to ask: 'What degree of over-inclusiveness is permissible in this context?' and 'Is an individual assessment required in this context?' And these questions need to be answered by looking to the actual effects of particular laws on the claimants. So the power of stereotypes per se to explain the unfairness of discrimination (through either their falsity, their over-inclusiveness, or their use as a substitute for individual assessment) seems very limited.

Moreover, it is unclear that these aspects of stereotypes could offer us the *kind* of explanation that we are looking for: namely, an explanation of why discrimination is unfair in some special sense, a sense that might explain why violations of these rights involve a failure to treat some people as equals. We might (and in fact do) object to a law's falsity, its over-inclusiveness, and its failure to give individual consideration as part of our analysis of violations of other constitutional rights; and in some constitutions, such as Canada's, we also investigate these properties of laws in the course of determining whether a government's action can be shielded by a limitation clause, as a justifiable violation of a right. So such facts about generalizations do not seem specific enough to the context of discrimination, and do not seem to have enough to do with

---

[14] F. Schauer, *Profiles, Probabilities and Stereotypes* (Cambridge, Mass.: Harvard University Press, 2003).

instances of denying one person a status that is accorded to others, to be able to offer the right kind of explanation of why discrimination is unfair.

But perhaps if we look to the harmful effects of stereotypes on groups that are marked out by a prohibited ground of discrimination, we might find the source of such an explanation. There are obviously many harmful effects of stereotyping these groups. But I shall focus on three in particular: being denied freedom or autonomy, being demeaned, and perpetuating and implicitly sanctioning long-standing prejudices. I shall argue that it is these effects that give the idea of a stereotype its apparent power in explaining cases of unfair discrimination: they are severe, they are persistent, and each of them is, on its own, sufficient to offer a plausible explanation of why discrimination is unfair in the special sense that involves a failure to treat people as equals. However, laws can harm people in these ways even without involving stereotypes; and I shall argue that there is therefore no need to appeal to stereotypes. Instead, we can look directly to whether a law treats members of a certain group differently, in a way that has one or more of these harmful effects and that therefore fails to treat them as equals.

I shall be focusing on these three effects, rather than others, for several reasons. First, they are the effects that seem to matter most to courts adjudicating cases of discrimination, perhaps because they are the most obvious and most severe of the harms in these cases. Second, each of them is, on its own, sufficient to offer a plausible explanation of why discrimination is unfair and, moreover, why it is unfair in some special sense that involves the failure to treat others as equals. And lastly, each of them has been invoked by legal theorists as the basis for a theory of why discrimination is unfair. So this discussion will pave the way for our discussion of what we might focus on, if we abandon the idea that stereotypes are a part of what makes discrimination unfair.

B. What are some harmful effects of stereotypes?

The harmful effects of stereotypes are very starkly exhibited by two sorts of discrimination that are frequently the subject of public discussion: racial profiling and prohibitions on nursing in public.

Consider first racial profiling, in which customs officials or police use generalizations about race as the basis for decisions about whom to stop and search. Although there is arguably much racial profiling that is motivated by prejudice and that appeals to stereotypes that are myths or that are much too over-inclusive, a more challenging test case for us involves those kinds of racial profiling that are based on statistically accurate and nuanced generalizations—for instance, that blacks or Latinos in a certain neighbourhood, who are of a certain age and hang out in certain streets, will be more likely to be involved with certain kinds of crimes. When people object to even this kind of racial profiling, they are objecting to the use of these people's race as a predictor of criminal behaviour. It may, in their view, be acceptable for officials to engage in what is called 'criminal profiling', which uses generalizations about the kinds of body language, flight patterns, or dress of people involved in certain kinds of crime. But using generalizations about *behaviour* or *dress* for these predictive purposes is, we want to say, categorically different from using generalizations about a minority group's *race*, for at least three reasons.

1. Stereotypes can perpetuate prejudice and express prejudicial messages

Part of what is so troubling about racial profiling is that it perpetuates prejudice towards the groups in question. We can think of 'prejudice' in the widest sense here, as involving either a desire to harm or just a desire to avoid associating with a particular group, which is based on misinformation about them. Racial profiling perpetuates prejudices about minorities in a number of ways. First, it reinforces the mistaken belief on the part of the public that members of racial minorities are more often perpetrators of crime than victims of it. In actual fact, racial minorities are just as likely to be victims of crimes as perpetrators, and much more likely to be victims of violent crimes than are whites. But racial profiling reinforces this erroneous connection in our minds between certain races and criminal behaviour, and so it feeds many of the suspicions that the general public has about minority groups: for instance, that young black men are aggressive and dangerous and one should keep clear of them, or that Latinos are thugs and drug dealers and untrustworthy. Moreover, because racial profiling focuses on race, and race is not a result of one's own actions or choices, the practice of racial profiling also tacitly sends the message that these minority groups are governed, not by their choices, but by their circumstances. It suggests that members of these groups are unable to rise above their circumstances and truly direct their own lives, and may therefore fuel the belief that they merit our animosity, or at any rate, our mistrust.

2. Stereotypes can demean people, in the specific sense of implying that they are less than fully mature moral agents, or possess less than full human value

As the case of racial profiling shows, stereotypes can also demean people. Sometimes, a stereotype demeans a particular group through the contrast that it implicitly sets up between that group and another group. In the case of racial profiling, the implied contrast is between those from 'criminally inclined' races such as blacks or Latinos, on the one hand, and whites, on the other hand, who are implicitly deemed to be insufficiently involved in any one area of crime to be the subjects of racial profiling themselves, and hence morally superior. But there is also another way in which stereotypes can demean. I mentioned earlier that, because racial profiling focuses on the race of people rather than on their behaviour, it tacitly sends the message that these minority groups are governed not by their choices, but by their circumstances. My point in mentioning this above was to call attention to the prejudices that this tacit message fuels. But it does a further thing. It demeans members of these racial groups, or lowers their status below that of a mature moral agent in our eyes. It implies that they are less good at doing what is essentially human, namely, living a life that you control through your own choices. Many stereotypes that are based on prohibited grounds of discrimination—on race, on gender, on disability—demean people in just this way. And part of the reason for this, I think, is that by focusing on a trait of someone that is not usually the result of past actions or choices and then appealing to this trait as a factor that determines members of the group's behaviour, the stereotype implies that this group is unable in a certain respect to choose otherwise. So it sends the message that there is a crucial respect in which members of this group are less than full moral agents. These reflections may help us understand, among other things, why so many instances of gender stereotyping seem so deeply demeaning. When states adopt protective labour laws requiring women to work reduced hours so that each woman will be able to 'discharge her maternal functions', or when courts deem female witnesses to be unreliable and more likely to exaggerate in sexual assault cases, they are implying that women develop certain psychological or emotional dispositions, *regardless* of their choices. The tacit assumption seems to be that while men's lives may be shaped by their own choices, there are important—in fact, defining—features of women that women are simply landed with, the way a person may be landed with a medical condition, through no choice or action of their own.

3. *Stereotypes can limit people's freedom and autonomy*

Stereotypes can also work to constrain people, to take away what is sometimes called their 'negative freedom', or their ability to live without interference from external pressures or external limitations on their movements or the options available to them. And likewise, they can work to limit what is sometimes called 'positive freedom' or 'autonomy', or a person's ability to shape her own life in accordance with her own beliefs and values. (For reasons of clarity, I shall use the term 'freedom' for negative freedom, and shall use the term 'autonomy' to cover various aspects of positive freedom.) While these harmful effects on freedom and autonomy are present in cases of racial profiling, they are even more vividly demonstrated in the second example that I indicated I wanted to discuss: prohibitions on nursing in certain public areas. Although nursing in public is socially acceptable, most women still feel social pressure to 'cover up', and some restaurants and hotels still gently redirect women to secluded areas or require, as Claridge's did recently, that a nursing woman drape a napkin over herself. This raises the interesting question of whether a government that permitted such restrictions on nursing mothers would be violating their equality rights. But the immediate issue for us is what effects this has on nursing mothers and their freedom or autonomy. The stereotype involved in such cases is a stereotype about the social meaning of the act of nursing and, ultimately, the social meaning of women's bodies: it says something like 'Women who nurse in public are being immodest' or 'Women who nurse in public are doing something disgusting'. The justification given for these generalizations usually appeals either to the claim that women's breasts are sex objects, or to analogies with urinating in public, thereby suggesting that nursing is somehow disgusting because breasts are unclean. Importantly, to accept these alternative characterizations of the breast is to deny women the chance to define what they are doing when they nurse. And in a very real sense, it is to deny them the chance to help define what their own bodies mean.

Of course, no one has complete freedom to make their body or their actions mean whatever they wish: such meanings are social and depend in large part on social conventions and shared practices. My claim here is not that women are denied autonomy in this case because they cannot make their bodies mean whatever they like. The claim is rather that women are denied autonomy because they are not given any role in determining what their actions or their bodies mean, and their quite plausible claims about the function of their own bodies are being ignored in favour of claims that are less plausible and carry with them a history of prejudice and inferiorization. Most women would say that really, all that they are doing when they nurse is 'nurturing their babies', and that breasts, when seen as receptacles of milk, do not need to be seen as playing any sexual role at all and certainly should not be likened to bodily organs involved in the elimination of waste. In accepting stereotypes over women's own views of their bodies and actions, the hotel or restaurant (or the state) is substituting another group's conception of these women's actions for their own—and moreover, substituting a conception of women's actions and their bodies that has historically been used to deny women an equal status and instead to give them the status of objects that can be manipulated in accordance with other people's desires.

I have tried to show that these stereotypes work to limit women's autonomy. They also, of course, limit women's negative freedom. Women are literally forced either to stop nursing, or to cover up, or to leave the location, so their actions are interfered with. And perhaps more importantly, their deliberations about what to do and how to go about making quite ordinary choices such as where to eat or where to shop are constrained in ways that other people's are not. So what we might call their negative 'deliberative freedom' is affected as well.

We have now looked at three particularly harmful effects of stereotypes in cases of unfair discrimination: they can perpetuate prejudice, they can demean, and they can limit a group's freedom and autonomy. We have also seen how each of these harms involves certain groups not being treated as equals. I think it is these harmful effects of stereotypes that give us the illusion that stereotypes can therefore play a helpful role in explaining why discrimination is unfair, and why it is unfair in the specific sense of failing to treat certain groups as equals. However, these harms are simply *effects* of exclusions based on stereotypes, and there seems in principle no reason why these harms could not arise in cases of discrimination that do not involve stereotypes. In other words, what is arguably doing the moral work here has nothing essential to do with a stereotype.

In the next section of the chapter, I shall further defend this claim by showing that stereotypes are not necessary conditions for unfair discrimination: there can be cases of unfair discrimination that are not helpfully explained in terms of stereotypes. The aim of this next section of the chapter is partly to support my conclusion that we should move our focus away from stereotypes and place it squarely on the harmful effects that matter. But this next section also has an additional aim. Some might argue that, even if stereotypes are not what *makes* discrimination unfair, they can still be what the Canadian Supreme Court has called 'useful guides' to whether unfair discrimination has occurred. But if certain kinds of discrimination are simply not best thought of as involving stereotypes, then requiring claimants to prove that they have been stereotyped in order to succeed in equality rights claims may result in some claimants being unjustly denied redress for real instances of discrimination.

IV. Discrimination without Stereotyping

It may seem impossible that there could be cases of discrimination that do not involve any stereotyping of the excluded or disadvantaged group. But, both in the law and in our ordinary moral lives, we recognize a form of discrimination known sometimes as 'indirect discrimination' and sometimes as 'adverse effect discrimination'. In such cases, a policy or act may be facially neutral but has a disproportionate negative impact on a particular group because they possess a certain trait, and that trait is a prohibited ground of discrimination. For instance, suppose a government institutes a height requirement for members of its ceremonial guard: they must be over six feet tall, because this will lend an appropriate gravitas to the guards. This requirement would likely be found by courts to be indirect discrimination on the basis of gender: although some women are over six feet tall, most aren't, and so the requirement disproportionately disadvantages women.

This hypothetical case is not an example of discrimination without stereotyping. For the picture of the ideal guard that seems to underlie the height requirement is a picture of someone who is strong and powerful and who lends gravitas to the state's image precisely because he has the features that are conventionally associated with men rather than women: height, physical strength, and authority. This height requirement therefore seems to express stereotyped ideas about men and women.

But there are many cases of indirect discrimination that are not plausibly understood as expressing or perpetuating stereotypes. Consider three examples.

Clean-shaven policies: In the United States and Canada, there has recently been considerable litigation over policies adopted by certain employers—most usually, clothing retailers and restaurants—requiring that employees appear clean-shaven. African-Americans have challenged these policies as disparate impact based on race, because a disproportionate number of African-Americans suffer from PFB or *pseudofolliculitis barbae*, a condition which makes shaving extremely painful. The facts about PFB and its connection to race are complex, however. While PFB is not a condition that any Caucasians suffer from, it is also not a condition that the majority of African-Americans suffer from. Roughly 45 per cent of African-Americans suffer from it, and roughly 25 per cent of African-Americans are unable to shave because of it. This means that, among the employees of any given store or restaurant, the majority will likely be able to comply with the policy without facing any disadvantage. And this suggests that it seems implausible to see such policies as based on a stereotype about whites or, by implication, blacks, or as fostering such stereotypes in the public conscience. One might object that there is a stereotype at work here, just as in my ceremonial guard example—an image of the perfect or 'put-together' employee, which is someone who is clean, smartly dressed, and *white*. However, what makes it plausible to think that there is a gender-based stereotype at work in the ceremonial guard example is that most women would fail to meet the relevant height requirement. Whereas the facts about the small number of African-Americans who are unable to shave because of PFB make it less plausible to see this case as embodying a stereotype about most African-Americans.

If you are unconvinced by this example, consider a different one.

Public library book transportation: Some municipalities, in running their public libraries, pay for books to be ordered online by members of the public and then delivered to their local library. This enables people in any district of the city to access books from any library in any other district. Suppose that in a particular district the policy is cancelled, because it proves too expensive to run. Anyone is still permitted to travel to any branch of the city to check out a book—but you have to get there yourself to pick up the book. This decision will likely have an adverse impact on a number of groups: poor families, single mothers, and people with many dependents or who are caregivers of those who cannot be left alone for extended periods. These groups will have less time to travel to another library, less money to spend on transportation, and certainly less money to use to buy the book they need as an alternative to borrowing it from the library. This seems to be a good example of prima facie discrimination on the intersecting grounds of race, family status, and gender (even though we might ultimately deem the policy to be justified for financial reasons). But it seems stretched to say that there are stereotypes about single mothers or racial minorities involved here, or that the policy would perpetuate such stereotypes.

As a third example, consider:

Public school bus drop-offs and pick-ups: Many municipalities provide a school bus service to transport children to and from school. But for reasons of practicality, some will only do pick-ups and drop-offs for a single child at a single location. So each family must decide which house its children are going to be picked up in front of, and dropped off in front of, each day. Obviously, this has a disparately negative impact on dual custody families in which children rotate between their two parents' homes. This seems to be discrimination on the grounds of family status. But is there a stereotype here? Again, as in the public library example, the length of the causal chain between the policy and the prohibited trait seems simply too long, and mediated by too many other facts about members of these groups, for us to plausibly say that the policy is best justified by, or has the effect of perpetuating, stereotypes about dual custody families.

Not every jurisdiction will deem all of these examples to be instances of unfair discrimination. As I have suggested, some of these policies may be found justifiable all things considered, for reasons such as financial ones. But any jurisdiction that has a concept of indirect discrimination will likely allow that *some* such cases are genuine cases of unfair discrimination. And these cases will constitute a problem for the view that stereotypes are a necessary condition for unfair discrimination, and also a problem for the view that all claimants must provide evidence of a stereotype in order to succeed in equality rights claims. For in these cases, the causal chain between the policy in question and the prohibited ground of discrimination (the chain that we refer to when we speak of discrimination 'based on' or 'because of' a certain trait) is too long. Or more precisely, it is not so long that we would deny that these are prima facie cases of unfair discrimination, but it is long enough that it is implausible to think that these cases embody or would perpetuate stereotypes about people with these traits. We might say, borrowing the language of torts, that the problem is one of remoteness. In some cases of indirect discrimination, the harm to people who possess a certain trait can only be traced back to the discriminator's act or policy through such a complex causal chain that the policy cannot plausibly be said to embody or perpetuate a stereotype about this trait. The harm is not so remote from the act or policy that we would deny that the victim has been wronged. But it is remote enough to make the idea of a stereotype less helpful in explaining why such cases of discrimination are unfair.

There is also another kind of discrimination whose unfairness seems recalcitrant to explanation in terms of stereotypes. It includes those cases that are thought of in the United States as 'failure to accommodate' cases, based on disability or religion. 'Failure to accommodate' cases are similar to cases of indirect discrimination in that they involve policies that are facially neutral. But, rather than denying a benefit to members of one group or making it difficult for members of the group to take advantage of that benefit, these policies simply fail to provide extra resources that members of these groups uniquely require, such as elevators or a private area for daily prayers. There is some controversy over whether there is actually such a deep difference between indirect discrimination and failures to accommodate.[15] Indeed, Canadian law denies that there is any difference and considers all cases of discrimination to be analogous to failures to accommodate. It is not my aim here to take a side on this debate. Rather, I want to suggest that, regardless of whether you think that failures to accommodate amount to true discrimination or whether you think that they amount merely to some other kind of unfair disadvantage, the unfairness here is not well explained in terms of stereotypes. Although some failures to accommodate may involve stereotypes, many do not.

First, consider *government buildings with no elevators*. Suppose a government determines that the cost of retro-fitting its older buildings with elevators is simply too great. It therefore decides not to install elevators in these buildings even though this has an obvious and significant impact on people with mobility issues. If this policy were widespread enough, and the cost of installing the elevators, low enough, this decision would certainly look like it embodied stereotypes about people with disabilities, and it would likely perpetuate such stereotypes: for instance, that not enough people with disabilities manage to get out and about for this to be a problem, or that it isn't important enough for the government to be seen to be promoting accessibility because the needs of people with disabilities don't really matter. But if the policy is not widespread and the cost is significant, then it seems artificial to suggest that the policy embodies a stereotype or that it would perpetuate such stereotypes. The natural description of this case would then be that a decision was made for financial reasons which significantly restricts the accessibility of certain important institutions. We can think of many reasons why this might amount to an unfairness, by appealing to the harmful effects that I considered

---

[15] See for instance C. Jolls, 'Accommodation Mandates' (2000) 53 *Stanford Law Review* 223; C. Jolls, 'Anti-Discrimination and Accommodation' (2001) 115 *Harvard Law Review* 642; S. Bagenstos, 'Rational Discrimination: Accommodation and the Politics of (Disability) Civil Rights' (2003) 89 *Virginia Law Review* 825; and S. Rabin-Margalioth, 'Anti-Discrimination, Accommodation and Universal Mandates—Aren't They All the Same?' (2003) 24 *Berkeley Journal of Employment and Labor Law* 111.

in section III of the chapter: it limits this group's access to important public buildings and thereby restricts their freedom, it limits their autonomy, and in implying that their access to public buildings is not a financial priority, it may demean them. But we can explain all of this without appealing to stereotypes.

Consider next *non-flexible break policies*, requiring employees to take breaks at certain fixed times. Members of certain religions are required to observe periods of prayer at particular times of the day; so non-flexible break policies have a disparate impact on members of these religious groups. But it seems stretched to say that these policies embody stereotypes. Most often the policies were adopted because this was most efficient and most cost saving. Like the other cases of failure to accommodate, if they amount to unfair discrimination, this seems best explained by appealing to the importance of the opportunities or freedoms that are denied to members of certain religious groups, or to the fact that because our jobs are such an important part of our identities, this limits their autonomy or is demeaning. But we can say all of this without appealing to the idea of a stereotype.

If these case analyses are correct, then there are important cases of discrimination, and in particular indirect discrimination and failures to accommodate, in which no stereotype is operative. Stereotypes cannot, then, be a necessary condition for unfair discrimination; and courts should be wary of requiring evidence of stereotypes as proof of unfair discrimination.

V. We Should Look Directly at Particular Harms to Victims

If we cannot look to the idea of a stereotype to explain the unfairness involved in cases of discrimination, where then should we look? Our discussion of particular cases of unfair discrimination in section III revealed a number of harms, both to the individuals who are directly excluded and to all of the members of the groups to which they belong. We saw that laws or policies that seem to involve unfair discrimination towards members of disadvantaged groups can: perpetuate prejudices and express prejudicial messages about the capacities or needs of members of that group; limit the negative freedoms or autonomy of members of these groups, in ways that others' freedoms are not limited; and demean them, in the sense of denying that they are full moral agents or possess full human value. We also saw that each of these three harms could form the basis of a plausible explanation of why discrimination is unfair—and moreover, an explanation that makes it clear why such discriminatory acts fail to treat people as equals. It is probably most obvious that laws that demean people fail to treat them as equals: for denying that some people are full moral agents or possess full human value is certainly failing to treat them as equal to others. But the other harms we considered can also explain this. When a law perpetuates prejudicial attitudes towards a group that has suffered long-standing stigma and disadvantage, and when it sends the message that members of this group are fundamentally different from others, less capable, or less trustworthy, it does fail to treat them as equals. And when it denies them an important freedom or an aspect of their autonomy, and this is something that they have a right to and that others in their society are given, then it also fails to treat them as equal to others.

There is an important objection one might make here, though, and this objection draws out a feature of the analysis that has so far remained implicit rather than explicit. My analysis of discrimination suggests that the kind of unfairness involved in cases of discrimination is highly historically contingent. That is, these three kinds of harms only seem to arise because, and insofar as, we are dealing with discrimination against socially marginalized groups that have historically faced stigmatization and disadvantage. That is why discriminatory laws often perpetuate prejudice; that is why, instead of simply denying someone a job or a pension or a single opportunity, they have more pervasive effects on her deliberative freedom or autonomy; and that is why they are not just mildly insulting but demeaning. And this may seem problematic. I began the chapter by suggesting that equality rights have a special claim to be recognized in a constitution, because respect for them seems to be required by political legitimacy. But hasn't our analysis of equality rights shown that they are highly historically contingent? So wouldn't a country that had no history of prior discrimination against such groups have no need for equality rights?

I think this objection trades on two different senses of 'need'. Of course such a country would have no practical need for equality rights, in the sense that its government would never actually violate them. But this does not mean that it would not 'need' equality rights in the sense of being under a moral obligation to respect them: it would still 'need' them in the sense that it would still be under such an obligation, and respect for these rights would still be intimately connected with the legitimacy of this government. So the three harms we have discussed are still, in my view, capable of explaining the unfairness of discrimination, and explaining it in the right sort of way. The fact that such explanations invite us to consider historical contingencies such as the past treatment of different minority groups seems, far from being a problem, to be a necessary feature of any accurate conception of discrimination and why it is unfair.

Each of the harms we have noted—the perpetuation of prejudice; the demeaning of certain groups; and the denial of freedom and autonomy—has been recently highlighted by some legal scholars working on discrimination law, and invoked as the basis for a particular theory of why discrimination is unfair. Some scholars, such as John Gardner, have argued that the perpetuation and expression of prejudice is at the heart of unfair discrimination.[16] Deborah Hellman has argued that discrimination is unfair insofar as it is demeaning, where this involves not just expressing a view about another less than human status, but actually *lowering* their social status.[17] Tarun Khaitan and I have, in different ways, argued that denials of certain kinds of freedom or autonomy are key to understanding what makes discrimination unfair.[18] If my criticisms of

---

[16] J. Gardner, 'Liberals and Unlawful Discrimination' (1989) 1 *Oxford Journal of Legal Studies* 9; and J. Gardner, 'Discrimination as Injustice' (1996) 3 *Oxford Journal of Legal Studies* 16, at 353. Gardner focuses primarily on the prejudicial intent of the alleged discriminator, and his aim here is to explain the unfairness of direct discrimination (he offers a very different account of indirect discrimination).

[17] D. Hellman, *When is Discrimination Wrong?* (Cambridge, Mass.: Harvard University Press, 2010).

[18] T. Khaitan, *A Theory of Discrimination Law* (Oxford: Oxford University Press, 2015); S. Moreau, 'What is Discrimination?' (2010) 2 *Philosophy and Public Affairs* 38, at 143; and S. Moreau, 'In Defense of a Liberty-Based Account of Discrimination', in D. Hellman and S. Moreau (eds), *Philosophical Foundations of Discrimination Law* (Oxford: Oxford University Press, 2013), 71–86.

appeals to stereotypes are correct, then we need to engage with the more substantive questions that these theories are asking, such as: which harms, really, are key to understanding the unfairness of discrimination? Is one of them primary, and can others be explained as side effects of one of them? Do they all work together to render discrimination unfair? Or are different harms salient in different cases of discrimination, or for different kinds of discrimination? Perhaps, for instance, direct discrimination is more deeply demeaning than indirect discrimination, whereas some forms of pervasive or systemic indirect discrimination may result in greater losses of freedom or autonomy than some discrete instances of direct discrimination. If this is true, then perhaps a pluralist account of discrimination is preferable.

One significant feature of all of the above theories of unfair discrimination is that they all resist a pluralist explanation of discrimination, and aim instead to appeal to some single kind of harm in explaining why discrimination is wrong. Each of them takes one of the types of harm that we have looked at and treats it as primary, and each tries to explain the relevance of the other harms either by suggesting that they are partly constitutive of the primary harm, or by suggesting that they are subsidiary effects of it. So, for instance, although Hellman acknowledges that victims of discrimination are certainly denied important freedoms and given less autonomy, she maintains that this is relevant to the unfairness of discrimination only insofar as it contributes to their being demeaned.[19] By contrast, I have argued that although unfair discrimination is often demeaning, this is usually because it involves deprivations of certain important freedoms that individuals are entitled to have.[20] One question that this raises, but that few scholars have to date addressed, is why exactly we feel under such pressure to invoke a theory of discrimination that is unitary in this sense, when discrimination as a concept covers so many different kinds of exclusions and disadvantage, based on so many different grounds.[21] One might suggest that we do think of all of these different cases as instances of some single phenomenon called 'discrimination', rather than as a collection of different social ills, and we need an understanding of discrimination that reflects this. We also want a theory that is principled rather than arbitrary, and one that simply conjoins together a number of different harms seems more likely to be arbitrary. Moreover, at least in our ordinary moral thought, we think of equality rights as special not just in the sense that I mentioned earlier in this chapter—namely, that they seem to be particularly closely connected to political legitimacy—but also in a further sense. We think of government violations of equality rights as being particularly egregious, particularly serious or urgent from a moral standpoint. It is not clear whether a pluralistic conception of unfair discrimination, one which simply appealed to a variety of different kinds of harms, would be able to explain the particular moral seriousness that

---

[19] Hellman, above n 17, chs 2 and 4.   [20] Moreau, 2010, above n 18, 177–8.
[21] Patrick Shin and Lawrence Blum have both questioned whether a unitary theory of discrimination can be given: see P. Shin, 'Is There a Unitary Concept of Discrimination?' and L. Blum, 'Racial and other Asymmetries', both in Hellman and Moreau, above n 18, 163–81 and 182–200. Neither paper, however, explores the prior question of why a unitary theory of discrimination is necessary or desirable; and it seems that until we know this, we will not be able accurately to judge just how cohesive a theory must be in order to be 'unitary' in the sense that should matter to us here.

attaches to unfair discrimination; for it seems unlikely that all of the different kinds of harms invoked by a pluralistic theory would be of the same moral urgency.

A further question that needs addressing is whether we need to (or can) integrate such theories of the unfairness of discrimination—all of which appeal to the harms done to the victims of discrimination—with recognition of the moral inappropriateness of the discriminator's beliefs in certain cases, particularly certain cases of direct discrimination. Scholars such as Larry Alexander and Matt Cavanagh have developed theories of wrongful discrimination that are based on the idea that it is morally wrong to act on certain kinds of beliefs about other people's lesser worth.[22] One might ask: where, in our harm-based theory of discrimination, is there a place for recognition of the inappropriateness of such attitudes or beliefs? I think we could respond to this challenge in several different ways.

First, we might respond that these theories are answering different questions. Alexander and Cavanagh are concerned with the question of whether it is moral to act on certain beliefs: they are seeking an answer to a problem in moral philosophy about which acts are morally permissible. By contrast, the harm-based theories of discrimination that I have been discussing are offering a principle specifically designed for the law. These theories are answering the question that legislators and judges ask, when they try to determine whether a particular legal policy should be regarded as unfairly discriminatory, in the sense that the victims are owed a remedy at law. We can answer this legal question without taking any stance on when and why discrimination is morally wrongful, and without needing to deny that it is the discriminator's intentions or beliefs that render his act wrongful from a moral standpoint.

Second, we might accept, in line with the Canadian Supreme Court's position that we examined in section II, and consistently with American constitutional law, that consideration of prejudicial motives is important in explaining why discrimination is unfair as a matter of constitutional law, and that any complete theory of the unfairness of discrimination must recognize that both the harmful effects on victims and the discriminator's inappropriate prejudicial intentions are relevant. Of course, this position would then make our theory pluralist in a further way: we would be appealing to two very different kinds of things—harms to victims and intentions of agents—as sources of the unfairness of discrimination, and so we would once again have to address the potential problems with pluralism that I discussed above.

Third, we might try to show that the discriminator's intentions are legally relevant, but only in an indirect way, in helping us understand the full nature and scope of some of the harms experienced by victims. So, for instance, in explaining how and why certain policies affect people's autonomy, or why a particular policy demeans someone, we do often need to make reference to the discriminator's prejudiced beliefs. On this view,

---

[22] For Alexander, these beliefs include erroneous judgments about another person's lesser worth, as well as the stereotypical thoughts that grow out of such judgments. See L. Alexander, 'What Makes Wrongful Discrimination Wrong: Biases, Preferences, Stereotypes, and Proxies' (1992) 141 *University of Pennsylvania Law Review* 149. Cavanagh appeals to what he calls 'unwarranted contempt' as the source of the moral wrongness of discrimination: see M. Cavanagh, *Against Equality of Opportunity* (Oxford: Clarendon Press, 2003).

the discriminator's intentions are often relevant in explaining why discrimination is unfair. But they have no independent explanatory power: it is the harms to the victims that explain why discrimination is unfair.

Clearly, scholars and practitioners of discrimination law have a great deal more work to do in clarifying the different kinds of harms that are involved in different cases of discrimination; in determining which harms really do contribute to the unfairness of discrimination; and in determining the legal relevance of the discriminator's intentions or beliefs. I hope that I have shown why we need to focus directly on these questions, without worrying about locating a stereotype in each case of unfair discrimination.

15

Proportionality

*Malcolm Thorburn**

I. Introduction

The practice of proportionality justification is a defining feature of the 'postwar paradigm'[1] of constitutional rights protection that was first developed in Germany and has since spread around the world.[2] According to that practice, the state may infringe constitutional rights[3] so long as it can show that doing so was a necessary and proportionate means for it to accomplish a legitimate public purpose.[4]

Many commentators in the English-speaking world have subjected the practice of proportionality to withering criticism. Proportionality justification, they suggest, is a triumph of expediency over principle, for it allows the state to infringe constitutional rights whenever they get in the way of its pursuit of important policy goals. And that seems to undermine the role of constitutional rights as rights. The point of rights, they insist, is not just to identify important interests that should weigh heavily in the balance but rather to exclude certain interests from interest balancing altogether.[5] So to invite the state to balance constitutional rights against its legitimate purposes, as proportionality seems to do, is to deny rights their proper function. It is to convert rights into mere 'rules of thumb'[6] to be disregarded whenever the balance of interests favours doing so.

* Faculty of Law, University of Toronto. Distant ancestors of the present chapter were presented at the Philosophical Foundations of Constitutional Law workshop at the University of Toronto, the New Scholars workshop at the University of Toronto, and the Los Angeles meeting of the New Voices in Legal Theory workshop. I am grateful to the participants at all these events for comments and criticisms. Thanks also to Aharon Barak, Vincent Chiao, Larissa Katz, and Arthur Ripstein for extremely valuable discussion.

[1] L. Weinrib, 'The Postwar Paradigm and American Exceptionalism', in S. Choudhry (ed), *The Migration of Constitutional Ideas* (Cambridge: Cambridge University Press, 2007), 84–111.

[2] Since its development in Germany, proportionality analysis has migrated to the European Court of Human Rights, Australia, Brazil, Canada, Hong Kong, Hungary, India, Israel, New Zealand, Poland, Portugal, Turkey, South Africa, South Korea, Spain, Switzerland, the United Kingdom, and elsewhere.

[3] The German Basic Law exempts the right to dignity from proportionality justification. This is unusual, however. The explanation for why this might be is complex. For more on this, see M. Kumm and A. Walen, 'Human Dignity and Proportionality: Deontic Pluralism in Balancing', in G. Huscroft, B. Miller, and G. Webber (eds), *Proportionality and the Rule of Law: Rights, Justification, Reasoning* (Cambridge: Cambridge University Press, 2014), 67–89.

[4] Canadian courts require the state to establish that its purpose was 'pressing and substantial' and not merely a legitimate public purpose; *R v Oakes* [1986] 1 SCR 103. But this has meant that Canadian courts rarely engage in proportionality analysis *stricto sensu*, since only pressing and substantial purposes qualify from the outset.

[5] As Richard Pildes has argued (using Joseph Raz's language of 'exclusionary reasons'), constitutional rights operate as second-order exclusionary reasons, telling the state not to act on the balance of first-order reasons where rights are at stake. See R. Pildes, 'Avoiding Balancing: The Role of Exclusionary Reasons in Constitutional Law' (1994) 45 *Hastings Law Journal* 711.

[6] I borrow this language from F. Schauer, *Playing by the Rules* (Oxford: Clarendon Press, 1993), 4, inter alia.

Much of the power of this sort of criticism comes from the contrast it seeks to draw between the constraints imposed by constitutional rights and the state's freedom otherwise to set and pursue whatever purposes it might like. And this contrast makes a good deal of sense in a tradition like the United States where constitutional rights are widely assumed to operate against a background of democratic majoritarianism. That is, much of US constitutional theory operates on the assumption that the people acting through their democratically elected representatives should usually be entitled to set and pursue whatever ends they might like. So if we suggest that the state may justify the infringement of a constitutional right on the basis of a legitimate state purpose, it sounds to many American ears as though we are saying that the state may infringe constitutional rights whenever the balance of reasons—any reasons—warrants it. And that, quite rightly, sounds like we have given up a commitment to constitutional rights in the name of expediency.

This sort of criticism has no bite when applied to the German constitutional tradition, however, because many of its framing assumptions simply do not apply. Most importantly, the German constitutional tradition does not begin with the majoritarian assumption that the state should generally be free to do as the majority wishes. Instead, it begins with the *Rechtsstaat* principle according to which the state and all the basic institutions of the constitutional order must be compatible with the status of all persons as free and equal bearers of certain basic rights. That is, in the German *Rechtsstaat* tradition, constitutional rights do not appear late in the account to constrain the power of the state which has already been defined on other terms. Rather, they appear at the very beginning, as the foundational idea—the unwritten principle—to which our understanding of legitimate state authority must conform.

Majoritarianism is at odds with the *Rechtsstaat* principle because it involves the majority imposing its will on free and independent rights-bearing persons. And in most cases, the imposition of the majority's will must involve interferences with individual freedom. Although there will be cases where state authority is consistent with the status of persons as free and equal rights bearers, there will be many more where it is not. In the German *Rechtsstaat* tradition, constitutional rights and proportionality justification work together as a filtering mechanism through which we can determine what sorts of treatment of persons by the state are consistent with their status as free and equal rights bearers. On this account, then, we do not use constitutional rights one by one, as a series of limits we impose on the otherwise unconstrained freedom of the majority to do as it would like. Rather, we use constitutional rights together as parts of a single coherent account of the conditions under which state action is consistent with respect for persons as free and equal rights bearers.[7] And proportionality justification is the mechanism we use to ensure that the specific rights can operate together as parts of that single, coherent account of legitimate state action.

* * *

---

[7] A. Hollerbach, 'Auflösung der rechtsstaalichen Verfassung?' (1960) 85 *Archiv des öffentlichen Rechts* 241, at 255 (cited in J. Bomhoff, *Balancing Constitutional Rights: The Origins and Meanings of Postwar Legal Discourse* (Cambridge: Cambridge University Press, 2014), 107): 'Every individual element always refers to the overarching whole; is only an element by reference to the whole.'

This chapter explores the place of proportionality justification in the German constitutional tradition (and, to a lesser extent, in those other jurisdictions that follow the postwar paradigm of constitutional rights protection). In so doing, I consider some of the challenges to proportionality justification put forward by a number of English-speaking constitutional scholars. I argue that many of their criticisms trade on a confusion about the nature and role of constitutional rights in the German constitutional tradition. Constitutional rights in the German *Rechtsstaat* tradition play a fundamentally different role from constitutional rights in the American constitutional tradition. So it should not be surprising to find that they are—indeed, they must be—subject to justified infringement on the basis of proportionality analysis. In exploring the differences between the American and the German understandings of constitutional rights, I also consider how this difference is related to a number of deep disagreements about other constitutional fundamentals, such as the role of courts, the justificatory power of the popular will, and the nature of the constituent power. Finally, I suggest that the understanding of rights and proportionality reasoning that is laid out explicitly in the German *Rechtsstaat* tradition is also a deep animating principle of the English common law constitution. Despite the many differences in institutional context between the German *Rechtsstaat* model and the English common law constitution, their conceptions of constitutional rights and their role in determining the limits of legitimate state power are strikingly similar.

II. Proportionality in German Constitutional Law

In the German constitutional tradition, the state may infringe on constitutional rights so long as it can justify doing so as a necessary and proportionate means to its pursuit of a legitimate state end. The proportionality procedure for determining when the state is justified in infringing constitutional rights is not set out in the text of the German Basic Law. Rather, it was developed by the German Federal Constitutional Court in a number of early cases reflecting on the nature of rights and their place within a *rechtsstaatlich* constitutional order.[8] Proportionality justification, on the German account, emerges 'basically from the nature of constitutional rights themselves'.[9] Of course, some later written constitutions that have followed the German model have set out the structure of proportionality justification more or less explicitly: some articulate the structure of proportionality reasoning in some detail;[10] others make explicit textual reference to 'reasonable limits' to constitutional rights;[11] yet others only invoke limitation clauses

---

[8] The first major case in the Bundesverfassunggericht to employ proportionality reasoning about constitutional rights was the Lüth case: 7 BVerfGE 198 [1958]. The German Constitutional Court was drawing explicitly on an earlier jurisprudence of proportionality from the Prussian *Oberlandesgericht* from the late nineteenth century.

[9] 19 BVerfGE 342 [1965], 348.

[10] Constitution of the Republic of South Africa 1996, art 36: 'reasonable and justifiable in an open and democratic society based on human dignity, equality and freedom'.

[11] Part I of the *Constitution Act 1982*, being Schedule B to the *Canada Act 1982* (UK), 1982, c 11, s 1: 'demonstrably justified in a free and democratic society'.

that are specific to particular rights.[12] But it is important to keep in mind that proportionality justification did not arise from an explicit textual provision; rather, it is a creature of judicial reflection on the nature of constitutional rights in a *Rechtsstaat*.

Before we consider questions of justification, of course, the party challenging the
state must establish that a constitutional right has, in fact, been infringed.[13] This simply
follows from the logic of justification: it is the justified infringement of constitutional
rights that we are concerned with here. Once this has been established, we proceed to
the analysis of justification itself. Over the years, the procedure to determine whether
the state was justified in infringing a given constitutional right has hardened into a
fairly definite set of tests that courts apply whenever it has been established that a constitutional right has been infringed.[14] Nevertheless, it is important to emphasize that
the proportionality procedure still retains a great deal of flexibility, working as it does at
a very high level of abstraction in guiding the reasoning of courts about justified rights
infringement.[15]

Proportionality justification addresses three concerns. The first is whether the party
infringing the constitutional right actually had the proper standing to claim a justification. Courts address this question by asking whether the infringement was 'prescribed
by law' and whether it was undertaken in furtherance of a legitimate state purpose.[16]
These considerations are often dismissed as mere threshold conditions, but they play
an essential part in the justification process. For together, they mean that no one can
use the powers of the state to infringe constitutional rights on his own private say-so
(where the act was not 'prescribed by law') or for his own private purpose (rather than
a legitimate public purpose). Furthermore, the requirement of a legitimate state purpose also excludes any purpose that is at odds with the regime of constitutional rights.
Although this first step does not establish that the infringement of a constitutional right
is justified, it determines at least that we are dealing with an entity that has the proper
standing—as a public authority pursuing a legitimate public purpose—to make a claim
of justification.[17]

---

[12] Council of Europe, *European Convention on Human Rights* (ECHR) 1950, section 8(2) enumerates the
grounds for limiting the right (set out in section 8(1)) to 'respect for his private and family life, his home
and his correspondence'.

[13] By this, I do not mean to suggest that postwar paradigm jurisdictions require a 'case or controversy'
in the manner of the US Supreme Court, since most do not. I mean only to suggest that the complainant
must establish at the very least that a constitutional right could in principle be infringed by the application
of a statute or practice.

[14] Although these specific tests vary somewhat from one postwar paradigm jurisdiction to another,
their underlying logic is strikingly similar. For a detailed treatment of these tests in various postwar paradigm jurisdictions, see A. Barak, *Proportionality: Constitutional Rights and their Limitations*
(Cambridge: Cambridge University Press, 2012), 243ff.

[15] Mattias Kumm and Alec Walen put the point as follows (Kumm and Walen, above n 3, 69–70): 'Balancing
is not a mechanical exercise: it is a metaphor we use to describe a residual category within rights analysis
that registers the importance of the various concerns at stake…. When balancing is misunderstood as a
technique that somehow allows lawyers and courts to avoid substantive moral reasoning or engagement
with policy, it is likely to lead to bad results'.

[16] For example: Israeli Basic Law, art 8: 'befitting the values of the state of Israel, enacted for a proper
purpose'.

[17] Put another way, this first step addresses the problem of vigilantism. I have discussed this concern in
the context of justified use of force in criminal law in M. Thorburn, 'Justifications, Powers and Authority'
(2008) 117 *Yale Law Journal* 1070.

With this claim of standing in place, the second set of considerations address the necessity of the constitutional rights infringement. Here, too, the courts have usually addressed this concern in two distinct sub-tests. One sub-test is concerned with the question of whether it was necessary to infringe the constitutional right at all in pursuit of the legitimate state objective (often phrased in the language of 'rational connection' between the infringement of the right and the pursuit of the objective). The other sub-test asks whether it was necessary for the state to infringe the right to quite the extent it did in pursuit of its legitimate purpose (often framed in terms of whether the state 'minimally impaired' the right in pursuit of its purpose). Although some courts and commentators have focused on these two necessity sub-tests as the heart of proportionality analysis,[18] their role is really just to establish that there is a genuinely unavoidable conflict between the state's pursuit of its legitimate purposes and the constitutional right in question. The difficult normative question—when and to what extent the state is justified in infringing the right in pursuit of its legitimate purposes—must be determined at the final stage of proportionality analysis, often referred to as 'proportionality *stricto sensu*'.[19]

Once the state has established that it was acting within its proper jurisdiction as a public authority and that there is a genuinely unavoidable conflict between its pursuit of a legitimate public purpose and a particular constitutional right, we turn finally to the question that is at the heart of philosophical debates about proportionality justification: the test of proportionality *stricto sensu*. Of course, although all of the prior steps are important to the analysis, they are all considerably less controversial. For no matter what our conception of rights or of legitimate state aims, it is hard to argue that officials could ever be justified in infringing rights without state authorization, or that the state may do so without proffering any justifying reasons for doing so, or that it may do so by putting forward aims that can be achieved without infringing rights as it did. But what is a good deal more controversial—the controversy that will occupy us for much of this chapter—is whether constitutional rights may be justifiably infringed when there is an unavoidable clash between the state's pursuit of a legitimate purpose and a constitutionally protected right. For it is at this stage—and only at this stage—that we must determine how rights must be reconciled with the state's pursuit of its legitimate aims when they are in direct conflict with one another.

III. Rights as Trumps

A number of influential commentators in the United States and elsewhere have attacked the practice of proportionality justification as antithetical to the very idea of

---

[18] Canadian constitutional scholar Peter Hogg suggests (P. Hogg, *Constitutional Law of Canada* vol II, 5th edn (Toronto: Carswell, 2007), 146) that '[t]he requirement of least drastic means has turned out to be the heart and soul of Section 1 justification'.

[19] As a descriptive matter, the stage of 'proportionality *stricto sensu*' actually plays very little role in the Canadian jurisprudence on proportionality. But my concern here is not to reproduce the jurisprudence of any particular jurisdiction. Rather, it is to trace the logic of proportionality justification as a principle of the *Rechtsstaat*.

constitutional rights.[20] A common theme running through most of these criticisms is that we must distinguish sharply between the logic of ordinary public policymaking and the logic of rights. That is, their arguments about the nature of rights are set within a framing assumption about the nature of the state's usual mode of operations. The assumption upon which much of the critical literature is based is that unless a constitutional right is at stake, the state is free to pursue whatever purposes the majority might like. Ronald Dworkin describes this assumption neatly in his famous 1970 essay, 'Taking Rights Seriously'. 'Normally', he argues, 'it is a sufficient justification [for state action], even for an act that limits liberty, that the act is calculated to increase what the philosophers call general utility'.[21] That is, under ordinary circumstances, the state is free to act in whatever way it deems to be most desirable—a matter that governments today will usually resolve by reference to a broad utilitarian calculus. So on this account, constitutional rights play no part in structuring the state's reasoning from the inside; if anything, they act only as external constraints on its pursuit of its own policy ends.

Now, once we have this open-ended conception of legitimate state aims in mind, it is not difficult to see why proportionality justification appears to be such a problem. For it tells us that constitutionally guaranteed rights must sometimes give way to the state's pursuit of its legitimate aims. But if we assume that the state is generally free to pursue whatever ends it might choose, that means that rights must sometimes yield simply because they are at odds with the state's chosen policy objectives. And that appears to undermine the very status of constitutional rights as rights. For, as Dworkin puts the point, '[t]here would be no point in the boast that we respect individual rights unless that involved some sacrifice, and the sacrifice in question must be that we give up whatever marginal benefits our country would receive from overriding these rights when they prove inconvenient.'[22]

If we are to 'take rights seriously', the argument goes, then we cannot think of them as mere aide-memoires to the state in its pursuit of whatever policy goals it has chosen for itself. Rights by their very nature must constrain our freedom to pursue our own ends in whatever way we like. Following this intuition, Dworkin and many others have argued that constitutional rights must not be amenable to the balancing of interests. Instead, they must act as firm and impenetrable constraints (variously described as 'side constraints'[23] or 'trumps'[24] or 'shields'[25] or 'firewalls'[26]) on the ordinary logic of state action. It would be inappropriate for the state to infringe constitutional rights simply because they are getting in the way of the state's self-chosen ends too much. And it would be even more inappropriate for the courts to create a proportionality doctrine

---

[20] S. Tstakyrakis, 'Proportionality: An Assault on Human Rights?' (2009) 7 *International Journal of Constitutional Law* 468; G. C. N. Webber, *The Negotiable Constitution: On the Limitation of Rights* (Cambridge: Cambridge University Press, 2009).

[21] R. Dworkin, *Taking Rights Seriously* new impression (London: Duckworth, 2000), 191.

[22] Ibid 193.   [23] R. Nozick, *Anarchy, State and Utopia* (New York: Basic Books, 1974), 29.

[24] R. Dworkin, *Is Democracy Possible Here? Principles for a New Political Debate* (Princeton: Princeton University Press, 2006), 48–9, calls proportionality justification clauses 'political compromises'.

[25] F. Schauer, 'A Comment on the Structure of Rights' (1993) 27 *Georgia Law Review* 415, at 429–30.

[26] J. Habermas, *Between Facts and Norms: Contributions to a Discourse Theory of Law and Democracy*, W. Rehg (trans) (Cambridge, Mass.: MIT Press, 1998), 256, 258–9.

out of whole cloth, as the German Constitutional Court appears to have done, that would permit the state to set aside our constitutional rights in the name of expediency.

IV. Rights and the Will of the Founders

Arguments of this sort—that proportionality reasoning is at odds with the very idea of rights because it allows the state to disregard constitutional rights when they get in the way of the state's self-chosen ends—trade on a certain understanding of the role of rights in the constitutional order. The first step toward making sense of the distinctiveness and the legitimacy of proportionality justification in the postwar paradigm is to challenge this conception of the role of constitutional rights.

A. The role of the constituent power

In US constitutional law theory, it is widely assumed that the best way to determine what rights people have is to determine what rights the constitutional text says they have. Indeed, more generally, most schools of thought on constitutional interpretation in the United States, despite their differences on many other questions, agree on one very basic assumption: that the primary task of a judge confronted with a constitutional question is to discern the meaning of the written constitutional text before her. They differ sharply in their answer to this question, of course: their theories of interpretation vary widely from 'original meaning'[27] to 'semantic originalism',[28] 'living originalism',[29] and many others. Advocates of the 'plain meaning' school insist that all we can know is that the founders chose to adopt the words we find in the constitutional text, so we must simply give them the meaning they appear to us to have; advocates of 'semantic originalism' will insist that we ought to give them the meaning that the words commonly had at the time, for that was the contemporary public meaning of the words; and so on. But these are still all variations on a common theme: that the primary task of a judge engaged in constitutional adjudication is to determine what the text before us, set down by the founding fathers, means.[30]

Now, this might seem like a fairly innocuous assumption to make. If we want to know what constitutional rights people have, surely we should look to the text of the written constitution to find out what rights it says that they have. Indeed, where else could we possibly look? But in fact, this is far from an innocuous assumption, for it is

---

[27] Antonin Scalia and Robert Bork are two of the most prominent proponents of this account. R. Bork, *The Tempting of America: The Political Seduction of Law* (New York: Free Press, 1990).

[28] Ronald Dworkin has indicated that he rejects all forms of originalism. Jeff Goldsworthy and others have suggested, however, that his theory of interpretation is best understood as 'semantic originalism'. See J. Goldsworthy, 'Dworkin as an Originalist' (2000) 17 *Constitutional Commentary* 49.

[29] J. Balkin, *Living Originalism* (Cambridge, Mass.: Harvard University Press, 2014).

[30] That is, it is the text, not the subjective will of the founders themselves that is dispositive. Bork, above n 27, 144: 'The search is not for a subjective intention. If someone found a letter from George Washington to Martha telling her that what he meant by the power to lay taxes was not what other people meant, that would not change our reading of the Constitution in the slightest. Nor would the subjective intentions of all the members of a ratifying convention alter anything. When lawmakers use words, the law that results is what those words ordinarily mean.'

founded on a certain (usually unspoken) assumption about the authority of the constitutional text that is highly suspect—and that is rejected by the *rechtsstaatlich* constitutional tradition in Germany and elsewhere. That unspoken assumption is that the constituent power (usually referred to as the 'founding fathers' in the United States) operates in a legal vacuum—for until there is a written constitution in place, there is no law.[31] So the only source of constitutional rights is the will of the founding fathers themselves. In Federalist 78, Alexander Hamilton puts forward an account of constitutional judicial review based on just this account of constitutional rights. He writes:

> It only supposes that the power of the people is superior to both [the legislature and the judiciary]; and that where the will of the legislature, declared in its statutes, stands in opposition to that of the people, declared in the Constitution, the judges ought to be governed by the latter rather than the former.[32]

Now, this account of the role of the constituent power has important implications for our understanding of the role of the state, as well. For if we understand the constituent power to have been acting in a legal vacuum when it drafted the written constitution, then we must conclude that the only legal constraints on the state must be those that the constituent power has set down in the text of the written constitution. That is, as Hamilton put the point: the people, acting through their elected representatives, are free to make whatever laws they might like so long as they are consistent with the constraints that the people themselves have imposed in the text of the written constitution.

According to this model, then, constitutional rights operate as constraints on the power of the state to set and pursue its own ends in precisely the same way that private rights operate as constraints on the power of private persons to set and pursue their own ends. Just as my claim right to Blackacre constrains others' freedom to wander on Blackacre as they might like, so my constitutional right to freedom of expression ought to constrain the freedom of the legislature to make laws that constrain my freedom of expression as it might like.[33] Under this conception, rights do genuinely constrain the state, just as private rights genuinely constrain private parties. But what is most noteworthy about this account of constitutional rights is the underlying (and usually unspoken) assumption about the general background freedom of the state to set and pursue its own ends as the majority sees fit.

B. The role of courts

If the written constitution exists in a legal vacuum, then the only legal limits on the state are those set out in the text of the written constitution. On this account, the job of courts in constitutional cases is clear: they should read the written constitution

---

[31] As Richard Stacey nicely points out in his chapter in this volume, this assumption is still alive in the constitutional discourse in many other jurisdictions outside the United States, as well. But for the reasons Stacey points out, it is just as unsustainable in the United States as it was in Egypt during the Arab Spring.

[32] A. Hamilton, 'No. 78', in C. Rossiter (ed), *The Federalist Papers* (New York: Penguin Putnam, 1999), 432–40.

[33] W. N. Hohfeld, 'Some Fundamental Legal Conceptions as Applied in Judicial Reasoning' (1913) 23 *Yale Law Journal* 16.

carefully and give effect to the constitutional rights enumerated in it. This fetishization of the constitutional text persists in much of American constitutional law theory today.

Perhaps the most eloquent defender of this approach to the judicial role is US Supreme Court Judge Antonin Scalia. In his work on statutory (rather than constitutional) interpretation, Scalia famously derides American legal education for its focus on common law reasoning, working out legal questions on the basis of some very abstract understanding of individual rights, rather than teaching students how to interpret explicit legislative provisions.[34] Teaching common law reasoning might be fine for a time when the legislature was neither democratic nor particularly prolific, he argues, but we now live in an age when the people speak clearly and often as to how legal relations should be structured within the jurisdiction. Recognizing the legislature's superior claim to democratic legitimacy, the argument goes, courts should act as servants of the legislature, articulating the meaning of its laws and applying them to the fact scenarios before them. When courts are called upon to construe constitutional provisions, the task is similar. Courts need not enter into the sorts of complex discussions of their role as guardians of the legal order that German courts so often do; rather, they should simply defer to the will of the constituent power that drafted the bill of rights, as expressed through the constitutional text it created.

V. Rights and the Rule of Law

The constitutional text plays a very different role in German constitutional law than it does in the United States. In the United States, the text of the constitution is usually thought of, in one way or another, as the source of all constitutional rights. As we saw above, there are many theories of interpretation that American constitutional scholars have used to 'find' rights in the text of the Bill of Rights. The right to privacy, for example, has been found to exist by implication from a number of explicitly guaranteed rights.[35] Again, the point here is not which theory of textual interpretation is best; rather, it is that in the United States, it is almost universally agreed that the question of what constitutional rights we have is answered by reference to the meaning of the canonical constitutional text.[36] And this widespread fetishization of the constitutional text arises from a framing assumption about the background freedom of the majority to make whatever laws it sees fit. That is: the constituent power must be the source of all constitutional rights because there are no legal rights until a constitutional order has been put in place by an act of will by the constituent power of the people. But does the constituent power act in a legal vacuum? Is it plausible to think that the constituent power is free to put in place any constitutional arrangements it wishes?

---

[34] A. Scalia, *A Matter of Interpretation* (Princeton: Princeton University Press, 1997), 3ff.

[35] L. Brandeis and S. Warren, 'The Right to Privacy' (1890) 4 *Harvard Law Review* 193. The authors find the right to be an implication of the right against search and seizure, which is explicitly guaranteed by the Fourth Amendment.

[36] Some have argued that, seen in the proper light, Ronald Dworkin is best understood as part of this group, as well. See K. E. Whittington, 'Dworkin's "Originalism": The Role of Intentions in Constitutional Interpretation' (2000) 62 *The Review of Politics* 197.

A. Judges and the rule of law

Implicit in the text-centred account of constitutional rights that dominates the debate in the United States is a certain account of the role of judges in the constitutional order. As Justice Scalia puts the point, common law reasoning might have been of some use in a bygone age when there were few canonical texts—neither a written constitution nor many statutes—to guide judicial reasoning; but in the modern era, the people speak loud and clear through authoritative documents. And when the people speak, the job of the courts is to interpret their meaning and to apply it as best they can to the situation at hand. David Dyzenhaus describes this account of the judicial role as follows:

> In sum, the conception of a judge...is Montesquieu's: judges are officials through whose mouths the law speaks its will. This conception of a judge is purely instrumental. Judges are no more than an instrument through which the (factual) content of the law manifests itself in the world.[37]

By contrast, in the German *Rechtsstaat* tradition, the role of the judge is not merely to discover the law that is already 'out there' fully formed, awaiting discovery. To think of the judicial role in this way is to reduce the role of judge to that of functionary: a person whose task is simply to carry out the will of her superiors as best she can. Whether that will is to be determined according to a literal reading of texts, a historical reading, or even a moral reading, her task remains that of a functionary. But in the *Rechtsstaat* tradition, the role of a judge is to do justice (of a certain sort) in the case before her. This does not mean that her task is to disregard all legal texts—written constitutions, statutes, and the like—and to decide all cases in light of her own understanding of what is just. On the contrary, judges in the *Rechtsstaat* tradition generally decide cases by following the rules set out in canonical texts quite precisely. But what is important to keep in mind is that the legitimate authority of those texts (like the legitimate authority of any legal source) is always in play in the judge's reasoning.

Now, for a judge to keep in mind the legitimacy of legal sources does not mean that she must consider the content of each law to see if it is sufficiently close to her own moral standards.[38] Rather than looking to the content of a particular law, judges must look to the place of that law within the larger legal order. That is, it is the place of each law within the legal order that is in play in each case that comes before a court. To see how this might be, it is useful to look again at the common assumption that our constitutional rights must emanate from the will of the constituent power.

B. The founders and the rule of law

In a democratic age, it is tempting to assume that the will of the people must be supreme in all things. Should the people choose to make laws that are at odds with our sense of

---

[37] D. Dyzenhaus, 'The Very Idea of a Judge' (2010) 60 *University of Toronto Law Journal* 61, at 65.

[38] Although judges must engage in normative analysis every time they decide a case, it is not the sort of normative analysis contemplated by Gustav Radbruch in his famous formula. G. Radbruch, 'Gesetzliches Unrecht und übergesetzliches Recht, Süddeutsche Juristenzeitung' (1946) 1 *Süddeutsche Juristen-Zeitung* 105, at 107.

the moral rights of individuals, that may be something to be regretted, but (we might think) it is no grounds for challenging the authority of the people to make such laws. To say that the laws do not conform to our conception of the rights people ought to have is to make a contribution to public debate, but it doesn't seem to affect the legitimacy of such laws. For if we believe that the people should be free to set laws for themselves, then we must accept the laws that they have chosen, no matter how morally objectionable they might be.

A somewhat more promising approach is to argue that the legislature was not entitled to make the law it did because in so doing, it violated someone's constitutionally protected rights. This, of course, is a standard strategy in the United States as it is in many other countries with the institution of constitutional judicial review. But in the United States, the invocation of constitutional rights as a mechanism to thwart the democratic will of the majority as expressed through their duly enacted laws, raises what Alexander Bickel famously called the 'counter-majoritarian difficulty'.[39] Much of American constitutional theory has focused on providing a satisfying solution to this problem. Although American constitutional theorists have proffered a number of different normative rationales for constraining the will of the majority in this way, they are all premised on the same underlying assumption that there is nothing beyond the will of the people (acting as the constituent power) that can constrain the will of the people (acting through the constituted state). The German *Rechtsstaat* tradition challenges this assumption.

When the people come together in their capacity as the constituent power to bring forth a new constitutional order, we may reasonably ask: by what authority does this entity make laws that claim authority over all those within its jurisdiction? One might reply that it is by the authority of any people to make laws for itself: it is the inherent authority of a people to rule itself. But, as John Stuart Mill points out, 'the "self-government" spoken of is not the government of each by himself, but that of each by the rest'.[40] Now, Mill is overstating the case somewhat: in a genuine democracy, there is some truth to the claim that we are at least part-authors of the laws under which we live. But Mill is also quite right to point out that there is a world of difference between the sort of authorship we bear toward our own private acts and that which we bear toward the laws under which we all must live. So although the status of each individual as co-author of the laws under which we live bears some justificatory weight, it remains the case that more work needs to be done to establish that such laws are compatible with our status as free and independent persons.

The German *Rechtsstaat* tradition proposes a different solution to this puzzle. It does not embrace the doctrine of popular sovereignty that seems to be at the root of at least some conceptions of the constituent power in the United States, but neither does it embrace political anarchism.[41] For even though political authority imposes obligations

[39] A. Bickel, *The Least Dangerous Branch: The Supreme Court at the Bar of Politics* 2nd edn (New Haven: Yale University Press, 1986).

[40] J. S. Mill 'On Liberty', in J. Gray (ed), *On Liberty and Other Essays* (Oxford: Oxford University Press, 1991), at 8.

[41] The classic modern defence of anarchism is R. P. Wolff, *In Defense of Anarchism* (Oakland: University of California Press, 1970).

on free persons, it need not be at odds with their status as free and independent. For not every act by a public authority necessarily represents an unjustifiable interference with individual freedom and independence. Indeed, in the *Rechtsstaat* tradition, it is generally accepted that a public authority is required in order to set in place the conditions under which it is possible for us to preserve our independence as we live in community together with others.[42] The way we ensure this is for courts to take into account at all times whether the particular legal rules that are in play in a given dispute are consistent with the status of each person as free and independent such that they form a legitimate basis upon which the courts may rest their decision in a particular case. In many cases, there will be no reason to question the consistency of particular legal rules with our conception of persons as free and independent; but in cases where that is an issue, the state must justify its actions to show that, appearances to the contrary, they are consistent with that conception of persons.

VI. Proportionality and Rights

A. Proportionality in the common law

The role of constitutional rights in the *Rechtsstaat* tradition, then, is to provide a framework within which courts may determine whether the actions of the state—whether it is executive action, regulation, legislation, etc.—can be recognized as legitimate, and therefore whether they ought to be recognized as the appropriate basis for the adjudication of disputes by a court. In this way, constitutional rights do not set up side constraints on the otherwise free choice of the state to pursue the public good as it sees fit. Rather, they set out regulative principles that serve to direct the activities of the state from the inside. Now, in case this sort of talk should sound too outré to English-speaking legal scholars, it is perhaps worthwhile to recall that something very much like this sort of thinking has been at work for centuries in the English common law constitution.[43]

The English common law constitution, like the German constitution, is directed to securing certain key constitutional rights. And in both cases, those constitutional rights are deemed to be central to our understanding of the constitutional order not because they have been set down by the constituent power in a canonical text, but rather because they are central to our understanding of what it is for a public authority to exercise legitimate power over free and independent rights-bearing persons. The broad right to liberty is at the very core of the English common law constitution, then,

---

[42] Arthur Ripstein makes clear just how broad this power of the state may be understood to be simply in virtue of its role as securing the conditions of equal freedom. A. Ripstein, 'Roads to Freedom', in A. Ripstein, *Force and Freedom: Kant's Legal and Political Philosophy* (Cambridge, Mass.: Harvard University Press, 2009).

[43] Weinrib, above n 1, 89ff and many others have argued that the German constitution's placement of the *Rechtsstaat* principle above even the constituent power to change (as well as the status of human dignity as absolute and not amenable to justified infringement, and the right of resistance in all Germans against those who would seek to undermine the constitutional order) was motivated by a feeling of 'never again' in response to the horrors of the Nazi regime, dedicated as it was to the denial of basic human dignity of so many. Nevertheless, I argue here, the rule of law ideas to which it appeals are far from new.

even though it is not explicitly guaranteed in any constitutional bill of rights. In this respect, then, constitutional rights play a role in the common law constitution that is similar to the one they play in the German *Rechtsstaat* constitutional order. This similarity has sometimes been difficult to see because the common law constitution does not explicitly guarantee any constitutional rights. But, given the discussion above concerning the role of rights in the German constitutional tradition—where they are basic structural features of the legal order whether or not they are recognized in any constitutional document—this ought not to be so surprising. As A.V. Dicey points out, the guarantee of rights in a constitutional document does not always mean that the constitutional order has a deeper commitment to rights protection; indeed, he insists, the opposite seems to be true. Contrasting the Belgian written bill of rights (that expressly guarantees the right to liberty) with the English tradition, he writes:

> The expression ... 'guaranteed,' is ... extremely significant; it suggests the notion that personal liberty is a special privilege insured to Belgians by some power above the ordinary law of the land. This is an idea utterly alien to English modes of thought, since with us freedom of person is not a special privilege ...[44]

In the common law constitutional tradition, the rights themselves go largely unspoken because the mechanisms of English constitutional law—judicial decisions, the great constitutional documents, etc.—do not take the time to articulate that underlying state aim; instead, they move directly to the business of putting it to work in specific cases. Discussing one of the great English constitutional documents, for instance, A.V. Dicey writes: 'The Habeas Corpus Acts are essentially *procedure* Acts, and simply aim at improving the legal mechanism by means of which the acknowledged right of personal freedom may be enforced.'[45]

These broad, general rights that play such a central organizing role in English constitutional law remain unspoken much of the time. But it is telling that at a moment of constitutional crisis, the Englishmen who rebelled in the thirteen colonies explained their reasons for rebelling against the British Crown in terms of its failure to live up to its justifying purpose: securing the basic rights of all persons. Or, as the Declaration of Independence put the same point rather more eloquently:

> We hold these truths to be self-evident, that all men are created equal, that they are endowed by their Creator with certain unalienable Rights, that among these are Life, Liberty and the pursuit of Happiness. – That to secure these rights, Governments are instituted among Men ...[46]

The primary complaint of the colonists was that the Crown had failed to act in a way that was consistent with its justifying purpose: to secure these rights to life, liberty, and so on. It was on this basis that they concluded that King George III was 'unfit to be the ruler of a free people'.

---

[44] A. V. Dicey, *Introduction to the Study of the Law of the Constitution* 8th edn (Indianapolis: Liberty Fund, 1982), 124.
[45] Ibid 134 (emphasis added).   [46] US Declaration of Independence (1776), para 2.

Common law courts have been at work for centuries considering the conditions under which particular acts of government are inconsistent with a commitment to those rights. And in many of these cases, the courts have had to address the question of proportionality quite squarely. Of course, the common law constitution allows the state to infringe on an individual's right to liberty in some circumstances: pre-trial detention, for example, is permissible under the right conditions. And the common law constitution even allows the state to infringe the right to life in certain limited circumstances, such as when this is necessary to prevent someone from committing a very serious criminal offence; and so on. What we find, time and again, is common law courts working out the conditions under which these basic rights may be justifiably infringed, by making reference to the same basic considerations we find in the practice of proportionality justification in German constitutional law: determining questions of standing (that the infringement was carried out in the state's name and for a legitimate public purpose), then determining whether the rights infringement was necessary for the state to pursue that purpose, and, finally, determining whether the purpose was proportionate to the rights infringement.

Recognizing that common law courts have made reference to the right to liberty for centuries both in deciding cases in the absence of statutory guidance as well as in their construction of statutes, some scholars have recognized the deep similarities between the *Rechtsstaat* tradition of proportionality justification and the one that is at work in the common law constitution. The difference between the two lies mainly in their institutional context: whereas the common law constitution operates in a context of parliamentary supremacy, the *Rechtsstaat* tradition now operates in the context of a written constitutional bill of rights coupled with constitutional judicial review. Notwithstanding these differences in institutional context, Trevor Allan points out, '[j]udgments of proportionality are ... intrinsic to the judicial process, with or without a bill of rights.'[47]

B. Proportionality in the *Rechtsstaat*

Although proportionality reasoning is a feature of common law constitutionalism, it operated for many years with a very narrow conception of what sorts of purposes it was legitimate for the state to pursue. In the early nineteenth century, many common law courts and commentators assumed that the only purposes for which state power could legitimately be exercised involved the protection of certain basic rights to life and liberty (through the workings of private law and the criminal law) and certain other very basic mechanisms for the protection of the legal order itself. As Isaiah Berlin put it, 'the State was reduced to what Lassalle contemptuously described as the functions of a night-watchman or traffic policeman.'[48] Many of the canonical writers in the tradition of the common law constitution such as Michael Oakeshott,[49] A.V. Dicey,[50] and

---

[47] T. R. S. Allan, 'Democracy, Legality and Proportionality', in Huscroft, Miller, and Webber, above n 3, 205–33, at 20.

[48] I. Berlin, 'Two Concepts of Liberty', in I. Berlin (ed), *The Proper Study of Mankind* (New York: Farrar Strauss and Giroux, 2000), 199.

[49] M. Oakeshott, 'The Rule of Law', in M. Oakeshott, *On History and Other Essays* (Indianapolis: Liberty Fund, 1999).

[50] Dicey, above n 44.

Friedrich Hayek[51] also had great difficulty in accepting that the state might legitimately be entitled to put in place the sorts of regulatory measures that we all take for granted today: redistributing wealth, regulating the workplace, protecting the environment, ensuring access to healthcare, education, and much else besides.

In the move from the early-nineteenth-century understanding of proportionality justification as permitting the state only to do what is necessary to secure individual rights in the most direct manner (through the institutions of the nightwatchman state) to the modern conception of legitimate state purpose as admitting a wide variety of public purposes, we may see a parallel in the move in English administrative law from a concern with questions of jurisdictions toward a broader concern with the reasonable-ness of the administrative agency's conduct. The touchstone of legitimate state action in both cases moves away from ensuring that the conduct is on a list of permissible purposes and toward a concern with whether the state's conduct is justifiable to the individuals affected in a manner that is consistent with their claims as rights holders.

Proportionality reasoning, then, is not just an adjustment to the procedures through which courts decide cases about constitutional rights. It is a necessary part of rights analysis in the postwar paradigm (just as it is in the common law constitution) because it is essential to the judicial role in overseeing the state's pursuit of its legitimate aims. State action cannot be neatly divided between areas where the state may do as it likes and areas where it is forbidden from acting altogether. Instead, the state must be able to justify itself to those who are subject to its power at all times, explaining how its actions can be justified as part of a coherent effort to set in place the conditions of freedom for all under law. The advance of the postwar paradigm, of which proportionality analysis is the central structuring concept, is truly a move away from what Etienne Mureinik calls the 'culture of authority' (according to which the state is entitled to do as it likes so long as it remains within the side constraints of constitutional rights) and a return to an older 'culture of justification' according to which all actions of the state call out for justification to each person as free and equal rights bearers.[52]

VII. Proportionality and Balancing

The US Bill of Rights occupies a curious position at the intersection of two distinct constitutional rights traditions. On the one hand, as we have seen, it is the home of a text-centred account of constitutional rights in which the only constraints on the legiti-mate authority of the state arise from the specific rights enumerated in the text of the constitution. On the other hand, however, many of those very rights are themselves the product of the sort of common law reasoning about rights that operates according to a very different logic. The right against unreasonable searches and seizures, for example,

---

[51] F. Hayek, *The Constitution of Liberty* (London: Routledge, 1960).

[52] E. Mureinik, 'A Bridge to Where? Introducing the Interim Bill of Rights' (1994) 10 *South African Journal on Human Rights* 31; and D. Dyzenhaus, 'Law as Justification: Etienne Mureinik's Conception of Legal Culture' (1998) 14 *South African Journal on Human Rights* 11. I differ from Mureinik's use of the term 'culture of justification', however, because whereas he suggests that it is new to the postwar paradigm, I sug-gest that it is a return to a constitutional culture that is centuries old.

is guaranteed by the Fourth Amendment to the US Constitution, but it is also a right that was developed over many years by common law courts according to the logic of proportionality. And this is true of a number of the other rights guaranteed by the US Bill of Rights, as well.

Recognizing these and other similarities in the protections actually guaranteed by these two different constitutional rights traditions, some scholars have suggested that the existence of a distinct justification procedure in Germany but not in the United States is only a difference in mode of exposition. As I shall argue below, there is a great deal of truth to that claim, but it is essential that we make clear precisely what it is that the two systems have in common. The usual way in which it is claimed that the two systems share a common way of thinking is premised on the assumption that proportionality reasoning is just open-ended interest balancing. Of course, if this were the case, it would be easy to find parallels to that sort of reasoning in American constitutional jurisprudence. The judgment of Justice Frankfurter in the case of *Dennis v United States*[53] is but one example of this sort of approach. In adjudicating the right to free speech guaranteed by the First Amendment, Justice Frankfurter insisted that '[t]he demands of free speech in a democratic society as well as the interest in national security are better served by candid and informed weighing of the competing interests...than by announcing dogmas too inflexible for the non-Euclidian problems to be solved.'[54]

On this reading, it is simply common sense that rights cannot be protected absolutely; courts must take into consideration other interests when deciding what limits to impose on state action. As Ronald Dworkin has pointed out, '[t]he metaphor of balancing the public interest against personal claims is established in our political and judicial rhetoric, and this metaphor gives the model both familiarity and appeal.'[55] Now, according to this image of 'balancing', constitutional rights recognize especially important interests, but when there are even greater interests that would be served by interfering with a certain right, the right must give way to the greater good of society.[56] Of course, given the structure of the American Bill of Rights, this sort of balancing must take place at the stage of defining constitutional rights, rather than recognizing justified infringements to defined rights. Nevertheless, it might seem that this sort of balancing of the interests protected by constitutional rights against the interests served by the state action in question is precisely the sort of enterprise that German courts are engaged in when engaging in proportionality justification.

But, as we have seen above, this is not the sort of reasoning that animates proportionality reasoning in the German constitutional order. Instead, the sort of proportionality that animates German constitutional thinking is concerned with articulating the contours of a theory of legitimate government action in light of a certain conception of persons as free and equal rights holders. But this sort of reasoning is precisely what was

---

[53] 341 US 494 (1951).   [54] Ibid 524–5.   [55] Dworkin, above n 21, 198.

[56] The metaphor of 'balancing' took on a dangerous cast in the McCarthy-era cases such as *Dennis*. It threatens to do so again in cases decided in the era of the 'war on terror' and the 'war on crime'. See J. Waldron, 'Security and Liberty: The Image of Balance', in *Torture, Terror and Trade-Offs: Philosophy for the White House* (Oxford: Oxford University Press, 2010).

at stake in the common law reasoning that gave rise to the recognition of rights against unreasonable search and seizure, cruel and unusual punishment, excessive bail, and so on. Common law courts had to determine when it was necessary and proportionate for the state to interfere with an Englishman's privacy in order to further the course of justice, which is itself required in order to secure all other rights.

Most of these proportionality principles that had developed in the common law constitution were given constitutional status of a different kind by their incorporation into the text of the US Bill of Rights. As a result, what had been the outcomes of proportionality reasoning about broad rights to life and liberty were turned into specific rights that depended for their constitutional status on their having been adopted by the constituent power in the canonical constitutional document. So one might be tempted to agree with Fred Schauer that the effect of the US Bill of Rights was to turn the fluid and indeterminate common law rights into concrete and specific rights under the new written constitution. He writes:

> Just as the common law has become substantially less fluid as dispute patterns have repeated themselves over hundreds of years, and just as codes in civil law countries have become more refined with more experience in the transactions that those codes must govern, so too does freedom of expression decision-making codify itself over time and with experience.[57]

But this temptation should be resisted. Of course, a jurisprudence of constitutional rights will become more detailed and determinate over time as cases accumulate on more and more different aspects of a particular doctrine. But the fact of codification in the US Bill of Rights should not have any effect on that. Instead, its effect has been to disconnect those common law rights from their normative foundations in a conception of persons as free and equal rights holders that shapes our very idea of legitimate government.[58]

VIII. Conclusion

In this chapter, I have argued that proportionality reasoning about rights is intrinsic to a certain conception of the role of rights in a constitutional order. In a rule of law legal order, where rights are understood as incidents of our understanding of the moral status of persons as free and equal, they regulate our understanding of legitimate state authority from the inside. In that capacity, rights function together as parts of a single, unified account of legitimate state authority. And this means that when the demands of that account come into unavoidable conflict with one another, there must be a mechanism through which we can ensure any resolution of that conflict is justifiable in

---

[57] F. Schauer, 'Freedom of Expression Adjudication in Europe and America: A Case Study in Comparative Constitutional Architecture', in G. Nolte (ed), *European and US Constitutionalism* (Cambridge: Cambridge University Press, 2005), 49–69, at 12–13.

[58] There are signs that some US scholars are looking to the origins of proportionality reasoning in a theory of limited government, and not just in utilitarian balancing. See, inter alia, A. Ristroph, 'Proportionality as a Principle of Limited Government' (2005) 55 *Duke Law Journal* 263.

terms of that same account of legitimate state action. Proportionality reasoning is that mechanism.

Seen at this level of abstraction, the practice of proportionality is common to the German *Rechtsstaat* tradition and to the English tradition of common law constitutionalism, despite their different institutional contexts. In addition, there are differences in how proportionality reasoning has been used over the centuries in the common law tradition, based on differences in their respective understandings of the necessary role of government—from the nineteenth-century conception of the nightwatchman state to the twentieth-century understanding of the regulatory state as necessary to secure the empirical conditions of our freedom (by preventing dependency based on illness, ignorance, poverty, and much else). So proportionality reasoning about constitutional rights does not guarantee a single set of results. But, seen in the right way, that should not be of concern. Proportionality's promise has never been that it will secure a particular set of outcomes. Rather, it promises a procedure through which the state is required to make explicit precisely how its conduct is consistent with our best conception of the rights that we, as a political community, take persons to have just in virtue of our personhood and in virtue of our membership in this particular political community. Seen in this way, the acts of government are not just expressions of the will of the majority. When filtered through the logic of proportionality, state action 'does not have to be politics, it can be law'.[59]

---

[59] J. Bomhoff, 'Lüth's 50th anniversary' (2008) 9 *German Law Journal* 121, at 124.

Index

Fried, C. 78
Friedrich, C. J. 179*n*, 195*n*
Frishman, O. 135*n*
Frost, R. 79
Fuller, L. L. 1*n*, 29*n*, 47*n*, 48, 171, 172*n*, 175,
    206–7, 218
functional concept of a constitution 145–7
fundamental freedoms 21, 40–1, 64, 67, 154,
    204, 208–10, 218–19

Gaddafi, M. 161
Galanter, M. 96*n*
Gandhi, I. 108
gap-filling doctrine 60
Gardbaum, S. 101*n*, 111*n*
Gardner, J. 11*n*, 15*n*, 19–20, 21*n*, 24*n*, 29, 30–1,
    45*n*, 226*n*, 228*n*, 232, 300
Garrison, W. L. 78
George III, King 317
George, W. R. 55*n*
Germany:
    Constitution 65
    emergency powers 90
    eternity clause 92–3
    Rechtsstaat 44, 176, 204, 214, 216, 219
    Weimar Constitution 90
    see also under proportionality
Gilbert, M. 142, 144
Ginsburg, T. 105*n*, 111*n*
Goldsmith, J. 186
Goldsworthy, J. 32*n*, 53*n*, 54, 56*n*, 58*n*, 61*n*,
    67*n*, 68, 71, 103*n*, 311*n*
Gözler, K. 65*n*
Graber, M. A. 247*n*, 264*n*
Greenawalt, K. 70*n*, 71*n*
Greenberg, M. 70*n*
Green, L. 40*n*, 230*n*
Greenwald, G. 186*n*
Grey, T. C. 37–8, 55*n*
Grice, H. P. 53, 69–71, 73
Griffith, J. 229*n*
Grote, R. 204*n*
Gurr, T. 161*n*
Gutmann, A. 77*n*, 273*n*
Gwyn, W. B. 225*n*

Habermas, J. 266, 266*n*, 273*n*, 274*n*, 310*n*
Hale, Lady 26
Hale, M. 34*n*, 188*n*
Haljan, D. 83–4
Hall, W. 122
Hamilton, A. 78*n*, 88, 312
Hamlin, A. 224*n*
Hansen, M. 224*n*, 225*n*
Harnish, R. M. 69*n*
Harrington, J. 179, 190, 191–3
Harris, B. 181*n*
Harrison Moore, W. 181
Hart, H. L. A. 2*n*, 3, 10, 15, 18–20, 23, 28–9, 34,
    40, 42–5, 75–6, 84, 167*n*, 173*n*, 175, 176*n*,
    201*n*, 212*n*, 230
    Concept of Law 17
    rule of recognition 9, 26*n*
    Separation Thesis 14
    utilitarianism 15

Hayek, F. A. 179, 195–8, 206*n*, 208, 211, 213–14,
    217, 319
Helfer, L. R. 101*n*
Hellman, D. 300–1
Heun, W. 225*n*, 237*n*
Hirschl, R. 76, 261*n*
Hobbesian 31, 170
    'civil science' 190
    institutional requirement 135
    legal point of view 133*n*
Hobbes, T. 28, 48, 121, 125, 127*n*, 128, 130–2,
    134*n*, 140, 154*n*, 162*n*, 164, 191–3, 215*n*
    legal order 126
    Leviathan 189–90
    state theory 179
Hoekstra, K. 125*n*
Hogg, P. 309*n*
Hohfeld, W. N. 312*n*
Holden, R. 108*n*
Hollerbach, A. 306*n*
Hollis-Brusky, A. 247*n*
Holmes, O. W. 85–6
Holmesian 'felt necessities' 88
Holmes, S. 97*n*, 198*n*
Hope, Lord 26*n*
hospitality, cosmopolitan right of 130
Huang, Y. 69*n*
Hueglin, T. 154*n*
Hughes, P. 63*n*
human dignity 63, 65, 171, 204, 218, 220
humanitarian decisions 123
human rights 103, 127, 128, 138, 139
    see also fundamental freedoms
Hurd, H. M. 70*n*
Huscroft, G. 318*n*

identity 143–4
illiberal constitutions 76–7, 82
immigration policies 126, 130
    see also migrants/migration
immutable rules 111
implications *see* constitutional implications and
    constitutional structure
implicit meaning 60–1
implied meaning 53–6, 57–62, 67–8, 70–2
    constituent power 152*n*
    indirect meaning 57–8
    indirect meaning and constitutional
        structure 58–9
    legal basis for constitutional implication 60–2
inclusion:
    legal 151–4
    recursive acts of 147
    unauthorized 155
incompatibility declarations 12–13, 101
India 96, 113
    Congress Party 108–9
    Constitution 106, 109, 168*n*
    Supreme Court 65, 108–9, 168*n*
individual's birth (*jus soli*) 120
individual's lineage (*jus sanguinis*) 120
integrity 27, 31, 213
intentionalism 54, 66–7, 68
Inter-American Court of Human Rights 138
inter-institutional comity 235–6

Printed and bound by CPI Group (UK) Ltd, Croydon, CR0 4YY